United in Diversity

Europäisch-jüdische Studien
European-Jewish Studies

―

On Behalf of the Moses Mendelssohn Center for
European-Jewish Studies, Potsdam

Edited by Miriam Rürup and Werner Treß

Volume 62

United in Diversity

Contemporary European Jewry in an Interdisciplinary Perspective

Edited by
Marcela Menachem Zoufalá and Olaf Glöckner

DE GRUYTER
OLDENBOURG

The book was supported by the grant UDISEJ – Erasmus+ 2018-1-CZ01-KA203-048165 – 'United in Diversity' – An Interdisciplinary Study of Contemporary European Jewry and Its Reflection.

This publication was supported by a generous contribution from Celia and Jack Michonik.

ISBN 978-3-11-221413-8
e-ISBN (PDF) 978-3-11-078321-6
e-ISBN (EPUB) 978-3-11-078330-8
ISSN 2192-9602
DOI https://doi.org/10.1515/9783110783216

This work is licensed under the Creative Commons Attribution-NonCommercial-NoDerivatives 4.0 International License. For details go to https://creativecommons.org/licenses/by-nc-nd/4.0/.

Creative Commons license terms for re-use do not apply to any content (such as graphs, figures, photos, excerpts, etc.) not original to the Open Access publication and further permission may be required from the rights holder. The obligation to research and clear permission lies solely with the party re-using the material.

Library of Congress Control Number: 2023913067

Bibliographic information published by the Deutsche Nationalbibliothek
The Deutsche Nationalbibliothek lists this publication in the Deutsche Nationalbibliografie; detailed bibliographic data are available on the internet at http://dnb.dnb.de.

© 2025 with the authors, editing © 2025 Marcela Menachem Zoufalá and Olaf Glöckner, published by Walter de Gruyter GmbH, Berlin/Boston.
This volume is text- and page-identical with the hardback published in 2023.
This book is published with open access at www.degruyter.com.

Cover image: Kazimierz, Kraków Old Town, Poland, September 2017 (Photo Archive: Marcela Menachem Zoufalá).
Printing and binding: CPI books GmbH, Leck

www.degruyter.com

Table of Contents

Acknowledgments —— VII

Introduction —— 1

Eduard Nižňanský and Katarína Bohová
Perceptions of the Holocaust in Slovak Historiography and Among the General Public after the Establishment of the Slovak Republic in 1993 —— 7

Jiří Holý
Trivialization of the Holocaust? The Elements of Pop Culture in Holocaust Fiction and Film —— 51

Dina Porat
A New Era? Christian-Jewish Relations in Post-Cold War Europe —— 71

Haim Fireberg
A "Jewish Problem" or a "Society Problem"? Understanding Contemporary Antisemitism in Europe from Jewish and Governmental Perspectives —— 87

Lilach Lev Ari
Feeling "At Home" or Just Privileged Minorities? Perceptions of Jewish and Non-Jewish Respondents in Contemporary Budapest —— 111

Olaf Glöckner
New Relations in the Making? Jews and Non-Jews in Germany Reflect on Shoah Memory, Unexpected Growing Jewish Pluralism, Israel, and New Antisemitism —— 133

Marcela Menachem Zoufalá
Ambivalence, Dilemmas, and Aporias of Contemporary Czech Jewish *Lived Experience* —— 161

Barbora Jakobyová, Eduard Nižňanský, and Olaf Glöckner
Jewish Experiences and New Encounters in Slovakia —— 181

Olaf Glöckner, Marcela Menachem Zoufalá
Jews in Poland: Between Cultural/Religious Renewal and New Uncertainties —— 199

Marcela Menachem Zoufalá and Olaf Glöckner
Afterword —— 213

Bibliography —— 217

About the Authors —— 235

Index of Persons —— 239

Acknowledgments

The research project "United in Diversity" has offered us an exceptional opportunity to continue our joint international studies on Jewish history and present, particularly in Central and Eastern Europe. Generous funding from the European Union's Erasmus+ program has made this project easier for us, as has financial support from Celia and Jack Michonik.

We would like to extend a special thanks to our home institutes, the Center for the Study of the Holocaust and Jewish Literature at Charles University in Prague and the Moses Mendelssohn Center for European-Jewish Studies in Potsdam. We were always assured of the support and encouragement of our directors Jiří Holý, Julius H. Schoeps and Miriam Rürup. We are also very grateful to our colleagues from the Center for the Study of Contemporary European Jewry at Tel Aviv University and from the Faculty of Arts at Comenius University in Bratislava, who have significantly contributed to the success of this project over the years.

For the progress of our empirical studies in the Czech Republic, Poland, Hungary, Slovakia and Germany, the openness and willingness to communicate of all our Jewish and non-Jewish interview partners was essential. Thanks also go to representatives of the Jewish communities and organizations who kept their doors open for us even in difficult times.

We also received important scientific (and organizational) advice from Joanna Dyduch, Artur Skorek, Libuše Heczková, Blanka Soukupová, Zbyněk Tarant, András Kovács, Lars Dencik, Sergio DellaPergola, Daniel Staetsky, Eliezer Ben-Rafael, Robert Řehák, Julia Bernstein, Kateřina Krejčířová, Roswitha Kuska, Werner Tress, Margi Schellenberg, John Ryan, Julia Brauch, and Alice Meroz.

However, our very special thanks go to our partners Mascha Lyamets and Karmi Menachem, who supported our writing phase with understanding and humor.

Marcela Menachem Zoufalá   Olaf Glöckner

Prague / Potsdam, September 2023

Introduction

For many years Jewish life in Europe has been viewed with skepticism and concern. The aftermath of the Shoah, demographic decline, trends of assimilation, and secularization gave reason to suspect that "the old continent" could not offer bright perspectives for those who desired to lead a distinct Jewish existence and build community. The disbelief was declared inside and outside the Jewish world. It appeared – for Jews and non-Jews – it was more achievable to guard Jewish heritage and memory than to hold high expectations in developing meaningful communal life anew. Some remaining demographic and cultural "Jewish Islands" were treated with care and respect, though visions for a full-bodied Jewish future in Europe were seen as unrealistic.

The wave of Jewish hope and revival starting in the 1990s was therefore rather unforeseen. The well-known events triggered by the end of the Cold War, followed by European unification, were primarily accompanied by massive euphoria in the Eastern block due to liberation from Communist repression. This historical breaking point included a surge of ethnoreligious and ethnocultural renewals. In this general context, some emerging concepts of a "Jewish renaissance" in Europe – as suggested by scholars like Diana Pinto[1] – might have overreached the target. Nevertheless, it cannot be denied that, since the 1990s, European Jewry has been in the process of dynamic transformation. These changes were inherently connected with external Jewish assistance on the one hand (for example, support programs by the American Jewish Joint Distribution Committee/JDC, the LA Pincus Fund, the Jewish Agency of Israel, and the Ronald S. Lauder Foundation) and new self-aware Jewish generations less affected by the shadows of the Shoah who search for their distinct individual and collective identities on the other.

Though comparatively limited by statistics, communities in Central and Eastern Europe in particular are seeking original directions of how to live their Jewishness. Despite rather bleak demographic forecasts, predominantly younger Jewish protagonists have shown a willingness to reconnect to the heritage of their ancestors and excavate the potentials of Jewish tradition.

This introduced collective monograph intended to explore the processes mentioned above from a transdisciplinary perspective. This intention was supported by European Education and Culture Executive Agency (EACEA) funds that material-

---

1 Diana Pinto, "The new Jewish Europe. Challenges and Responsibilities," *European Judaism: A Journal for the New Europe* 31, no. 2, European Jewry – Between Past and Future (Autumn 1998): 3–15.

ized in the "United in Diversity. A Study of Contemporary European Jewry and its Reflection" project. Part of the work constituted of qualitative anthropological research carried out in Jewish communities in five different countries: Poland, Hungary, Slovakia, the Czech Republic, and Germany. The examination revolved around self-perception, sense of belonging, transnationalism, future expectations, and inevitably antisemitism. The interactions with the majority of societies in the respective countries represented one of the additional significant focus areas.

Parts of previous generations whose identity survived cumulative traumas of the twentieth century eventually regained their ethnic awareness that was attentively cultivated afterward. The subsequent trends identified prevalently among younger generations of Central and Eastern European Jews embody an urgent call for visible participation in civil societies, however, not necessarily always on behalf of Jewish communities. Building meaningful relations based on shared ethnicity may even be interpreted as outdated. Moreover, introducing Jewishness into non-Jewish settings and opening up to the majority of society might be perceived as an inherited responsibility that under certain circumstances, represents unbearable weight.

An ongoing rapprochement between Jews and Christians certainly belongs to the relevant factors of the Jewish quality of life. As an outcome of these attempts, accompanied by an atmosphere of togetherness, synagogues and other Jewish institutions in Europe seem to be experiencing higher respect and recognition than ever before. In parallel, remarkable political and societal efforts to commemorate the Shoah receive more attention every year. Considering the regional angle, Jews in all five scrutinized countries might feel there are growing opportunities for full integration into said countries. Taking into account the broader perspective, a discussion of whether European Jewry is disposed to become the third pillar of the global Jewish community, aside from Israel and the American Jewish community, could be cautiously reopened.

Simultaneously, post-War Jewry in Europe has remained, at least in some places, fragile and unsafe. There are frequent anti-Jewish incidents across the continent, with many of them allegedly justified as political action against the State of Israel. In particular, the studies of the Fundamental Rights Agency (FRA) have proven that a majority of European Jews feel antisemitism is on the rise, subsequently expecting a deteriorating situation in the near future.[2] Many Jewish communities, families, and individuals in Europe have close connections to Israel.

---

[2] Experiences and perceptions of antisemitism – Second survey on discrimination and hate crime against Jews in the EU, published December 10, 2018, accessed May 18, 2023, https://fra.europa.eu/en/publication/2018/experiences-and-perceptions-antisemitism-second-survey-discrimination-and-hate.

Thus, any escalations of violence in the Middle East involving Israel cause deep concern among them, a sentiment that also increases as anti-Israeli rallies multiply also in the EU.

Gradually, while Jewish people or institutions are under attack by antisemitic extremists from different camps or at the margins of political demonstrations, growing public outrage is detected. Politicians, churches, and protagonists of civic society attempt to strengthen the affected Jewish institutions and persons and moderate the repercussions. This might be perceived as a new quality of solidarity arising in the midst of a non-Jewish environment. Further research will be necessary to reveal to what extent this positive reverse trend stabilizes and, in case, how balanced and long-lasting conditions enable the undisturbed development of Jewish life.

This observed antagonism constitutes one of the significant aspects of life for members of Jewish communities today. In other words, two seemingly opposing streams have surfaced in the European continent in the first decades of the twenty-first century. This collective monograph abundantly testifies that Jewish cultures and religious traditions are witnessing a unique and unforeseen rise in the living experience for many involved actors. On the other hand, however, the same study confirms that Europe's Jews – even those of Central and Eastern Europe – are experiencing new threat scenarios.

Suppose we pause momentarily during these highly turbulent times (in Europe as elsewhere). In this case, we can realize that Jewish life on the continent was almost always present, albeit in varying degrees and geographical distribution. Employing this point of view, securing the sources, traditions, and knowledge of European-Jewish history from late antiquity to the present day is essential. This large arc of events in general, and the developments since 1933, 1945, and 1989 in particular, sufficiently illustrate that historical scholarship can only rarely be apolitical. In this case, a major topic with critical implications lies at the interface of contemporary history and research involving scientific controversy but also the burden of raw emotions.

There is a pressing need for immediate attention and critical scholarship to the matters mentioned above. Otherwise, phenomena such as whitewashing will infiltrate the political culture and mainstream society, specifically in so-called Visegrad countries even further. The term competitive victimhood is still awaiting thorough exploration in this context. Attempts at Holocaust relativization and Holocaust denial, not yet entirely uncommon today, are apparent consequences of a lack of awareness of these issues.

How certain is the Jewish future in Europe? This is a question that is asked more often than almost any other. Undoubtedly, many cultural, religious, social, and intellectual resources are "manufactured anew" with often enthusiastic participation and engagement of the non-Jewish environment. Consequently, our study also explored what "essential issues" and values Jews in Poland, Hungary, the Czech Republic, Slovakia, and Germany attribute to their lived experience, in which manner they consider themselves part of a wider European community, and how they define their relations to other ethnocultural and ethnoreligious groups.

The present publication is comprised of the main findings of the mentioned study. In the book's first part, the texts and contributions dealing with historical, literary, and intellectual works on the Shoah in European space can be found. In this frame of reference, the authors uncovered vigorous efforts to keep the memory of the Shoah alive, countering falsifications of history and sensitizing upcoming generations to the vulnerability of contemporary Jewish life. The second part of the collective monograph mainly lists socio-empirical and anthropological results from the abovementioned qualitative research in five European countries.

Eduard Nižňanský and Katarína Bohová describe the perceptions of the Holocaust in Slovak historiography and among the general public after the establishment of the independent Slovak Republic in 1993. The authors underline that not all details of this historiography have been explored and that – at the same time – a difficult fight against new trends of nationalism and historical revisionism has to be waged. The authors also strongly consider the impact of revisionism on the formation of national symbols as well as the historiography situated between science and the Catholic Church's interpretation of history (of the Slovak state and the beatification of bishop Ján Vojtaššák).

Jiří Holý examines changes in the representation of the Holocaust/Shoah in Czech literature and film over the past few decades and focuses in particular on elements of pop culture in Holocaust fiction and film. Pop culture elements have become a typical feature of literature in the last few decades. According to Holý, they extend the creative possibilities for speaking about the Holocaust while raising many problematic questions. However, the author argues that second and third-generation artists and writers consciously use a variety of pop culture methods to respond to the increasing forgetfulness of history.

Dina Porat describes the manifold attempts by European Jewry and Israel, on the one hand, and the Vatican in Rome, on the other, to improve their historical relationship and examine possibilities for mutual theological appreciation. According to the author, efforts beginning in 1965 to reverse problematic relations and start a genuine dialogue of mutual respect with both sides have continued for several decades and in recent years have gained momentum. Since the beginning of the 2000s, several open letters and statements have been formulated and published by the Jewish side, illustrating the willingness to accept the extended hand and reach the reconciliation phase.

Haim Fireberg reflects on new antisemitism, especially in Poland, Hungary, and Germany. The author states that certain forms of new antisemitism in Central Europe are underestimated or suppressed and argues that the level of violent antisemitism, as indicated by statistics, is not necessarily correlated with the perceptions of antisemitism in those countries. Furthermore, Fireberg identifies particular "paradoxes" in Hungary and Poland. Despite having relatively low levels of antisemitic violence, the two countries perceive antisemitism differently in light of their understanding of domestic, political, and social conditions.

Lilach Lev-Ari, in her paper "Feeling 'At Home' or Just Privileged Minorities?", describes how Jewish people search for their place in contemporary Budapest. Lev-Ari's findings, based on qualitative research, including a series of interviews, imply that Jews in Hungary today are well integrated into various societal fabrics; most feel a sense of belonging and perceive themselves as an integral part of Hungarian society, at least in the micro perspectives. However, some would be aware of undercurrents of old and contemporary antisemitism at the macro level – sentiments which, according to the author, affect Hungarian Jews' sense of integration and affiliation.

Olaf Glöckner introduces the current environment of reunified Germany's heavily transformed Jewish community. The research results' analysis offers diverse perspectives on Jewish developments, much enhanced by immigration from the Former Soviet Union during the 1990s. In parallel, non-Jewish society actors reflect on overall processes of still ongoing public reconsideration and memory politics, comprehending Jewish heritage and the present as an essential part of German culture and self-understanding.

Marcela Menachem Zoufalá presents anthropological research that attempts to deconstruct and interpret the meaning of Jewishness as a lived experience among the members of the Jewish minority in the Czech Republic today. The results show the situation of Czech Jews as simultaneously dynamic, hopeful, and fragile. The study confirms that the social climate in the Czech Republic is more open to Jews in particular, though uncertainties about how tolerant and reliable the majority of society's attitudes are towards minorities persist.

Barbora Jakobyová, Eduard Nižňanský, and Olaf Glöckner trace how veteran Jewish leaders and intellectuals are shaping Jewish communities in Slovakia while simultaneously working towards political awareness-raising. In parallel, they refer to new forms of cooperation and reconciliation between Jews and non-Jews, for example in arts, literature, and intercultural exchanges. Furthermore, the research results distinctly reconfirm that painful and complex debates about the past continue and that the striving for historical repression has not ceased.

Finally, the country-specific study in Poland (Glöckner, Menachem Zoufalá) reveals how especially committed Jews inside and outside local communities work on concepts of religious, cultural, and intellectual renewal, but also search for new forms of intercultural exchange, in particular at places with a rich Jewish history. These projects are also understood as efficient means against a strong trend of new Polish nationalism which does not make the life of ethnocultural minorities any easier. Remarkably, key figures of the Jewish communities see the future of Jewish life in Poland as firmly intertwined with the future of Europe.

As in other research projects, the voices of participating scientists and authors represent pluralistic assessments concerning the status quo and future perspectives of Jewish life in Europe. This involves inter alia the inner dynamics and cohesion of the Jewish communities, insecurities, and potential external threats. In particular, in the empirical part of the book, readers will encounter parallel, sometimes conflicting, views and interpretations, so they can form their own opinion of a Jewry that is seeking its authentic path while shaping the developments of Europe.

Eduard Nižňanský and Katarína Bohová
Perceptions of the Holocaust in Slovak Historiography and Among the General Public after the Establishment of the Slovak Republic in 1993

This text and study presents a brief overview of the most important trends in the Slovak historiography of the Holocaust within recent three decades. Prior to 1989, the Holocaust was a topic marginalized in the country's historical research. The most important finding that emerges from the analysis of Slovak literature on the Holocaust is that, besides its obvious historiographic dimension, it was frequently meant to serve political purposes (including in the area of education). The works published after 1989 can be categorized as follows: collections of documents; memoirs; the perspective of the minority; the problem of local aggressors; the social background of the Holocaust; legal analysis of anti-Jewish legislation; oral history; the so-called Slovak revisionism; and connection between the historiographic and political levels. In this text, we analyze the link between historiography and politics in the example of Vladimír Mečiar's cabinet and revisionist publications. We also consider the impact of revisionism on the formation of national symbols (the case of a memorial of Ferdinand Ďurčanský) as well as the historiography situated between science and the Catholic Church's interpretation of history (of the Slovak state and the beatification of bishop Ján Vojtaššák).

Historical Review: Politics of Antisemitism and the Holocaust in Slovakia 1939–1945

In March 1939 Nazi Germany decided to take advantage of its geopolitical dominance in Central Europe and intervene against the Second Czechoslovak Republic. The result was the occupation of Bohemia and Moravia and the establishment of the Protectorate of Bohemia and Moravia, as well as the establishment of the Slovak State.[1]

---

[1] By the Constitution adopted on July 21, 1939 the state was officially called the Slovak Republic, the name used in official documentation. Slovak politicians and print media would commonly refer to it as the Slovak State.

The HSPP[2] leadership was able to implement its political agenda: "(...) One nation, one party, one leader for a united advance in the service of the nation."[3] The regime of the dictatorship of one political party, the HSPP, was created.

The foundation of the state subsequently defined its entire existence. The Slovak Republic was a satellite state of Nazi Germany. The Slovak Republic signed a "Treaty of Protection" with Nazi Germany, in which it allowed pledged German troops into Slovakian territory, to coordinate its foreign and military policy with Nazi Germany.[4]

The antisemitic policy of the Slovak Republic between 1939 and 1945 was based on the inherent antisemitism of the HSPP representatives who came to power after the Munich Agreement in 1938. This type of antisemitism has several levels.

The first level was the Christian level that emerged from earlier anti-Jewish stereotypes, such as the deicide myth or the Jews' refusal to accept Jesus as the Messiah, etc. Slovakia was a Catholic country,[5] so these stereotypes used by HSPP politicians, based on Christian anti-Judaism, greatly affected the population.

---

2 Hlinka's Slovak People's Party (HSPP) (Hlinkova slovenská ľudová strana; HSĽS), established in the year 1913 as the Slovak People's Party (Slovenská ľudová strana, SĽS) by Catholic priest Andrej Hlinka. HSPP was a far-right clerical-fascist political party with a strong Catholic fundamentalist, nationalist, and authoritarian ideology. HSPP was antisocialist, anti-communist, and against the influence of liberalism. After the formation of the Czechoslovak Republic (1918), the party preserved its conservative ideology, opposing Czechoslovakism and demanding Slovak autonomy. In the second half of the 1930s, the rise of totalitarian regimes in Europe and the party's inability to achieve long-term political objectives caused a loss of the party's faith in democratic procedures and saw the party turn towards more radical and extremist ideologies such as fascism. The HSPP never won more than a third of the electoral votes during the parliamentary elections in the democratic Czechoslovak Republic. At the time of Slovakia's autonomy (October 6, 1938–March 14, 1939), it created a system of dictatorship of one political party (HSPP). During the existence of the Slovak state (1939–1945) it was the only Slovak political party allowed, which was also confirmed in the Constitution of the Slovak Republic (1939). After World War II its activities were banned.
3 See Eduard Nižňanský, "Die Machtübernahme von Hlinkas Slowakischer Volkspartei in der Slowakei im Jahre 1938/39 mit einem Vergleich zur nationalsozialistischen Machtergreifung 1933/34 in Deutschland," in *Geteilt, besetzt, beherrscht*, ed. Monika Gletter et al. (Essen: Klartext Verl, 2004), 249–287.
4 Eduard Nižňanský et al. (eds.), *Slowakisch-deutsche Beziehungen 1938–1941 in Dokumenten I. Von München bis zum Krieg gegen die UdSSR* (Prešov: Universum, 2009), 304–309 (Vertrag über das Schutzverhältnis zwischen dem Deutschen Reich und dem Slowakischen Staat – 18. März Wien, 23. März Berlin).
5 According to A. Štefánek, the religious composition in Slovakia in 1940 was as follows: 1,956,233 Catholics (73.64 percent), 183,736 Greek Catholics (6.91 percent), 403,073 Protestants of all denominations (15.13 percent), and 9,994 non-denominational (0.37 percent). Anton Štefánek, *Základy sociografie Slovenska* [Foundations of the Sociography of Slovakia] (Bratislava, 1944), 179–180.

There were also national, economic, and political stereotypes. The national-linguistic stereotypes argued that "the Jews are not Slovaks" (or that the Jews spoke Hungarian, German, Yiddish), which was representative of the magyarization of Slovaks during the Austro-Hungarian Empire. *The New York Times* commented on the difficult position of Jews in Slovakia in Autumn 1938 as follows: "The Slovaks accuse them (Jews) of supporting Czech centralism and also of being pro-Hungarian and for using the Hungarian language. Hungarians accuse them of having betrayed Hungary."[6]

The economic (social) stereotypes included beliefs such as that the Jews exploited and exploit the Slovaks, living off their manual labour and at their expense, and that Jewish pub owners made alcoholic beverages out of the Slovaks. President Jozef Tiso[7] said in September 1940: "Concerns are raised, for instance, that what is done to the Jews is unchristian. But I say: Matters will have become most Christian after they have been thoroughly dealt with. Furthermore, they reproach us for violating the right to private property. They say we seize the Jews' radios. They say we seize Jewish stores, businesses, and that is allegedly unchristian. But I say: it is

---

6 *New York Times*, November 6, 1938.
7 Jozef Tiso (1887–1947) was a Roman Catholic priest and Slovak politician who acted as the Prime Minister of the Slovak Autonomous Region (from October 6, 1938 until March 14, 1939), the Prime Minister of the Slovak State (from March 14, 1939 until October 26, 1939), President of the Slovak Republic (1939–1945), and Chairman of Hlinka's Slovak People's Party, the only Slovak political party legalized during the Nazi occupation (1938–1945). After 1942, Tiso was styled as "Vodca" (Leader), a Slovak imitation of Führer. He eradicated democracy, replacing it with a totalitarian clerical-fascist regime embodied by the "One God, one nation, one organization" slogan. Tiso collaborated with Nazi Germany during WWII. Under Tiso and Prime Minister Tuka (from 1939 until 1944), the Slovak leadership aligned itself with Nazi policy by implementing anti-Semitic legislation. In 1942, Slovakia deported approximately 58,000 Jews to Nazi concentration camps and ghettos. After WWII, Tiso was sentenced to death. See: Milan Ďurica, *Jozef Tiso (1887–1947), Životopisný profil* [Jozef Tiso 1887–1947. A biographical profile] (Bratislava: Lúč, 2006); Miroslav Fabricius and Ladislav Suško (eds.), *Jozef Tiso: Prejavy a články 1913–1938* [Jozef Tiso: Speeches and Articles 1913–1938] (Bratislava: Historický ústav SAV, 2002); Miroslav Fabricius and Katarína Hradská (eds.), *Jozef Tiso: Prejavy a články 1939–1944* [Jozef Tiso: Speeches and Articles 1939–1944] (Bratislava: Historický ústav SAV, 2007); Ivan Kamenec, *Tragédia politika, kňaza a človeka* [Jozef Tiso: The Tragedy of a Politician, Priest and Man] (Bratislava: Premedia, 2013); James Mace Ward, *Priest, Politician, Collaborator: Jozef Tiso and the Making of Fascist Slovakia* (Ithaca and London: Cornell University Press, 2013); Eduard Nižňanský, "Die Vorstellungen Jozef Tiso über Religion, Volk und Staat und ihre Folgen für seine Politik während des Zweiten Weltkriegs," in *Religion und Nation: Tschechen, Deutsche und Slowaken im 20. Jahrhundert*, ed. Kristina Kaiserová et al. (Essen: Klartext, 2015), 39–83; Eduard Nižňanský, "Anti-Semitic Policies of Jozef Tiso during the War and before the National Court," in *Policy of Anti-Semitism and Holocaust in Post – War Retribution Trials in European States*, ed. Stanislav Mičev et al. (Banská Bystrica: Múzeum SNP, 2019), 113–148.

indeed Christian, for we only seize what they had seized from our people since long ago."[8]

Political stereotypes saw Jews as "liberal," leftist (or "Jewish-Bolshevik"), capitalist, and Marxist. From the perspective of the conservative, nationalist, clerical, and Catholic HSPP, Jews stood for liberal or left-wing ideologies. In this respect, the statements and practice of HSPP were based on the notion of "Jewish Bolshevism," the idea that essentially all Jews are adherents to radical communism. This claim has no rational basis because the Jews in Slovakia, in fact, belong to the traditional middle class and supported a large variety of political parties (including a Jewish one). In contrast, president Tiso called for a struggle against "all evildoers of the Slovak people, against Jewish Bolshevism."[9]

Such autochthonous antisemitism combined with the image of the Jew as the enemy of the Slovaks and the Slovak state.[10] This formed the basic intention of the Slovak antisemitism policy.[11] There were two political wings in the HSPP: "moderate" (Jozef Tiso) and radicals (Vojtech Tuka,[12] Alexander Mach[13]).

The "moderate" approach is reflected in a speech in January 1939 by Tiso: "The Jewish question will be resolved such that Jews in Slovakia will be left only as much influence as corresponds to their number in proportion to the entire population of Slovakia. Slovaks will be educated as such that they will be able to fully

---

8 *Slovák*, September 9, 1940, 4.
9 *Slovák*, June 6, 1939, 1.
10 Eduard Nižňanský, *Obraz nepriateľa v propagande počas II. svetovej vojny na Slovensku* [Image of the enemy in propaganda during World War II in Slovakia] (Banská Bystrica: Múzeum SNP, 2016).
11 For a chronology and phases of the Holocaust in Slovakia, see Eduard Nižňanský, "Der Holocaust in der Slowakei," in *Unterrichtsbeispiele zu den Verbrechen im Nationalsozialismus*, ed. Ulrich Habermann, Jörg Kayser, and Henrich Scheller (Berlin: Cultus e.v., 2005), 7–17.
12 Vojtech "Béla" Tuka (1880–1946) was a Slovak politician of the HSPP who served as Prime Minister (1939–1940) and Minister of Foreign Affairs (1940–1944), as well as a collaborator with Nazi Germany. Tuka was one of the main forces behind the deportation of the Jews from Slovakia to Nazi concentration camps in German occupied Poland. He was the leader of the radical wing of the HSPP. He was executed after WWII.
13 Alexander Mach (1902–1980) was associated with the far right wing of HSSP. Mach came to the fore in 1938 after the Munich Agreement and subsequent upsurge in Slovak nationalism as a close associate of Vojtech Tuka and Ferdinand Ďurčanský. He was the head of the Slovak Office of Propaganda (1938–1939). Mach was a member of the Slovak parliament from 1938 to 1945. He was an important representative of the paramilitary organization Hlinka Guard. In the years 1939–1944 he was its main commander. Hlinka Guard organized violent actions against the "enemies of Slovakia," including Jews. From July 1940 he was also Minister of the Interior. As a minister, he organized the creation of Jewish labour camps in Slovakia. As a minister, he was responsible for organizing the deportation of Jews in 1942. After WWII he was sentenced to 30 years in jail.

enjoy economic control and be able to gradually take over all positions heretofore occupied by Jews."[14]

The "moderate" promoted antisemitic policies were based on a quota that limited Jews in the social, economic, and other spheres of life to about four percent. This was implemented from the onset of Slovakia autonomy in Autumn 1938 to the Salzburg negotiations in 1940. However, after antisemitic policy became radicalized, the moderates did not express themselves or protest against the deportations of Jews in 1942.

In 1939, the radical Alexander Mach declared: "They've dealt with the Jews who have gold, wealth everywhere, and we will take care of them as well (...) he who does not work will not ever eat. He who has stolen something will have it taken from him! This is the practical solution to the entire Jewish question!"[15]

This was socio-economic antisemitism. Radicals wanted to exclude the Jewish community from society at all costs, despite the consequences for the majority of the community.

From the beginning of its existence, the Hlinka Guard[16] was also radically antisemitic.

With the intervention of Nazi Germany in Slovak state politics, political radicals rose to power in the summer of 1940. However, the "moderates" were not opposed to the radicals' attitude to "solving" the Jewish question. The politics of radical antisemitism resulted in a radical pauperization of the Jewish community in the wake of the liquidation and Aryanization of Jewish companies and businesses, as well as a continuous ban on issuing various licenses. The political program culminated with the organizing of Jewish deportations in 1942.

If it was aimed at Jews, the Slovak State first defined "who a Jew was" and then adopted legislation that infringed on Jewish property rights or professional activity.

On 18 April 1939, the Slovak government headed by Tiso passed Act no. 63/1939 Coll. regarding the definition of the term Jews and the limitation of Jewish activity in some professions. The definition of "Jew" covered all individuals professing a Jewish religion (unless they were christened before 30 October 1918), individuals without the sacrament of confession who had Jewish parents, as well as the children of such individuals. According to the historian Ivan Kamenec, this definition is based on religious (confessional) criteria.[17] The definition of "Jew" according to

---

14 *Slovenská politika*, January 27, 1939, 2.
15 *Slovák*, February 7, 1939, 4.
16 The Hlinka Guard (Hlinkova Garda) was a militia (fighting organization of non-professional soldiers, citizens of the Slovak State) maintained by the Hlinka's Slovak People Party.
17 Ivan Kamenec, *Po stopách tragédie* [On the trial of tragedy] (Bratislava: Archa, 1991), 48.

Act no. 63/1939 Coll. was later specified by Regulation no. 102/1939 Coll. of the Office of the National Ministry of Justice and Internal Affairs from 26 April 1939. The regulation stated that the term "Jew" was defined till the end of the rearranging of social, economic, and political circumstances in the Slovak State, as well as in accordance with national tradition and in view of national subsistence, so that the Slovak nation could take over all public, economic and cultural positions crucial for its continued existence. The term "Jew," defined in social and economic terms, was not intended to sort people by confession. The legislative body purported to move from a confessional definition toward a national one. The government made leeway for exceptions. This model was symptomatic for Slovak State politicians, including Tiso: on the one hand, there were sanctions (restrictions, disqualifications); on the other hand, there was the handing out of exceptions to those whom they chose at their own whim because, for instance, their profession made them necessary for the majority of society to properly function (doctors, veterinaries, engineers, etc.).

The Slovak State, in fact, aimed to regulate every aspect of life of the Jewish community. The Jews, as pariahs, could only stand by and watch what the state authorities would come up with next in an attempt to persecute them. The process of excluding Jews from public life began with the adoption of several government decrees between April and July 1939. The number of Jews active in some liberal professions (advocacy, medicine, pharmacy, journalism, public employees) was also regulated, and the method was supposed to reduce Jewish participation within each profession to the above-mentioned four percent (numerus clausus). The situation became even worse when German armed troops arrived in Slovakia in late August 1939.[18]

In July 1940, the radicals gained a footing within the country, which had a catalyzing effect of the implementation of antisemitic politics. The Interior Ministry issued a series of discriminatory regulations. Jewish citizens were denied the right to own inns, hunting and fishing licenses, guns, passports, driving licenses, radios, and optical apparatuses. Jewish persecution intensified, and punishments for officials and Slovak citizens who attempted to help them were made more severe. The wave of discriminatory measures continued with the expulsion of Jewish students from schools, in accordance with Regulation no. 208/1940 Coll. from 30 August 1940. This method of intervention against Jewish citizens was also approved by president Tiso. On the topic of limiting educational opportunities to the Jewish

---

[18] It was in preparation for the war against Poland. The arrival of the Wehrmacht in Slovakia was based on the "Protection Treaty, March 1939."

community, he made the following extreme nationalist (perhaps even Judeophobic) remarks:

> Do not let them into schools, do not give Jews an opportunity for education. I say: if I want to protect my people so it is never despoiled by the Jew again, I must prevent him from doing so. I do not want our townsman to go to a Jewish innkeeper who sells on credit, then to sign a note and go to a Jewish banker, from the banker to an advocate, from him to court, and so, without violence, without theft, without blood they seize the property of the Slovak man. If I want to protect the Slovak, I must sever this Jewish chain. We must prevent Jews, armed with every sort of scholarly knowledge, from being able to pounce at the Slovak man in the future.[19]

Jews were expelled from all schools except public schools, where they were taught in separate classes.

In the autumn of 1940, Dieter Wisliceny, a German adviser (in German – Berater) on the Jewish question, came to Slovakia.

In September 1940, Constitutional Law 210/1940 Coll. was adopted, which enabled the government to "solve" the Jewish question in one year. It was a classic Enabling Act.[20] Thus, from September 1940 until September 1941, we can only find government regulations "solving" the Jewish question. Subsequently, the government adopted Regulation no. 222/1940 Coll. which created the Central Economic Office (CEO, in Slovak "Ústredný hospodársky úrad") which had: "performed everything that was necessary for the exclusion of Jews from Slovak economic life and for the transfer of Jewish property into Christian ownership, according to specific instruction."[21] Its first chairman was Augustín Morávek.[22] The CEO functioned side by side with the Cabinet Office.

All Jewish organizations besides the official Jewish religious communities were disbanded after September 1940. A single authorized organization was established by the state – the Jewish Central (JC, in Slovak "Ústredňa Židov," Regulation

---

19 *Slovák*, September 25, 1940, 4.
20 Constitutional Act No. 210/1940 Coll. adopted on September 3, 1940: "Section 1 (1) The Government is authorised to take all the measures necessary in order to: a) exclude Jews from the Slovak economic and social life, b) transfer the Jewish assets into the Christian property, (2) Authorisation according to Sec. 1 shall be valid for one year since the date this Act entered into force." Slovak Law Code 1940, Constitutional Act No. 210/1940 Coll.
21 Ivan Kamenec, *Po stopách tragédie* [On the trial of the tragedy], 95.
22 Augustín Morávek (1901–?) was a Slovak politician and head of the Central Economic Office (CEO; Ústredný hospodársky úrad) from 1940 to 1942. Morávek actively participated in anti-Jewish measures and anti-Semitic legislation. Through the CEO, he managed the process of aryanization and liquidation of Jewish businesses. However, during the war, in connection with the investigation of the corruption of the CEO, he escaped (probably abroad) and thus avoided the post-war trials.

no. 234/1940 Coll.) – of which every Jew was required to be a member. The JC basically imposed state orders on the Jewish community.

Another anti-Jewish measure concerned Slovak housemaids employed in Jewish households: "On the basis of Art. 2 § 2 of Act no. 190/1939 Coll., the interior Ministry prohibits the employment of Aryan women under 40 years of age in Jewish households from 15 September 1940." This affected many Slovaks who subsequently could not find another source of income.

Anti-Jewish measures enacted in 1941 also concerned Jewish immovable property. Jews in Slovakia were forbidden to live on streets and squares named after Anton Hlinka or Adolf Hitler. Apparently, Jews were not forced to move house for this reason.

On 9 September 1941, the Slovak government passed Regulation no. 198/1941 Coll. (the so-called Jewish Codex) on the legal status of Jews. With 270 articles, it was the most extensive legal norm ratified during the entire existence of the Slovak Republic. Similar to the Nazi Nuremberg laws, it determined Jewish identity on the basis of a racial principle. Whoever was descended from at least three ethnically Jewish grandparents was considered Jewish, and whoever was descended from at least one was considered a Jewish mixed-blood.[23] The Codex was opposed by Catholic bishops, and the Vatican diplomatically protested.[24] President Tiso was entitled to grant an exemption to certain individuals.[25]

Provisions on the mandatory marking of Jews under Regulation no. 198/1941 Coll. came into being on 18 September 1941 with the publication of a decree of the Interior Ministry that specified the marking method. Jewish individuals were required to sew a visible Jewish mark on the left side of their outer garment, a yellow star made of felt, linen or other material, with a diameter of six cm and a light blue border 0.5 cm wide. Mandatory marking did not apply to children under six years of age, Jewish spouses of non-Jews, Jews retained in state services, Jews possessing a valid employment permit, and Jews baptized prior to 10 September 1941.[26]

---

[23] See Slovak Law Code 1941, Govt. Reg. 198/1941 Coll.
[24] Ivan Kamenec, Vilém Prečan, and Stanislav Škorvánek (eds.), *Vatikán a Slovenská republika (1939–1945) Dokumenty.* [Vatican and Slovak Republic 1939–1945. Documents] (Bratislava: SAP, 1992), 56–66.
[25] This discretion followed from § 255 and § 256 of Regulation 198/1941 Coll.
[26] *Úradné noviny*, September 9, 1941, 1573.

Aryanization

From the very beginning of the existence of the Slovak Republic, its leading politicians promised that they would take Jewish businesses into "Aryan" hands by means of Aryanization and liquidation. These claims were based on the aforementioned socio-economic antisemitism. A state-guaranteed mechanism intended to despoil Jews of entrepreneurial, immovable, and movable property was systematically prepared – effectively, an encroachment on Jewish property rights. As the state legitimized Aryanization, its occurrence always fell within the confines of law, as well as the actions of Aryanizers. The regime created conditions under which Aryanization was considered permitted, commonplace, without risk of punishment, and, of course, backed by leading political figures. Aryanization was supported even by the president and Catholic priest Tiso. They cast away all moral principles, and the majority of the community, who took part in the process, gradually sunk into immorality, where everyone's desire was simply to "hoard" as much as possible. The practical consequences of Aryanization and liquidation of Jewish property was the impoverishment of the Jewish community, which was then ghettoized and, in the end, deported to the concentration camps.

The Slovak Republic's encroachments on Jewish property concerned: a) agricultural property (Act. no. 46/1940 Coll., and subsequent decrees of the State Land Office); b) Jewish companies and businesses (Act no. 113/1940 Coll., Government regulation no. 303/1940 Coll., a.o.); c) the Jewish housing fund (Government decree no. 238/1941 Coll. from 1 November 1941, a.o.); d) Jewish bank accounts (Regulation no. 271/1940, 272/1940, 186/1941, 199/1941, a.o.); e) Jewish movable property (a large number of regulations encroaching upon property rights, up to and including regulations from 1942, when tax offices auctioned the deportees property).

Other severe restrictions covered professional activity in certain fields (e.g., doctors, pharmacists, lawyers, etc.), which debarred Jews from earning a living on their own.

Of approximately 12,000 Jewish businesses and business licenses, about 2,000 were aryanized and the rest were liquidated.[27] The Slovak Republic aryanized agricultural property, bank deposits, real estate, and movable property, which it then sold off in various ways. If the Slovak Republic instrumentalized and institutional-

---

27 Ivan Kamenec, *Po stopách tragédie* [On the trial of the tragedy], 111–112; Jean-Marc Dreyfus and Eduard Nižňanský, "Jews and non-Jews in the aryanization process comparison of France and the Slovak State, 1939–1945," in *Facing the catastrophe: Jews and non-Jews in Europe during World War II* (Oxford: Berg, 2011), 13–39.

ized economic antisemitism, then it is not surprising that the majority of the population participated in the confiscation of Jewish property.

The aryanization and liquidation of Jewish companies and businesses, as well as bans on certain professions, meant that Jews were pauperized by their own state and by fellow citizens.[28] These results of Slovak antisemitic politics, put into practice by the executive and the legislative bodies of state, had the consequence that the "Jewish question" became a social problem across the state from autumn 1941.[29] The results of Slovak antisemitic politics crossed paths with the Nazi Holocaust plan in autumn 1941, and the outcome were the deportations of Jews from Slovakia under mutual cooperation of both sides.[30] After all, Nazi Germany did not expect any complications in Slovakia, as one can judge by the protocols from the Wannsee conference.[31] In 1942, the words of the German adviser Wisliceny were fulfilled: "Ridding 90,000 Jews of property will give rise to a problem that can only be solved by deportation."[32]

---

28 Eduard Nižňanský, "On relations between the Slovak majority and Jewish minority during World War II," *Yad vashem studies* 42, no. 2 (2014): 47–89.

29 To support this historical construction, we quote an explanatory report from the Interior Ministry on April 1, 1942. According to this report, out of 88,951 Jews (Government regulation no. 198/1941 Coll. cited a number of 89,053 Jews) that made for approximately 22,000 households, 32,527 (36.3 percent) were initially gainfully employed. Another 4,000 Jews lived off income gained from their property without active employment (altogether 41 percent). Aryanizations and liquidations of companies and businesses, as well as rejections of work permits and various other anti-Jewish measures, led to the exclusion of 22,267 individuals, and 2,500 individuals (out of 4,000) lost the opportunity to live off income from their property (24,767 – meaning 71.7 percent). The explanatory report noted that about two thirds of these individuals were heads of families or households. The report concluded that 16,000 households (that is to say 72 percent of the original 22,000) lost the opportunity to earn a living. It also estimated the cost of supporting 16,000 pauperized Jewish households at 160 million Slovak Kron per year (10,000 per household) – comprising about 64,000 Jews. If we compare this number with the number of deportees – approximately 58,000 – and add an approximate number of 4,500 Jews interned in Jewish labour camps and Jewish labour centers, we may conclude that deportations allowed the government to deal with the Jewish social problem successfully. See Eduard Nižňanský and Ivan Kamenec (eds.), *Holokaust na Slovensku 2. Prezident, vláda, Snem SR a Štátna rada o židovskej otázke (1939–1945). Dokumenty.* [Holocaust in Slovakia 2. President, government, parliament SR and State Council about Jewish question (1939–1945). Documents] (Bratislava: NMŠ, 2003), 180–181.

30 Eduard Nižňanský, "Expropriation and deportation of Jews in Slovakia," in *Facing the Nazi genocide: non-Jews and Jews in Europe* (Berlin: Metropol, 2004), 205–230.

31 ADAP Serie E, Tom 1, p. 272 (Document no. 150); Eduard Nižňanský, "The discussions of Nazi Germany on the deportation of Jews in 1942 – the examples of Slovakia, Romania, and Hungary," *Historický časopis* 59 (suppl. 2011): 111–136.

32 Ivan Kamenec, *Po stopách tragédie* [On the trial of the tragedy],141.

Deportations of Jews from Slovakia 1942

Despite extensive research, we still cannot determine if the Slovak side first offered its pauperized Jews to Nazi Germany or if it only reacted promptly and positively to a German offer.[33] Slovak documents show that Prime Minister Tuka and Interior Minister Mach detailed the planned deportations at a government meeting on 3 March 1942.[34] We believe that the 1942 deportations represent the climax of the antisemitic politics of the Slovak Republic. The technical aspect of deportations from Slovak territories was ensured by the Slovak Republic authorities themselves.

From March 25 to October 20, 1942, 57 transport trains left Slovakia, of which 19 went to Auschwitz and 38 to the Lublin region. According to a report of the Slovak Ministry of Transportation and Public Works on January 14, 1943, the trains carried 57,752 Jews: 39,006 to the Lublin area and 18,746 Jews to Auschwitz.[35] Documents from the Ministry of Interior and the Ministry of Foreign Affairs refer to 57,628 deported Jews.[36]

Before the final transports left Slovakia in August 1942, President Tiso declared the following at a harvest home celebration in Holíč:

> I would like to bring up one more question. Whether what is being done is Christian. Is it humane? Is not it robbery? But I ask: is it Christian for the Slovak nation to want to eliminate its eternal enemy the Jews? Is it Christian? Love of self is a commandment of God, and that love of self compels me to get rid of everything that harms me, that threatens my life. I do not think anyone needs to be convinced that the Jews element threatens the life of a Slovak. (...) Slovak throw them off, get rid of the bad one![37]

The standpoints of the radical and conservative wings of HSPP thus drew surprisingly close. Political responsibility for organizing deportations remained with the

---

33 Eduard Nižňanský (ed.), *Holokaust na Slovensku 4, Dokumenty nemeckej proveniencie. 1939–1945* [Holocaust in Slovakia 4. The documents of German origins. (1939–1945)] (Bratislava: NMŠ, 2005), 113, 114, 207–212.
34 Eduard Nižňanský and Ivan Kamenec (eds.), *Holokaust na Slovensku 2. Prezident, vláda, Snem SR a Štátna rada o židovskej otázke (1939–1945). Dokumenty* [Holocaust in Slovakia 2. President, government, parliament SR and State Council about Jewish question (1939–1945). Documents], 142.
35 Eduard Nižňanský (ed.), *Holokaust na Slovensku 4, Dokumenty nemeckej proveniencie. 1939–1945* [Holocaust in Slovakia 4. The documents of German origins. (1939–1945)], 487–488, 532–533.
36 Eduard Nižňanský and Ivan Kamenec (eds.), *Holokaust na Slovensku 2. Prezident, vláda, Snem SR a Štátna rada o židovskej otázke (1939–1945). Dokumenty* [Holocaust in Slovakia 2. President, government, parliament SR and State Council about Jewish question (1939–1945). Documents], 234–235.
37 *Slovák*, August 18, 1942, 4.

Slovak political representation, which during the war agreed to deport (but not to murder) its citizens of Jewish origin to an uncertain fate, where they could come to bodily, familial, and human harm and where they could certainly not fare as well as in Slovakia. The Slovak Republic even paid 500 RM to Nazi Germany for each deported Jew.[38]

The German Ambassador H. Ludin had already wrote to Berlin in April 1942: "The Slovak government agreed to transport all Jews from Slovakia without any pressure from the German side. The President himself personally agreed with transportation, despite the intercession of the Slovak episcopate."[39]

The literature is rife with speculations and discussions on who stopped the deportations. A social analysis of the remaining Jewish community reveals that most of those who held exceptions were professionally indispensable (e. g., doctors, veterinaries, engineers, etc.), or were employed at Aryanized businesses as "economic Jews," because the new owners were either uninterested or incapable of running the company. Some Jews were stationed in Jewish labour camps (Nováky, Sereď, Vyhne), where they worked for the benefit of the state.[40] After the deportations in 1942 20,000 Jews lived in Slovakia.

The "Peaceful Years": 1943–1944

In February 1943, Interior Minister and HG Commander Alexander Mach spoke at a county meeting of the Hlinka Guard in the town of Ružomberok and declared: "But March will come, April will come, and transports will leave."[41]

In 1943, an attempt was made to recommence deportations of Jews in Slovakia, but these did not ultimately take place. The attempt came after the defeat of the German Wehrmacht by Stalingrad and the defeat of Nazi Germany and fascist Italy in Africa. The situation on the front slowly began turning to the advantage of the anti-Hitler coalition (USA – Great Britain – USSR).

---

38 Eduard Nižňanský, "Payment for the deportations of Jews from Slovakia in 1942," in *Discourses – diskurse* (Praha, 2008), 317–331.
39 Eduard Nižňanský (ed.), *Holokaust na Slovensku 4, Dokumenty nemeckej proveniencie. 1939–1945* [Holocaust in Slovakia 4. The documents of German origins. (1939–1945)], 127–128.
40 See Igor Baka, *Židovský tábor v Novákoch 1941–1944.* [The Jewish Camp in Nováky 1941–1944] (Bratislava: Zing Print, 2001); Ján Hlavinka and Eduard Nižňanský, *Pracovný a koncentračný tábor v Seredi 1941–1945* [The Labor and Concentration camp in Sereď 1941–1945] (Bratislava: DSH, 2009); Eduard Nižňanský, "Die Aktion Nisko, das Lager Sosnowiec (Oberschlesien) und die Anfänge des 'Judenlagers'" in Vyhne (Slowakei), *Jahrbuch für Antisemitismusforschung 11* (Berlin: Metropol, 2002), 325–335.
41 *Gardista*, February 9, 1943, 2.

Slovak National Uprising and Jews

In the autumn of 1944, the situation changed. The Slovak National Uprising[42] broke out on August 29, facing Waffen-SS, Wehrmacht, and Einsatzgruppe H under the command of the SS-Obergruppenführer Gottlob Berger.[43] At a meeting on September 1 that included Berger, German Ambassador H. Ludin,[44] and other Embassy staff, as well as other German officials, it was decided to radically resolve the "Jewish question." Einsatzgruppe H (head Jozef Witiska)[45] would imprison the Jews in camps, which would be guarded by the Hlinka Guard. The fate of Jews and the "rebels" thus "overlapped" and often resembled each other.

Witiska's report of Einsatzgruppe H activities by December 9, 1944 mentions that the number of people arrested had reached 18,937, of whom 9,653 were Jews and 3,409 partisans (others included deserters and a variety of other people). Some 8,975 Jews and 530 "others" (in German "sonstige") were deported to German concentration camps, while 2,257 of those arrested were murdered (in German "Sonderbehandlung"). Jews, Slovaks, Roma, soldiers, partisans, "rebels," and civilians were found in mass graves. According to historian Mičev, there were 211 mass graves with 5,306 victims in Slovakia.

Sometime at the end of September 1944, one of Adolf Eichmann's trusted subordinates, SS-Haupsturmführer Alois Brunner,[46] came to Slovakia, took command of Camp Sereď, and organized the renewed deportations of Jews. According to the last research, 11,719 Jews were deported from Sereď on 11 transport trains (Auschwitz, Bergen-Belsen, Oranienburg, Ravensbrück, Mauthausen, Theresienstadt).

---

42 The Slovak National Uprising was an anti-fascist political and military uprising (August 29–October 26, 1944). Slovak political leaders (communists and democrats) who were in opposition to the regime of Jozef Tiso prepared the uprising, by which they declared themselves to the anti-Hitler coalition. The military action was carried out by part of the Slovak army in conjunction with the partisans. The uprising was mainly concentrated in central Slovakia. It was defeated by the military forces of Nazi Germany.
43 Gottlob Christian Berger (1896–1975) was a senior German Nazi official who held the rank of SS-Obergruppenführer und General der Waffen-SS (lieutenant general) and was the chief of the SS Main Office responsible for Schutzstaffel (SS) recruiting during World War II.
44 Hanns Elard Ludin (1905–1947) was a German diplomat and German ambassador in Bratislava in 1941–1945. After World War II he was convicted and executed by the National Court in 1947.
45 Josef Witiska (1894–1945), SS-Obergruppenführer, who from September 1944 was Chief of Einsatzgruppe H in Slovakia (paramilitary death squads of Nazi Germany).
46 Alois Brunner (1912–?), joined Eichmann in 1939 in the Zentrallstelle für jüdische Auswanderung in Vienna. He organized deportations from Vienna, Berlin, Salonica, Paris, and Slovakia.

Apostolic Delegate Giuseppe Burzio[47] discussed the tragic situation of Jews in a telegram on October 26, 1944:

> Steps to save the Jews before the occupation were ineffective; deportations is [sic] ongoing and the search for Jews in hiding continues. As a result of the occupation, the remnants of Slovak independence have also disappeared. The government and the President of the Republic servilely carry out the orders of the occupation forces' administrative offices. Good Catholics are dismayed by the president's attitude and are asking what he is waiting for, why does he not submit his resignation.[48]

Burzio's comment reflects Tiso's personal and political failure. As quoted above, Burzio had earlier commented that Tiso has "no understanding and not even one word of sympathy for the persecuted: he sees the Jews as the source of all evil." Clearly, the Italian and Slovak Catholic priests judged the tragedy of the Jews completely differently.

The policy of antisemitism, deportations, and the Holocaust in Slovakia meant the end of the existence of an organized Jewish community in Slovakia. After World War II, most of the surviving Jews emigrated from Slovakia (for example to Israel).

Introduction: The Relations Between History and Politics

The mutual influence of historiography and politics (or even national memory) is a phenomenon that occurs in every state. It affects more than just interpretations of contemporary history. The pursuit of monuments, busts, and street names – elements that aspire to be the symbols of a state or nation – is a tendency that we may encounter throughout the age of ideology, i.e. in the nineteenth and twentieth centuries, as well as in earlier periods (secular or ecclesiastical monuments). We are confronted with it. When it comes to Slovakia, the interpretation of antisemitism and the Holocaust as well as their perception in historiography and in relation to actual politics are also linked to the fall of communism in 1989. Until that point, the Holocaust had been a marginal topic, both for the historiographical community and society (i.e. in school education). The fall of communism meant not only the

---

47 Giuseppe Burzio (1901–1966), Vatican diplomat, *Chargé d'affaires* in Slovakia in 1940–1945. He repeatedly intervened with the Slovak government to stop deportations of the Jews.
48 Ivan Kamenec, Vilém Prečan, and Stanislav Škorvánek (eds.), *Vatikán a Slovenská republika (1939–1945) Dokumenty* [Vatican and Slovak Republic 1939–1945. Documents], 202–203.

formation of new political institutions and the creation of parliamentary democracy in Czechoslovakia (and from 1993 onwards, in Slovakia itself, as the two countries separated), but also – importantly for this analysis – a brief ideological vacuum which was then gradually filled with the ideas of nationalism and Christianity.[49] Slovakia had essentially no liberal tradition to follow, even going back to the interwar period. From the perspective of forming and developing a sovereign state after a period of de facto dependence on USSR, it seemed logical that after the establishment of the Slovak Republic in 1993, Vladimír Mečiar's[50] cabinet actually tapped into the latent nationalism.

The Holocaust in Slovak Historiography

In general, it can be said that prior to 1989 the Holocaust was among several topics marginalized by Slovak historiography. While the seminal Slovak work on the Holocaust was written by Ivan Kamenec[51] back in the early 1970s as a doctoral dissertation, it was only published as a monograph in 1991. The most important finding that emerges from the analysis of Slovak literature on the Holocaust is that, besides its obvious historiographic dimension, it was frequently meant to serve political purposes (including in the area of education).

After 30 years of research, it can be acknowledged that the basic facts of the Holocaust in Slovakia are already reliably established and reconstructed, both in domestic and foreign historiography. They are being further elaborated, with a

---

49 Timothy Byrnes, *Transnational Catholicism in Postcommunist Europe* (Landham; Boulder; NY; Oxford: Rowman and Littlefield Publishers, 2001); Pedro Ramet, "Christianity and National Heritage among the Czechs and Slovaks," in *Religion und Nationalism in East European Politics*, ed. Pedro Ramet (Durham/London: Duke University Press, 1989), 264–285; Agáta Šústová Drelová, "Čo znamená národ pre katolíkov na Slovensku?" [What does the "nation" mean to Catholics in Slovakia?], *Historický časopis* 67 (2019): 385–412.

50 Vladimír Mečiar (1942) is a Slovak politician who served as Prime Minister of Slovakia three times, from 1990 to 1991, from 1992 to 1994, and from 1994 to 1998. He was the leader of the People's Party – Movement for a Democratic Slovakia (Ľudová Strana – Hnutie za demokratické Slovensko/ HZDS). Mečiar led Slovakia during the dissolution of Czechoslovakia in 1992–1993.

51 Ivan Kamenec, *Po stopách tragédie* [On the Trial of Tragedy]; see: Nina Paulovičová, "Pokus o komparáciu monografie Ivana Kamenca "Po stopách tragédie" s niektorými významnými dielami o holokauste v zahraničí" ["An attemp to compare Ivan Kamenec's monograph On the Trial of Tragedy with some important works on the Holocaust abroad"] in Edita Ivaničková et al., *Z dejín demokratických a totalitných režimov na Slovensku a v Československu v 20. Storočí* (Bratislava: HÚ SAV, 2008), 18–29.

focus on the chronological, regional, or thematic perspective.[52] Works of Slovak historiography published after 1989 can be categorized in the following way.

Collections of Documents

A five-volume edition, "Riešenie židovskej otázky na Slovensku" ("The Solution of the Jewish Question in Slovakia"), was published by the Museum of Jewish Culture in Bratislava.[53] This collection does not meet the basic criteria for the editing of scientific sources. In the case of the first three volumes, the author misrepresented the content of the documents and did not inform the readers of the changes made. There are also issues with document signatures as well as missing names and geographical and nominal entries in local registers.

The Milan Šimečka Foundation (Nádácia Milana Šimečku, Bratislava), with support from the Holocaust Documentation Centre (Dokumentačné stredisko holokaustu – DSH, Bratislava), has already published eight volumes in the thematically arranged "Holokaust na Slovensku" [*Holocaust in Slovakia*] series. Given the fact it was co-authored by one of the authors of this chapter, we will refrain from evaluating it here, but merely make a brief note of its existence. A German publication, "Die Verfolgung und Ermordung der europäischen Juden durch das nationalistische Deutschland 1933–1945, volume 13 (Slovakei, Rumänien und Bulgarien),"

---

[52] On the historiography of the Holocaust in Slovakia, see Ivan Kamenec, "Phenomenon of the Holocaust in Historiography, Art and the Consciousness of Slovak Society," in *Holocaust as a Historical and Moral Problem of the Past and the Present*, ed. Monika Vrzgulova and Daniela Richterová (Bratislava: DSH, 2008), 331–339; Eduard Nižňanský, "Der Holocaust in der Slowakei in der slowakischen Historiography der neunziger Jahre," *Bohemia* 44 (2003): 370–388; Nina Paulovičová, "The Unmasterable Past? Slovaks und the Holocaust: The Reception of the Holocoust in Post-communist Slovakia," in *Bringing the Dark Past to Light. The Reception of the Holocaust in Post-Communist Europa*, ed. John-Paul Himka and Joanna Michlic (Lincoln/London: University of Nebraska Press, 2013), 549–590; Nina Paulovičová, "Mapping the Historiography of the Holocaust in Slovakia in the Past Decade (2008–2018). Focus on the Analytical Category of Victims," *Judaica et Holocaustica* 10, no. 1 (2019): 46–71; Tomas Sniegon, *Vanished History. The Holocaust in Czech and Slovak Historical Culture* (Berghahn Books, 2017); Miloslav Szabó, "Zwischen Geschichtswissenschaft und Wissenschaft. Der Holocaust in der slowakischen Historiographie nach 1999", *Einsicht* 11 (2014): 16–23.

[53] L. Hubenák, ed. *Solution of the Jewish Question in Slovakia 1938–1945*. 5 volumes (Bratislava, n.d.).

makes extensive references to the aforementioned series, using it as a source of more than seventy percent of analyzed documents on Slovakia.[54]

Another publication of historical and, unusually, political significance is a collection of documents entitled "Vatikán a Slovenská republika" ["Vatican and the Slovak Republic"].[55] It gives Slovak readers access to the Vatican's diplomatic documents ("Actes and Documents du Saint Siège relatifs à la Second Guerre Mondial") which show the Holy See's approach to the "solution" of the Jewish question in Slovakia. However, materials regarding Vatican's internal matters, such as instructions issued to Slovak bishops during their visits to Rome, remain uncovered.

Memoirs

Memoirs provide insight into the perspective of the victims. Their publication throughout the post-World War II period played an important role for the development of historiography of this subject. Among the most notable positions were books co-authored by Alfred Wetzler[56] and Rudolf Vrba.[57] The authors of this memoir successfully escaped from the Auschwitz-Birkenau concentration camp in 1944. Their testimony about the situation in the camp and the mass killings there played an important role and was published as the "Auschwitz-Report."[58] After 1989, more of such accounts were published, coming from people who stood at different levels of hierarchy among concentration camp prisoners, from "ordinary häftlings" (Hilda Hrabovecká[59]) to individuals positioned much higher

---

54 Mariana Hausleitner and Souzana Hazan and Barbara Hutzelmann (Hg.), *Die Verfolgung und Ermordung der europäischen Juden durch das nationalsozialistischen Deutschland 1933–1945*. Band 13 Slowakei, Rumänien und Bulgarien (Berlin/Boston: Walter de Gruyter GmbH, 2018).
55 Ivan Kamenec, Vilém Prečan, and Stanislav Škorvánek, *Vatikán a Slovenská republika /1939–1945/. Dokumenty* [Vatican and the Slovak Republic 1939–1945].
56 Alfred Wetzler, *Čo Dante nevidel*. [What Dante Did not See] (Bratislava, 1964).
57 Rudolf Vrba, *I Cannot Forgive* (Vancouver, 1997).
58 Eduard Nižňanský, "The history of the escape of Arnošt Rosin and Czeslaw Mordowicz from the Auschwitz-Birkenau concentration camp to Slovakia in 1944," in *Uncovering the shoah:*
   resistance of Jews and their efforts to inform the world on genocide [Odhaľovanie Šoa : odpor a úsilie
Židov informovať svet o genocíde], ed. Ján Hlavinka and Hana Kubátová (Bratislava: HÚ SAV, 2016), 113–134; Ivan Kamenec, "The Escape of Rudolf Vrba and Alfréd Wetzler from Auschwitz and the Fate of Their Report," in Ján Hlavinka and Hana Kubátová (eds.), *Uncovering the shoah: resistance of Jews and their efforts to inform the world on genocide* [Odhaľovanie Šoa: odpor a úsilie Židov informovať svet o genocíde] (Bratislava: HÚ SAV, 2016), 101–112.
59 Hilda Hrabovecká. *Ruka s vytetovaným číslom* [Hand with a Tatooed Number] (Bratislava: Marenčin PT, 1998).

(Manca Schwalbová[60]). There have also been several memoirs authored by politicians of the war-time Slovak republic. Most of them, however, sidestep the subject of the Holocaust. We learn most about the "solution" of the Jewish issue from the works of Gejza Medrický[61] (Minister of Economy) and Imrich Karvaš[62] (Chairman of the National Bank).

Minority Perspectives

Most of the scholarly and popular literature on the Holocaust in Slovakia published after 1989 analyzes Jews in Slovakia[63] as a minority and an object of antisemitic policies of the Slovak leadership represented in the parliament (1939-1945) by Hlinka's Slovak People's Party [HSĽS – Hlinková slovenská ľudová strana].[64] The authors describe, in chronological or thematic order, the systematic elimination of Jews in that period – their exclusion from civic, political, and economic life, all the way to the tragic culmination in the shape of deportations to extermination camps. Most writers analyze history by looking at three main groups: victims (Jews), perpetrators (across the broader spectrum of the HSĽS ruling elite), and the silent majority. In doing so, they adopt a well-known scheme proposed by R. Hilberg: victims – murderers – bystanders.[65] In terms of attributing responsibility for the events, they tend to see the majority of Slovak population as something of a background element, a difficult-to-describe silent majority. Some present specific examples of violence (or the organization of violence) on the part of said majority, such as the Hlinka Guard (HG) or the paramilitary offshoot of the Deutsche Partei (DP),[66] the Freiwillige Schutzstaffeln (FS).[67] Sometimes, they focus on the role of

---

60 Schwalbová Manca, *Vyhasnuté oči* [Quiescent Eyes] (Bratislava, 1964).
61 Gejza Medrický, *Minister spomína* [The Minister's Reminiscence] (Bratislava: Litera, 1993).
62 Imrich Karvaš, *Moje pamäti (V pazúroch Gestapa)* [My Memories (In the Clasp of the Gestapo)] (Bratislava: NKV International, 1994).
63 The reference is to Jews in Slovakia, or the Jewish community in Slovakia, and not to Slovak Jews, since only a small minority of Jews declared themselves to be Slovaks. See: Livia Rothkirchen, "The Situation of Jews in Slovakia between 1939 and 1945," *Jahrbuch für Antisemitismusforschung* 7 (1998): 46–71.
64 The only legalized Slovak political party during the existence of the Slovak state in 1939–1945.
65 Raul Hilberg, *Perpetrators, Victims, Bystanders: The Jewish Catastrophe, 1933–1945* (New Work: HarperCollins, 1992); idem: *The Destruction of the European Jewry*, third edition (New Haven: Yale University Press, 2003).
66 The Deutsche Partei (DP) was a political party of the German minority (Volksdeutsch) in Slovakia, which had become fascist.
67 Freiwillige Schutzstaffeln (FS), Engl.: Voluntary Protection Corps.

individuals, e.g. Jozef Tiso (Prime Minister and, later, President of the Slovak Republic), Vojtech Tuka (Prime Minister) or Alexander Mach (Minister of the Interior). Although many works take their roots from or are influenced by the perspective of the Jewish minority, one should also take note of numerous studies, monographs as well as master and doctoral dissertations about particular Jewish communities (Bratislava – Petra Lárišová; Igor Baka, Zuzana Ševčíková, and Eduard Nižňanský; Banská Bystrica – Eduard Nižňanský and Michala Lônčíková; Dolný Kubín – Barbora Jakobyová and Eduard Nižňanský; Dunajská Streda – Atilla Simon; Komárno – Miroslav Michela; Medzilaborce – Ján Hlavinka, etc.). Some books have also been written in English. The Israeli Chamber of Commerce supports the publication of local monographs under its "Lost City" project. A special place within this thematic category is held by works about the system of forced labor and Jewish work camps in Slovakia (Nováky – published by Baka[68]; Sereď – published by Jan Hlavinka and Eduard Nižňanský[69]).

Local Aggressors

To fully reflect the trends in the historiography of the Holocaust, we have to mention the work of Katarína Hradská, who wrote a book about Dieter Wisliceny,[70] who acted as a Nazi advisor ("Berater") for the "solution" of the Jewish issue in Slovakia.

Social Background of the Holocaust

The first works capturing the social environment and, specifically, the relations between the Jewish minority and the Slovak majority population appeared after 2000. They present changes and processes that led to the exclusion of Jews from the Slovak economy: Aryanization, liquidation of Jewish businesses and the craft industry as well as deportations. They also describe a shift in the stratification of the Slovak majority which occurred as the proponents of Aryanization benefitted from taking over Jewish property and used it to reap new profits. It seems that the above-mentioned phenomena provide a more fitting basis for the analysis of

---

68 Igor Baka, *Židovský tábor v Novákoch 1941–1944* [The Jewish Camp in Novák 1941–1944].
69 Ján Hlavinka and Eduard Nižňanský, *Pracovný a koncentračný tábor v Seredi 1941–1945* [The Labour and Concentration camp in Sereď 1941–1945].
70 Katarína Hradská, *Prípad Wisliceny. Nacistickí poradcovia a židovská otázka na Slovensku* [The Wisliceny Case: Nazi Advisors and the Jewish Question in Slovakia] (Bratislava: AEPress, 1999).

the minority-majority relations than Hilberg's classification. One also needs to identify which exact groups within the Slovak majority actually replaced the Jews after their elimination from economic, professional, and social life. This question is linked to another topic: the formation of a middle class. This is because, in terms of their economic and social position as well as their representation in freelance professions, Jews in Slovakia represented a typical middle class. Here, the analysis necessarily enters the realm of politics, as the group which became the new middle class owed their status to the help from the country's only legal party, HSĽS, and its connection to the regime. This is why more attention needs to be paid to local aggressors and perpetrators, primarily the lower-level representatives of the public administration and party structures, including the Hlinka Guard (HG). We can examine the upward mobility of these local groups which used their political connections and exploited the circumstances by coming into the possession of wealth and property removed from Jews.[71] The results of such research done to date show that is it best to analyze these events locally, with a focus on a particular town or city.

Legal Analysis of Anti-Jewish Legislation

Historians of law (e.g. Katarína Zavacká, Ladislav Hubenák) have published several volumes on this subject. We can only remark that the first of such works was published as early as the 1960s.

Oral History

A separate part of research on the Holocaust is the work done by ethnologists (Peter Salner, Monika Vrzgulová) rather than historians. The Milan Šimečka Foundation, with the support of Yale University, recorded 150 spoken accounts from Holocaust victims. The Holocaust Museum in Sereď and the Museum of the Slovak National Uprising in Banská Bystrica have also made similar efforts worthy of attention.

---

[71] For more detail, see: Eduard Nižňanský and Ján Hlavinka, *Arizácie* [The Aryanization] (Bratislava, 2010); Eduard Nižňanský and Ján Hlavinka, *Arizácie v regiónoch Slovenska* [The Aryanization in the regions of Slovakia] (Bratislava, 2010).

Generally About the Works of the Holocaust

Historians (Ivan Kamenec, Ladislav Lipscher)

So far, only three monographs have attempted to capture the Slovak antisemitic policy and the Holocaust in Slovakia in its entirety.

With his interest in the persecution and elimination of the Jewish population in Slovakia, Ivan Kamenec has essentially been a lone crusader in Slovak historiography since the 1960s. His classic work "Po stopách tragédie" ["On the Trail of Tragedy"] to this day constitutes a seminal piece of research on the Holocaust in Slovakia. We see Kamenec's work, influenced by Marxism, as analysis of not only the Holocaust but also the war-time Slovak Republic. He pointed to the problem of autochthonous antisemitism in Slovakia and its implications for the formulation of antisemitic policies – whether among the moderates[72] or the radicals.[73] He also examined how the authorities of the Slovak Republic defined Jews as an enemy and what consequences that attitude had for the Jewish community. He presented, in chronological order, the institutionalization and implementation of antisemitic policies by the war-time state. From a broader perspective, he also showed the solution of the Jewish question as part of a domestic power struggle between the so-called moderates and radicals, as both groups sought to gain the support of Nazi Germany and secure their political power. He wanted to distinguish genuinely autochthonous antisemitic policies of the war-time Slovak Republic from those that emerged as a result of Nazi pressure (e.g. deportations). Naturally, political realities of the times prevented Kamenec from researching foreign archives (e.g. Politisches Archiv des Auswärtiges Amt, Berlin). Prior to 1989, he had only been allowed to publish some of the results of his extensive work.

For similar reasons, Ladislav Lipscher's book *Židia v slovenskom štáte* [Jews in the Slovak State] was only published in Slovakia after 1989. After the author's emigration, the book was also translated into German and English editions. After leaving Slovakia, Lipscher himself ceased his work as a historian and abandoned his research on the Holocaust.

---

72 For example, President Jozef Tiso.
73 Specifically, Prime Minister Vojtech Tuka and Minister of the Interior Alexander Mach.

The Problem of the So-called Slovak Revisionism

Even in the case of a subject such as the Holocaust, there have been attempts at politicizing it. After Slovakia's democratic transition, a group of nationalist-minded historians returned to Slovakia. In principle, there have been no revisionist works published in Slovakia – no publications fundamentally question the existence of the Holocaust. The "revisionism" that one might encounter is a certain defense mechanism adopted by some within the historiographic community, whereby the responsibility for the deportation of Jews is attributed to Nazi Germany or, possibly, individual figures among the radicals (Prime Minister V. Tuka or Minister of the Interior, A. Mach). According to this line of thought, President Tiso supposedly helped many Jews through "thousands of exemptions" and bore no responsibility for antisemitic policies adopted in Slovakia. Examples of such perception include a collection entitled "Zamlčaná pravda o Slovensku" ["The Concealed Truth about Slovakia"] and Milan Stanislav Ďurica's[74] book *Slovenský podiel na európskej tragédii Židov* [The Slovak Share in the European Tragedy of Jews]. Ďurica exclusively used sources that suited his line of argument, ascribing the responsibility for the "solution of the Jewish question" to Nazi Germany and presenting Tiso as well as most of the Slovak ministers (with the exception of Tuka and Mach) as champions of Slovak independence in the face of Nazi pressure. The author frequently replaced the term "deportation" with "evacuation" and interpreted the Constitutional Act No. 68/1942 Coll. as a form of "resistance," while it was this exact legal document that, by means of retroactivity, legalized the deportation of Jews (about 58,000 Jews were deported between March and October 1942). The Act reflected the supposed pursuit of the so-called lesser evil – a trend that so often manifested itself during the times of the Slovak Republic. By adopting it, the country's politicians wanted to at least partially save their faces by showing that Slovakia was not deporting all Jews. A political dimension can also be recognized in another book by Ďurica, *Dejiny Slovenska a Slovákov* [The History of Slovakia and Slovaks], published in 1995 as a supplementary school textbook, in which one finds antisemitic sentiment.

Similar notions were voiced by František Vnuk. In his biography of Alexander Mach (Minister of the Interior), Vnuk devotes merely 25 pages to antisemitic policies and the Holocaust, while almost entirely avoiding mentions of Mach's radical

---

74 Milan Stanislav Ďurica (1925) is a Slovak historian and theologian, professor of theology at the Salesian Theological College in Abano Terme (Italian), and since 1993 professor of scholastic history at the Cyril and Methodius Theological Faculty of the Comenius University in Bratislava (Slovakia). He retired from teaching in 1997. He has been criticized as an "ultranationalist."

antisemitic rhetoric and statements. There are barely a few lines on the 1942 deportations, with no specific numbers of affected people.[75]

As was already mentioned, the entire topic is connected with a broader discussion about the character of the war-time Slovak Republic's regime and the responsibility of Slovak politicians for the events of that time. In this context, the aforementioned works represent the defensive line of the argument whereby President Tiso, the government, and the parliament saved the Slovak nation, even if "other" things also happened as a consequence. It is also stressed that the situation of the Jews in the Protectorate of Bohemia and Moravia, or in Poland, was much worse.

The So-called Slovak Revisionism and its Impact on Historical Literature Abroad

It is worth noting how the Slovak version of revisionism has influenced historiography outside of Slovakia. In this context, one should consider, for instance, a book written by Walter Brandmüller[76] called *Holocaust in der Slowakei und die katholische Kirche* [Holocaust in Slovakia and the Catholic Church], published in 2003.[77] Interestingly, Brandmüller is a German medieval scholar and a cardinal of the Catholic Church, with close ties to the Vatican. The list of sources cited in the book makes it more or less evident that he does not have command of the Slovak language, while his advisers (Emília Hrabovec and the aforementioned Milan Ďurica, among others) only provided him with selected works on the topic. In all likelihood, this explains the conspicuous absence of well-known publications by Ivan Kamenec, Katarína Hradská, Eduard Nižňanský or Peter Salner. Brandmüller's book draws heavily on a selection of Vatican documents, "Actes et Documents du Saint Siege relatifs a la Seconde Guerre Mondiale,"[78] which the author supplements with several other documents. It must be pointed out that the book does not mention the fact that some of the documents regarding Slovakia were originally presented to the Slovak audience by Ivan Kamenec, Viliam Prečan, and Stanislav Škorvánek in a volume of documents entitled "Vatikán a Slovenská republika"

---

75 František Vnuk, *Mať svoj štát znamená život* [Having own state means life] (Bratislava: Ozveny, 1991).
76 Walter Brandmüller (1929) is a German prelate of the Catholic Church, a cardinal since 2010. He was the president of the Pontifical Committee for Historical Sciences from 1998 to 2009.
77 Walter Brandmüller, *Holocaust in der Slowakei und die katholische Kirche* [The Holocaust in Slovakia and the Catholic Church] (Ph. C. M. Schmidt, 2003).
78 P. Blet, R.A. Graham, A. Martini, and B. Schneider (eds.), *Actes and Documents du Saint Siège relatifs à la Second Guerre Mondial. Ed. I – XI* (Cita del Vaticano, 1970–1981).

["The Vatican and the Slovak Republic 1939–1945. Documents"]. Brandmüller comprehensively fails to refer to post-Munich political changes in Slovakia. The book's title suggests it should contain information on the number and role of Catholic priests active in Slovak politics (e.g. in the Parliament, State Council or Hlinka's Slovak People's Party) or spiritual leaders of the Hlinka Guard in the times of the Slovak Republic. However, such data is simply absent. In a similar fashion, the author does not analyze the relations between Nazi Germany and the Slovak state. In fact, the book may leave readers with an impression that until 1940 there were essentially no developments regarding Slovak Jewry that warrant any discussion. Brandmüller adopts certain nationalist stereotypes by implying that in the era of the Austro-Hungarian Empire, Jews were pro-Hungarian and anti-Slovak, while later, during the times of the interwar Czechoslovakia, they favored the Protestant Czechs over Slovaks. He also claims that Slovak Catholics' resentment towards the Jews was socially (or economically) motivated, rather than religiously. However, anti-Judaist sentiments can be heard in many statements made by Catholic theologians, such as Jesuit Provincial, Jozef Mikuš, a professor of theology, Štefan Zlatoš, and President Jozef Tiso himself. The only element acknowledged in the German cardinal's analysis is the dramatic episode from 1942. Brandmüller refers to a letter supposedly written by bishop Ján Vojtaššák[79] to stop deportations. It is not clear from the text, however, whether the bishop wrote the letter in 1942 or 1943. The authors glosses that in fact the author of the letter from March 1943 was an unnamed Jewish citizen and that Bishop Vojtaššák was only its intended addressee. This issue will be dealt with in more detail in the following text. With regard to the Constitutional Act 68/1942 Coll., the author uses Ďurica's thesis that the law was an act of resistance, since it allowed exceptions on religious grounds (e.g. for converts). He closes his analysis with a reference to a documented statement from Hanns Elard Ludin (German ambassador), dated June 1942, in which it is claimed the deportations have ceased. The information, however, is false, as four more transports are known to have left Slovakia in July, while further instances occurred throughout September and October. Brandmüller mentions neither the number of post-June transport nor the number of deported people. He states that President Tiso stopped the deportations in 1942 after protests from the Vatican, yet cites no documents to support such a claim. He describes in detail interventions made by Giuseppe Burzio, Holy See's chargé d'affaires in Bratislava from 1940 to 1945, who took up the issue with President Tiso.

---

[79] Ján Vojtaššák (1877–1965) was a Roman Catholic bishop of the Spiš Diocese. From 1940 to 1945 he was a Vice-President of the State Council, which at the time was understood as the second chamber of parliament.

He proceeds to dissect Tiso's letter to Pope Pius XII, dated November 1944, in which the President attempted to exculpate himself from personal responsibility. Brandmüller concludes that the contents of the letter were shaped by Tiso's powerlessness, blindness, or even cynicism. In the final parts of his book, he ponders over whether excommunicating Tiso could have been an effective disciplinary measure, adding that even in medieval times such acts did not fulfil their purpose. In doing so, he calls into question his aptitude as a medieval scholar and cardinal.

The Relationship Between Governmental Power and Historiography. The Case of M. S. Ďurica's book: "History of Slovakia and Slovaks"

To illustrate the links between historiography and politics, we will present three examples of how political power has been used to endorse a certain historiographic approach or how the government has used an interpretation of history to not only strengthen its position, but also attempt to reshape the national memory and influence the school education process. Naturally, one may also ponder whether this type of approach was not a throwback to the practices of the previous regime.

M. S. Ďurica is among the representatives of the revisionist approach in Slovak historiography. Ďurica returned from exile in Italy after 1989 and acted from a national-Christian position. In doing so, he primarily tried to reinterpret the history of the Slovak Republic (1939–1945). When Slovakia was re-established as an independent country in 1993, its ruling elite scrambled to look for ways to strengthen the country's legitimacy. In that pursuit, it sought historical symbols, figures, and episodes that could be used to justify the dissolution of Czechoslovakia and the existence of a new state. The government's desire was even more understandable given the fact that during the 1992 election campaign, none of the competing political parties openly advocated independence. Hence, the burden of legitimizing Vladimír Mečiar's cabinet and Slovakia's rebirth as a sovereign entity was shifted onto the interpretation of the history of the Slovaks. It is in this context that the "Old nation – young state" slogan emerged into the public discourse, which implies that Slovaks have been present as a nation in European history since approximately the ninth century, but were constantly under someone else's rule: first, the Hungarians (for roughly 1,000 years) and later, for much of the twentieth century, by the Czechs (with parallel pressure from the USSR) under the Czechoslovak state. Once the independent Slovak Republic was established in 1993, its political elites were looking for symbols that would help vindicate that decision. They hence attempted to reinterpret the history of the war-time Slovak Republic (1939–1945) as a positive model for the 1990s.

It is important to note that, in general, the existence of various historiographical approaches is not wrong *per se*, as it helps push our knowledge and understanding of history forward. Our view of Ďurica's book does not stem from our unwillingness to engage with a different interpretive model or methodology. Ďurica's story is connected to the question of education. It is understandable that after the fall of communism it was necessary to write new history textbooks – the previous regime had distorted interpretations of history, especially the twentieth century. After 1993, the Slovak government was primarily influenced by Vladimír Mečiar's nationalist vision. Its implementation could be seen, for instance, in the battle for national symbols. Even though the Slovaks became a political nation thanks to the existence of the First Czechoslovak Republic (1918–1938), the anniversary of its establishment (October 28, 1918) was not set as a memorial day in independent Slovakia.

From 1993 onwards, the ideological vacuum was gradually filled with nationalism and Christian theology. Prime Minister Mečiar's cabinet was formed in cooperation with the Slovak National Party (SNS). SNS representative Eva Slavkovská[80] served as the Minister of Education and Science from 1994 to 1998. In 1995, the Ministry commissioned Ďurica to develop an auxiliary history textbook for schools. Once again, it needs to be emphasized that we do not question the need to replace the previous textbooks which had clearly been ideologically influenced by the previous regime. Given Slovakia's gradual opening towards the EU, the European Commission decided to assist in the effort by providing funds for the creation of new teaching aids, using the PHARE Education Support scheme.

As it turned out, Ďurica's book, entitled *History of Slovakia and Slovaks*, is problematic in nearly all respects. It was prepared as an annotated chronological manual. It contains factual errors and imbalances. Its ethical dimension is also questionable, as it presents a biased, manipulated interpretation of historical events. Ďurica tries to prove the thousand-year-existence of the "Slovak ethnic group" and the long-standing provenance of the Slovak nation – a spirit that permeates the entire textbook. In relation to antisemitism and the Holocaust, the author glorifies the totalitarian regime of the Slovak Republic in 1939–1945 and its President, Jozef Tiso, as a Catholic leader at the head of a Christian state. Ďurica even tries to cynically distort the persecution of the Jewish minority by disregarding the repressive nature of those measures. He claims the deportation of Jews

---

[80] Eva Slavkovská (1942); member of Slovak National Party (Slovenská národná strana/SNS); Ministry of Education and Science 1994–1998.

from Slovakia was exclusively initiated by the German side. He tries to put the blame for antisemitic policies adopted in Slovakia (including the aforementioned deportations) on the Nazis. He presents Slovak politicians as "the good guys" of that story, as opposed to the Nazi figures, whom he casts as villains. There are several examples of this bias. In relation to a Government Decree no. 198/1941 (the so-called "Jewish Code," Decree no. 198 Sl. Coll. from September 9, 1940), which introduced racial prejudice as a foundation for antisemitic legislation, Ďurica argues that Tiso did not sign the Decree. He tries to create an impression that the President was somehow defiant and did not approve of antisemitic policies. However, he does not mention that under the 1939 Constitution a presidential signature was simply not required on governmental regulations (such as decrees) – only on acts adopted by the parliament. Ďurica also omits the fact that Tiso did sign the Constitutional Act no. No. 210 Sl. Coll., dated September 3 1940, which enabled the cabinet to use governmental regulations (rather than parliamentary acts) to shape policy towards Jews. A direct consequence of this constitutional law was the adoption of Government Decree no. 198/1941 Sl. Coll. The political responsibility that both Tiso and the Assembly of the Slovak Republic bore for these legal moves simply cannot be ignored. Moreover, Tiso signed Constitutional Act no. 68 Sl. Coll., dated May 15 1942, legalizing the deportations that took place that year. The book makes no mention of Tiso's anti-Jewish statements or the propaganda spread by Hlinka's Slovak People's Party (HSĽS). Another highly questionable portion of content refers to the conditions in labor camps set up throughout Slovakia (Nováky, Sereď, Vyhne). Ďurica goes so far as to present the Jewish inmates' experience almost in terms of having a normal life. He also refers to an insidious argument made by the Minister of Interior, Alexander Mach, and Prime Minister Vojtech Tuka, who suggested the transports to concentration camps that took place in April 1942 were made with the purpose of "keeping families together." At the beginning of 1997, the Ministry of Education distributed Ďurica's book through district offices to individual primary schools. The existence of this book and its use in the educational process was basically supported by all political parties (HZDS, SNS, Christian Democratic Movement – KDH). The only parties to openly oppose it were SDĽ (Party of the Democratic Left) and the communists. The textbook and its use in schools was also endorsed by Matica slovenská, or the Conference of Bishops of Slovakia.

The Institute of History of the Slovak Academy of Sciences published an analysis of Ďurica's book,[81] in which they pointed out the conceptual and factual errors of this publication. Further criticism can also be found in other sources.

---

81 Kolektív Historického ústavu SAV, "Stanovisko ku knihe M. S. Ďuricu: Dejiny Slovenska a Slová-

Even though Slovakia was not yet an EU member state, the fact that the contentious textbook was co-funded by Brussels drove three members of the European Parliament to submit written interpellations.

In his interpellation, Hedy d'Ancona[82] asked: "Is the Commission aware of the existence of a textbook on Slovakian history for Slovakian primary schools which glosses over the mass deportation of Jews to the extermination camps?"[83]

Elsewhere, Leonie van Bladel[84] asked the European Commission: "Has the Commission considered how it can prevent PHARE programme subsidies from being misused in the future for the publication of xenophobic views, as has happened in Slovakia with the publication of a history book for primary schools?"[85]

Otto Bardong's[86] questions were: "Is it [the Commission – E.N.] aware that this book seeks to create a national mythology out of Slovakian history since prehistoric times, constructs a hostile image towards neighbouring countries, particularly the Czechs, and emphasizes antisemitic tendencies? In particular, is it aware

---

kov [Expert opinion on the book by M. S. Ďurica: History of Slovakia and Slovaks]," Studia historica Nitriensia 5 (1996): 285–291.

82 Hedwig "Hedy" d'Ancona (1937) is a retired Dutch politician of the Labour Party (PvdA) and political activist. From 1994 to 1999 she served as a Member of the European Parliament.

83 Hedy d'Ancona wrote question no. E-2343/97 to the European Commission on July 10, 1997: "Subject: Anti-Semitism in a Slovakian school textbook: 1. Is the Commission aware of the existence of a textbook on Slovakian history for Slovakian primary schools which glosses over the mass deportation of Jews to the extermination camps? 2. Can the Commission confirm that this textbook, written by Milan Ďurica, a Catholic priest, has been published with money from the European Union? 3. If so, can the Commission indicate the programme under which these funds were provided? Can it also indicate how it monitors the use of such funds? 4. Does the Commission see any prospect of withdrawing the funding, and can it ensure that the book is taken out of circulation? 5. Does the Commission share the view that the message of this controversial textbook runs counter to the objectives of the European Year Against Racism? 6. What action is the Commission intending to take to ensure that in future aid to third countries is not misused for purposes which are at variance with the criteria for accession to the European Union in respect of democracy and civil rights?" See: webside of Members of the European Parliament, accessed October 2021, https://www.europarl.europa.eu/sides/getDoc.do?pubRef=-//EP//TEXT+WQ+E-1997 2343+0+DOC+XML+V0//DE.

84 Leonie van Bladel (1939) is a Dutch politician; from 1994 to 1999 she served as Member of the European Parliament.

85 Question no. E-2469/97, subject: "Misuse of a PHARE programme subsidy by Slovakia." See: website of Members of the European Parliament, https://www.europarl.europa.eu/sides/getDoc.do?type=WQ&reference=E-1997-2469&language=EN, accessed October 31, 2021.

86 Otto Bardong (1935–2003) was a German politician and historian who from 1994 to 1999 he served as a Member of the European Parliament in the ranks of PPE – Group of the European People's Party (Christian-Democratic Group).

that the Tiso Regime (1939–1945), a satellite state of national socialism, is described in altogether favourable terms?"[87]

From our point of view, the problem touches on at least two important levels. The first one is the questioning of Ďurica's textbook, written on the basis of a revisionist concept. The second one is the reaction that it evoked from the European Commission. Brussels not only forced Mečiar's cabinet to withdraw the book from schools, but also stated that

> When the Commission was informed that the book contained negative anti-Semitic material also by defending the activities of the Tiso's regime, they implemented immediate measures and achieved the withdrawal of the book. The Commission does not intend to finance educational programs such as the "Education Support Program" in Slovakia in the future. Similar programs in other Central and Eastern European countries ended in 1996.[88]

---

[87] Otto Bardong, question no. E-2644/97 to the Commission, dated September 1, 1997. Subject: "Subsidy from PHARE funds for a book on the history of Slovakia and the Slovaks. The Commission has subsidized with PHARE funds publication of the book by M. S. Ďurica: "History of Slovakia and the Slovaks" (Dejiny Slovenska a Slovákov), Bratislava, 2/1996 (Ministry of Education), which contains materials for teaching history in primary, secondary and upper secondary schools. The Commission is asked to state: 1. What was the size of this subsidy and in which year was it granted? 2. Is it aware that this book seeks to create a national mythology out of Slovakian history since prehistoric times, constructs a hostile image towards neighbouring countries, particularly the Czechs, and emphasizes anti-Semitic tendencies? 3. In particular, is it aware that the Tiso Regime (1939–1945), a satellite state of national socialism, is described in altogether favourable terms? 4. Has it since received international reviews of this book? 5. Can subsidies for such publications intended for use in schools be scrutinized more thoroughly in future?" See: website of Members of the European Parliament, https://www.europarl.europa.eu/sides/getDoc.do?pubRef=-//EP//TEXT+WQ+E-1997-2644+0+DOC+XML+V0//DE, accessed October 31, 2021.

[88] Answer given by Hans van der Broek on behalf of the European Commission on September 4, 1997: "Under the Phare "Renewal of education programe" for Slovakia, funding was provided for curriculum development. The Slovak ministry of education requested funding for the printing of a schoolbook on Slovak history, described as a chronological description of historical events to be used as a supplementary teaching aid. The request letter contained three recommendations of the book by historians teaching in Canada, Germany, and Slovakia, all of Slovak origin. The Commission relied on the recommendations and approved funding (ECU 80,000) for the printing of the book. When the Commission was made aware that the book contained offensive material of an antisemitic nature which misrepresented Slovakia's wartime role, it took immediate action. The responsible member of the Commission in a meeting with the Slovak Foreign Minister on 25 June 1991 requested urgently the withdrawal of the books from Slovak schools. Replying to this request the Slovak Prime Minister announced on 27 June 1997 in Amsterdam that the book would be withdrawn. On 1 July 1997 the Slovak ministry of education published a statement, saying that the book "will not be used in the educational process." On 2 July 1997, the Foreign Minister informed the Commission in a letter about this decision of the Ministry of education after the issue had been raised at a regular government meeting. The Commission has focused its efforts on having the book withdrawn rather than having the funds reimbursed. The Commission agrees that the con-

SNS Chairman Ján Slota[89] described the Commission's approach as a "method of burning books." A spokesperson for the HZDS described the decision as an insult to the work of a renowned historian. The Slovak Ministry of Education also vigorously protested the Commission's statements. At the beginning of July, during a meeting in Amsterdam, Prime Minister Mečiar had to promise to withdraw Ďurica's book from schools.[90]

The Statements of Revisionist Historians and their Consequences in Relation to the Actions of Representatives of Regional Self-government. The Case of Ferdinand Ďurčanský

One example of a connection between revisionist historiography and regional-level politics is the problem of installing a monument to Ferdinand Ďurčanský[91] in the town of Rajec. Ďurčanský was the Minister of Foreign Affairs and the Interior of the Slovak Republic from 1939 to 1940. He actively cooperated with Nazi Germany in the autumn of 1938. His signature can be found on all antisemitic regulations and laws adopted between 1939 and 1940. After World War II, he fled Slovakia. The National Court sentenced him to death *in absentia*, as capital punishment was not yet abolished at that time and Ďurčanský was not rehabilitated.

In 2009, the council of Ďurčanský's hometown, Rajec, approved a proposal for the construction of a monument to commemorate the former Minister – a decision

---

tents of this book run counter to the objectives and principles embodied in the "year against racism." The Commission stresses the importance of compliance with the democracy criterion set out at the Copenhagen Council in all its contacts and co-operation initiatives with applicant countries. Every effort is being made to support Slovakia in its objective to comply fully with this criterion." See: website of Members of European Parliament: https://www.europarl.europa.eu/sides/getAllAnswers.do?reference=E-1997-2343&language=EN. accessed October 31, 2021.

89 Ján Slota (1953) is the co-founder and former president of the Slovak National Party (Slovenská národná strana; SNS), a nationalist formation. Slota was the leader of SNS from 1994 to 1999 and from 2003 to 2013. He was the mayor of the city of Žilina from 1990 to 2006.

90 Grigorij Mesežnikov, "Prezentácia vzťahu Európska únia – Slovensko hlavnými politickými aktérmi" [Presentation of the European Union – Slovakia relations by the main political actors], *Medzinárodné otázky* 8, no. 1 (1999): 17–51.

91 Ferdinand Ďurčanský (1906–1974) was a Slovak nationalist leader who for a certain time served as a minister in the government of the Axis-aligned Slovak State in 1939 and 1940. He was known for spreading virulent anti-Semitic propaganda, although he left the government before the Holocaust in Slovakia was fully implemented.

that allows us to legitimately consider the societal impact of Slovak revisionist historiography and its influence on regional-level policy.

As we indicate earlier in this study, since the 1990s the historiographic community in Slovakia has been divided (in a somewhat simplified view) into the "national movement" which defended the record of the 1939–1945 Slovak Republic and "other" historians. This polarization is still, to this day, visible in the field of art. In 1996, the History Department of Matica slovenská[92] organized a conference to commemorate an anniversary of Ďurčanský's birth. Only historians grouped in the revisionist movement were invited to the event. After the conference, the organizers published what is practically a hagiographic collection on Ďurčanský's life and a staunch defense of his actions as the official of the war-time Slovak Republic, including justifications of his antisemitic policies.[93]

Subsequently, in 2009, the municipal council in the town of Rajec unanimously decided to place a monument in honor of Ďurčanský in front of the building of the local Municipal Museum. When explaining the decision, the mayor of Rajec, Ján Rybárik, referred to the above-mentioned conference publication, which only sees contributions from the revisionists. He went on to comment: "Given the information I have, I try to look at it objectively. For being a Rajec citizen, I see more positives in that person than negatives. My opinion is that Mr. Ďurčanský can have a bust displayed in Rajec."[94]

In Slovakia, municipalities decide on the installation of local monuments as self-governing bodies/institutions. The decision of authorities in Rajec brought forth both protests and positive reactions. State, religious, and academic institutions joined citizen-led initiatives (including by residents of Rajec) in objection to Ďurčanský's monument. The decision was protested, for instance, by the Central Union of Jewish Religious Communities, the Slovak Union of Anti-Fascist Fighters, the Tilia Civic Association, and the Human Movement. The Institute of History (IH) of the Slovak Academy of Sciences issued an official statement, endorsed by the

---

92 Matica slovenská is Slovakia's scientific and cultural institution focusing on topics around the Slovak nation. This all-nation cultural institution was established in 1863 as a result of the Slovak national efforts to lay the foundations of Slovak science, libraries, and museums. Nowadays, it is governed by the "Act on Matica slovenská" of 1997.
93 Štefan Baranovič (ed.), *Ferdinand Ďurčanský (1906–1974). Zborník zo seminára o Dr. Ferdinandovi Ďurčanskom, ktorý sa konal pri príležitosti jeho nedožitých deväťdesiatych narodenín v Rajci 8.12.1996* [The yearbook from seminar about Dr. Ferdinand Ďurčanský, which was held on the occasion of his ninetieth birthday in Rajec on December 8, 1996] (Martin: Matica Slovenská, 1998).
94 "Ďurčanského sochu zatiaľ neodstránia. Mesto chce stanovisko od historikov" [The monument of Ferdinand Ďurčanský will not be removed yet. The city wants an expert opinion from historians], *Denník Sme*, February 24, 2011, acceseed October 2021, https://myzilina.sme.sk/c/5781369/durcanskeho-sochu-zatial-neodstrania-mesto-chce-stanovisko-od-historikov.html.

Military Historical Institute (Bratislava), the Slovak National Uprising Museum (Banská Bystrica) as well as several professional historians. The Human Movement initiated dialogue with representatives of the region and later sought to reach out to state-level and European legislative and judicial authorities.

After the 2010 municipal election, the newly chosen members of the city council buckled under the pressure and requested expert opinion from IH, the Nation's Memory Institute (ÚPN), and Matica Slovenská. March 2011 saw a symposium devoted to Ferdinand Ďurčanský's issue, attended by historians from IH, ÚPN, the Comenius University (Bratislava), and Matica Slovenská.

IH and other historians stated that, in their opinion, commemorating Ďurčanský with a statue constituted a denial of modern Slovakia's democratic principles and humanist values. They further claimed the act was an attempt to justify the war-time regime:

> The principles to which F. Ďurčanský subscribed and which he embodied in practical politics are in sharp conflict with the democratic principles of today's Slovak Republic. We are convinced that this dispute is not only about the person of F. Ďurčanský, or his bust, but for a sophisticated attempt to justify the totalitarian regime of the war-torn Slovak Republic. We state that the report by Peter Mulík from the Slovak Historical Institute of Matica slovenská does not correspond to the content of the colloquium, where there were many more critical objections about the public and political activities of F. Ďurčanský than about his positives. Revealing the bust will be a denial of the principles on which our democratic society is based today.[95]

At that time, historian Martin Lacko, who now openly supports the Tiso regime, spoke on behalf of the *UPN*. He commented on Ďurčanský's antisemitism in only one sentence: "As Minister of the Interior, however, he was enforcing restrictive anti-Jewish measures, especially in the economic field." He highlighted Ďurčanský's further political activities and did not comment on the issue of the politician's proposed bust.[96]

Mayor Ján Rybárik refused to change his position on the matter. He continued to refer to the conference publication authored by revisionist historians in 1998. In June 2011, the city council, now with a new line-up of deputies, upheld the 2009 decision. Only one of 13 deputies voted in favor of removing Ďurčanský's bust.[97]

---

[95] An expert opinion of the Institute of History the Slovak Academy of Sciences to the Ferdinand Ďurčanský: http://www.history.sav.sk/index.php?id=durcansky, accessed October 31, 2021.
[96] An expert opinion of the Nation Memory Institute: https://www.upn.gov.sk/data/pdf/historicke-hodnotenie-FD.pdf, accessed October 31, 2021.
[97] The summary from the meeting of the Municipial Council in Rajec, held on May 19, 2011: http://www.rajec.info/files/16995-ZAPIS20110609.pdf, accessed October 31, 2021.

In response, the Human Movement reported a suspected crime – an act that prompted Slovak police to launch an investigation into the offence of "supporting and promoting groups aimed at suppressing fundamental rights and freedoms." However, the criminal proceedings were dropped in August 2011.[98]

Even Prime Minister Iveta Radičová's[99] liberal cabinet could not remove the monument, having no executive powers in this respect. It took the government several months to issue an official statement, "Government Declaration on the Placement of a Bust of F. Ďurčanský in Rajec." The document reads:

> Pursuant to the Act on Municipal Establishment, the decision on the location of historical monuments on the territory of a town or municipality is within the competence of the local self-government. In this case, the city council of Rajec. The Government of the Slovak Republic cannot change the decision of self-government bodies. In the discussion on the person of Ferdinand Ďurčanský, the members of the Government of the Slovak Republic consider as decisive the statement of the Historical Institute[100] of the Slovak Academy of Sciences, which states, among other things, that 'F. Ďurčanský acted as a supporter of the German Empire (...) and in his state functions he cooperated in consolidating the undemocratic regime, as well as in the preparation, adoption and implementation of anti-Semitic legal norms'. The Government of the Slovak Republic condemns any attempts to downplay responsibility, or even indirectly rehabilitate the symbols or ruling elites of any totalitarian system that have participated in crimes and gross violations of human rights.[101]

At this point, we would like to repeat what several other historians have also pointed out. Building monuments to the figures who were directly involved in the political persecution of the Jewish community and other members of society is something we consider unacceptable. As an added element of the tragic irony of Ďurčanský's case, his bust sits in a square named after the Slovak National Uprising – an act he, a former minister collaborating with Nazi Germany, explicitly condemned at the time of its outbreak in 1944. We see attempts at honoring and commemorating such people as an effort to rehabilitate the totalitarian regime of the war-time Slovak Republic, of which Ďurčanský was a representative – an effort

---

98 "Odhalenie busty Ďurčanského spustilo policajné vyšetrovanie" ["The unveilling of a bust of Ferdinand Ďurčanský started a police investigation"], *Denník Pravda*, June 14, 2011, accessed October 31, 2021: https://spravy.pravda.sk/regiony/clanok/210914-odhalenie-busty-durcanskeho-spustilo-policajne-vysetrovanie/.
99 Iveta Radičová (1956) is slovak sociologist who served as the Prime Minister of Slovakia from 2010 to 2012. In 2012 she also briefly held the post of Minister of Defence. Previously she served as Minister of Labour from 2005 to 2006.
100 The official English version of its name used by the institution itself is "Institute of History."
101 See also Statement by the Slovak government: https://www.vlada.gov.sk/vyhlasenie-vlady-sr-k-umiestneniu-busty-f-durcanskeho-v-rajci/, accessed October 31, 2021.

which, in this case, is made by local- and regional-level politicians. Political actors always seek to legitimize their intentions and actions through "historical logic." Here, revisionist historiography became a launch pad for specific political steps by the mayor and the city council. Their efforts were motivated by the desire to find stronger national and state-building continuity by linking the history of the war-time republic to the contemporary state, established in 1993. We also consider this an attempt to create new symbols that distort historical memory and national awareness – at the very least among the residents of Rajec.

As a counterbalance to the actions of the local politicians, we have a government statement which refers to professional analysis of critical historiography, represented by the Institute of History of the Slovak Academy of Sciences (or other academic institutions). However, these two standpoints on the same historical episode have had completely different impacts and only one of them is actually reflected in reality. The Ďurčanský Memorial stands in the town of Rajec to this day. It might be worth adding that the government continues to financially support both IH and Matica slovenská.

In conclusion, we would like to quote an opinion from a Slovak sociologist, Michal Vašečka. In 2018, he highlighted the phenomenon of relativization of values that may emerge as a result of the society's struggles to cope with national history – construction of monuments to controversial figures being one example of this. Vašečka claims that, as such tendency continues and civil society is not able to set sufficient boundaries, we can expect even more of such monuments in the future:

> Unless there is a nationwide consensus that Ďurčanský on the one hand and Biľak on the other are problematic personalities and have – albeit perhaps indirectly – blood on their hands, such busts will continue to be built. Unfortunately, people have taken different values from past times, they try to preserve the best of everything, but it also brings relativization of values. And in some cases it is simply necessary to set a limit.[102]

The year 2020 saw a change in law, as the National Council of the Slovak Republic attempted to reconcile the country's collective conscience with its troubled history under communist rule (1948–1989), but also with the 1939–1945 episode. According

---

[102] Miroslav Kern, "Sociológ Vašečka o 70 rokoch od nástupu komunizmu: Chýba nám tu múzeum totality" [Sociologist Vašečka on 70 years since the start of the communist rule: we lack a museum of totalitarianism], *Denník N*, February 23, 2018, accessed October 31, 2021, https://dennikn.sk/1034803/sociolog-vasecka-o-70-rokoch-od-nastupu-komunizmu-chyba-nam-tu-muzeum-totality/.

to the new regulations, monuments and streets cannot be named after the representatives of both these totalitarian regimes.[103]

The Links Between Historiography and the Position of the Catholic Church in Slovak Society

In order to further discuss the relationship between historiography and politics, we shall consider a dispute that erupted around the activities of bishop Ján Vojtaššák. This particular example not only illustrates potential implications of how we form our knowledge of the history of Slovakia's statehood and its nation, but also the position of the Catholic Church. Under communist rule, the Church was suppressed by the regime. After 1989, it emerged from decades of oppression in a position of great authority, commenting on various social and state-related problems. According to the 2001 and 2011 censuses, more than sixty percent of citizens specifically identified as members of the Catholic Church. This number made Slovakia, in statistical terms, a denominational country.[104] The preamble to the 1992 Constitution of the Slovak Republic explicitly refers to the "spiritual bequest of Cyril[105]

---

103 Act No 338/2020 Coll. of November 4, 2020 amending Act No. 125/1996 Coll. on the immorality and illegality of the communist system and amending and supplementing certain acts. See: https://www.slov-lex.sk/pravne-predpisy/SK/ZZ/2020/338/ [quot. 2022–05–05], accessed May 31, 2022.
104 "The Slovak Republic is religiously neutral, that is, there is no official religion existing in it. Freedom of religious denomination is ensured under law. The degree of the population religiosity is high. At the population census of 2011, 75.97 % of people ranked among the believers, 13.44 % were declared as persons with no religion and 10.59 % did not show any religion. Majority of believers are of Roman-Catholic denomination." "Slovakia. Population: Demographic Situation, Languages and Religions" website of the European Education and Culture Executive Agency: https://eacea.ec.europa.eu/national-policies/eurydice/content/population-demographic-situation-languages-and-religions-72_en [quot. 2021–10–08], accessed October 31, 2021.
105 Saints Cyril (also called Constantin, 829–869) and Methodius (815–885) were brothers from Solun and theological missionaries, who were sent to Great Moravia by byzantine Emperor Michael III in the ninth century, at the request of Rastislav, the Prince of Great Moravia. They were key figures who evangelised the Slavs. Constantine created the Glagolitic script, an early form of Slavic alphabet, and was the first to translate parts of The Bible as well as liturgic texts to Slavic languages. Methodius, in turn, founded a school that became a centre of Slavic education, culture, and literature. He was appointed as archbishop of Pannonia and Great Moravia. In 1980, Pope John Paul II declared the two brothers co-patrons of Europe. See: Gyula Moravcsik (ed.), *Constantine Porphyrogenitus: De Administrando Imperio* (2nd revised ed.) (Washington D.C.: Dumbarton Oaks Center for Byzantine Studies, 1967); Francis Dvorník, *Byzantine Mission among the Slavs: SS. Constantine-Cyril and Methodius* (Rutgers University Press: New Brunswick, New Jersey, 1970), 484.

and Methodius."[106] However, the same document states that the Slovak Republic is a secular state.[107]

When the President of Slovakia Zuzana Čaputová[108] spoke on the occasion of Pope Francis I's visit in September 2021, she mentioned the country's democratic and European character, but also its Christian tradition: "Slovakia is an integral part of a large family of democratic states of the European Union, which provides us with important international guarantees of our security and prosperity. Christianity and the Catholic Church have been an integral part of our cultural identity for centuries."[109]

The President's remarks included references to Pope Francis' encyclicals and his rejection of all forms of antisemitism as well as other religiously motivated hatred which, in his opinion, are in direct contradiction with Christian values.[110]

We are of the view that, up until now, the hierarchy of the Catholic Church has not expressed a direct criticism of the historical record of the war-time Slovak Republic (1939–1945). Such reluctance is likely motivated by the fact that it was a Catholic priest, Jozef Tiso, who headed the state. Furthermore, other representatives of the Church held several important positions (including at the regional level, i.e. in cities, districts, and counties) within the ruling political formation, Hlinka's Slovak People's Party. Thus, they were directly involved in governance processes, effectively representing a single-party dictatorship. In that sense, they also influenced or partook in certain forms of antisemitic policies and the Holo-

---

106 The Preamble to the Constitution of The Slovak Republic, "We, the Slovak Nation, Bearing in mind the political and cultural heritage of our predecessors and the experience gained through centuries of struggle for our national existence and statehood, Mindful of the spiritual bequest of Cyril and Methodius and the historical legacy of Great Moravia, Recognizing the natural right of nations to self-determination, Together with members of national minorities and ethnic groups living on the territory of the Slovak Republic, In the interest of continuous peaceful cooperation with other democratic countries, Endeavouring to implement democratic form of government, to guarantee a life of freedom, and to promote spiritual culture and economic prosperity, Thus we, the citizens of the Slovak Republic, have, herewith and through our representatives, adopted this Constitution." See website of President of Slovak Republic, https://www.prezident.sk/upload-files/46422.pdf, accessed October 31, 2021.
107 "Title one: Article 1 (1) The Slovak Republic is a sovereign, democratic state governed by the rule of law. It is not bound to any ideology or religion." https://www.prezident.sk/upload-files/46422.pdf, accessed October 31, 2021.
108 Zuzana Čaputová (1973) is a Slovak politician, lawyer, and environmental activist. She has served as the President of Slovakia since 2019.
109 See website of The President of the Slovak Republic: https://www.prezident.sk/en/article/papez-frantisek-vidi-slovensko-ako-posla-pokoja-v-srdci-europy/, acceseed October 31, 2021.
110 The statements of The President of the Slovak Republic: https://www.prezident.sk/page/prejavy/ , accessed October 31, 2021.

caust in Slovakia – regardless of whether they were acting as state officials or from the position of spiritual authority.

In 2012, the Conference of Bishops of Slovakia[111] issued a statement on the deportation of Jews from Slovakia in 1942:

> (...) The then-responsible politicians espoused Christianity and its values, but some of them violated them by persecuting Jews in practice. They either completely succumbed to the idea of the correctness of their radical approach, or they remained more or less passive. What strikes, in particular, is the indifference with which they approached the fate of people who left for more than precarious conditions. As it turned out soon after the deportations, it was not about settling Jews in the reserved areas – although many were convinced it was – but about their systematic liquidation.[112]

It is worth pointing out the bishops failed to specifically mention Tiso – the man who, after all, headed the war-time Republic – by name. In light of all these facts, we can only remind readers that some historians have described the 1939–1945 regime as clero-fascist.[113]

The dispute we wish to present in the following paragraphs concerns controversy among historians who have written in critical terms about a representative of the war-time Catholic hierarchy in Slovakia, bishop Ján Vojtaššák. In addition to being a member of the ruling Hlinka's Slovak People's Party, he also held the position of Vice-President of the State Council, which at the time was understood as the second chamber of parliament, but only had advisory functions.[114] In relation

---

111 The Conference of Bishops of Slovakia (Konferencia biskupov Slovenska, abbreviation: KBS) was established on March 23, 1993 and is composed of the Catholic Bishops, both Latin Catholic and Greek Catholic, in the Slovak Republic.

112 See the statement on the website of the Conference of Bishop of Slovakia: https://www.tkkbs.sk/view.php?cisloclanku=20210913093, accessed October 31 2021.

113 Miloslav Szabó, *Klérofašisti. Slovenskí kňazi a pokušenie radikálnej politiky (1935–1945)* [Clerofascists. Slovak priests and the temptation of radical politics] (Bratislava: Slovart, 2019); Miloslav Szabó, "Clerical Fascism? Catholicism and the Far-Right in the Central European Context (1918–1945)," *Historický časopis* (Bratislava: Slovac Academic Press, 2018) 66, no. 5, 885–900; Eduard Nižňanský and Barbora Jakobyová, "Lokálni aktéri počas holokaustu. Prípad dvoch katolíckych kňazov z Dolného Kubína: Ignác Grebáč-Orlov a Viktor Trstenský" [The local actors during the Holocaust. The case of two catholic priests from Dolný Kubín: Ignác Grebčč-Orlov and Viktor Trstenský], in *Historik a dejiny: v československom storočí osudových dátumov* (Bratislava: Veda, 2018), 59–86.

114 Eduard Nižňanský and Ivan Kamenec (eds.), *Holokaust na Slovensku 2. Prezident, vláda, Snem SR a Štátna rada o židovskej otázke (1939–1945). Dokumenty* [Holocaust in Slovakia 2. President, government, parliament of the SR and State Council on the Jewish question (1939–1945). Documents]; Ivan Kamenec, *Štátna rada v politickom systéme Slovenského štátu v rokoch 1939–1945* [The State Council in political system of the Slovak state from 1939 to 1945] *Historický časopis* (Bra-

to Bishop Vojtaššák, we would like to present the four most common lines of argument in the dispute.

The first issue are his statements as a member of the State Council on the subject of Jews and the "solution" of the Jewish question. Several documents published in the *Vatican and the Slovak Republic*[115] volume hint at the Vatican's position on the persecution of Jews in Slovakia and describe the Holy See's interventions in this regard. Among them are reports from the Vatican's charge d'affaires in Bratislava, Giuseppe Burzio, who reflected on the situation in Slovakia and criticized Vojtaššák's actions. Another volume, *The Holocaust in Slovakia*, includes a collection of Vojtaššák's speeches in the State Council.[116] Historians Ján Hlavinka and Ivan Kamenec published a monograph on Vojtaššák's activities in the years 1938–1945, pointing to particularly serious problems in the interpretations of his work in the period.[117]

There are certain facts that have been uncovered and verified by historians. The authenticity of Vojtaššák's statements as a State Council member is unquestionable. Moreover, research has revealed documents proving that the Bishop was responsible for the Aryanization of the village of Baldovce and the lands in Betlanovce. Hlavinka and Kamenec consider Vojtaššák as an essential figure behind the fate of Alexander Lörinc, a Jew from Spišské Podhradie who was transported to a labor camp. The Catholic hierarchy directly spoke out against Lörinc at a State Council meeting in 1943 to draw the attention of Anton Vašek,[118] the head of the fourteenth Department of the Ministry of the Interior. Since deportations were no longer taking place at this point in time, Lörinc was placed in a labor camp instead.

---

tislava: Slovac Academic Press, 1996) 44, no. 2, 221–242; Igor Baka, *Politický systém a režim Slovenskej republiky v rokoch 1939–1940* [The political system and regime of the Slovak Republic in 1939–1940] 9Bratislava: VHÚ, 2010), 322 s.

115 Ivan Kamenec and Vilém Prečan and Stanislav Škorvánek (eds.), *Vatikán a Slovenská republika /1939–1945/. Dokumenty.* [Vatican and Slovak republic /1939–1945/. Documents].

116 Eduard Nižňanský and Ivan Kamenec (eds.), *Holokaust na Slovensku 2. Prezident, vláda, Snem SR a Štátna rada o židovskej otázke (1939–1945). Dokumenty* [Holocaust in Slovakia 2. President, government, parliament SR and State Council about Jewish question (1939–1945). Documents].

117 Ján Hlavinka, Ivan Kamenec, and Martin Styan, *The Burden of the Past. Catholic Bishop Ján Vojtaššák and the Regime in Slovakia (1918–1945)* [English translation] Prepracované vydanie v angličtine (Bratislava: Dokumentačné stredisko holokaustu, 2014).

118 Anton Vašek (1905–1946) was a Slovak journalist and politician. From 1942, he headed the fourteenth Department of the Ministry of the Interior – the so-called "Jewish Department" which was responsible for technical and administrative organisation of the "solution" to the Jewish issue, including deportations.

In reaction to the above-mentioned revelations, several historians of the Catholic Church, nationalist-leaning researchers, and representatives of the Church itself decided to defend not only Vojtaššák's reputation and actions, but also the Slovak Church's effort to beatify him. According to Vatican's procedures, the beatification process calls for a collection of biographical data on the candidate. The first monograph about Vojtaššák was penned by another Catholic priest, Viktor Trstenský.[119] After World War II, Vojtaššák was persecuted by the communist regime. In a staged trial that took place in 1951, he was sentenced to 24 years in prison, while his co-defendants – two other bishops, Michal Buzalka[120] and Pavel Gojdič[121] – were handed life imprisonment.

The impulse for Vojtaššák's beatification came from Pope John Paul II, who during his 1995 visit to Slovakia praised him in a sermon delivered in Levoča: "The older amongst you certainly remember the venerable figure of Bishop Ján Vojtaššák, while the Greek Catholic brothers the figure of Bishop Pavel Gojdič. Both were imprisoned after pseudo-trials. Today, they deserve the process of beatification, as they gave a testament to the faithful service of the Church in Slovakia."[122] In order for the process to start, all diocesan bishops of Slovakia had to give their consent. The beatification proceedings were launched in 1996 by the Bishop of Spiš, František Tondra, with the approval of the Congregation for the Causes of Saints in Rome.[123] In November 2001, the diocesan phase of the process was concluded and the matter was handed over to the Congregation in Rome. In 2003, the State Secretariat of the Holy See sent a letter to František Tondra, stating

---

119 Viktor Trstenský, *Sila viery, sila pravdy: Život a dielo najdôstojnejšieho biskupa Jána Vojtaššáka, mučeníka cirkvi a národa* [The power of faith, the power of truth: The life and work of the most diginified Bishop Ján Vojtaššák, a martyr of the Church and the nation] (Bratislava: Senefeld-R, 1990).

120 Michal Buzalka (1885–1961) was an assistant bishop of the Trnava Archdiocese. From 1940 to 1945 he was the military vicar of the Slovak Army. He was persecuted by the communist regime and imprisoned. 2000 saw the start of his beatification process.

121 Pavel Gojdič (1888–1960) was a Rusyn Basilian monk and the eparch of the Slovak Catholic Eparchy of Prešov. In 1940, the Pope appointed him the Bishop of Prešov. Prior to that, in 1939, he served in Mukachevo. He was imprisoned by the communist regime in Czechoslovakia. In 2001, he was beatified by Pope John Paul II. In 2007, he was recognized as Righteous Among the Nations by Yad Vashem.

122 Pope John Paul II in Slovakia and his speech: https://www.kbs.sk/obsah/sekcia/h/dokumenty-a-vyhlasenia/p/dokumenty-papezov/c/navsteva-svateho-otca-v-sr-1995 (accessed October 31, 2021).

123 In the Catholic Church, the Congregation for the Causes of Saints (Latin: Congregatio de Causis Sanctorum) is the congregation of the Roman Curia that oversees the complex process that leads to the canonization of saints, passing through the steps of a declaration of "heroic virtues" and beatification.

that 'the Holy See respects Bishop Vojtaššák, but so far does not consider his beatification to be appropriate."

At the same time, historians with nationalist or Christian leanings[124] as well as certain representatives of the Catholic hierarchy[125] jumped to Vojtaššák's defence by questioning the findings and conclusions from the research and documents mentioned earlier. At first, they tried to cast doubts over the events that took place in Baldovce. However, after Hlavinka and Kamenec published their two books, they were forced to admit Vojtaššák's role and culpability. At the same time, they failed to respond to the findings about the Aryanization of Betlanovce, even though other historians published documents that revealed how President Tiso intervened with the chairman of the State Land Office, Karol Klínovský, in order to enable Vojtaššák to acquire that land. In a similar fashion, they either did not comment or denied that the Bishop was involved in the persecution of Lörinc.

It should also be said that Vojtaššák's defenders published what was supposedly a letter penned by the Bishop and sent to the Minister of the Interior, Alexander Mach, to stop deportations of prevent further ones from happening in 1943. In reality, the author of the letter was an unnamed Jewish citizen who escaped from a concentration camp, while Vojtaššák was an intended recipient whom the victim tried inform about the atrocities occurring in the camp. The supposed letter from the Bishop was merely a cover letter Vojtaššák added when forwarding the Jew's testimony to Mach. It is, therefore, impossible to verify whether Vojtaššák himself wrote anything about the suffering of Slovak Jews.

Any attempt to provide a monocausal explanation of the developments regarding the preparations for further deportations in 1943 is, in our opinion, bound to be a gross oversimplification. The argument that deportations did not take place because Vojtaššák had supposedly pleaded with Mach is also highly questionable. There are several other factors and elements that one should take into account. Firstly, there are several documents which reveal the Vatican's intervention in the matter.[126] There is also the pastoral letter from March 8 1943, in which the authors defended not only Jewish converts (those who converted to Christianity), but also other Jews living in Slovakia. One should also consider political and military

---

124 For example, František Dlugoš, Ján Duda, Milan S. Ďurica, Emilia Hrabovec, Ivan Chalupecký, Stanislav Májek, Peter Mulík, Ivan Petranský, and František Vnuk.
125 For example, Cardinal Ján Chryzostom Korec, Bishop of Nitra Mons., Viliam Judák, Mons. Ján Kuboš – the administrator of the Spiš Diocese, Mons. Cyril Vasiľ – Bishop of Košice eparchy, Peter Jurčaga, the postulator for the cause of beatification of the Servant of God, Bishop Ján Vojtaššák.
126 Ivan Kamenec, Vilém Prečan, and Stanislav Škorvánek (eds.), *Vatikán a Slovenská republika /1939–1945/. Dokumenty* [Vatican and Slovak Republic /1939–1945/. Documents].

developments of that time, as the tide of war was turning against the Axis. The defeats in the battles of Stalingrad and Kursk forced Wehrmacht into the defensive on the Eastern front. Italian and German armies were also defeated in North Africa (Tunis, May 1943). The Allies landed in Sicily and pressed north, prompting the fall of Mussolini's regime. When Churchill and Roosevelt met in Casablanca earlier that year (January), they determined "the war will be fought until the unconditional surrender of Nazi Germany and its allies."[127] All these direct and indirect pressures led Mach to state at a cabinet meeting in August that no further deportations of Jews would take place.[128] Finally, there have not been any identified documents of German provenance that would confirm that Nazi Germany pressed Slovakia to resume deportations.[129]

A final controversy emerged after the publication of a book entitled *Pio XII e gli Ebrei. L'archivista del Vaticano rivela finalmente il ruolo del Papa Pacelli durante la seconda guerra mondiale*,[130] authored by Johan Ickx, the Director of Historical Archives in the Section for Relations with States at the Holy See's Secretariat of State. Ickx's book contains some revelations and claims regarding Vojtaššák's actions. In response, historians defending the Bishop penned a text entitled *For the true image of Bishop Vojtaššák*[131] in which they criticized the Vatican historian's work. In their effort to counter Ickx, they focused on the role and position of the State Council. They attempted to downplay both the importance of the institution of which he was a member and the statements he made in this capacity. For instance, they did not bother with analyzing his remarks at the State Council meeting on March 26 1942. Indeed, they selected only those of Vojtaššák's speeches that suited their arguments. They failed to comment on the episodes of Aryanization or the Bishop's role in the persecution of Alexander Lörinc. From our point of view, the purpose behind the rebuke of Ickx's book is to further the case for Vojtaššák's beatification. In the interest of fairness, it should be noted that their argumenta-

---

[127] The conclusion of the Casablanca Conference: https://www.britannica.com/event/Casablanca-Conference (accessed October 31, 2021).
[128] Eduard Nižňanský and Ivan Kamenec (eds.), *Holokaust na Slovensku 2. Prezident, vláda, Snem SR a Štátna rada o židovskej otázke (1939–1945). Dokumenty.* [Holocaust in Slovakia 2. President, government, parliament of the SR and State Council on the Jewish question (1939–1945). Documents].
[129] Eduard Nižňanský (ed.), *Holokaust na Slovensku 4, Dokumenty nemeckej proveniencie. 1939–1945* [Holocaust in Slovakia 4. The documents of German origins. (1939–1945)].
[130] Pius XII and the Jews. Vatican archivist finally reveals Pope Pacelli's role during the Second World War.
[131] The text signed: Mons. Ján Kuboš, the administrator of diocese in Spiš, Mons. Viliam Judák, Bishop of Nitra, Mons. Cyril Vasiľ, apostolic administrator of the Košice eparchy, Peter Jurčaga, the postulator for the cause of beatification of the Servant of God Bishop Ján Vojtaššák.

tion with regard to certain errors and inaccuracies in the book may, indeed, be considered relevant. However, they consistently failed to admit and discuss the antisemitic (or anti-Judaic) sentiments in Vojtaššák's statements and actions.

Vojtaššák's case is about more than just his beatification. It is a window that shows society's understanding of the relationship between religion and politics – in this case, the antisemitic policy that led to the Holocaust. Members of the Catholic clergy who were politically involved in the functioning of the Slovak Republic (1939–1945) are co-responsible for the situation and developments that took place at that time. As a Deputy Chairman of the State Council, Bishop Vojtaššák certainly belonged to that group. We believe the Slovak Church's efforts to defend him amount to an attempted rehabilitation of a totalitarian regime and its leading figures.

In our view, the significance of the situation is further emphasized by the fact that in 2002 the Slovak Republic and the Holy See concluded an agreement which regulates, among other issues, public holidays. The treaty clearly states that both parties recognize "the contribution of the citizens of the Slovak Republic to the Catholic Church."[132]

During his visit to Slovakia, Pope Francis I said: "Here, in front of the history of the Jewish nation, marked by this tragic and indescribable confrontation, we are ashamed to admit it: how many times the (...) Lord's name was used for indescribable acts of inhumanity! How many oppressors declared: 'God is with us'; but they were not with God."[133] While Francis did not specifically name any of the politically involved Catholic priests (such as Tiso or Vojtaššák), the Vatican's future decisions as to the continuation of the beatification process will show the Slovak society how we can (both now and in the future) perceive the historical record of such controversial figures and its evaluation by the Catholic hierarchy.

Conclusion

After the fall of communism, historiography, enjoying a newly found freedom, began to fill some of the blank pages in Slovakia's history. Specifically, it began to deal with previously marginalized topics such as antisemitism and the Holocaust. In particular, the dissolution of Czechoslovakia made it possible for nation-

---

132 Treaty between the Slovak Republic and the Holy See. http://spcp.prf.cuni.cz/dokument/kon-sr.htm (accessed October 31, 2021).
133 Pope Francis's statement: https://www.kbs.sk/obsah/sekcia/h/dokumenty-a-vyhlasenia/p/dokumenty-papezov/c/sk2021-prihovor-papeza-frantiska-pri-stretnuti-so-zidovskou-komunitou (accessed October 31, 2021).

alist-oriented historiography, represented by M. S. Ďurica and F. Vnuk, to establish itself very quickly. From there on, historiography dealing with the war-time Slovak Republic (1939–1945) became divided into two approaches. Later, it became apparent that the nationalist-clerical narrative could also be used for political purposes. The three examples discussed above show various possible interpretations of certain historical episodes. Naturally, they also show how we might be able to prevent such a distorted take on history from becoming a norm in a civic society. In the 1990s, the dangerous interference of revisionism was only stopped with the help of the European Commission.

In the case of a monument to F. Ďurčanský, it became apparent that a local-level decision to honor a figure obviously linked with antisemitic policies could be stopped neither by a civic movement nor by the opinions of scientific institutions, nor even by the position of the central government. It seems that the only way to prevent similar situations in the future is to change the law so as to make it impossible for regional politicians and decision-makers to affect the collective national memory in such a way or create symbols and commemorative spaces for radical political movements.

The example of Bishop Vojtaššák reveals how historiography overlaps and/or collides with the views of the Catholic hierarchy. In our opinion, this particular issue largely stems from the fact that the Church has so far not denounced the actions of the authorities of the war-time Slovak Republic and its totalitarian regime headed by Jozef Tiso, a member of the Catholic clergy. While the Church has frequently distanced itself from antisemitism and the Holocaust, it did not do the same with regard to Tiso's regime. Even the latest speeches from the Catholic hierarchy show that the Church is unwilling to stop the Bishop's beatification process. In this case, only the future may show to what extent the dispute around Vojtaššák's role will resonate with Slovak society which is, at least formally, very religious (predominantly Catholic).

Overall, all three examples discussed throughout the chapter indicate that Slovakia's struggle with the interpretation of its twentieth-century history is bound to continue, as will the effort to build a civil society. Efforts to rehabilitate the war-time Slovak Republic are associated with a hidden form of antisemitism, still present in Slovakia. Historiography, as it turns out, is also a part of this conflict.

Jiří Holý
Trivialization of the Holocaust? The Elements of Pop Culture in Holocaust Fiction and Film

1

This reflection examines changes in the representation of the Holocaust/Shoah in literature and film over the past few decades. Aleida Assmann has noted that the culture of the Holocaust memory has undergone (what she calls) an "ethical turn" from the figure of a hero or martyr to that of a traumatized victim. Categorizations like survivor, victim, and witness have gained high moral status since the 1990s. This focus has pushed the experience of the victim to the center of consciousness and culture. The Holocaust is recognized as a collective trauma and has been transformed into a global icon in European-American civilization. It represents inhumanity in general, related to values of universal morality, and is perceived as a part of transnational memory.

Some years before Assmann, in 1998, the Israeli historian and scholar Yehuda Bauer declared in his speech to the *Bundestag* in Germany:

> The Holocaust has assumed the role of universal symbol for all evil because it presents the most extreme form of genocide, because it contains elements that are without precedent, because the tragedy was a Jewish one and because the Jews [...] represent one of the sources of modern civilization. (Bauer 2001, 270)

Later he wrote: "In the past two decades or so, an amazing phenomenon has happened. The Holocaust has become a symbol of evil in what is inaccurately known as Western civilization, and the awareness of that symbol seems to be spreading all over the world" (Bauer 2001, 270). He criticized the idea that the Holocaust was "just another genocide." Nevertheless, this universalization of the Holocaust has been evident in many literary works as well as films over the past decades. It has turned out to be one of the key components in the formation of postmodern Western culture. Films from the 1980s such as *Cannibal Holocaust* (1980, directed by Ruggero Deodato) or *Porno Holocaust* (1981, directed by Joe D'Amato) testify to this process. Neither of these films mentions Jews or their extermination. However, they capitalize on the Holocaust "brand" as a terrible, incommensurable, but also alluring event.

The term "Americanization" or "Americanizing" of the Holocaust was probably first used in 1983 by Lawrence Langer, the preeminent U.S. scholar of Holocaust literature. Langer's article entitled "Americanization of the Holocaust on Stage and Screen" was published in the collective volume *From Hester Street to Hollywood*. Langer analyzes the enormous impact of two crucial events of the presentation of the Holocaust in the United States: the theater and film adaptation of *The Diary of Anne Frank* (premiered on Broadway in 1955, with the film version in 1959) and the 1978 NBC mini-series *Holocaust*. He argues that both alleviate the brutal reality of the Shoah by adapting it to Hollywood's broadly accepted mainstream conventions in America. For instance, in the 1959 film, the feelings that the teenagers Anne Frank and Peter van Pels have for each other are presented in long, sentimental sequences. The last of these scenes comes immediately before the discovery of the hiding place and the arrest of the whole group. However, in her original diary entries, a coolness between Anne and Peter in the final few months is evident. It is significant that the film version of the Anne Frank diary ends with her words, "In spite of everything, I still believe that people are really good at heart." According to Langer, this expression of hope and optimism in extremely difficult circumstances separates the presented narrative from its historical context:

> There is no final solace, no redeeming truth, no hope that so many millions may not have died in vain. They have. But the American vision of the Holocaust, in the works under consideration here, continues to insist that they have not, trying to parley hope, sacrifice, justice, and the future into a victory that will mitigate despair. (Blacher Cohen, 1983)

Langer states that the truth of the Holocaust is about the defeat of hope and the victory of anonymous and mass death. On the other hand, Langer seems to ignore the fact that it is a part of traditional American ethos to emphasize the predominance of goodness, optimism and liberty. The final words of Anne Frank in the film, spoken as if from heaven, express this ethos.

Michael Rothberg also uses this term in the essay "The Americanization of the Holocaust" (1995), later included in his well-known and respected monograph *Traumatic Realism* (2000). Rothberg declares that the Holocaust is being simplified by American popular culture. He lists some parameters of these changes:

> ...the predominance of media and information technologies; the hegemonic position of American media in a global media environment; the "sequencing" of the Shoah in various spheres of the media with other genocides and histories of oppression, as well as with other images and commodities of a postmodern consumer culture. (Rothberg 2000, 201)

Other scholars or survivors have recorded similar changes. In 1998, the Hungarian Holocaust survivor, writer, and *Nobel Prize* winner Imre Kertész wrote that the Holocaust was getting out of hand of the survivors and was becoming a subject of mass media stories, "a cheap commodity".

Polish literary scholars Monika Adamczyk-Garbowska and Magdalena Ruta also write about "Shoah business" and about the universalization of Jewish phenomena in culture, the material world ("Jewish" pubs and cafes for tourists), and politics. Often it is a "virtual Jewish world" instead of the authentic world created by Jews.

According to Alvin Hirsch Rosenfeld, the Holocaust has been transfigured, losing its specificity. This view is close to Yehuda Bauer's above-mentioned statement. He argues that today the culture of the Holocaust is constituted by alternative forms of narrative, art, and film mainly created by television writers, journalists, and filmmakers. National myths and reigning ideologies in each country shape the response to the extermination of Jews in different ways. Unlike Aleida Assmann, Rosenfeld states there is not "anything like a shared memory of the Holocaust, we find a multiplicity of historical memories and often a clash among them." American culture is a dominant shaper of popular images in the West. It dictates the process of imagining and presenting the Holocaust to a great extent for the rest of the world. This is how the Nazi persecution of Jews has been changed from an authentic historical event into just a symbol, or even "entertainment" (2011, 15). Rosenfeld warns of the possible "end of the Holocaust" in the cultural consciousness, and Judy Chicago and Steven Spielberg (see below) can serve as examples for him. *The Holocaust Project* (1985–1993), an artistic installation, made by Chicago in cooperation with her husband, the photographer Donald Woodman, consists of 16 large scale works made of different mediums (tapestry, metal, wood, photography, painting) using the tragic event of the Holocaust as an area where discrimination, injustice, and human atrocities take place (e.g. parallel to the slaughter of Native Americans, the Vietnam War, environmentalism, aggressive patriarchal power of men against women). It was also presented as a book with historical and contemporary photographs and the personal journal of the author (1993). I assume Judy Chicago's project should not be thought of as "entertainment." It provokes emotion because of its use of the topic of the Holocaust as a platform for controversy by utilizing the traditional representation of the Shoah. Moreover, it can bring the Holocaust closer to younger people by comparing it to issues that could be more personally relevant to them.

Sophia Francesca Marshman reflects analogously on Rosenfeld in her study "From the Margins to the Mainstream? Representations of the Holocaust in Popular Culture" (2005). She describes how depictions of the Holocaust have been sliding into the realm of entertainment, following Lawrence Langer and others in calling it the "Americanization of the Holocaust." The phenomenon of the Holocaust has become an object of popular culture and has led to mass Holocaust tourism. As a result, these historical events have been perverted and trivialized. She writes: "The Holocaust has been brought to the attention of millions of people, yet in a softened and distorted guise" (Marshman 2005, 1). She demonstrates this shift with two works, *Sophie's Choice* (novel by William Styron in 1979; film by Alan J. Pakula, 1982) and, similar to Rosenfeld, *Schindler's List*. Marshman attributes this shift to the fact that the Holocaust memory is no longer able to be presented by the witnesses' testimony. Almost all of the witnesses and survivors of the Holocaust have already passed away and the authoritative voices of Primo Levi, Elie Wiesel or Imre Kertész have been marginalized. The popular media tamper with history to make it more accessible to the audience.

However, other scholars have expressed a different opinion. Ernst van Alphen, Professor at Leiden University, published the essay "Playing the Holocaust" in 2001, in which he discussed the role of toy-art works inspired by Nazis atrocities and the Holocaust: David Levinthal's photographs in his *Mein Kampf* (1996), where mass murders, gas chambers or crematoriums are presented by toys and figurines, Ram Katzir's wandering installation *Your Coloring Book* (1996), and Zbigniew Libera's *Lego Concentration Camp* (1996) arousing a lot of controversy. It seems that the devices Levinthal, Katzir, and Libera use are too disrespectful to depict these horrible events. Nevertheless, van Alphen concludes that such a playful presentation of the Shoah does not necessarily lead to its trivialization. It can evoke emotional imagination and lead to engagement with the shocking past. The Polish researcher and writer Leszek Engelking, who refers to van Alphen's original essay, called his own article "Playing the Holocaust and Holocaust Business." He comments on this issue:

> For a generation entering the artistic arena in the 1980s and 1990s, that of grandchildren of the victims and bystanders of the Holocaust, the situation was different. In any case, some of their representations were focused on demonstrative violations of taboos, bordering on profanation. The dolls [...] appear in the works of several artists dealing with the subject of the Holocaust, above all with a Pole Zbigniew Libera (born 1959) – with the creation of the *Lego Concentration Camp*. They are action figures of executioners and victims, prisoners and guards of the German camp, and the whole work is a set of Lego blocks to build a death camp. It is undoubtedly a hugely controversial artifact. (Engelking 2007, 89)

The thesis of this reflection, in part related to van Alphen's and Engelking's arguments, is as follows: it is an indisputable fact there are fewer and fewer eyewitnesses of the extermination of the Jews and of the Holocaust in general. As a consequence, the Holocaust is becoming more and more of a universal theme and more often the subject of fiction. Nevertheless, is this fact alone causing a slide to entertainment? Is it not also a challenge for new artistic expression or new provocative approaches? Is it not correct to generalize and consider using pop culture Holocaust literature and culture en bloc? Connecting the Holocaust to poetic, literary, and aesthetic devices has often been discussed as taboo, or at least as inadequate, as reflected in the controversy surrounding Art Spiegelman and his graphic novel *Maus* (1980–1991) that eventually won a Pulitzer Prize. I suppose that the patterns of American (and in general Western) mass and popular culture are more heterogeneous and multifaceted than Langer and the other researchers mentioned have assumed. Devices of pop culture can also be used for dismantling sentimental superficiality, as well as black and white characters (see Quentin Tarantino's film *Inglourious Basterds*, 2009).

2

The shortcomings and strengths of pop culture paradigms can be demonstrated by Steven Spielberg's film *Schindler's List* (1993). It was warmly received by audiences (approximately 120 million viewers) and contributed to strengthening the role of the Holocaust in collective memory. The film is a free adaptation of Thomas Keneally's novel *Schindler's Ark* (1982, later *Schindler's List*), which presented an idealized figure of the "good Nazi German" who rescued more than a thousand Jews. While the novel is more authentic, the film distorts some historical facts, for example, Schindler's mission to save his Jews in Auschwitz and Schindler's sentimental farewell to prisoners in Brünnlitz. In contrast, Schindler's antagonist, the brutal commander of the Płaszów camp Amon Göth, becomes the embodiment of ultimate evil. In this way, the film utilizes archetypes as in myths or fairy tales which are already well known from Hollywood storytelling: the struggle of absolute good versus absolute evil, a black and white vision of the world, the character of a moral hero, and the happy ending. The figure of the little girl in a red coat, killed by Nazis, uses a favorite motif of Holocaust literature and film: the death of an innocent child. This scene is shot as a color sequence in the mainly black-and-white film. Therefore, the film is a sophisticated mixture of horror or thriller (liquidation of the ghetto in Kraków, sequences in Auschwitz), noble goodness, and sentimentality (the last scene in the cemetery in Jerusalem). *Schindler's List* emphasizes the basic goodness of human beings, like the aforementioned theater and film adaptation of *The Diary of Anne Frank*. Nevertheless, it is not possible to agree with Claude Lanzmann's assessment of *Schindler's List* as a "kitschy melodrama," or with Imre Kertész, who did not allow for the possibility of life in a Nazi concentration camp to be accurately portrayed by anyone who had not experienced it first-hand.

Marshman's and Rosenfeld's statements are to some extent inconsistent with Assmann's "ethical turn" in her view of the Holocaust. While Assmann notices the dominance of the experience of a victim, Marshman and Rosenfeld claim that the contemporary Holocaust memory eliminates survivors' voices. However, all of them agree with the idea of the universalization of the Holocaust. Currently, the Holocaust appears in forms and genres that are incompatible with how it was presented in the several first post-war decades. These topics are addressed not only in middle-brow novels and films like *Sophie's Choice* but are also integrated into popular culture in genres like mainstream romance film, musical, operetta, etc. From Polish literature, examples can be mentioned such as Bogdan Rutha's novels *Wyspa psów* (The Island of Dogs, 1971) and *Szczurny palac* (The Rat Palace, 1973) or Jerzy Stegner's romance and crime novel from the Warsaw Ghetto *Żydówka Noemi* (Jewess Noemi, 2010). Slawomir Buryła states that Stegner is betrayed by his inability to write a good literary work, not by the popular genre. All these novels are stereotypical and monotonous. Neither Stegner nor Rutha managed to use the opportunities that these genres offer. This assessment can also be applied to works of the Czech Holocaust survivor and writer Arnošt Lustig, at least to a certain extent. This will be examined in detail in the next chapter.

Nevertheless, in contrast to Marshman, it can be argued that this universalization and popularization of the Holocaust is not only focused on the so-called soft versions of life-affirming "escape stories," sentimental stories with beautiful Jewish girls or innocent children, which allow the audience to hide themselves from the harsh realities of the Holocaust. Sometimes, authors and filmmakers utilize elements of thriller, romance, magic realism, fairytale, fantasy, comics or horror to address the young generation and to create original works. The following authors belong to this group: the American novelist Michael Chabon (*The Amazing Adventures of Kavalier and Clay,* 2000; this work won the Pulitzer Prize), the Czech writer Jáchym Topol (*Chladnou zemí*, 2009; in English *The Devil's Workshop*, 2013) or the Polish novelist Igor Ostachowicz and the Slovak writer Peter Krištúfek whose works are discussed in detail below.

They endeavor to revise classical images and devices of the representation of the Shoah. This integration of pop culture forms is a special literary or cinematic strategy. It can be used as an approach that appeals more to contemporary generations. Moreover, it can also be used as an element of provocation, seeking to be taboo-breaking in style. These works are often connected with innovative narrative techniques, irony, grotesque, or comedy – or in contrast with demonstrative "unpoetic" style. This is the way a "de-" and "re-" constructing of the Holocaust is presented.

Sometimes, these works adapt and modify motifs of Jewish magical tradition and folklore. In this way, Michael Chabon uses the figure of the Golem in *The*

Amazing Adventures of Kavalier and Clay. The Golem, a larger-than-life creature made by a man, was most associated with the sixteenth century Prague rabbi Judah Loew ben Bezalel. Loew allegedly modeled the Golem from clay and brought him to life to protect the Jews. According to legend, Loew stored the Golem in the attic of the Old New Synagogue in Prague. In Chabon's novel, in 1939, one of the protagonists, the young Jewish artist Josef (Joe) Kavalier, has escaped from Nazi-occupied Prague while also smuggling the Golem out with him. Joe leaves the Golem in the city of Vilnius in Lithuania and then eventually makes his way to Brooklyn, where his aunt Ethel and cousin Sammy live. While the members of Kavalier's family in Europe all become victims of the Holocaust, Joe and Sammy create a modern graphic novel centered on their hero, the Escapist, who fights against the Nazis.

Another creature connected with the Jewish tradition is the dybbuk which originated from the Hasidic folklore. It is the malicious spirit of a dead person who is able to possess living beings and manipulate them. It became known from the Yiddish play written by S. Ansky *The Dybbuk, or Between Two Worlds* (premiered in Warsaw in 1920) and has grown into being a favorite subject of adaptations by writers and film directors. For instance, in Romain Gary's 1967 novel *La Danse de Genghis Cohn* (The Dance of Genghis Cohn), a former concentration camp SS officer, Lieutenant Schatz, is haunted by the dybbuk of the Polish Jew Genghis Cohn, whom he had killed. The Polish author Hanna Krall published the short story "Dybbuk" as a part of her book *Dowody na istnienie* (Proofs of Existence, 1995; in English in *The Woman from Hamburg and Other True Stories*, 2005). The protagonist is an American scientist, Adam S., born after the war. He is probably possessed by the spirit of his stepbrother, who apparently died in the Warsaw Ghetto during the war and who has come to rouse him to awareness of his Jewish roots and family history.

In several works, the Holocaust only appears as a backstory. In the works of younger authors, the Holocaust is often presented as one of several topics, "embedding the Holocaust in a broader narrative."

3

In this section, the work of the Czech writer Arnošt Lustig (1926–2011), who is a good example of changes in the presentation of the Holocaust literature in the few last decades, will be discussed. Lustig survived the Holocaust. When he was 16, he was imprisoned in Terezín, then in Auschwitz for a short time (several days), and later in Buchenwald. Thus for him, the Shoah became the theme of his life's writing. His first works belong to his best: *Noc a naděje* (1958, Night and Hope, translated into English in 1962) and *Démanty noci* (1958, Diamonds in the Night, translated into English in 1962, with a new translation in 1977). Lustig's characters are not heroic figures, especially in these first short stories. They are often outsiders, children, or old men and women. Despite the bleakness these people must repeatedly undergo, by donning an outer shell just to survive, the majority of them try to maintain their fundamental moral values.

Arnošt Lustig's later books, however, accentuate the more abrasive sides of life in the camps: physical and mental cruelty, violence, homo- and heterosexual prostitution, a lack of solidarity among the prisoners, and so on. He often records the stories of young Jewish girls and women. Their beauty and youth form a moving contrast to the horrors of the Shoah. He first applied this approach in the novellas *Dita Saxová* (1962, translated into English in 1966, a new translation in 1993) and *Modlitba pro Kateřinu Horovitzovou* (1965, A Prayer for Kateřina Horovitzová, translated into English in 1973), and also in *Nemilovaná*, subtitled *Z deníku sedmnáctileté Perly Sch.* (1979, The Unloved: From the Diary of 17-Year Old Perla S., translated into English in 1985). *Nemilovaná* won the prestigious American National Jewish Book Award in 1986. It is the story of a young Jewish prostitute named Perla in the Terezín ghetto, written as her fictional diary, capturing the period from August to December 1943 with both naïveté and immaturity as well as abrasive matter-of-factness.

> November 16. Twice. Candle and matches. Hairnet. A box of spirit. Three times. Solid alcohol. A quarter of rye bread. Twenty grams of margarine. Thermometer. Tin cup. Liter thermos. (Lustig 1991, 63)

These are rewards for sex.

Perla is a young and beautiful girl, initially submissive in her relations with men. One of her "clients" is a German SS officer who humiliates her by behaving in a superior manner that is condescending to her. This character fulfills the stereotype of the sadistic Nazi. However, Perla's behavior changes towards the end – as does Kateřina Horovitzová's in Lustig's earlier work. When Perla learns she has to leave Terezín with a transport to the East, she kills the Nazi officer by biting through his throat while they are having intercourse.

In general, Perla belongs to the well-known and popular character type of the selfless courtesan or prostitute (e.g. Marguerite Gautier in Dumas's *La Dame aux camélias*, or Sonia Marmeladov in Dostoevsky's *Crime and Punishment*). In Holocaust literature, Ladislav Mňačko's Marta or Maria Nurowska's Elżbieta can be seen as examples. In *Smrť sa volá Engelchen* (Death Is Called Engelchen, 1959), Marta is a beautiful and mysterious woman with a hidden Jewish identity. She works for the Gestapo as a secretary and sleeps with Nazi officers to gain information that she then passes on to the partisans in Moravia. After the war, Marta is still traumatized by the events that she experienced and commits suicide. Elżbieta Elsner in *Listy miłości* (Letters of Love, 1991), a sixteen-year-old Jewish girl, comes voluntarily to the Warsaw Ghetto where she becomes a prostitute in a whorehouse to save her father from starving. After escaping from the ghetto, she assumes a new identity. Both of these novels use a mixture of innocence and sexuality while being set among the horrors of the war and Holocaust.

Unloved could be considered to be, in part, original. Instead, Lustig's later novels repeat and replicate his earlier types of characters and devices. Like in the diary *Unloved*, laconic records of sexual partners appear in the first part of the novel *Krásné zelené oči* (2000, Lovely Green Eyes, translated into English in 2001): "Fifteen: Herrmann Hammer, Fritz Blücher, Reinhold Wupperthal, Siegfried Fuchs..."

The main figure is also a youthful Jewish prostitute, the fifteen-year-old Hana Kaudersová, named "Kůstka" (in the English translation "Skinny"), from Prague. After spending some cruel months in Auschwitz, she stays three weeks in a German military field brothel in Poland. Every day, Hanna is forced to serve a dozen soldiers, some of whom are distraught and violent. In this novel, on the one hand, the long dialogues of the characters contain trite ideas; on the other hand, Hana's experiences in Auschwitz and in the brothel are extreme, harsh, and cruel.

> Anything that is not specifically permitted is forbidden. [...] The soldier is always right. Kissing is forbidden. Unconditional obedience is demanded. [...] With immediate effect, it is forbidden to provide services without a rubber sheath. Most strictly prohibited are: Anal, oral or brutal intercourse. Taking urine or semen into the mouth or anus. Re-using contraceptives. (Lustig 2002, 10–11)

Eroticism, an attractive woman, and teenage sexuality also appear in Lustig's so-called Jewish Trilogy, edited in the years 1992 to 2000 (*Colette, dívka z Antverp*, 1992; *Tanga, dívka z Hamburku*, 1992; *Lea z Leeuwardenu*, 2000). Here, the female figures are in many ways similar. In all these works, the author uses conventional narration: long, dull dialogues, stiff repetitions of motifs, and trivial reflections and remarks by the narrator.

> "Am I?"
> "You are," answered V. F.
> "From flesh and blood?"
> "From flesh and blood." (Lustig 2013, 76–77)
>
> "Why did God create you and me?" (Lustig 2013, 151)

The narrator comments on these clichés: "These words have ten different meanings," even later, "Any reference to 'purity' has a hundred different meanings." Such dialogues and remarks should provide an impression of considerable depth. However, they are banal. Likewise, in his later novels, Lustig's narrative uses many conventional images. On the first page, he already makes an initial comparison of Colette with birds:

> The wing-span of flying birds was in her eyes. The course of flight from somewhere to somewhere. [...] She resembled a bird whose magnetic needle failed for the whole nine months that she was known to several people in Auschwitz-Birkenau. (Lustig 2013, 5)

Similar images can be found approximately 40 times in the novel: for example, "She felt like a bird caught in a huge cage." This comparison is well-known from prison stories (e.g. from Dostoevsky, *The House of the Dead* to Anne Frank) and has reached the point of triviality.

The narrator uses these and analogous rhetorical devices (also images of ashes, chimneys, trains, crematorium ovens) on almost every page. He tries to compensate for these conventional images by using devices of thrillers and erotic novels. For example, in *Colette*, the extermination camp in Auschwitz-Birkenau is described in many scenes, most of which are violent and cruel. The Nazi warden Weissacker, like Amon Göth in *Schindler's List*, kills prisoners for pleasure and rapes female prisoners. His person is the embodiment of the ultimate evil. A pretty 19-year-old Belgian Jewess named Colette is also among his sexual victims. However, she falls in love with a Czech prisoner named Vili Feld. Risking their lives (forbidden love!), Colette and Vili sneak off together and make love. These love scenes provide a strong contrast to Colette's and Vili's harsh life in Auschwitz. Critics have stressed the author's personal experience of Nazi concentration camps as a guarantee of the novel's authenticity and credibility. But in fact, his emphasis on erotic and sexual scenes is quite implausible. Furthermore, as Alvin H. Rosenfeld writes, sexual scenes set in an extermination camp present an improper trivialization and even abuse of tragic events.

> In the camps themselves, as virtually all survivor accounts indicate, the central, most frustrating, and hence most abiding appetite was for food. Other passions were secondary and, it seems, for most were held in abeyance. As a result, one of the characteristics of Holocaust writings at their most authentic is that they are peculiarly and predominantly sexless. (Rosenfeld 1980, 164)

Moreover, the plausibility of the main characters in *Colette* is often questionable. Vili and Colette are "omnipresent" (like the famous Forrest Gump in Robert Zemeckis' film) and also "omniscient." Lustig writes that "V. F. knew there was a forgery workshop where Nazis produced English and American money ..."

Colette who was known only to "several people in Auschwitz-Birkenau," "knew men from the Sonderkommando who worked in the crematoria, bakers from bakeries, cobblers from shoemaker's workshops, wagon unloaders and employees from the ramp" (Lustig 2013, 65). She even knew about Himmler's secret order to stop the gassing of Jews. By using this information and these statements, the author constructs a kind of encyclopedia of life in Auschwitz-Birkenau. Nevertheless, on the one hand, the improbable sexual scenes and the omniscience of the characters misrepresent the harsh reality in the camp. On the other hand, the exaggerated use of highly improbable situations defiles the reality of the Shoah. The result is a loss of authenticity and plausibility of the characters and situations that are presented. At the same time, much of this "encyclopedic data" turns out to be inaccurate when compared with known historical facts.

The film adaptation of the novel, created by director Milan Cieslar in 2013 (allegedly with Lustig's participation; however, Lustig had died in February of 2011), stresses the brutality of some of the scenes and emphasizes eroticism. While the lovers in Auschwitz in the well-known Polish film *Pasażerka* (Passenger, 1963) hold each other's hands, the film version of Colette presents hetero- and homosexual intercourse in Auschwitz in a variety of positions. Some sequences and the last-minute rescue of the two main characters are reminiscent of thriller and Hollywood movies.

In the novella *Colette*, for instance, Lustig's narrative uses many conventional images. The plausibility of his characters is very often lost.

4

The Polish-American historian Jan Tomasz Gross has questioned the Poles' self-image during World War II. He has raised the issue in his books *Neighbors* (Polish edition 2000, in English 2001), *Fear* (in English 2006, in Polish 2008) and *Golden Harvest* (with Irena Grudzinska Gross; Polish 2011, English 2012), which are all based on testimonies and documents. He has described cases of Polish complicity and enrichment through the murder of Jews and has accused the Polish society after 1945 of failing to come to terms with what he considered to be widespread antisemitism. Gross claimed that Polish people killed more Jews than Germans during the war.[1] His works have aroused numerous controversies and polemics by conservative Polish historians and politicians.

As Przemysław Czapliński states, the publication of these books also became a turning point in Polish literature dedicated to the persecution of Jews and the Holocaust. Currently, in literature, Poles appear as either persecutors, helpers or witnesses. The Poles are not only victims of the Nazi regime, but they also have to deal with their own guilt. The events in Jedwabne in July 1941 where the Polish villagers murdered more than 300 Jews by burning them in a barn has inspired several works either directly or indirectly – Tadeusz Słobodzianek's theater play *Nasza klasa* (2009, Our Class), Władysław Pasinowski's film *Pokłosie* (2012, Aftermath), Krystian Piwowarski's short stories *Więcej gazu, Kameraden!* (2012, More Gas, Comrades!) and Igor Ostachowicz's novel *Noc żywych Żydów* (2012, Night of the Living Jews), which is analyzed below in more detail. The barn in Jedwabne has become a symbol, like the gas chambers in Auschwitz. Marta Tomczok calls these stories "post-Jedwabnie narrations."

Similar statements are also presented in Slovak and Czech Jewish studies and literary works. In the Czech Republic, the memory of the Holocaust had to compete with the memory of Czechs enduring the Nazi occupation. In Slovakia, the new political elites condemned the persecution of the Jews and distanced themselves from the clero-fascist administration of the Slovak Republic during the war (Hiemer et al. 2021, 26). The Slovak Catholic Church and its supporters, however, often defended the wartime leader, the priest Jozef Tiso and his regime. Several Slovak historians and other intellectuals argued against this distortion of history and demonstrated the responsibility of the Slovak clero-fascist administration for persecution and deportations of the Jews. The sharpness of the debates illustrates something about the fragile status of the Jewish cultural tradition that has to be constantly renegotiated and protected. This is what recent literature undertakes through imagination, pop culture, and entertainment elements linking history and the present in a surprising way.

Concerning these problems, another writer to be analyzed closer is the Polish author Igor Ostachowicz (born in Warsaw in 1968). He served as an advisor to the former Polish prime minister Donald Tusk and debuted under the pseudonym Julian Rebes with the novel *Potwór i panna* (2009, Monster and Miss), "the bloody story of a monster in love" with a setting that spans from ancient Rome to contemporary Warsaw. His following novel, *Noc żywych Żydów* (2012, Night of the Living

---

[1] Jan T. Gross, "Eastern Europe's Crisis of Shame," September 13, 2015, https://www.project-syndicate.org/commentary/eastern-europe-refugee-crisis-xenophobia-by-jan-gross-2015-09?barrier=accesspaylog.

Jews), was nominated for the most prestigious Polish literary prize, *Nagroda Literacka Nike*. It contains elements of horror or thriller. The title was probably inspired by the famous horror film *Night of the Living Dead* (1968, directed by George A. Romero), which depicts the fight of a few townspeople against the "living dead" zombies in Pennsylvania, or by the short horror film *Night of the Living Jews* (2008), which depicted an invasion of Jewish zombies attacking a gentile family while hungering for human flesh (a parody on zombie films). In 2014, Marek Kalita adapted Ostachowicz's novel for the theater in a staging at the Teatr Dramatyczny in Warsaw.

The fictional world of Ostachowicz's novel is set in the twenty-first century, in the present-day Warsaw district of Muranów, where the Warsaw Ghetto was located. The Jews who were killed during the Holocaust and have been forgotten now come back as zombies.

> Only those who are forgotten break out of the floor and crawl out of their basements, those who don't have any family. Nobody will remember them over their grave. People need a little warmth or interest in them after their death, especially after a tragic one. (Ostachowicz 2012, 203)

Forgetting about the Jews contrasts with Aleida Assmann's statement about memorializing the Holocaust as a collective trauma and a common European transnational memory. Although it is an important part of the Jewish tradition to bury deceased relatives and to remember them, Jewish graves have not been tended to after the War, in contrast to those of the murdered Poles.

In the novel *Noc żywych Żydów* Jews emerge from the cellar and flood contemporary Warsaw, trying to integrate into Polish society. The history of Polish Jews returns in the form of zombies, like horror, disgusting and harsh. Polish neo-fascists and skinheads rise against them and a battle between the forces of good and evil takes place in the Arkadia shopping center. Like in *Schindler's List* and other works, archetypes of myths or fairy tales are exploited: the struggle of good versus evil. In contrast with the film *Night of the Living Dead* and other works, the zombies are not aggressive; on the contrary, they are besieged and must defend themselves. These Jewish zombies can speak and feel, and they are presented as victims. They cannot rely on the help of the Polish police or the public too much. Like other authors of his generation, Ostachowicz uses devices of magic realism and fantasy. Miraculous props play an important role in this fight, for example, a silver heart that brings happiness to its owner. The heart belonged to the Jews but was stolen by fascists, and eventually it is returned to the Jews and their allies. The antisemites manage to set the roof of the shopping center on fire, but it seems they will be defeated, and the Jews will be able to leave and go home to their former houses in Warsaw.

The narrator is the unnamed main character, "a worker with a university diploma" and the son of an antisemitic father. He lives in a modest apartment in Warsaw with his philosemitic girlfriend, whom he calls "Skinny" ("Chuda"). Suddenly he finds himself involved in a big conflict, almost against his will. Eventually, he decides to help the Jews, and he joins them in fighting against the forces of evil. He probably dies during this fight and becomes a zombie too. Nevertheless, the reader cannot be sure, just as it is unclear whether or not the Jews will be saved. Images of "white light" suggest that it is possible the whole story was only a vision caused by amphetamines or other drugs.

Like Lustig in *Colette*, Ostachowicz uses devices of the thriller in the novel. Ostachowicz also exploits popular cultural references, elements of fantasy, comics, and even computer games, horror, and porn films. At the same time, however, the narration mocks these genres and plays with their clichés and stereotypes.

The narrator's language is a specific feature of *Noc żywych Żydów*. It is spoken Polish, on occasion rude, sometimes difficult to understand for those who are not native speakers of Polish. Nevertheless, the style is consistent with the general perspective of the text and with the harsh situations that are depicted. In this novel, as in almost all the books mentioned, there often occur scenes of violence and open depictions of sex, both voluntary and forced, and both hetero- and homosexual. But from time to time, humor and laughter also emerge. As an example, at one point a "living dead" Jewish Polish officer sitting in a cafe wants to light a cigarette. The narrator tells him that smoking is not allowed there, and the officer wonders if it was a remnant of Nazi regulations. In the novel, the news media present sensational headlines like "Living Corpses in the Streets" or "Jewish Corpses Obstruct the Living Poles."

A Polish physician who tried to save his Jewish fiancé during the war is an interesting minor character. After a brutal act of the Nazi Gestapo, he is forced to kill her to save her from further torture. Then he decides to get revenge and murder the Nazis. This type of fierce avenger is not common in the Holocaust literature. It recalls, for example, figures in Jurek Becker's novel *Bronsteins Kinder* (1986, Bronstein's Children; film adaptation by Jerzy Kawalerowicz, 1991) or the famous film by Tarantino *Inglourious Basterds* (2009). According to Marta Tomczok, Ostachowicz's novel is far from any of the usual martyrology and melancholy, both significant for Polish Holocaust literature. The author found in pop culture – like Art Spiegelman in *Maus* and other younger artists – a perfect innovative medium for evoking the past.

The scenes situated in Auschwitz are especially remarkable in the Ostachowicz's novel. They are perhaps only comparable with the "Auschwitz chapter" in the novel *Sestra* (1994, in English *City, Sister, Silver*, 2000) by Jáchym Topol. Ostachowicz's narrator and his girlfriend "Skinny" find themselves in the transport to Auschwitz-Birkenau in the phantomatic, unreal fictional world of *Noc żywych Żydów*. Their enemies, the protagonists of evil, wait for them on the ramp and welcome them by roaring and beating them. The narrator goes through harsh experiences (*Appell, Bunker*), and suffers from hunger. He says:

> ...I feel like this is some infernal version of Auschwitz, improved on by the devil, because I don't know how it was in the real one. But it seems to me that [there] is not even a little sparkle of positive human emotion here, not even pity or willingness. And I am among the deceived. (Ostachowicz 2012, 137)

He can see a lot of cages into which naked female and male prisoners are driven. He finds himself in one of the cages with his girlfriend. She is apathetic to him, and he watches her having sex with other men, and he feels like an animal. Eventually, their stay in Auschwitz turns out to be the devil's performance of the forces of evil. They want to seize the silver heart that is said to bring happiness to its owner and thereby force the narrator to surrender to them.

These scenes could have, in fact, been inspired by the chapter "I had a Dream" in Topol's novel *Sestra*, where the characters also find themselves in the Auschwitz camp and this "visit" is presented as something unreal but overwhelmingly impressive. Topol's novel *Sestra* was published in Polish in 2002 (a decade before the publication of *Night of the Living Jews*) in the brilliant translation of the aforementioned Leszek Engelking. Engelking has also analyzed *Sestra* and other works by Topol.

5

The novella *Ema a Smrtihlav* (Emma and the Death's Head Hawkmoth), written by the Slovak author Peter Krištúfek (1973–2018), was published in 2014. Krištúfek worked as a moderator in various radio stations, filmed documentaries as well as feature films, and wrote short stories and novels. In his works, he often presented a controversial view of modern Slovak history using dramatic storylines and fantastic motifs. He died prematurely due to a traffic collision in Central Slovakia.

The beginning and the end of the story are set on the coast of the Black Sea in Bulgaria in 1961. The main character, Šimon, almost 30 years old, is spending his holiday there with his wife, daughter, and son. However, the main storyline returns to the pre-war and war years in Slovakia. Before the war, the then little Šimon lives with his parents and younger brother in Bratislava. His father is a Czech architect and his mother a Slovakian Jew making fashionable dresses for women. The happy life of the family ends with the breakup of Czechoslovakia, the formation of the Slovak clero-fascist republic, and the outbreak of World War II (1939). Because his father is Czech, he must leave his family behind and move out of the Slovak state and back to the Czech lands. His wife and children are endangered by discrimination for being Jews. In 1942, the transports of the Slovakian Jews begin. Šimon's mother tries to save her family. She flees with her younger son Leo to Central Slovakia, where she has acquaintances. Šimon, a black-haired and more "Jewish" looking boy, is taken to a village near Bratislava where Marika Sándorfiová, a friend of his mother, lives. Šimon spends three years there hiding in her barn. All four members of the family survive and come back together after the war.

The novella is narrated in the third person but completely from Šimon's point of view. During his hiding, Šimon is ten to 13 years old. The whole time he must stay alone in the barn with smelly pigs and goats. Marika "néni" (aunt) only comes to the barn in the early morning and late evening to feed the cattle. Šimon suffers from the cold in the winter, his toes get frostbitten. He is still afraid of being found out; one day, the barn is searched by German soldiers, but they do not discover his hiding place.

Throughout his three years in hiding, Šimon's only distraction is reading colorful magazines, listening to music from nearby houses, and watching a death's head hawkmoth in the barn. Based on the pictures in magazines, adventure books, and fairy tales, Šimon invents his own fantastic story. He imagines a pretty brown-haired woman named Ema lying on the beach near the sea in a yellow swimsuit (this picture is also depicted on the frontispiece of Krištúfek's book). Like in the magazine, she smiles and puts Nivea Creme from a blue tin on herself. Šimon's fear of being discovered is transferred into another figure, a German General wearing the picture of a death's head hawkmoth on his uniform. Šimon calls him General Death's Head Hawkmoth. The General threatens Ema, kidnaps her in a tank, and imprisons her in his house. Šimon manages to free her and they run away together.

The tale imagined by Šimon is similar to many fairy tales and romances based on the archetypical story about "the princess and a dragon." A "damsel in distress" and her saving is also an essential part of Hollywood films, and pop culture in general (see the above-mentioned films *Schindler's List* or *Colette*). Ema embodies beauty, peace, and love, while the General incorporates danger and evil. Šimon's tale is connected with two popular sentimental or even kitschy songs about love and death. They are the Hungarian "Szomorú vasárnap" (Gloomy Sunday) and the German "Lili Marleen." Šimon can hear the first coming from the neighbors while he is in hiding; the second he can only play in his head while he imagines Ema's story. The author quotes both of them in their respective original languages.

He adds the Slovak translations and explanations at the end of his book. He writes that "Lili Marleen" became "a fateful hit of German soldiers fighting in World War II." In fact, it was also popular among American and British units. Marlene Dietrich performed it live for the Allied troops during the war and sang it many times later. Two films of the same name were made, the British *Lilli Marlene* (1950) and the German *Lili Marleen* (1981).

Krištúfek's integration of these sentimental songs into his novella is another example of how he used pop culture elements in his writing. On the other hand, his construction of *Emma and the Death's Head Hawkmoth* is very sophisticated. For instance, the death's head hawkmoth is a moth which Šimon had seen in his father's collection of butterflies. The eagles with spread wings on the uniforms of Slovak fascists also evoke memories of this moth in him. He later watches its hatchings grow and develop in the barn. In a magazine, he sees a picture of the Nazi general who "has the skull and crossbones on his cap." All these experiences are projected onto his image of the German General.

Šimon's daydreams are blended with actual events. Whereas the Germans are searching the barn for hiding places, Šimon imagines how Ema and he would escape from the General and his soldiers. At the moment the German officer says "Nichts!" and leaves the barn, Ema and Šimon are saved and return to the beach.

It is worthy of attention that later in 1961, in the frame story, Šimon's real wife is very similar to his boyish image of Ema:

> The pretty woman lay in a beach chair under a colorful parasol. Ema, he recognized her at once. She was happily stretched, with sunglasses on her face, brown hair braided in a chignon.
> A beachside dressing room made from canvas stood nearby, with red and white stripes. (Krištúfek 2014, 48)

When compared to his adult life in the frame story:

> In the middle of the beach shone a dressing room made from red and white canvas. [...]
> A colourful parasol stood nearby and under it a beach chair.
> The brown haired woman in yellow swimsuit was sunbathing on the chair. (Krištúfek 2014, 50)

Krištúfek depicts an idyllic life before the war, like many Holocaust writers (Josef Škvorecký, Ota Pavel, Piotr Szewc or Marek Bieńczyk). In contrast, the experiences of the main protagonist during the war are very brutal and leave him both physically and mentally traumatized. Šimon suffers from frostbite on his feet and fears water; he has never learned to swim.

According to Polish survivor and researcher Michał Głowiński, documentaries, as well as works of fiction thematizing the Shoah, cannot effectively apply the principles of traditional poetics. The events that are evoked in Holocaust literature are unbelievable and horrible, and it is impossible to communicate them as required, for instance, by Aristotle. Igor Ostachowicz, Peter Krištúfek, and other authors respond to Głowiński's statement, with their various approaches to writing. They each disturb the illusionistic imitations and conventional images in the public consciousness connected with the Holocaust. As Darren Sush, one of the "third generation," that of the grandchildren of survivors, expresses:

> Growing up as the grandson of Holocaust survivors, I've heard countless stories about the atrocities that took place during the Holocaust. My mind was bombarded with images and visions that I could not possibly fathom as truth.

This is the reason why the current generation is searching for new narrative treatments, i.e., imaginative and fantastic scenes, metafiction, and the grotesque. They also use stereotypes involving elements of pop culture.

Conclusion

This article examines changes in the presentation of the Holocaust/Shoah throughout the past few decades. First, several theoretical concepts of these changes are analyzed. Yehuda Bauer, Aleida Assmann, and others state that the Holocaust has become a universal symbol of evil in Western culture. Nevertheless, various researchers, mainly American (Lawrence Langer, Michael Rothberg, Alvin Hirsch Rosenfeld, and Sophia Francesca Marshman), warn about the trivialization of the Holocaust using the term "Americanization of the Holocaust." According to them, the Shoah has become a part of popular culture, even "entertainment." They support their judgment by listing globally popular books and films like *Schindler's List*. The extermination of Jews has been glossed over, and the tragic deaths of millions of people have been replaced with happy endings. Not only world-famous books and films but also popular media tamper with the history of the Shoah to make it more convenient for Western audiences.

In spite of that, all these critical views fail to distinguish between the vast variety of works. Middle-brow novels and films (*Sophie's Choice*) or artistic works like *The Holocaust Project* by Judy Chicago should never be identified as "entertainment" or even "kitschy melodramas." Moreover, these critics seem to ignore the fact that it is an important part of traditional American ethos to emphasize the predominance of goodness, optimism, and liberty.

However, other researchers (Ernst van Alphen, Leszek Engelking or Slawomir Buryła) express a different opinion. They believe that the use of elements of pop culture can be a chance for new artistic expression and new provocative approaches to be developed. For them, this also applies to the topic of the Holocaust. For instance, Art Spiegelman's graphic novel *Maus* (1980–1991) aroused many controversies but eventually won the Pulitzer Prize. It is not correct to generalize and consider using pop culture in Holocaust literature and culture *en bloc*.

This article agrees with the second statement. It is true that the Shoah is gradually changing into a universal theme and the subject of fiction. This fact causes many works thematizing the Holocaust to descend into trivialization in their efforts to be popular. Nevertheless, the elements of pop culture, its genres and devices, can also be utilized to create innovative works. It may be a challenge for younger artists who do not want to repeat stable motifs and images connected with the Holocaust.

Therefore, the following sections deal with three writers (one Czech, one Polish, and finally one Slovak) and their works in greater detail. The stories and novels written by the Czech author Arnošt Lustig (1926–2011) are a good example of the integration of pop-culture forms, like thrillers or mass-market romance novels, into Holocaust literature. Unlike his first books from the 1950s, Lustig's later works accentuate the more abrasive sides of life in the camps (violence, brutality, hetero- and homosexual prostitution, as well as a lack of unity among the prisoners). He often recorded the stories of young Jewish girls and women whose beauty and youth form a moving contrast to the horrors of the Shoah. In the novella *Colette* (1992), for instance, Lustig's narrative utilizes many conventional images. The plausibility of his characters is very often lost.

While Lustig uses elements of thriller and romance, other authors also apply elements of thriller or fantasy, comics, and horror as well as pornographic films (the Polish novelist Igor Ostachowicz, born 1968) when writing about the Holocaust. The works of both Lustig and Ostachowicz are full of violence, brutality, and sexual scenes. In contrast to Lustig, however, Ostachowicz's *Noc żywych Żydów* (2012, Night of the Living Jews) is more original and impressive. It also puts forward actual questions concerning the past and the relations between Poles and Jews. The Poles are not only victims of the Nazi regime, but they also have to cope with their own guilt. Ostachowicz's novel belongs to the group of works that discusses the controversial issues of the Poles' past after historian Jan Tomasz Gross questioned the self-image of the Poles during World War II.

The Slovak author Peter Krištúfek (1973–2018) published his novella *Ema a Smrtihlav* (Emma and the Death's Head Hawkmoth) in 2014. It is narrated from the point of view of a Jewish boy, Šimon, in Slovakia during the war. Šimon is forced to spend three years in hiding in a barn. In his imagination, inspired by pictures in color magazines and popular songs, he invents fantastic stories. His trashy stories about a beautiful young woman called Ema and a German general are blended with actual events.

Krištúfek integrates sentimental German and Hungarian songs as well as pinup pictures from magazines in his narration. The novella *Ema a Smrtihlav*, similar to Ostachowicz's novel and other works of younger writers, disturbs the illusionistic imitations and conventional images in the public consciousness connected with the Holocaust.

Pop culture elements have become a typical feature of literature in last few decades. They extend the creative possibilities for speaking about the Holocaust while raising many problematic questions. Second and third generation artists and writers use a variety of pop culture methods to respond to the increasing forgetfulness of history. These books may sometimes appear trivial, but their poetics can appeal to younger generations for whom the Holocaust represents the distant past.

Dina Porat
A New Era? Christian-Jewish Relations in Post-Cold War Europe

In December 2015, during a festive gathering at Tel Aviv University, a book – the first of its kind – was launched: *In our time: Documents and Articles on the Catholic Church and the Jewish People in the Wake of the Holocaust*.[1] The volume includes papal and Vatican announcements, sermons, declarations, and agreements, all concerning a dramatic change in the attitudes of the Catholic Church towards the Jewish people and Israel, issued within a 50-year span: from the conclusion of the Second Vatican Council (1965) until the end of 2015. Taking a look at more recent declarations and papal addresses issued since 2015, the main research questions that arise now, in the 2020s, are: how were the unprecedented changes occurring within the Church implemented? Have they filtered down to the vast number of Catholic believers – a billion and a quarter worldwide – and changed the deep-seated, centuries long negative attitudes towards the Jewish people? Has the downfall of the former Eastern Bloc, that opened a new era in so many aspects, affected Christian-Jewish relations, particularly in Europe? Finally, what are the present formal and informal Jewish reactions? Attempts to find some of the answers will rely on the analyses of texts and interviews with officials and activists on both sides. This text traces some recent developments and also sheds light on a certain change in attitudes on both the Christian and the Jewish side.

A number of key documents have recently been published by the Vatican and its officials. On 15 July 2021, in a session dedicated to "the Power of Religious leadership," held during the seventh Global Forum for Combatting Antisemitism in Jerusalem, Msgr. Tomasz Grysa, the first Counsellor of the Apostolic Nunciature in Israel, said: "The Holy See reiterates (…) its position against antisemitism and invites every person of good will to embrace the golden rule of loving one's neighbour, as a solid foundation for fraternity and social friendship."[2] In order to enhance the message, he quoted Cardinal Kurt Koch, president of the Commission for Religious Relations with the Jews, the Vatican's central body for dealing with these matters. The Cardinal pointed out that antisemitism was re-emerging, but "we can overcome it by opening ourselves to the other, by building fraternity and deepening

---

[1] *In Our Time: Documents and Articles on the Catholic Church and the Jewish People in the Wake of the Holocaust*, ed. Dina Porat, Karma Ben Johanan, and Ruth Braude (Tel Aviv University Press, 2015).
[2] Msgr. Grysa kindly entrusted me with his message on the session, in which I took part (D.P.).

the common heritage with Judaism."³ Moreover, he said this in the presence of more than 50 of the world's top leaders, who gathered in Jerusalem to mark the international Holocaust Memorial Day on 23 January 2020. Two years earlier, in January 2018, Pope Francis had told the Organization for Security and Cooperation in Europe (OSCE) conference in Rome that he would never grow tired of the "struggle against antisemitism and crimes associated with antisemitic hatred." Later that year, on 13 June, he called upon his followers to never forget the Shoah, using the Hebrew term, and to remember it as "a constant warning for all of us, of an obligation to reconciliation, of reciprocal comprehension and love toward our 'elder brothers,' the Jews."⁴

While more such declarations have been made recently, let us concentrate on the events of 2015 which are of special interest and relevance to this analysis. On December 10, during a press conference held in the Vatican, with two Rabbis standing in attendance, the Pontifical Commission for Religious Relations with the Jews issued an unprecedented declaration – one of utmost historical importance. Entitled *"For the Gifts and the Calling of God are Irrevocable" (Rom.11:29): A Reflection on Theological Questions Pertaining to Catholic-Jewish Relations*, it marked the fiftieth anniversary of the *Nostra Aetate* (*In Our Time*) – the 1965 declaration which, upon its issuing, was a watershed moment in Jewish-Christian relations and will be discussed in detail further in this chapter.

It should be noted that prior to the release of the December 2015 declaration, "a very special general audience" was organized at Pope Francis' wish. It took place on 28 October, the day which marked 50 years since the promulgation of *Nostra Aetate*. A major conference, with hundreds of participants, was held at the Pontifical Georgian University in Rome, where the Pope spoke quite emphatically about interreligious dialogue and cooperation.⁵ Why was there a need to issue the De-

---

3 Cardinal Koch spoke at the Fifth World Holocaust Forum, held on January 23 at Yad Vashem, in the presence of more than 50 world leaders, https://www.vaticannews.va/en/world/news/2020-01/holy-see-yad-vashem-forum-koch-antisemitism.html.

4 The Pope spoke on January 29, 2018 to the OSCE conference participants during an audience he granted them in his chambers. Half a year later, he sent one more message via the Vatican's Secretary of State to Berlin to mark the fortieth anniversary of the Neo-catechumenal Way, June 13, 2018, https://www.vaticannews.va/en/pope/news/2018-06/pope-message-anniversary-neocatechumenal-way-berlin.html

5 The presentation of an eight-page abstract of the December 10, 2015 document by Cardinal Kurt Koch took place on December 14–15 at Tel Aviv University, during a special conference which I had the honor to chair (D.P.). For the text of the abstract, see the Vatican site: vatican/Roman curia/pontifical councils/doc 20151210/ebraismo/nostra aetate. For more on the 2015 events see: Porat, "Recent Efforts by the Catholic Church to Abate Antisemitism in the Wake of the Holocaust," *Justice* no. 58 (2016): 7–11.

cember declaration, in addition to the clear address the Pope had delivered barely a few weeks earlier?

In search for an answer, one needs to take a close look at *Nostra Aetate* which serves as a binding foundation for documents issued by the Catholic Church in its wake. Then, one can turn their attention to the 10 December Pontifical document, while also taking into consideration changes occurring within the Church and attempts to implement them.

Nostra Aetate (Engl.: *In Our Time*), the *Declaration on the Relations of the Church to non-Christian Religions*, was proclaimed at the end of the second synod, better known as the Second Vatican Council. This impressive gathering which spanned three years, from 1962 to 1965, attended by some 3,000 cardinals and bishops from the world over, was initiated by Pope John the XXIII, formerly Angelo Giuseppe Roncalli. In his capacity as the Vatican's delegate in Istanbul during the 1940s, Roncalli met the members of a rescue delegation from the Yishuv, the Hebrew community under the British Mandate between the two world wars, who told him about the horrors of the Holocaust. Roncalli, a warm and open person, was deeply moved and in tears when he heard about the sinking of the "Struma," a boat carrying hundreds of refugees that was denied access to Turkish ports. He was even more shaken when presented with the Protocols of Auschwitz, written by two escapees who described, for the first time, the realities of the mass killing of Jews. He did his best to extend help, writing intensively to Pope Pius the XII and to European heads of state he had contacts with, in an attempt to alleviate the plight of their Jewish communities.[6] Once WWII was over and the prospects of establishing the state of Israel were at stake, Roncalli became willingly instrumental in behind-the-scenes diplomatic efforts to gain US members' votes, by facilitating audiences of Zionist activists with high-level Vatican officials.[7]

When Roncalli became Pope in 1958, he did not forget the Holocaust and its implications for the Jewish people. The Second Vatican Council he initiated revolutionized the life of the Church at large. A volume published in its wake included a page and a half that came to be known as "the Jewish Document," or the *Nostra Aetate Declaration*. This short document marked a theological shift and a watershed moment in Christian-Jewish relations. Given the importance the wording of such a declaration carries and the fact it serves as a binding basis for subsequent Papal documents, it is important to spell out its most significant parts: "The Church [...] cannot forget that she received the revelation of the Old Testament through the

---

[6] See: Dina Porat and David Bankier, *Roncalli and the Jews During the Holocaust: Concerns and Efforts to Help* (Jerusalem: Yad Vashem, 2014), 135.
[7] See: Moshe Jaeger, Yoseph Govrin, and Arie Oded (eds.), *The Foreign Ministry: the first 50 Years* (Jerusalem: Keter, 2002), 998.-1002.

people with whom God in His inexpressible mercy concluded the Ancient Covenant." Maria and her son Jesus were Jews, the text goes on, and the Church "also recalls that the Apostles, the Church's main-stay and pillars, as well as most of the early disciples who proclaimed Christ's Gospel to the world, sprang from the Jewish people." Moreover, "Since the spiritual patrimony common to Christians and Jews is thus so great, this sacred synod [the Second Vatican Council] wants to foster and recommend [...] mutual understanding and respect."

The above-mentioned statements are placed in the introduction, providing context and background for further content. Further on, *Nostra Aetate* presents three points, each of which has been awaited for almost two thousand years by Jews, both as individuals and as a group:

First, it states that during the time of the Second Temple, "the Jewish authorities and those who followed their lead pressed for the death of Christ; still, what happened in His passion cannot be charged against all the Jews, without distinction, then alive, nor against the Jews of today."

The second point is no less surprising given the centuries-long persecution of Jews and the way the Church had fostered their thoroughly ugly, almost demonic image: "Although the Church is the new people of God, the Jews should not be presented as rejected or accursed by God, as if this followed from the Holy Scriptures."

Finally, the document reads that the Church "decries hatred, persecutions, displays of antisemitism, directed against Jews at any time and by anyone."[8]

Such words were unheard of during the long history of Christian-Jewish relations and went contrary to popular, deeply rooted, centuries-long Christian beliefs. The charge of deicide is revoked, while the right of the Jewish people to continue the covenant with God in a manner equal to that of His new people, the Christians, is reinstated. Antisemitism in all forms and under any circumstances is outright denounced.

Numerous Papal documents written over the following years continued in the spirit of *Nostra Aetate*, each referencing the 1965 Declaration. This insistence on a consistent wording by several Popes and Vatican committees shows that the change in the attitude of the Catholic Church towards the Jewish people was not a momentary trend, spurred by a well-attended meeting (such as the Second Vatican Council), but rather the outcome of a long and genuine process. Indeed, in 1974, during the papacy of Pope Paul VI, the Commission for Religious Relations with the Jews issued directives and suggestions aimed at helping the believers in-

---

8 *Nostra Aetate* has been formally translated into Hebrew under Paulus VI (Second Vatican Council): *A declaration on the Church's attitude to non-Christian Religions, 'In our Time'*. For the English text, see the Vatican site: Vatican/archive/hist_councils/19651028/nostra-aetate.

ternalize *Nostra Aetate:* this was a milestone in the history of Jewish-Christian relations, according to the Commission's members, a milestone that was influenced by the memory of the persecution of Jews and their annihilation in Europe before and during World War II. The Commission reminded the believers that the spiritual and historical ties that bind the Church with Judaism mean every form of antisemitism and discrimination is contrary to the spirit of Christianity. It strongly recommended that Christians strive for a better knowledge of the components of the Jewish tradition.[9] These words were indeed a new development, reflecting a profound change: antisemitism as contrary to the Christian spirit!

In 1985, the same Commission issued a much longer and detailed document on "the Right Way" to present Jews and Judaism in Catholic education and preaching. The text relies, again, on *Nostra Aetate*; it emphasizes that the uniqueness of the Jewish people is a fact and should not be questioned; that Jesus was and always remained a Jew, a person of Jewish Palestine who shared its concerns and hopes; and – again – that any form of antisemitism and discrimination is contrary to the very spirit of Christianity.[10] This document was issued during the long papacy of John Paul II, who insisted time and again on rapprochement between the two religions and advanced it in a variety of ways. Much as for John XXIII, the Holocaust had a deep impact on his conduct as a pope: he had witnessed the disappearance of his childhood Jewish friends from his home town in Poland and was a member of the Polish underground during the war.

Among the many speeches, addresses, and documents issued during his long papacy (1978–2005), some stand out with special significance and highlight the continuing change, well into the post-Cold War years. The Commission for Religious Relations with the Jews carried on its work and in March 1998, on the eve of the third millennium, published the Pope's letter to the believers, *'We Remember': Reflections on the Holocaust.* This long address, which by now is considered one of the most important expressions of the development of the Vatican's position in this regard, outlines the long history of Jewish-Christian relations. While some parts of the Pope's thoughts and historical facts, as he presented them, might be considered debatable by Jewish and other historians, certain elements of his rhetoric are starkly unequivocal. He described the Holocaust as a merciless, indelible crime, an indescribable tragedy never to be forgotten. He also appealed to the Jewish peo-

---

9 Commission for Religious Relations with the Jews, Guidelines and suggestions for implementing the Conciliar Declaration "Nostra Aetate" (n. 4). See the Vatican site: Vatican/roman_curia/ pontifical _councils/ doc_19741201/nostra _aetate.
10 Commission for Religious Relations with the Jews, Notes on the Correct Way to present the Jews and Judaism in Preaching and Catechesis in the Roman Catholic Church. See the Vatican site: Vatican_curia/pontifical_councils? Doc_19820306_jews-judaism.

ple to hear Christians out with open hearts, despite the fact that during WWII many did not protest against the persecution and killing of their Jewish neighbours. On behalf of the Church, he apologized for the mistakes and failures of these believers. The letter, it should be noted, does not mention that many Christians collaborated with the Germans in the actual round-ups and killings, nor does it speak about the Church as an entity during the Holocaust, but rather about individual believers. The address reminds its readers that Jesus was a descendent of king David, that the Jews "are our very beloved brothers," if not elder brothers, and warns against the evil seeds of anti-Judaism and antisemitism that should never again take root in any human heart.[11]

The basic agreement between the state of Israel and the Holy See signed in 1993 – a historic milestone in itself – includes in its second item a commitment of both sides to an appropriate cooperation in the struggle against all forms of antisemitism as well as all types of racial and religious intolerance. The Holy See used this opportunity to reiterate its renouncement of hate, persecution, and other expressions of antisemitism directed against the Jewish people and against Jews as individuals at any time, in any place.[12] By signing this agreement, the Catholic Church acknowledged, for the first time, the legitimacy of the Zionist movement (as opposed to Pope Pius X, who outright rejected Theodor Herzl's plea in 1904), and of the Jewish state it built. The Vatican confirmed its wish to maintain contacts, ambassadors included, between the two states. The demise of the Soviet Bloc made it easier for the Church to conclude such an agreement with Israel, since the necessity to choose between East and West was no longer a factor.

Other documents, such as the 1990 *Antisemitism: A Sin towards God and Humanity* and the 2003 *Antisemitism: A Wound to be healed* declarations, should also be mentioned. Along with a host of other declarations and statements, they were issued while John Paul II was still Pope. In March 2000, during his visit to Israel, he left a moving personal note among the Western Wall stones. In it, he asked God, the God who chose Abraham and his offspring to bring His name to all nations, to forgive those who caused suffering to God's children. Pope Benedict XVI went along the same *Nostra Aetate* lines in his two-volume biography of Jesus, in which he reiterated Jesus' and his disciples' Jewish origins, as well as the exoneration of the Jews from the deicide accusation that affected their lives for centuries.[13]

---

[11] Pope John Paul II, Apostolic Letter *Tertio Millennio Adveniente*, November 10, 1994, 33: AAS (acta apostolicae sedis) 87 91005, 25.
[12] AAS, vol. LXXXVI (1994), vol. 9, 716–728.
[13] Joseph Ratzinger, Pope Benedict XVI, *Jesus of Nazareth*, three volumes (Ingnatius press, 2011–2012).

The above-mentioned documents form an incomplete list, as one could go on quoting more speeches, addresses, letters, and the like. This brings us back to the question of why Pope Francis issued one more emphatic statement in December 2015, given so many already existing documents that were written after 1965. A close look at the contents of Pope Francis' declaration might perhaps provide an answer.

The document of over 30 pages was first issued in Rome on 10 December. Its abstract was brought to Tel Aviv a few days later by Cardinal Kurt Koch who leads, as was already mentioned, the Jewish-Christian relations in the Vatican. Cardinal Koch presented it at the opening of a special conference held in the Diaspora Museum, attended by the heads of most religious denominations in Israel. He emphasized it was the Pope's wish to have it presented in the Holy Land right after it was first published in Rome. This is a unique document that summarizes all the documents that preceded it and still depicts Jewish-Christian relations in an unprecedented manner, imbued with deep respect towards the Jewish people, in a clear and unequivocal manner.

This declaration, like the former ones, takes up *Nostra Aetate* as a starting point, yet it "broadens and deepens" its principles, while especially remembering the Jewish roots of Christianity and the fact that "Jesus and his early followers were Jewish, shaped by the Jewish tradition of their time" (page 1 in the abstract). This is a study document, said and wrote Cardinal Koch, "whose aim is to deepen the theological dimension of the Catholic-Jewish dialogue" (3). As the Cardinal argued, the dialogue finally had a good chance of succeeding, since over the recent decades "from enemies and strangers we have become friends and brothers" (4). Moreover, a very close and unavoidable family relationship has developed, so much so that the present dialogue is not inter-religious but rather an intra-familial one (5).

There are indispensable harmonies between the two testaments, the Old and the New one, and special relations between the Old and the New Covenants: "The covenant offered by God to Israel is irrevocable [...] the new Covenant has its basis and foundation in the Old one [...] the New Covenant is neither the cancellation nor the replacement but the fulfillment of the promises of the Old Covenant" (5–6).

Both the original full document and its abstract do not sweep thorny problems under the carpet: how can Jews be part of God's salvation if they do not believe in Jesus as Christ and Messiah? This, says the Pope, "remains an unfathomable divine mystery" (6). Another issue is the Church's traditional wish to convert the Jews. "The Catholic Church neither conducts nor supports any specific institutional mission work directed towards Jews," while it may be directed at members of other religions. This is an additional issue, since for centuries Christians had prayed for the conversion of Jews and tried their hand at forcing it, sometimes in a cruel fashion. Moreover, if Christians choose to approach Jews in order to explain the principles of Christianity, they should do so in "a humble and sensitive manner," because Jews are the bearers of God's word and had undergone the great tragedy of the Shoah (7). The ending to the document follows what has become almost a traditional form: it is a wish for a common struggle against any manifestation of racial discrimination against Jews and all forms of antisemitism (7).

The December declaration includes more statements, some of which have not been included in the abstract. A Christian can never be an antisemite, mainly because of the Jewish roots of Christianity; mutual respect is both a pre-condition for inter-religious dialogue and its purpose; one more basic purpose of the dialogue is learning about each other. In this regard, the document contains the following, inspiring sentence: 'one can only learn to love what one has gradually come to know, and one can only know truly and profoundly what one loves." A repeated emphasis is being put on the Holocaust as the starting point for the process of change in the Vatican. It was the dark, terrible shadow of the Holocaust that hovered over Europe after the Nazi era, says the declaration, that has led the Church to re-think its ties with the Jewish people.[14]

* * *

The documents discussed above reflect an enormous change, practically a revolution, in the Catholic Church's attitude towards the Jewish people – from centuries-long hostility and antisemitism in a variety of forms to expressions of friendship, kinship, and respect. The change is of utmost importance. There are more than a billion and a quarter of Catholic believers worldwide today and such declarations, coupled with Papal visits to Jerusalem and Auschwitz, are bound to have a positive impact on Christian-Jewish relations. Moreover, the manner and tone – et c'est le ton qui fait la musique – in which the change is introduced are essential to its reception by the audiences in various countries. Indeed, successive popes' behaviour, their warm, open personalities, and the history of contacts with Jews has played a vital role. Roncalli met with the rescue delegation in Istanbul. John Paul II had close friendships with Jews, some of which lasted throughout his life. Francis befriended Rabbi Avraham Skorka during his tenure as the cardinal in Buenos Aires. These three men, much more than other popes in office during and after the Holocaust, initiated and maintained the momentum of the revolutionary change towards the Jews.

---

[14] For the abstract see footnote 5.

Nonetheless, these positive developments have not eradicated all problems, not least the reactions from the Jewish side and the practical implementation of the improved relations.

One of the issues concerns timing: Pope Francis' declaration of 2015 was issued in the midst of the so-called refugee crisis, a wave of immigrants, arriving mainly from Muslim countries. Terrorism and antisemitism have been on the rise for the last decade. Radical Muslim circles have been greatly concerned by the process of rapprochement between the Church and the Jewish people, and the December 2015 document was no exception.[15] Is the current pope looking to form something of a Jewish-Christian coalition that would form a barrier against violence and terror originating from extreme Islamism? Or will he have to find a way to preserve co-existence with the Muslim world in order to maintain some balance in the Vatican's foreign relations? The Pope's visit to Budapest in September 2021 exemplifies the dilemma: he came (but for seven hours only) to demonstrate that his views on Judaism and the refugee problem are opposite to those of prime minister Victor Orbán, telling Jewish and Christian leaders in an ecumenical meeting that he thinks "of the threat of antisemitism still lurking in Europe and elsewhere. This is a fuse that must not be allowed to burn. And the best way to defuse it is to work together, positively, and to promote fraternity." Subsequently, he travelled for a three-day visit to Slovakia, where he said that the "horrors of the Holocaust must not be forgotten."[16]

Another problem concerns politics: today, half of all Catholics reside in countries of the third world, where political leadership traditionally supports the Palestinian cause. Moreover, prior to 1989 these leaders had for decades been under the Soviet umbrella and now President Putin's Russia is trying to maintain its influence – not necessarily or specifically with regard to the Israeli-Palestinian conflict, but more generally. Given all this, is the Vatican taking a political risk when issuing such pro-Jewish declarations? Part of the answer lies in the wish and duty of the Church to defend and protect its followers in the Middle East, especially on Israeli territory, where the holy sites are located. Christian communities, living as a minority under the daily pressure from radical Islamists around them, are dwindling and good relations with Israel are needed, since the Israeli authorities are their main source of support and security.

Perhaps one can find a hint elsewhere. Israel is bound to defend all of its citizens, with or without Papal declarations. The Vatican's statements are intended for

---

15 Meir Litvak and Esther Webman, *From Empathy to denial, Arab Responses to the Holocaust* (London: Hurst & Company, 2009), ch. 4.
16 https://www.bbc.com/news/world-europe-58533533.

internal Catholic use – they are part and parcel of the theological debate taking place among the high echelons of the Church. Since such discourse is defined as being theological, rather than political, it does not need to take the Arab and Muslim world into consideration. In fact, documents do not mention Israel as a state (except, naturally, for the basic agreement signed in late 1993 by the Holy See and State of Israel). Instead, they refer to the Jewish people as elder, beloved brothers, as they indeed reflect inner theological exchange. Still, Pope Francis told members of the World Jewish Congress delegation very clearly that "to attack Jews is antisemitism, but an outright attack on the State of Israel is also antisemitism. There may be political disagreements between governments and on political issues, but the State of Israel has every right to exist in safety and prosperity."[17] Such words suggest the Pope combines Israel and the Jewish people into one entity.

The third issue concerns implementation: the documents are not distributed to the outside world, beyond the realm of the Catholic believers – nor are they translated to many vernaculars so as to be accessible to non-Catholic audiences. This at least partly explains why these astonishing documents, imbued with respect and well-wishing for the Jewish world, are almost unknown, even in Israel or among Jews. To the extent that this information does filter into the Jewish and Israeli public's knowledge, it is met with suspicion caused by previous experiences. However, implementation is not only an external problem affecting the non-Christian world. It is also relevant to the Vatican's primary audiences. It remains to be seen how much of the message trickles down to the Christian population at large (be it Catholic, Protestant or Orthodox), including, for instance, small villages and conservative communities in Latin America and Eastern Europe. We also do not know how long it will take for the process and its good intentions to be understood and fully accepted by large audiences.

In order to try and tackle some of these problems, a number of personalities, from both the Jewish and the Catholic sides, were interviewed by the author of this article. Among the representatives of the Church: Cardinal Koch; Msgr. Tomasz Grysa; and Archbishop Pierbattista Pizzaballa; on the Jewish side: Rabbi David Rosen; Rabbi Avraham Skorka; and Dr. David Stolov.

---

[17] The World Jewish Congress (WJC) visit to the Vatican was held on October 28, 2015: https://www.worldjewishcongress.org/en/news/world-jewish-congress-leaders-to-gather-in-rome-meet-with-pope-francis-10-5-2015.

The Catholic Side

Cardinal Kurt Koch and Msgr. Tomasz Grysa are of the same opinion. When asked in January 2020 about the Vatican's efforts to implement the changes and instil them in believers, Koch – the person in charge of the matter as head of the International Commission for Religious Relations with the Jews – pointed out the many documents, including the above-mentioned ones, that were issued and distributed as the Pope's binding words.[18] In addition, similar to Msgr. Grysa, the First Counsellor in the Apostolic Nunciature in Israel, he emphasized the cooperation between two key bodies appointed first within the Vatican and then with participation of Jewish representatives. Chronologically, the first one was the Commission for Religious Relations with the Jews, set up in the Vatican in October 1974. The International Catholic-Jewish Liaison Committee was established a few years before, in November 1970, but only started actual work in 1973–74. Addressing the opening ceremony of a Liaison Committee session in Rome, on 13 May 2019, Koch expressed his great satisfaction and pride: this was the twenty-fourth meeting in 54 years [*Nostra Aetate*, dated 1965, is always the milestone, D.P.] – "we have written history," he told his listeners.[19] In other words: here is an ongoing effort to maintain contacts that can further the changes, as we meet every other year and constantly carry out work in this regard.

The second body is a permanent bilateral commission for dialogue between the Chief Rabbinate of Israel and the Vatican's Commission for Religious Relations with the Jews. It was proposed by John Paul II and established in 2002, in the wake of the Pope's very successful visit to Jerusalem in 2000. Despite the suspicion and the initial reluctance, a request of a pope who was eager to come for a visit (as opposed to Paul VI, who would not even set foot in Israeli Jerusalem in 1964) could not have been refused. The commission meets annually, alternating between Rome and Jerusalem, which means that its members have already met almost 20 times. When asked about whether he sees a change among the participating Rabbis, Cardinal Koch emphatically answered that relations are warmer and friendlier each year, with personal friendships created and maintained.

---

18 I interviewed him in Yad Vashem, on January 23, 2020, during the Fifth World Holocaust Forum (D.P.).
19 Opening Ceremony on the International Catholic-Jewish Liaison Committee Meeting, Rome, May 13, 2019, http://www.christianunity.va/content/unitacristiani/it/commission, for religious relations with the jews.

Msgr. Grysa added an important point.[20] When asked in July 2021 about practical ways to spread the Church's message against antisemitism, he answered that papal addresses are taken up by the bishops, for whom they are binding and who are tasked with finding ways to implement them into practice. In Israel, he says, the Latin Patriarchy in Jerusalem is active, as are the Benedictine Brothers in Abu-Gosh, the Neocatechumenal believers in the Galilee, the Community of Beatitude in Latrun, and many others. Msgr. Grysa was optimistic – he said a lot of work was being done and some progress was already visible, with Cardinal Koch leading the effort.

Archbishop Pierbattista Pizzaballa, the newly appointed Latin Patriarch of Jerusalem, is less optimistic. In a candid interview in December 2021, he stated that the change was very slow, with the Catholic public at large knowing almost nothing about it and not familiar with papal documents. Most believers did not search for them, even though they were available on the Vatican's website. Only those interested in Catholic-Jewish relations were familiar with their contents. In fact, he went on, there was an increasing distance and disconnect between the Catholic establishment, the high echelons and officials, and the public at large, as the younger generations of believers were no longer keen to hear about Catholic morality and ethics – in every respect, not just with regard to relations with the Jewish people.

Since the change is very slow, it will take at least two generations – it is an extremely sensitive issue with heavy historic baggage. Archbishop Pizzaballa said he felt people were tired of hearing that Jesus, Maria, and the apostles were all Jewish. His saw a need for a fresh approach: "something new should be built by a courageous religious leadership on both sides." As a member of the joint Rabbinate-Vatican commission, he saw similar developments among Jewish activists (he mentioned the intense efforts of Rabbi David Rosen, to be discussed later): they were trying to further the dialogue with the Church, but they also needed a public that would trust and follow them. As far as he could observe having lived in Israel for decades, the Israeli public at large was not aware of the change and the documents – in that observation, he is quite right. Moreover, relations with the Jews are not currently considered an urgent or central issue. It is the Muslim immigrants arriving in large numbers to Europe and North America that, being a far larger group, are now much more relevant to the Christian way of life and its future. Nonetheless, Pizzaballa was keen to identify an appropriate topic

---

20 I interviewed him during the Fifth Global Forum on Antisemitism in July 2021 in the Ministry for Foreign Affairs in Jerusalem, and again via telephone on September 3, 2021.

that he, together with his own staff and the public in Jerusalem, could place in the right context and elaborate on from a Jerusalemite perspective.[21]

The Jewish Side

There is an unusual, less known initiative taking place in Israel. In order to discuss it, I approached Dr. David Stolov, the executive director of the Interfaith Encounter Association (IEA) which this year celebrates 20 years of its activity.[22] This Jerusalem-based association, working to bring together Jews, Christians, and Muslims living in Israel, is a perfect example of a grassroots undertaking. Led by a triple advisory council made up of representatives of the three religions, it has so far formed 112 groups numbering 10–15 participants each, consisting of Jews and Christians who meet regularly, four to five times a year, to study the new Testament. A Dutch priest positioned in Israel, Aart Brons, organized these meetings for a number of years on behalf of the Netherlands-based Center for Israel Studies and the IEA. Archbishop Pizzaballa used to frequent them when he still served as the Franciscan Custos of the Holy Land; other people who have participated in the meetings include Russell MacDougal, rector of the Tantur Ecumenical Institute (located between Gilo and Beth Lechem) as well as a few Rabbis, e.g. David Stav and Dan Eisik. The former Latin Patriarch, Michelle Sabach, met with both the participants and the activists, while the Apostolic Nuncio, Archbishop Leopoldo Girelli, hosted the activists for a visit. In addition, IEA has been in constant contact with the Austrian hospice in Jerusalem.

All in all, one can say this interfaith initiative has been welcomed by the main Christian leaders and Jewish Rabbis in Israel. However, when interviewed in September 2021, Dr. Stolov said contacts with religious leaders were intermittent and did not result in any kind of practical or formal support. There were no approaches to or from the Israeli ministry of education, although the headmasters and staff of several Arab and Jewish high schools partnered with the Association to create programmes that would enrich their students' knowledge about Islam and Christianity.

"We are unknown," summed up Dr. Stolov and I quote him, "we are not political, we threaten no one's position, we live on donations and grants from foundations, and try to do the best we can, and to hold as many activities and encounters as possible besides the study groups."

---

21 A Zoom interview with the archbishop, December 22, 2021 (D.P.).
22 I interviewed him via Zoom, because of coronavirus restrictions on September 3, 2021 (D.P.).

Rabbi David Rosen, the international director for interreligious affairs in the American Jewish Committee (AJC) and honorary president of the International Council of Christians and Jews (ICCJ), represents the institutional side among stakeholders involved in the process. He is a key figure to the development of Christian-Jewish relations. Honoured by the Holy See and Elizabeth II, he is even more critical in his assessment and points to a number of problems.[23] Regarding efforts to implement the changes in the Vatican, he argues that their success varies depending on socio-economic conditions. Those who live close to Jews, mainly in large urban centres, as well as those who enjoy higher education, especially in the USA, internalize the change better than the population in Europe (particularly the eastern part) and the less educated parts of society in general. Rosen makes a reference to studies on American Catholic religion textbooks, conducted in the 1970s (and re-published in the 1990s) by two American scholars inspired by the legendary Sister Rose. The research charted a dramatic reversal in Catholic teachings about the Jews which began with *Nostra Aetate*, to the extent that Jews may now also use these textbooks.[24] However, said Rosen, most people still had "pre-conciliar perceptions," by which he meant perceptions forged long before the 1965 change brought about by the Second Vatican Council. Although syllabi for clerical students incorporate the changes, in most seminars worldwide knowledge about the post-Council shift is not a required part of the studies and the topic itself is covered in a rather vague manner. Rosen met bishops – most notably in Far East Asia and Latin America – who, astonishingly, had never heard about *Nostra Aetate*.

Formal Jewish reaction to the changes is no less challenging. First of all, it took a long time to come. Rosen pointed out two major statements – both of which he was involved in – that reflect the attitude on the Jewish side. The first one, written and issued in 2002, entitled *Dabru Emet (Speak the Truth), A Jewish Statement on Christians and Christianity*, was initiated and signed by 250 US-based Reform and Conservative Rabbis as well as Jewish scholars and leaders. It called upon Jews and Christians to work together towards justice and peace. The second one was written

---

23 I interviewed him via telephone on September 1, 2021 (D.P.). See also an interview he had with Yair Sheleg published on April 18, 2016 in Shabbat of Makor Rishon. See also *Turning the Tide of Christian-Jewish Relations, The Delegations of the Holy See's Commission for Religious Relations with the Jews and the Chief Rabbinate of Israel's Commission for Relations with the Catholic Church, Joint Statements 2003–2013*, ed. Rabbi Dr. David Rosen (AJC) and State Secr. (ret.) Konrad Adenauer Stiftung (English and Hebrew, no place or date of publication mentioned).

24 Rose Thering, "Potential in Religion Textbooks for Developing a Realistic Self-concept" (PhD diss., St. Louis University, 1961) was a milestone on the way to the Nostra Aetate. The research inspired by her work was conducted by Eugene Fisher, associate Director of the Secretariat for Ecumenical and Interreligious affair, US Conference of Catholic bishops, and Prof. Philip Cunningham, director of the institute for Jewish-Catholic relations at St. Joseph's University in Philadelphia. .

in 2015. Entitled *La'asot Retzon Avinu Shebashmaim – to do the will of our Father in Heaven: Toward a partnership between Jews and Christians*, it constitutes a significant step forward. It was presented to Pope Francis on 31 August 2017, with the subtitle reading *Between Jerusalem and Rome: Reflections on 50 Years of Nostra Aetate*. It was authored and signed by three bodies: the Conference of European Rabbis (CER), the Chief Rabbinate of Israel, and the Rabbinical Council of America (RCA). It marked a wider reaction to the changes. The signatories, including Rabbi Rosen, admitted that many Jewish leaders were skeptical of the sincerity of the Church's overtures towards the Jewish community due to the long, painful history between Christians and Jews. However, over time, it became clear to them that the Church's teachings were sincere and increasingly profound. The Orthodox Jewry – i.e. those who still consider Christianity outright paganism – has remained skeptical and suspicious, in line with their deep concern that by accepting the hand extended by the Vatican, liberal, Reform and Conservative Jews weaken the unity and power of Judaism.

The letter presented to the Pope included the following key sentence: "Despite the irreconcilable theological differences, we Jews view Catholics as our partners, close allies, friends and brothers in our mutual quest for a better world, blessed with peace, social justice and security."[25] Such words, coming from three organisations representing a large number of Rabbis across three continents, demonstrate that a change is gradually occurring also on the Jewish side.

Rabbi Avraham Skorka, a close personal friend of Pope Francis (both were born in Buenos Aires and lived there for many years) sent his remarks in writing. He is now a faculty member of Saint Joseph's University in Philadelphia, where a sculpture, showing the Ecclesia and the Synagoga sitting together as equal friends, was located in front of the local chapel to celebrate 50 years since *Nostra Aetate*.[26] While answering the questions in his written interview, Rabbi Skorka referred to many of the documents mentioned above, which he considers a testimony to the "unfolding theological developments, including a re-evaluation of traditional approaches to Jews and Judaism." He draws special attention to an international research project that was supported by the Commission for Religious Relations with Jews, resulting in a volume of essays, with an introduction by Cardinal Kasper, then president of the Commission.[27] More research and educational programmes, wrote

---

25 6, 8. See the text in Dialogika, Jewish sources, the richest site on Christian-Jewish relations: https://www.ccjr.us/dialogika-resources.
26 Sculptor Joshua Koffman designed it as an answer to the famous "Ecclesia and Synagoga" at the entrance to the Strasburg cathedral. See: https://sju.edu/ijcr/.
27 *Christ Jesus and the Jewish People Today: New Explorations of Theological interrelationships*, ed. Phillip A. Cunningham et al. (Grand Rapids: Eerdmans Publishing, 2011).

Skorka, add to the emergence of a new relationship, similar to the "Sant'Egidio" and "Focolare" movements within the Catholic Church which made important contributions to the interfaith dialogue.

Nevertheless, Rabbi Skorka, just like Rabbi Rosen, raises a number of troubling points. Published sermons and suggested themes for homilies regularly include inaccurate and even polemical presentations or assumptions about Jews and Jewish practice. Although there are Vatican instructions to assign Jews and Judaism a central place in theological teachings, this has not happened yet. Skorka is also aware of analogous problems on the other side: the same holds true in educational Jewish settings and curricula in most Jewish day schools in the US. Rabbinical seminaries give little, if any, attention to Christianity. It is hard to disagree with his concluding remark that Jews and Catholics are merely taking their first steps on a long path to overcoming history.[28]

Having taken one more look at the documents and the interviews, the question at stake is whether the time has come to offer concluding remarks, insights, and expectations for the future of Jewish–Catholic relations? It seems that the effort, which started in 1965, to change these relations and start a genuine dialogue of mutual respect handled by both sides has been continued along a number of decades, and is gaining momentum in recent years. Since the beginning of the 2000s a number of open letters and statements were formulated and published by the Jewish side, stating the readiness to accept the extended hand; Pope Francis has emphatically expressed his warm wish to further and deepen the dialogue; and there has been common work by the bi-lateral committees, active since the 1970s, as well as the joint committee established following the visit of John Paul II in Jerusalem, to keep the dialogue ongoing.

Still, as we have above mentioned, major questions are still centre stage: the process is a slow one, especially the instilling of these positive developments in the hearts and minds of the vast number of Catholic believers worldwide, who carry centuries long convictions; and, parallelly, instilling trust among Jews, especially the more religious ones, who carry deep suspicions against the Church, in the good intentions of the Church, especially given the complex reality in the Middle East. Therefore let us end by re-emphasizing that both sides have still a long journey to take, and therefore the issue should be re-visited in a number of years, by both researchers and activists.

---

28 Skorka wrote to me on October 3, 2021 – DP.

Haim Fireberg
A "Jewish Problem" or a "Society Problem"? Understanding Contemporary Antisemitism in Europe from Jewish and Governmental Perspectives

Antisemitic violence is always a reminder of the fragile balance between Jewish life and society. It happens even in the most thriving communities. Jews are experiencing an increasing fear of violence, a feeling almost ingrained in their identity by the memory of the Holocaust. When reviewing antisemitic incidents around the world, it becomes clear that hatred of Jews results in growing violence or worries about the future of Jewish life in Europe. The comparison of current antisemitism in EU member states reveals several peculiarities which are almost paradoxical. I have argued in a previous publication that the number of violent incidents is not necessarily indicative of the intensity of antisemitic sentiments in the country where this happens. Undoubtedly, it is a necessary condition for defining antisemitism, but it is not sufficient.[1]

Perceptions driven by the hatred of the Jews – i.e. antisemitism – were collected and encapsulated in the "Working Definition of Antisemitism" published in 2004 by the European Monitoring Centre on Racism and Xenophobia. Although not legally binding, the definition was meant to provide a practical guide to identifying incidents, collecting data and supporting future antisemitism-related legislation.[2] Few governments have accepted and used the definition, even if only for the purpose of training law enforcement organisations – the United Kingdom de-

---

[1] Haim Fireberg, "The Antisemitic Paradox in Europe: Empirical Evidences and Jewish Perceptions. A Comparative Study Between the West and East," in *Being Jewish in 21st Century Central Europe*, ed. Haim Fireberg, Olaf Glöckner, and Marcela Menachem Zoufala (Berlin: de Gruyter, 2020), 269–279.
[2] The most comprehensive information and discussion on the definition can be found today at: https://en-humanities.tau.ac.il/sites/humanities_en.tau.ac.il/files/media_server/0001/unedited.pdf; "The Working Definition of Antisemitism – Six Years After" (2010). The definition itself can be found in the opening pages. The original definition cannot be found online anymore, because the FRA decided it was not its mandate to deal with definitions. For other views and analyses on the definition, see: https://rm.coe.int/opinion-ecri-on-ihra-wd-on-antisemitism-2755-7610-7522-1/1680a091dd; https://www.holocaustremembrance.com/sites/default/files/inline-files/legal%20analysis%20IHRA%20working%20definition%20of%20antisemitism.pdf; https://www.inss.org.il/publication/ihra/.

∂ Open Access. © 2023 the author(s), published by De Gruyter. [CC BY-NC-ND] This work is licensed under the Creative Commons Attribution-NonCommercial-NoDerivatives 4.0 International License.
https://doi.org/10.1515/9783110783216-006

serves to be mentioned as one such country. However, the definition became a core reference for any discussion on antisemitism and the hatred of the Jews.³ As a result of its adoption by the International Holocaust Remembrance Alliance (IHRA) in 2016, it has also been embraced by hundreds of civic organisations and governments worldwide.⁴

There are many types of antisemitism that are frequently mentioned today, including traditional antisemitism, secondary antisemitism, etc. This essay does not examine each of them separately. It discusses antisemitism in contemporary Europe as it is experienced by the Jews. When people encounter hate on the street, online, at work, or in social settings, they are uncertain what it means. They should not attempt to categorize it and decide whether or not they fit into a specific category. Our basic assumption is that when there is a "Jewish problem" it often indicates that the society has a problem: a deep-seated hatred of the Jews, often disguised as something else.

Concentrating my research on Central Europe, I have chosen to analyze the current situation in three countries – Poland, Hungary, and Germany – as well as to study the overall policy of the EU towards antisemitism. All three states mentioned above have long-term, ambivalent relationships with their Jewish populations: a flourishing Jewish culture on the one hand, and a history of persecutions and antisemitism on the other. One should not forget the events during World War II, when Germany was responsible for the extermination of millions of Jews and Hungary actively collaborated, while Poland became a venue for the tragedy of the Holocaust and, shortly after the war, for deadly pogroms. Continuing antisemitism experienced by the European Jewry provides a context in which we can study this type of conflict in order to shed some light on the contradictory factors influencing antisemitic perceptions among individuals, organizations, and governments.

The Case of Poland

For centuries, Polish Jews had functioned as a prosperous society that was then virtually wiped out during the Holocaust. In extermination camps on Polish soil, the Germans executed millions of Jews deported there from all over Europe, in ad-

---

3 For comprehensive analysis about the definition and its legal significance, see: Adv. Talia Naamat, *The Legal Significance of the Working Definition: Recent Trends and Case Law* (Justice, Spring 2020), 27–31, https://www.ijl.org/justicem/no64/#27/z
4 For more information about the process and updated situation, see: https://www.holocaustremembrance.com/resources/working-definitions-charters/working-definition-antisemitism.

dition to the overwhelming majority of Polish Jews themselves. Even today, when speaking about the "death machine," many people confuse the German death camps, or concentration camps on Polish soil, with Polish death camps.[5] I argue that there can be no effective way to address contemporary antisemitism in Poland without neutralizing the war years per se as much as possible and a debate about the restitution of Jewish property in Poland to descendants of the pre-war owners. Global politics, emotional inclinations, and preconceptions also influence the relations between Jews and non-Jews in today's Poland.[6]

In 2015, there were around 7,500 Jews that are defined as enlarged Jewish population, of them approximately 3,500 Jews that are recognised as the core Jewish population – only a fraction of the country's pre-war Jewish population.[7] The Kantor Center's Annual Reports on Worldwide Antisemitism indicate that compared to other countries formerly part of the Soviet Union and/or Warsaw Pact (e.g. Latvia, Romania, Czechia, Slovakia, Estonia), violent antisemitic incidents are significantly more common in Poland. The numbers are even higher than in Hungary, where the Jewish population is 15 times larger. Between 2012 and 2018, the Kantor Center recorded 85 major violent incidents in Poland and only 57 significant incidents in Hungary.[8]

---

[5] For more about President Obama's remarks, see: https://www.bbc.com/news/world-europe-18264036. Even after official protests from the Polish government and Obama's apologies, such mishaps are still common: https://www.nytimes.com/2018/08/23/world/europe/fox-news-polish-death-camps.html. When serving as the head of opposition in the Israeli parliament, Yair Lapid tweeted: "There were Polish death camps and no law can ever change that": https://twitter.com/yairlapid/status/957208421794709504?lang=en. This was a declaration that caused a diplomatic crisis between the two countries: https://www.timesofisrael.com/auschwitz-museum-slams-lapid-lie-after-he-claim-poles-helped-run-death-camps/.

[6] The debate over the abandoned property of Poland's Jews can easily be found all over the Internet, including the official stance of the Polish government, the changing attitudes of Israeli governments as well as opinions of academics and laymen. Few examples: https://www.jta.org/2021/08/25/global/yair-lapid-says-the-holocaust-defined-him-thats-adding-fuel-to-the-fire-in-israel-poland-relations; https://www.jpost.com/israel-news/israels-lapid-vs-polands-holocaust-restitution-law-analysis-673157; https://notesfrompoland.com/2021/08/12/us-and-israel-condemn-property-restitution-bill-passed-by-polish-parliament/; https://notesfrompoland.com/2021/08/30/polands-new-restitution-law-explained/; https://www.clevelandjewishnews.com/columnists/ben_cohen/time-to-cut-ties-with-poland-s-government/article_a63548ae-e415-11eb-8c51-7f25126c7692.html.

[7] Sergio DellaPergola, "Jewish Demography in the European Union – Virtuous and Vicious Paths," in *Being Jewish in 21st Century Central Europe*, ed. Haim Fireberg, Olaf Glöckner, and Marcela Menachem Zoufala (Berlin: de Gruyter, 2020), 26.

[8] The Kantor Center General Analysis of the Year, volumes from 2012 to 2018. https://kantorcenter.tau.ac.il

On average, there are about 12 cases of violent antisemitism every year, but it is yet lower than in other EU member states (France, Germany, and Belgium) and the United Kingdom that have a large Muslim population. Further evidence of this can be found in a Fundamental Rights Agency (FRA) survey published in 2018 which asked respondents if they were afraid of becoming a victim of verbal insults, harassment or physical attacks due to their Jewish identity. Among the 12 countries that participated in the study, Poland ranked in the top four with affirmative responses.[9]

Only a few of the violent incidents in Poland were directed at people, according to the Kantor Center data. Most manifestations primarily targeted Jewish facilities, such as synagogues, or desecrated Jewish cemeteries and memorials of Holocaust victims. But the quantitative data on violent antisemitism does not fully explain the phenomenon. In addition to public attitudes and sentiments towards Jews, antisemitism is also influenced by government policies and practices. Furthermore, information on violence alone is not sufficient to reveal people's (Jews' and non-Jews') views regarding Jewish integration into society and the ethos of the nation.

According to Rafal Pankowski, a professor of sociology and one of the founders of the Never Again Association,[10] the Polish government led by the Law and Justice party (PiS) is seen as pro-Catholic. The party "is not [an] ideologically antisemitic party," he claims; however, several members of the party have made antisemitic remarks without the PiS leadership condemning them explicitly.[11] Antisemitism is generated in Poland in several ways: a) via the Internet and media[12]; b) by public figures such as politicians, clergymen, and journalists[13]; and c) street demonstra-

---

[9] https://fra.europa.eu/sites/default/files/fra_uploads/fra-2018-experiences-and-perceptions-of-antisemitism-survey_en.pdf, 34, 47.
[10] https://www.nigdywiecej.org/en/.
[11] https://kantorcenter.tau.ac.il/wp-content/uploads/2021/07/Doch_full_2018_220418.pdf, 75, 77–78.
[12] The notorious Catholic-nationalist radio station, Radio Maryja, regularly airs antisemitic utterances from its columnist, Stanislaw Michalkiewicz. For more about the broadcaster and its anti-Jewish attitudes and political involvement, see: https://en.wikipedia.org/wiki/Radio_Maryja.
[13] Few examples: in June 2017, PiS MP from Kalisz, Jan Mosiński, referred to the allegedly Jewish origin of his political opponents. Mosiński had already been known for making xenophobic and antisemitic statements in the past. In July 2017, the former Democratic Left Alliance (SLD) presidential candidate and current supporter of the PiS government, Magdalena Ogórek, referred to the Jewish origin of an erstwhile SLD leader, Marek Borowski, by emphasizing the alleged family name of his ancestors in her hostile Twitter post. On August 2, 2017, another PiS MP, Bogdan Rzońca, wrote on his Twitter account: "I am on my vacation reading books. I am thinking why, despite the Holocaust, there are so many Jews among those abortionists." https://kantorcenter.tau.ac.il/wp-content/uploads/2021/07/Doch_full_2018_220418.pdf, 77–78.

tions led by radical nationalist groups such as the National Rebirth of Poland (NOP) and the National Radical Camp (ONR).[14] Main antisemitic themes include: a) Christian prejudices; b) the claim that Jewish identity is not Polish; and c) distortion and trivialization of the Holocaust. Jews have reported tropes such as: "Jews have too much power," "Jews exploit Holocaust victimhood for their own gain," and "Jews in Poland have different interests than the rest of the population."[15] In the FRA survey, 53 percent of respondents identified their persecutors as "someone with right-wing political views" and 34 percent identified them as "someone with Christian extremist views." The proportion of Polish respondents in both of these categories was the highest in the EU.[16]

The conclusion from the survey is that Polish Jews' real concerns about antisemitism are caused by the combination of violence and antisemitic atmosphere in public and political arenas. Eighty-five percent of respondents said it was "a very big problem" or "a fairly big problem." Poland lags behind both France (95%), and Belgium (86%), while recording the same percentage as Germany. In Hungary, only 77% of respondents believe that antisemitism is a serious problem.[17] Internet and private broadcasting networks such as Radio Maryja are the main sources of antisemitic material.[18] Nevertheless, Jews in Poland have "little chance" of encountering antisemitic expressions. Only 37% of Jewish respondents said antisemitic harassment is a part of their daily lives.[19]

Poland's unique history before and after the Holocaust has influenced and sometimes overshadowed the current relationship between Christian Poles and Jewish Poles. Jews believe antisemitism is rampant in Polish society, although many blame those who adhere to old Catholic Church doctrines and nationalists who seek a purely ethnic Polish society.

Is the current regime in Poland encouraging antisemitism and supporting antisemites? There is no doubt that members of the ruling party, PiS, attend events containing antisemitic symbols or participate in antisemitic public events.[20] At

---

14 https://kantorcenter.tau.ac.il/wp-content/uploads/2021/07/Doch_full_2018_220418.pd, 77.
https://www.timesofisrael.com/polish-officials-condemn-antisemitism-at-nationalist-rally/; https://notesfrompoland.com/2021/11/12/death-to-jews-chanted-at-torchlit-far-right-march-in-polish-city/.
15 https://fra.europa.eu/sites/default/files/fra_uploads/fra-2018-experiences-and-perceptions-of-anti semitism-survey_en.pdf, 26.
16 Ibid., 54.
17 Ibid., 17.
18 Ibid., 28.
19 Ibid., 22.
20 One recent example of public trivialization of the Holocaust by five MPs: https://notesfrompoland.com/2021/12/15/polish-far-right-mps-appear-under-auschwitz-style-sign-at-anti-vaccine-protest/.

the same time, the government takes harsh action against antisemitic, homophobic, and nationalist demonstrators and condemns antisemitism. In a Twitter post, Polish interior minister Mariusz Kamiński said that the Polish government does not accept antisemitism or hatred. In an earlier statement, he called a march commemorating Poland's independence, which featured antisemitic chants such as "Death to Jews," shameful.[21] Many Jewish people still believe that not enough has been done. Only seven percent of Polish Jews think the government combats antisemitism effectively, according to the FRA survey.[22]

In the last few years, two important debates have taken place regarding two controversial laws proposed by the Polish regime. The first one is the "Restitution Law" that ended the right of descendants of Jewish Polish citizens to claim property lost during the period of German occupation and Communist rule. Despite the Israeli Government's assertions that this law is antisemitic, such claims cannot be substantiated.

The second law in question pertains to the Institute of National Remembrance (Instytut Pamieci Narodowej, or IPN). The international community only became aware of it in 2018, after the Polish parliament passed an amendment to the act governing the work of IPN. The amendment, which penalizes statements implying Polish involvement in Nazi crimes, is sometimes referred to by international media outlets as the "Holocaust Law." Observers have called it a dangerous step towards restricting freedom of expression in Poland. Therefore, it is no surprise that the law proved to be short-lived; after one year, thanks to the efforts of the Israeli and Polish governments, very little remains of its most controversial provisions. However, it is likely that the long-term impact of this attention-grabbing development on the Polish political scene will outlive its immediate appearance.[23]

For Poland and its Jews to resolve the overburdened relationship, it required a unique and deep understanding of the future. The following summary of Genevieve Zubrzycki's extensive research into the efforts to create a modern Polish state and citizenship shows that conflicts emerged and were deeply embedded in that process:

> A symbolic category – here Jewishness – can serve as a foil to construct not only an exclusive ethnic nation, but also to build an inclusive, civic, and secular nation. [...] in Poland the na-

---

21 https://notesfrompoland.com/2021/11/15/three-organisers-of–march-in-polish-city-arrested-amid-widespread-condemnation/.
22 https://fra.europa.eu/sites/default/files/fra_uploads/fra-2018-experiences-and-perceptions-of-anti semitism-survey_en.pdf, 41.
23 For a comprehensive analysis of the law, the debates, and solutions: https://www.cultures-of-history.uni-jena.de/politics/the-polish-holocaust-law-revisited.

tional self is being built not only against the Other (the Jew), but also through that indigenous Other in opposition to an alleged primordial 'self' – the ethno-Catholic Pole. This is more than the simplistic story of philosemitism opposing antisemitism – or 'anti-antisemitism.' Rather, Polish philosemitism is part of a larger process of redefining national identity.[24]

Prof. Zubrzycki asserts that, while Jewish culture is just one thread within an intricate tapestry of civic national counter-narratives about the Polish nation, it is a prominent motif given both the long history of Jews in Poland and the trauma of their extermination. Moreover, it enables the authorities to rebrand Poland on the international stage, which is an important motivation that cannot be overlooked. As the Polish case shows, redefinition of national identity can be a complex process, since to enhance the definition of Polishness differences between groups must be introduced and legitimized. This means that various boundaries must be maintained. Therefore, Zubrzycki emphasizes, "The inclusion of Jews within the symbolic perimeter of the nation in order to redefine Polishness does not, and cannot, de-Otherize the Jew. The Jew must irremediably remain Other."[25]

The Case of Hungary

Hungary has the fourth largest Jewish community in Europe, between 47,700 Jews (core Jewish population) and 75,000 Jews (descendants of Jewish families).[26] Similarly to Poland, Hungary had long been home to thousands of Jews who formed a prosperous and highly integrated society that was then destroyed and wiped out in just four months during the Holocaust, with active participation of Hungarian paramilitary forces. Consequently, I believe it is impossible to deal with antisemitism in modern Hungary without neutralizing the war years per se to the extent possible. Hungarian Jewry's tragic fate may obscure any discussion of the issue and pre-

---

[24] Genevieve Zubrzycki, "Nationalism, 'Philosemitism' and Symbolic Boundary-Making in Contemporary Poland," https://www.cambridge.org/core/journals/comparative-studies-in-society-and-history/article/nationalism-philosemitism-and-symbolic-boundarymaking-in-contemporary-poland/3BEF2AB1798A5399D1F686C7F45DE439.
[25] Ibid.
[26] Sergio DellaPergola, "Jewish Demography in the European Union – Virtuous and Vicious Paths," in *Being Jewish in 21ˢᵗ Century Central Europe*, ed. Haim Fireberg, Olaf Glockner, and Marcela Menachem Zoufala (Berlin: de Gruyter, 2020), 24. To better understand the Jewish community and its demographics, see another paper in the same volume: Zsófia Kata Vincze, "The 'Missing' and 'Missed' Jews in Hungary," 115–143.

vent it from being exposed to the political, social, and cultural developments that are shaping it.²⁷

Based on the Kantor Center's Annual Reports on Worldwide Antisemitism, the number of violent antisemitic incidents in Hungary, where the Jewish population is 15 times larger than in Poland, is moderate in comparison. The Center recorded only 57 such cases from 2012 to 2018. On average, Hungary only registers about eight violent incidents per year.²⁸ In fact, this is also indicated in the results of the FRA survey published in 2018. Hungary ranked bottom among the surveyed countries for the frequency of affirmative responses to the question about being afraid of becoming a victim of a verbal or physical attack.²⁹

According to an opinion survey conducted by the Median Institute for Public Opinion and Market Research in 2019–2020 on antisemitism in Hungary, which was initiated by the Federation of Hungarian Jewish Communities (Mazsihisz) and published in July 2021, antisemitism is present in all aspects of the Hungarian society.³⁰ According to András Heisler, Head of Mazsihisz, there are fears among the Jewish community, but there is no antisemitism in Hungary today from which these fears would "directly" result. Therefore, in this regard, Hungary is in a better position than Western Europe or other European nations, since there have been no physical atrocities.³¹

Analysis of the data reveals a more complex Hungarian society. In the category of cognitive antisemitism, referred to as "antisemitic perceptions" in this article, it has been discovered that only 16 percent of Hungarians are "strongly cognitive antisemites" (a further 20 percent exhibited moderate antisemitic attitudes). Consequently, "the proportion of those resistant to this form of antisemitism increased from 38 to 44 % [in comparison with previous surveys]."³² "According to a comprehensive aggregate indicator," concludes the survey, "… two-thirds (64 %) show no

---

27 See also: Andras Kovács, "Hungarian Intentionalism: New Directions to the Historiography of the Hungarian Holocaust," in Randolph Braham and Andras Kovács, *The Holocaust in Hungary: Seventy Years Later* (Central European University Press, 2016), Kindle edition, 443–459.
28 The Kantor Center General Analysis of the Year, volumes from 2012 to 2018, https://kantorcenter.tau.ac.il.
29 https://fra.europa.eu/sites/default/files/fra_uploads/fra-2018-experiences-and-perceptions-of-anti semitism-survey_en.pdf, 34, 47.
30 For the press conference, see: https://www.wzo.org.il/antisemitism/index.php?dir=site&page= articles&op=item&cs=9313. The full survey, its methodology, and results is available at: https://drive.google.com/file/d/1fvboWRLQmvJmDGo8qPCVhwhOKQTo2G5k/view. I have chosen to use the Hungarian survey. For an ADL survey that covers the same topic with almost similar result, see: https://global100.adl.org/country/hungary/2019.
31 Ibid.
32 Ibid., the survey, 46.

antisemitic attitudes at all. This value is also not a significant shift from the average of previous years."[33] When considering public attitudes towards other minorities or strangers as a whole, it turns out that the sympathy index towards Jews is only slightly lower than the sympathy index towards Germans (5.38/9 and 5.89/9, respectively). In comparison, the sympathy index towards Black people is 3.91/9; for Arabs, it stands at 3.37/9, for Roma people at 3.33/9, while towards the mythical category of "migrants" at 2.76/9.[34]

The survey also found that when data for Hungary is compared to the rest of the Western world, especially Western Europe, "the fear of physical attack is much less common among Jews, but Holocaust denial and relativization are more prevalent."[35] Hungarian Jewish communities experience antisemitism strongly, even though the number and frequency of violent incidents is low. Nationalist discourse and the revisionism of Hungary's wartime past are viewed by many as the causes of an unhealthy atmosphere. In this case, the debate is not restricted to academic circles and closed groups; it extends to the media and to public demonstrations.[36]

András Kovásc, Professor for Jewish Studies at Central European University (CEU) in Budapest, emphasizes that the government is not antisemitic.[37] His research suggests that the rise in prejudice in Hungary is related to the 2009 emer-

---

33 Ibid., 46–47.
34 Ibid., 59, Table 2.
35 Ibid., 111. It should not come as a surprise. I had discovered this paradox years ago: the number of violent antisemitic incidents cannot predict the level of antisemitic perceptions in a society. See my article: "The antisemitic Paradox in Europe: Empirical Evidences and Jewish Perceptions. A Comparative Study Between the West and East," in *Being Jewish in 21st Century Central Europe*, ed. Haim Fireberg, Olaf Glockner, and Marcela Zoufala (Berin: De Gruyter, 2020), 269–279.
36 The Kantor Center, http://www.kantorcenter.tau.ac.il/sites/default/files/Doch2014-2.pdf;

Randolph Braham, "Hungary: The Assault on the Historical Memory of the Holocaust," in *The Holocaust in Hungary: Seventy Years Later*, ed. Randolph Braham and András Kovács (Budapest: CEU press, 2016), 261–309;

Hungarian Free Press, http://hungarianfreepress.com/2015/05/07/budapest-politicians-tour-new-holocaust-museum-described-as-shocking;

The Kantor Center, http://www.kantorcenter.tau.ac.il/sites/default/files/Doch2014-2.pdf, 55.

Another controversy referred to the anti-George Soros campaign in Hungary that deepened the gap between the Government and the veteran Jewish establishment, currently led by Andras Heisler.

The Times of Israel, https://www.timesofisrael.com/decrying-netanyahu-betrayal-hungary-jews-say-pm-ignoring-them/.

https://www.dw.com/en/rising-anti-semitism-in-hungary-worries-jewish-groups/a-55978374;
https://balkaninsight.com/2020/11/30/sense-of-impunity-lies-behind-hungary-officials-antisemitic-attack-on-soros/.

37 https://www.dw.com/en/rising-anti-semitism-in-hungary-worries-jewish-groups/a-55978374.

gence of Jobbik, a party which is more or less openly antisemitic.[38] There is a significant correlation between antisemitism and certain attitudes such as xenophobia and nationalism, which adequately explains its influence. However, these attitudes do not produce the same degree of antisemitism in every social milieu and in every region of the country. There are differences that correlate with the strength of support for Jobbik support in a given region. The assumption is that "support for a far-right party is not a cause of antisemitism, but rather – on the contrary – should be regarded as a factor that mobilizes attitudes leading to antisemitism and that directs people towards antisemitism." Therefore, antisemitism is, at least in part, the result, rather than a cause, of attraction to the far right.[39] As a result of its partial defeat in the 2018 parliamentary election, Jobbik was no longer perceived as an authentic home for the right-wing of Hungary and many have sought out other platforms to express their hate and nationalism.[40]

Hungary's discourse primarily pertains to the quest for national identity in the twenty-first century, to the uncertainty regarding its common values and the place of minorities, including Jews, within a nation-state. In 2017, religion became the main marker of Hungarian cultural identity. Hypothetically, the change was a result of the resurrection of the Christian-national idea which appears as a foundation of the Hungarian constitution. This vision assumes that Christian culture is the unifying force of the nation, giving the state its essence and meaning. Similarly to how denomination is linked to national identity in Poland, in Hungary being Christian is equivalent to being Hungarian. Christian religiosity symbolizes the acceptance of the national-conservative identity discourse as well as belonging to the

---

[38] András Kovács, *Antisemitic Prejudices and Dynamics of Antisemitism in Post-Communist Hungary*, https://www.jmberlin.de/sites/default/files/antisemitism-in-europe-today_4-kovacs.pdf (2013), 22.
[39] Ibid.
[40] Barna Ildikó and Árpád Knap from Eötvös Loránd University, Budapest, suggested that the extreme right continued to support Jobbik even though in 2016–2017 the party seemed to turn away from its original agenda. Jobbik was portrayed as the leader of the opposition and the arch enemy of the governing Fidesz, the latter being accused of resorting to dirty tricks in order to defeat Jobbik. The turning point came after Jobbik was defeated in a parliamentary election in April 2018, and especially after its most extreme politicians left the party to establish the "Our Homeland Movement" (Mi Hazánk Mozgalom). See: Ildikó Barna and Árpád Knap, *Antisemitism in Contemporary Hungary: Exploring Topics of Antisemitism in the Far-Right Media Using Natural Language Processing* in: https://www.theo-web.de/archiv/archiv-ab-juni-2017/news/antisemitism-in-contemporary-hungary-exploring-topics-of-antisemitism-in-the-far-right-media-using/?tx_news_pi1%5Bcontroller%5D=News&tx_news_pi1%5Baction%5D=detail&cHash=98e44e842b1e2d38f1692d89d2f0a7c8; *The Jobbik Party in Hungary: History and Background*, https://www.humanrightsfirst.org/sites/default/files/Jobbik-Party-Fact-Sheet-final.pdf.

Christian-nationalist political camp, where antisemitism is more prevalent than in other sectors of society.⁴¹

The regime developed by Viktor Orbán after his ascension to power in 2010 has been viewed as being ethnically nationalist and authoritarian. Culture-wise, it is necessary to note the creation of some public institutions, national strategy research institutes, museums, and public universities, as well as many monuments (many of them honouring antisemitic "heroes" of the Horthy era).⁴²

For instance, a statue constructed at Budapest's Freedom Square in 2014 depicts a German imperial eagle striking down Hungary's guardian angel, Gabriel – an image meant to symbolize Hungary's innocence in the face of Nazi aggression and commemorate German occupation which began on 19 March 1944. Wide segments of the Hungarian public, not just among Jews, continue to oppose the statue, arguing that it downplays Hungary's responsibility for the Holocaust.⁴³ In September 2021, Pope Francis visited the site and, speaking to a large crowd, denounced the incorporation of Christian values into the Hungarian political system. "The cross, planted in the ground, not only invites us to be well-rooted: it also raises and extends its arms towards everyone," said Francis.⁴⁴

Even if the Fidesz cabinet led by Prime Minister Viktor Orbán is not considered antisemitic, it is obvious enough that it uses the same "anti"-rhetoric for domestic political gains. Budapest (and Poland) and the EU establishment are at odds over several issues, including whether European identity imposed by EU regulations takes precedence over national identity. Both Hungary and Poland refused to allow "refugees" to settle in their countries, claiming their Christian and national identities were being threatened.⁴⁵ After a meeting with his Polish counterpart Mateusz Morawiecki in November 2020, Hungarian Prime Minister Viktor Orbán declared: "There are a number of topics on which we disagree with the other EU countries, such as immigration and gender, and this would mean we could

---

41 Barna Ildikó and András Kovács, *Religiosity, Religious Practice, and Antisemitism in Present-Day Hungary*, https://archive.jpr.org.uk/download?id=7149/. A similar trend is obvious in Polish society. Being Christian, especially Catholic, appears as a typical feature of being "truly Polish."
42 Ibid., 124.
43 For more examples of the rift between the Jews and the Government, see: https://www.timesofisrael.com/budapests-new-30m-holocaust-museum-sits-in-limbo-as-hungary-debates-its-contents/.
44 https://www.dw.com/en/pope-francis-meets-hungarys-viktor-orban-on-4-day-europe-trip/a-59156880.
45 An interview by Madeleine Janssen with Michael Roth, German Minister of European Affairs:
https://www.t-online.de/nachrichten/ausland/eu/id_88431006/eu-europastaatsminister-michael-roth-will-polen-und-ungarn-sanktionieren.html;
https://balkaninsight.com/2020/11/27/democracy-digest-poland-and-hungary-refuse-to-back-down-over-eu-veto/.

be forced to accept their interpretation of all these matters. My patriotic duty is to defend Hungary and its vital interests."[46]

Nonetheless, in an article published on the pro-government news site *Origo* at the same time, Szilárd Demeter, the government's cultural commissioner and director of the Petőfi Literary Museum, pointed out how much antisemitism, the Holocaust, and the Jewish fate are embedded in the political rhetoric in Hungary. According to Demeter, in defending their way of life against the EU, Poles and Hungarians have become outcasts and are therefore the new Jews of Europe. As if that was not enough, he also compared George Soros to Adolf Hitler, calling him "a liberal Führer." His opinion piece made headlines in the Hungarian media. Eventually, Demeter retracted, saying he did not mean to "relativize the Holocaust."[47] Therefore, it is not surprising that the most frequent response in the ADL survey on antisemitism attitudes in Hungary is the statement that "Jews still talk too much about what happened to them during the Holocaust."[48] Hungarian society is definitely experiencing a "Jewish problem."

We have seen that the Holocaust is always present in Hungary's public life and political discourse. But do the political conditions in Hungary and the unclear societal attitudes towards minorities encourage Jews to go beyond the surface and learn more about their Jewish heritage and tradition? Hungarian government's rhetoric covertly contains antisemitism, while some extreme political parties openly employ it in their agendas and politics.[49] International Jewish organizations offer cultural and other programs to support Jewish communities in Hungary.[50]

---

[46] https://balkaninsight.com/2020/11/27/democracy-digest-poland-and-hungary-refuse-to-back-down-over-eu-veto/; https://abouthungary.hu/news-in-brief/heres-the-joint-declaration-of-the-prime-minister-of-poland-and-the-prime-minister-of-hungary.

[47] https://balkaninsight.com/2020/11/30/sense-of-impunity-lies-behind-hungary-officials-antisemitic-attack-on-soros/; https://www.szabadeuropa.hu/a/nyilatkozathaboru-utan-visszavonta-gazkamrazos-irasat-demeter-szilard/30974746.html.

[48] https://global100.adl.org/country/hungary/2019. A similar indication that the Holocaust is the most bothering issue for Hungarians who could be identified as antisemites was found by a research group in a recent publication: Barna Ildikó, Tamás Kohut, Katalin Pallai, Olga Gyárfášová, Jiří Kocián, Grigorij Mesežnikov, and Rafal Pankowski, *Modern Antisemitism in the Visegrád Countries – Countering Distortion*, https://www.researchgate.net/publication/349360020_Modern_Antisemitism_in_the_Visegrad_Countries_-Countering_Distortion/link/602c7321a6fdcc37a82fffb5/download.

[49] For analysis of antisemitic groups' rhetoric: Barna Ildikó, Tamás Kohut, Katalin Pallai, Olga Gyárfášová, Jiří Kocián, Grigorij Mesežnikov, and Rafal Pankowski, *Modern Antisemitism in the Visegrád Countries – Countering Distortion*, https://www.researchgate.net/publication/349360020_Modern_Antisemitism_in_the_Visegrad_Countries_-Countering_Distortion/link/602c7321a6fdcc37a82fffb5/download.

It is commonly believed that this "revival" of Jewish culture and the vibrant Jewish life in Hungary, primarily in Budapest, reflects a robust Jewish community in an encouraging environment. Even so, with all the changes in Jewish institutional life and in spite of the Jewish institutional boom, the number of Hungarians who identify themselves as Jews or are more committed to Jewish communal life has remained relatively unchanged. "The "missing Jews" were targeted again," concluded Kata Vicze, "but most of them remained missing (perhaps for their protection of their own privacy or deliberate choice of not declaring themselves Jewish, among other reasons)."[51]

A conservative Rabbi in Budapest, Gábor Fináli, analyzes the difficulties that hidden Hungarian Jews face when attempting to embrace Judaism. In his view, people often seek companionship. They wish for company first, and yearn for the consolation of spirituality that religion offers. Asked why they do not seek and call upon God in the synagogue, they respond that they view the synagogue with disdain and that they dislike it. The root of the problem is the absence of a living Hungarian Jewish identity – the one that exists is based on the Holocaust and the success of Israel, so it does not relate to current events or life in Hungary. As Fináli states, "Even in the third and fourth generations of Jewish families, the Holocaust is a greater force for community formation than Torah morality, beauty and richness, and Auschwitz is more influential than Mount Sinai."[52] Fináli suggests that there should be a communication strategy. Books should be translated thoughtfully and systematically, films should be imported, and Hungarian Jews should become more involved in the Jewish world.[53] The quest to reach the "missing Jews" sometimes becomes grotesque, for instance when elements as prosaic as Cholent – a stew of slow-cooked meat that simmers overnight and is often made by observant Jews, in accordance with the laws that prohibit cooking on the Sabbath – are used to attract Jews and part-Jews, in addition to building bridges with gentile Hungarians.[54]

---

50 https://ejpress.org/after-years-of-rebuilding-budapests-jewish-community-sees-growth-in-size-and-shuls/.
51 Zsófia Kata Vincze, "The "Missing" and "Missed" Jews in Hungary," in *Being Jewish in 21st Century Central Europe*, ed. Haim Fireberg, Olaf Glöckner, and Marcela Menachem Zoufalá (Berlin: de Gruyter, 2020), 115–143, 126.
52 See in the same context in this volume especially the text by Lilach Lev-Ari, who also argues that the Holocaust continues to strongly affect the life and intellectual world of the Jews in Hungary.
53 Gábor Fináli, "We have no example of being able to live as Hungarians," https://www-szombat-org.translate.goog/hagyomany-tortenelem/nincs-mintank-hogy-lehet-magyar-zsidokent-elni?_x_tr_sch=http&_x_tr_sl=hu&_x_tr_tl=en&_x_tr_hl=en .
54 https://www.jns.org/cholent-festival-brings-jewish-culture-to-hungary-via-food-music-traditions/.

The Case of Germany

The unique history of Germany in the twentieth century has prompted me to focus on antisemitism there, examining the changes and evolution that occurred over the course of the last decade. Germany is home to approximately 117,500 to 250,000 Jews (depending on how Jewishness is defined).[55] Berlin has the largest Jewish community in the country. The Jewish community in Germany consists primarily of post-Soviet immigrants, who arrived here in the 1990s, and their children. Additionally, many young Israelis (10,000–30,000) have viewed Germany, and particularly Berlin, as a liberal haven from the pressures of life in Israel and have decided to stay, live, and work here for longer.[56]

By 2011, the problem of violent antisemitism had largely ceased to exist for the majority of German Jews. Violent incidents were relatively rare, as antisemites instead chose vandalism as their preferred method of operation. Evidently, old Jewish cemeteries and memorial sites were the primary targets of desecration (16 cases were recorded in 2011 by the Kantor Center). These few incidents did not receive much attention in Germany at the time and were not presented in an alarmist tone in the Kantor Center's 2011 annual report.[57] However, in a statement released on October 9 2012 by Petra Pau, vice-president of the German Bundestag and a member of the Die Linke party, the Federal Government announced that 82 attacks on synagogues had occurred in Germany between 2008 and 2012.[58] A similar number was recorded in the Kantor Center Database. However, at that point, there was very little chance that a Jew would be subjected to physical violence. It appears that violent manifestations of antisemitism have increased in frequency since 2013, but most of them have still taken the form of desecration, happening far from the public eye.[59]

---

55 Sergio DellaPergola, "Jewish Demography in the European Union – Virtuous and Vicious Paths," in *Being Jewish in 21st Century Central Europe*, ed. Haim Fireberg Haim, Olaf Glöckner, and Marcela Menachem Zoufala (Berlin: de Gruyter, 2020), 26.
56 For an updated estimation of the numbers of Israelis in Berlin, see: Dani Kranz, *Israelis in Berlin: Wie viele sind es und was zieht sie nach Berlin?* (Bertelsmann Foundation, 2015), 11, accessed January 10, 2022, https://www.bertelsmann-stiftung.de/de/publikationen/publikation/did/israelis-in-berlin-1.
57 https://en-humanities.tau.ac.il/sites/humanities_en.tau.ac.il/files/media_server/humanities/kantor/research/annual_reports/GA-ALL_8.pdf
58 Deutscher Bundestag, 17. Wahlperiode, Drucksache 17/14813, 04.10.2013. Antwort auf die Anfrage der Abgeordneten Petra Pau (DIE LINKE) (Wie viele Anschläge auf Synagogen hat es in Deutschland in den letzten fünf Jahren gegeben?).
59 https://en-humanities.tau.ac.il/sites/humanities_en.tau.ac.il/files/media_server/humanities/kantor/Doch_2013.pdf. Admittedly, in 2019, the German parliament (Bundestag), when answering an of-

Germany was included in an FRA study conducted in 2013 that provided some insight into antisemitism in German society from a Jewish perspective. The survey indicated that 61 percent of the participants believed antisemitism was a real problem in Germany – a figure lower than in France and Hungary, but higher than in the United Kingdom.[60] At the same time, 32 percent of respondents believed that antisemitism had increased significantly over the previous five years. Compared to other European countries, Germany scored at the bottom on both criteria.[61] Even though the likelihood that a Jew living on the streets of Germany would experience antisemitic violence was extremely low (if not non-existent), a feeling of urgency led scholars, politicians, and other public figures to investigate the nature of these perceptions and feelings, and how they differed from the reality on the streets.

Rabbi Daniel Alter, a prominent member of the Berlin community who is responsible for combating antisemitism, emphasized that the problem was present all across the society. Ludwig Schick, the Archbishop of Bamberg at the time, foresaw the latent danger of antisemitism, even though it had not yet escalated into violence, while also adding that "anti-Jewish attitudes are no longer exclusively hidden from view; they are openly expressed, and they are less hidden these days."[62]

An extensive study conducted by Professor Monika Schwarz-Friesel at the Technical University of Berlin has since substantiated this claim by examining thousands of antisemitic hate messages, letters, and emails addressed to Israel's Embassy in Berlin and the German Central Council of Jews.[63] According to Schwarz-Friesel, most of the material contained in the examined sources was generated by "ordinary members of the mainstream society." The language used by academics, lawyers, doctors, bank employees, clergymen, and students demon-

---

ficial inquiry of the Vice President of the Bundestag, Petra Pau (The Left), confirmed that a Jewish cemetery in Germany was desecrated every other week. See: *Jede zweite Woche wird ein jüdischer Friedhof geschändet* in Jüdische Allgemeine Online, August 2, 2019, aaccessed January 10, 2022, https://www.juedische-allgemeine.de/unsere-woche/jede-zweite-woche-wird-ein-juedischer-friedhof-geschaendet/.

60 https://fra.europa.eu/sites/default/files/fra-2013-discrimination-hate-crime-against-jews-eu-member-states-0_en.pdf, 16.
61 Ibid., 17.
62 Ibid. 42.
63 Prof. Monika Schwarz-Friesel and her team started their research in 2002, using extensive linguistic methods. Their conclusion was initially published in German in 2013. Lately, the updated English edition was published: Monika Schwaez-Friesel and Jehuda Reinharz, *Inside the Antisemitic Mind; The language of Jew-hatred in contemporary Germany* (Brandeis University Press, 2017).

strated rejection, hostility, and defensiveness which decades of memory work have failed to alleviate.[64]

In 2018, the FRA published a follow-up survey to its 2013 study.[65] It marked the first time that the majority of respondents (85 percent) in Germany perceived antisemitism as a serious issue. This represented a significant increase of over 39 percentage points in this category. Around 60 percent of respondents reported that antisemitic incidents had increased "a lot" over the previous five years. This represented the second highest increase among European nations. In terms of these two criteria, the 2018 results took Germany closer to what is, on average, found throughout Europe today.[66] Data provided by the Kantor Center indicated 35 incidents of violent antisemitism in Germany in 2018. In comparison with 2013, one of the major differences was that almost half of the attacks targeted individuals.[67] Antisemitic violence has become a reality for Jews living in Germany, threatening their sense of security and turning their lives upside down.[68]

The huge migration wave from 2015 onwards gave rise to the question of how the growing number of Muslim refugees in Germany affects the presence of antisemitism.[69] In a meeting with Chancellor Angela Merkel, Josef Schuster, the head of the Central Council of Jews in Germany, expressed concern about Jew-hatred among immigrants and refugees from predominantly Muslim countries.[70] The German government (and Jewish organisations) was accused by critics of underplaying or even denying the growing involvement of Muslims and Islamists in antisemitic activities in Berlin and elsewhere in Germany. Migration was a very

---

64 Ibid. Preface to the 2013 edition.
65 https://fra.europa.eu/sites/default/files/fra_uploads/fra-2018-experiences-and-perceptions-of-antisemitism-survey_en.pdf. For a detailed analysis of FRA 2018, see: Sergio DellaPergola, *Jewish Perceptions of Antisemitism in the European Union, 2018: A New Structural Look*, in: https://www.degruyter.com/document/doi/10.1515/actap-2020-2001/html.
66 Ibid., 17, 19.
67 https://kantorcenter.tau.ac.il/wp-content/uploads/2021/07/Antisemitism-Worldwide-2018.pdf, 138.
68 Ronen Steinke, *Terror gegen Juden. Wie antisemitische Gewalt erstarkt und der Staat versagt* (Berlin verlag, München, 2020).
69 According to Benjamin Weinthal Germany's security and intelligence agencies officially expressed alarm in October 2015: "We are importing Islamic extremism, Arab anti-Semitism, national and ethnic conflicts of other peoples as well as a different societal and legal understanding. ... [T]he integration of hundreds of thousands of illegal migrants in Germany is no longer possible in light of the number and already existing parallel societies," https://www.jpost.com/Diaspora/German-intel-Migrants-will-bring-anti-Semitism-430058.
70 Ibid. For a comprehensive analysis of the 2015–2018 situation, see: James Kirchick, *Is Germany capable of protecting its Jews*, https://www.theatlantic.com/international/archive/2018/04/germany-jews-muslim-migrants/558677/ (April 2018).

controversial topic in Germany at the time.⁷¹ President Joachim Gauck addressed the issue of antisemitism among Muslim immigrants when he left office at the end of 2017, in a Public Lecture at the University of Düsseldorf:

> I feel ashamed (...) when antisemitism among people from Arab states is ignored or made understandable with reference to Israeli politics. Or when criticism of Islam is immediately suspected of growing out of racism and hatred of Muslims. Am I right that in these and other cases consideration for the other culture is seen as more important than the protection of basic and human rights? Yes, there is hatred and discrimination against Muslims in our country. What is required to oppose this resentment and generalisation is not only schools and politics, but each individual. But appeasers who disregard reprehensible behaviour of individual migrants in order not to promote racism only confirm racists in their suspicion that freedom of expression is restricted in our country.⁷²

President Gauck recommended that in order to change migrants' attitudes towards democracy, liberalism, and other groups living in Germany "and to agree on a future in this country together, we need one thing above all else – the same as it once was between native and displaced Germans – more knowledge about one another. More dialogue. More debate. More willingness to meet in the respective other our own fears, but also new opportunities."⁷³

Following the Islamist terror attack in Berlin on 19 December 2016, in which a truck was intentionally driven into the Christmas market killing 12 people and in-

---

71 https://www.dw.com/en/anti-semitism-in-germany-as-muslims-we-must-tackle-this/a-57578758; https://www.nytimes.com/2019/05/21/magazine/anti-semitism-germany.html; https://www.timesofisrael.com/germany-is-accused-of-downplaying-anti-semitic-attacks-by-muslims/.
72 https://rp-online.de/nrw/staedte/duesseldorf/joachim-gauck-an-heinrich-heine-uni-duesseldorf-mich-erschreckt-der-multikulturalismus_aid-17821655. Translation by the author. The original quote of Joachim Gauck in German: "So finde ich es beschämend (...) wenn Antisemitismus unter Menschen aus arabischen Staaten ignoriert oder mit Verweis auf israelische Politik für verständlich erklärt wird. Oder wenn Kritik am Islam sofort unter den Verdacht gerät, aus Rassismus und einem Hass auf Muslime zu erwachsen. Sehe ich es richtig, dass in diesen und anderen Fällen die Rücksichtnahme auf die andere Kultur als wichtiger erachtet wird als die Wahrung von Grund- und Menschenrechten? Ja, es gibt Hass und Diskriminierung von Muslimen in unserem Land. Und sich diesem Ressentiment und dieser Generalisierung entgegenzustellen, sind nicht nur Schulen und Politik gefordert, sondern jeder Einzelne. Beschwichtiger aber, die kritikwürdige Verhaltensweisen von einzelnen Migranten unter den Teppich kehren, um Rassismus keinen Vorschub zu leisten, bestätigen Rassisten nur in ihrem Verdacht, die Meinungsfreiheit in unserem Land sei eingeschränkt."
73 Ibid. Translation by the author. Original speech in German: "Um uns gemeinsam auf eine Zukunft in diesem Land zu verständigen, brauchen wir – wie einst zwischen einheimischen und vertriebenen Deutschen – vor allem eines: mehr Wissen übereinander. Mehr Dialog. Mehr Debatte. Mehr Bereitschaft, im jeweils Anderen unseren eigenen Ängsten, aber auch neuen Chancen zu begegnen."

juring at least 50 more, general fear and reservations towards the Muslim population in Germany increased.[74] A long-standing fear of far-right extremist terrorism also appeared after a right-radical young man had tried to conduct a massacre in the synagogue of the city of Halle (Central Germany) on Yom Kippur in 2019.[75]

In Berlin, which is home to the largest Jewish community in Germany, antisemitic incidents have been reported most frequently. It is true that the overall numbers for the first half of 2018 remained high in most parts of the city. However, in Friedrichshain-Kreuzberg, a district with a high Muslim population and new immigrants, antisemitic incidents rose by more than 50 percent, according to the Research and Information Office on Antisemitism in Berlin (RIAS).[76] There was (and is) a belief that the increase in antisemitic incidents is related to the growing number of immigrants from the Middle East living in the city. Felix Klein, the German national Antisemitism Commissioner, also admitted the statistics presented by RIAS would support a sense among Jews that Muslims were far more involved in antisemitic incidents than official statistics suggested.[77] Thus, the results of the FRA survey in 2018, also based on a comprehensive survey among German Jews, were not unexpected. The research found that almost 75 percent of German respondents chose not to carry attributes that would identify them as Jewish.[78]

Antisemitic violence and hostility are directed not only toward adult Jews. Recent studies have revealed an increase in antisemitism in German schools. Germany had for many years invested a great deal of resources and effort into school education in order to counter the young generations' hostility towards Jews. In fact, according to surveys, the situation paradoxically produced a new phenomenon re-

---

[74] https://www.marshallcenter.org/en/publications/occasional-papers/aftermath-terror-attack-breitscheid-platz (accessed January 10, 2021).

[75] On October 9, 2019, on Yom Kippur, the most important Jewish holiday, a heavily armed right-wing extremist tried to enter a packed synagogue in the East German city of Halle. Only the insuperable, thick, wooden door prevented a huge bloodbath. The invader, after realising that he could not breach the door, started a gun rampage on the streets and killed two random passengers.

[76] https://report-antisemitism.de/documents/2019-04-17_rias-be_Annual_Antisemitische-Vorfaelle-2018.pdf. RIAS – an NGO that tallies expressions of hatred against Jews, 15 (accessed January 10, 2021).

[77] https://www.jpost.com/Opinion/Berlin-Europes-antisemitism-capital-580076. For further analysis on Muslim antisemitism and its influence on German politics, see: https://en-humanities.tau.ac.il/sites/humanities_en.tau.ac.il/files/media_server/humanities/kantor/Antisemitism%20Worldwide%202018.pdf, 73 (accessed January 10, 2021). In addition to the national antisemitism commissioner most of the 16 federal states have installed their own antisemitism commissioners who work at the interface between Jewish communities, the state, and society.

[78] https://fra.europa.eu/sites/default/files/fra_uploads/fra-2018-experiences-and-perceptions-of-antisemitism-survey_en.pdf, 37 (accessed January 10, 2021).

ferred to as "Holocaust Fatigue" or "Shoah Fatigue."[79] Using these curricula, German educators attempted to address the youth of the new immigration wave in such a way as to at least reduce the deep-seated prejudice toward the Jews. However, many indicators suggest that the approach does not appear to be accepted by the students. Although no formal studies are yet available, it has been evident that schools (such as mosques) were used as breeding grounds for growing antisemitism.[80]

Abraham Lehrer, the director of the synagogue of the Cologne Jewish community, explained that "the number of young members of our community reporting hostility is increasing (...) Teachers of the school say that 'Du Jude' is used as a dirty word on the playground, despite the fact that no Jewish child attends the school." Often, ignorance, inability to deal with the phenomenon or indifference to it are the reasons for such reaction. Furthermore, educators are increasingly encountering antisemitism relating to Israel, predominantly (but not exclusively) among Muslims. Despite the 75 years that have elapsed since the Holocaust, "Du Jude" is still a commonly used insult on school playgrounds and in classrooms.[81]

During a meeting held in Heidelberg, Germany on February 29, 2019, the German commissioners dealing with antisemitism, together with Jewish and Hebrew teachers, discussed ways to combat the increasing verbal and physical antisemitism in German schools. School headmasters have been accused of failing to act in response to antisemitic incidents for fear of damaging their reputations. Antisemitism in schools has become a real issue – not just in Berlin, but throughout Germany.[82] According to Marina Chernivsky, the founder of the Berlin-based organisation "Kompetenz-Zentrum für Prävention und Empowerment,"[83] which offers counselling for individuals, families, and organizations experiencing antisemitic or discriminatory incidents, the lack of expertise on how to deal with antisemitism in the classroom means that even Jewish teachers do not always re-

---

79 https://www.deutschlandfunkkultur.de/studie-zu-70-jahre-nach-auschwitz-junge-deutsche-sind-des-100.html (accessed January 1, 2015).
80 Monica Vitale and Rebecca Clothey, "Holocaust Education in Germany: Ensuring Relevance and Meaning in an Increasingly Diverse Community," *FIRE: Forum for International Research in Education* 5, no. 1 (2019): 44–62, https://files.eric.ed.gov/fulltext/EJ1207646.pdf;
    https://www.i24news.tv/en/news/international/122372-160811-study-german-universities-neglect-holocaust-studies.
81 https://en-humanities.tau.ac.il/sites/humanities_en.tau.ac.il/files/media_server/humanities/kantor/Kantor%20Report%202020_130820.pdf, 103 (accessed January 10, 2021).
82 https://en-humanities.tau.ac.il/sites/humanities_en.tau.ac.il/files/media_server/humanities/kantor/Antisemitism%20Worldwide%202018.pdf, 74.
83 Marina Chernivsky is also leading the Berlin based Advisory initiative OFEK. See: https://ofek-beratung.de/.

port incidents concerning themselves, for fear of revealing their own religious identity.[84]

Research conducted in 2018 by Professor Julia Bernstein from the Department of Social Work and Health at Frankfurt University of Applied Sciences (Frankfurt UAS) produced significant findings regarding antisemitism in German schools. Bernstein led an extensive qualitative study, whereby Jewish students were asked about their experiences with antisemitism in schools and how teachers responded to it.

This study revealed that: a) among school children and teachers, it is not uncommon to find that antisemitism is normalized in relation to Israel; such "criticism of Israel" conceals deeper aggression and hatred towards the Jews; b) antisemitism is not always considered as a unique phenomenon and is sometimes mistaken for racism; in fact, the similarities and differences between those two phenomena are frequently overlooked; and c) there is a tendency to explain contemporary antisemitism through the lens of National Socialist antisemitism and the Shoah. Nonetheless, surprisingly, many young people use National Socialist symbols and fantasize about the extermination of the Jews in a manner directly related to the Holocaust.[85]

As for contemporary Germany, it should be acknowledged that violent antisemitism is not yet the crux of the problem. The number of incidents involving face-to-face violence is still relatively low, as could be seen from the numbers mentioned earlier.[86] The true face of antisemitism is presumed beneath the sociological and cultural surface, as it disguises itself as a kind of open and liberal society. Professor Monika Schwarz-Friesel and Professor Jehuda Reinharz explained it as follows:

> Here once again, antisemitism proves to be a chameleon: it changes its colors according to the social and political situations, but stays the same at its cognitive and emotional core. ... In spite of all the efforts to erase the distorted and false pictures of Jews and Judaism after the Holocaust, our data reveal the shocking truth about the continuity and persistence of the age-old hostility toward Jews ... Deeply rooted in the Western tradition of thinking ... it

---

[84] See: Marina Chernivsky, Friederike Lorenz, and Johanna Schweitzer, Antisemitismus im (Schul-)Alltag. Erfahrungen und Umgangsweisen jüdischer Familien und junger Erwachsener, https://zwst-kompetenzzentrum.de/wp-content/uploads/2021/04/Forschungsbericht_Familienstudie_2020.pdf.

[85] https://en-humanities.tau.ac.il/sites/humanities_en.tau.ac.il/files/media_server/humanities/kantor/Kantor%20Report%202020_130820.pdf, 105–106. The full outcome of the research was published in: Julia Bernstein, Antisemitismus an Schulen in Deutschland (Juventa Verlag GmbH, 2020).

[86] Although recent years have seen several deadly attacks (such as in Halle and Berlin), the majority of incidents continue to take the form of desecrating memorial sites or cemeteries.

proves to be a central part of ... culture.... To cope with contemporary hatred of Jews, to find a solution so as to seriously and effectively fight it, must take it [the Western culture] into account.[87]

The EU Perspective: The Challenges of Managing and Confronting Antisemitism

Antisemitism is not ignored by the European authorities. It is generally accepted that antisemitism, especially in its violent form, is perpetrated by the same individuals and groups – whether from the far left, far right or Muslim fundamentalists – that are responsible for extremism, hate crimes, and violence in general. The challenge of fighting antisemitism in Europe requires a coordinated effort against perpetrators. However, Irwin Cotler, former Minister of Justice and Attorney General of Canada, is more skeptical as to the level of commitment from governments and international organisations. "Jews are the canary in the mine shaft of global evil," he declares. "It begins with Jews, but it does not end there. Universal public values – and the humanity they uphold and protect – are also at risk."[88]

"Antisemitism has been on the rise in Europe and beyond these past few years, and the European Commission has adopted a firm policy to utilize all resources at its disposal to prevent and combat antisemitism and other forms of hatred and intolerance," said Katharina von Schnurbein, Coordinator of the European Commission for Combating Antisemitism.[89] Before taking any further steps, the Commission wanted to verify the results of the FRA 2018 survey and get a sense of what the general public thought about antisemitism. Published in January 2019, the Eurobarometer Survey on Antisemitism in Europe provided an interesting overview of the situation. The results showed a significant difference between the general public's perceptions of antisemitism and the experiences of the Jewish community as indicated by the FRA survey. Nine out of ten (89 percent) Jews surveyed by the FRA believe that antisemitism has increased, and eight out of ten (85 percent) consider it a serious issue. Jews in Europe rate antisemitism as

---

[87] Monika Schwaez-Friesel and Jehuda Reinharz, *Inside the Antisemitic Mind; The language of Jew-hatred in contemporary Germany* (Brandeis University Press, 2017), preface to the English edition (2016).
[88] https://en-humanities.tau.ac.il/sites/humanities_en.tau.ac.il/files/media_server/humanities/kantor/Kantor%20Report%202020_130820.pdf, 155–156 (Irwin Cotler, *The Laundering of Antisemitism under Universal Public Values*).
[89] Ibid. (Katharina von Schnurbein, *European Union Activities in Combating Antisemitism in 2019*), 152.

their biggest social or political problem. However, according to Eurobarometer results, only 36 percent of the general public believe that antisemitism has increased in recent years.[90] Therefore, the basic assumption behind bridging the results of the two FRA surveys with Eurobarometer was that there is a social problem that should be addressed.

On June 1, 2017, the European Parliament adopted an important resolution on the fight against antisemitism. It envisioned the appointment of national special envoys, the adoption of the IHRA working definition of antisemitism, and a call for increased efforts at the local, national, and European levels. In December 2018, Justice and Home Affairs Ministers of all 28 EU Member States adopted a joint declaration entitled "EU Council Declaration on the fight against antisemitism and the development of a common security policy for protecting Jewish communities, institutions and individuals in Europe." The declaration addresses a wide range of issues that require action.[91] It recommends that the Member States: a) develop and adopt comprehensive national strategies on preventing antisemitism that are integrated into their overall strategies to combat racism; b) adhere to the IHRA definition; c) safeguard and secure Jewish communities, while also providing them with adequate funding; d) implement all existing European legislation regarding racism and xenophobia; and e) promote education about the Holocaust and Jewish life in the modern world, including integration courses for newcomers, as well as ensure adequate teacher training.[92]

On October 20, 2021, the European Commission submitted its "Strategy on combating antisemitism and fostering Jewish life" in Europe.[93] "The Strategy we are

---

90 https://ec.europa.eu/commission/presscorner/detail/en/MEMO_19_542. It was also revealed by the Eurobarometer that antisemitism is more of an issue in countries with large Jewish populations. In countries where physical attacks against the Jewish community have occurred, such as Sweden, France, Germany, the Netherlands, Italy, the United Kingdom, and Belgium, antisemitism has also been cited as a problem. Swedish (81 percent) and French (72 percent) respondents are most likely to state that antisemitism is a problem in their country. People with Jewish friends and acquaintances are more likely to be aware of the issues as well as the rise of antisemitism.
91 https://ec.europa.eu/commission/presscorner/detail/en/MEMO_19_542.
92 Ibid. It should be noted that although the European Commission and EU Member States have adopted the IHRA definition, the document itself has no legal authority. One of the most compelling aspects of the working definition is its moral affirmative stance which may be the key to convincing politicians and decision-makers to support the Jewish cause as justified in its own right. While the political game allows for flexibility, it is still very difficult to reverse court decisions, especially if they are considered constitutional precedents. However, the European Union still prefers not to deal with antisemitism as a distinct phenomenon, but rather by utilizing the laws and national regulations dealing with hate crimes, hate speech, and racism.
93 For the detailed plan see: https://ec.europa.eu/info/sites/default/files/eu-strategy-on-combating-antisemitism-and-fostering-jewish-life_october2021_en.pdf.

presenting today marks a major step change in the approach the EU takes to counter antisemitism," said Ursula von der Leyen, President of the European Commission.[94] The implementation is anticipated to take place within the next decade and all EU member states will be required to prepare detailed plans. The Commission has made no recommendations as to how legislation is to be used as a tool against antisemitism.

Conclusions

A careful review of the current antisemitic situation in three EU Member States – Germany, Hungary, and Poland – allows us to draw several conclusions. The level of violent antisemitism, as indicated by the number of violent incidents, is not necessarily correlated with the perceptions of antisemitism in those countries. Some "paradoxes" can be observed in Hungary and Poland. Despite having relatively low levels of antisemitic violence, the two countries perceive antisemitism differently in light of their understanding of domestic political and social conditions. The situation in Germany is quite similar. Although there have been very few violent incidents in the past, there is a growing feeling of a threat of antisemitism, both in the social sphere and on the streets. According to the FRA survey conducted in 2018, German Jews experience a greater sense of insecurity in almost all measurable aspects. A high degree of estrangement from the national identity ethos is expressed by respondents in Poland and Hungary.

There is frustration with the political establishment, the ruling parties, and their solutions to antisemitism. Another contributing factor is the failure to create a standard platform on which all segments of society can unite. When Jews lack confidence in the future of their country of residence and do not recognize themselves as valuable members of its society, they feel abandoned. This sense of disillusionment also drives their perceptions of antisemitism which is evident in research results.

Even though antisemitism is a serious problem, it is only one of many issues which European governments and societies are facing now, and not necessarily the most urgent one. In light of the special "relations" between Europe and its Jews, particularly in the twentieth century, it is imperative that Jews do not confuse sympathy with action. In the context of increasingly complex European societies, with Western and Eastern nations increasingly divided over nationalism, the human

---

94 https://ec.europa.eu/commission/presscorner/detail/en/ip_21_4990.

texture is changing rapidly.[95] Given that the Jewish population of Europe ages and decreases rapidly, in parallel with the entire European population,[96] Jews should no longer expect special treatment in the future. Whenever the "Jewish problem" occurs, it does so due to Europe's own challenges such as building nations, combating disintegration, and coping with expanding cultural disparities between a rapidly growing Muslim population and an aging European population. These difficulties are causing political turmoil in Germany and France – the two largest countries in Europe – as well as widening rifts between these Western states on the one hand and Hungary and Poland on the other. As a result, the Jews may once again become scapegoats for societal and political problems faced by the countries in which they live.

---

[95] *A comparative analysis of changes in anti immigrant and anti-Muslim attitudes in Europe: 1990–2017*, https://comparativemigrationstudies.springeropen.com/articles/10.1186/s40878-021-00266-w; Bichara Khader, *Muslims in Europe: The Construction of a "Problem"*, https://www.bbvaopenmind.com/en/articles/muslims-in-europe-the-construction-of-a-problem/; https://www.pewresearch.org/fact-tank/2017/11/29/5-facts-about-the-muslim-population-in-europe/.

[96] Sergio DellaPergola and Daniel Staetsky, *Jews in Europe at the turn of the Millennium: Population trends and estimates*, https://www.jpr.org.uk/documents/JPR_2020.Jews_in_Europe_at_the_turn_of_the_Millennium.pdf; https://ec.europa.eu/eurostat/statistics-explained/index.php?title=Ageing_Europe_-_statistics_on_population_developments; https://ec.europa.eu/eurostat/statistics-explained/index.php?title=Ageing_Europe_-_statistics_on_population_developments#Older_people_.E2.80.94_population_overview; *Measuring active aging within the European Union: implications on economic development*, https://www.ceeol.com/search/viewpdf?id=925494.

Lilach Lev Ari
Feeling "At Home" or Just Privileged Minorities? Perceptions of Jewish and Non-Jewish Respondents in Contemporary Budapest

Introduction

The purpose of this paper is to analyze patterns of integration and inter-relations in contemporary Hungary, as perceived by Jewish and non-Jewish leaders and involved community members from the academia, religious organizations, and the media.

Most diaspora Jews can be defined as belonging to native-born minorities; they perceive themselves as distinct national minorities that became minorities due to political and social changes in their homeland, while others are immigrants (Barak 2006). Thus, Jews constitute mainly an ethnic, native-born minority group, i.e., a group whose culture and religion are different from that of the majority and that is liable to experience relative discrimination (Lev Ari 2022; Macionis 2017; Yiftachel 2001). Jews generally prefer to live in large cities that provide opportunities for economic, social, and cultural development. Within these cities, Jews tend to concentrate in neighborhoods that match their socioeconomic status, provide nearby employment opportunities, facilitate social mobility, and offer religious services and the presence of Jewish organizations (DellaPergola 2011).

Currently, the majority of Hungarian Jews – approximately 90 percent (a number even higher than the worldwide average for Jews' presence in large cities) – live in Budapest and constitute five percent of the city's total population (Kovács 2010). Thus, this study will focus on Jews residing in Budapest as representing contemporary Hungarian Jewry as a whole.

Hungary is one of the post-communist countries in Central Europe. Three decades after the demise of totalitarian regimes and the fall of the Iron Curtain, the term "Central Europe" has a different meaning in terms of the construction of territorial identities and the politics of memory. Jews have played a very important role in creating the central European space which, at a certain point, also became destructive for them, as it became the scene of the Holocaust. In recent years, the debate on the concept of "Central Europe" has somehow lost its significance. Soon after 1989, the term was replaced by a new one, oriented more towards examining the influence of central European countries' economic inclusion in the European

ð Open Access. © 2023 the author(s), published by De Gruyter. [CC BY-NC-ND] This work is licensed under the Creative Commons Attribution-NonCommercial-NoDerivatives 4.0 International License.
https://doi.org/10.1515/9783110783216-007

Union than with developing a central European heritage stretching from Slovenia to the borders of Belarus and Ukraine. However, some central European frameworks continue to exist: for example, the alliance of the Czech Republic, Slovakia, Hungary, and Poland, known as the Visegrad Group (V4). The Group has gradually become a central European voice representing specific regional interests within the overall European framework (Vago 2020).

After the fall of the communist regime in 1989, quite a few Jewish religious, educational, cultural, and political organizations were revived or newly founded in Hungary. In 2000, Jewish communities were organized all over the country, in 26 different settlements. The first Reform community – Sim Shalom – was founded in Budapest in 1992. The Lubavitch movement established its institutions, too, operating a synagogue, a kindergarten, and a school in Budapest. In addition to the high school of the Neolog community named after Sándor Scheiber, there is also an Orthodox American Foundation School in Budapest as well as the largest Jewish school, the liberal-secular Lauder Javne elementary and high school, which also has a kindergarten. More than 1,000 students were attending these Jewish schools in 2003 (Kovács and Forrás-Biró 2011).

According to Barna and Kovács, "it is impossible to define the exact number of Jews in Hungary" (2019, 1). The obstacles to estimating the size of the Jewish population in Europe in general, including Hungary, stem from the fact that in response to a census question regarding religion, many respondents (including Jews) prefer to declare no religion (DellaPergola 2020a). Estimations made in 2019 showed that 47,300 Jews resided in Hungary, which rated the country as the world's thirteenth largest Jewish community (DellaPergola 2020b). Almost all Hungarian Jews (95 percent) are native-born, similar to the total population – 96 percent (Graham 2018).

The majority of contemporary Hungarian society is composed of three main Christian denominations: the Catholic, the Reformed, and the Evangelical Lutheran Church. Fifty-four percent defined themselves as Catholic, 16 percent as Reformed, and three percent as Evangelical Lutheran (Kovács and Forrás-Biró 2011). After 1990, the Hungarian Parliament passed a number of acts regulating individual and collective reparations for persecutions during the Holocaust. Another law, guaranteeing reparations to all religious communities for previously confiscated property, settled the matter of collective reparations for the Jewish community. According to this act, religious communities – including the Jewish community – could reclaim previously confiscated real estate if they wished to use it again. The Hungarian state took responsibility for maintaining more than 1,000 Jewish cemeteries that were not maintained by the community. The Hungarian Jewish Heritage Foundation was established in 2003 to deal with legal issues regarding collective reparations (Kovács 2010).

Through semi-structured interviews, perceptions of Jewish and non-Jewish respondents residing in Budapest were analyzed on micro and macro levels. On the micro-personal level, the focus was on interviewees' feelings of being "at home," namely cultural integration within the Hungarian society and in the structure of social networks. On the macro-level, findings demonstrate interviewees' perceptions regarding the relations between the Jewish community and the non-Jewish majority within the Hungarian society, the centrality of Jews in Budapest as a privileged minority or an integral part of the Hungarian society, versus implicit and explicit antisemitism. It should be noted, however, that the results are based on a small-scale version of participants and thus are not representative of the entire Hungarian population.

Theoretical Concepts

The main theoretical terms are related to socio-cultural integration of Jews in Hungary. The terms ethnic minorities, social networks, transnationalism, and antisemitism will be briefly presented in this section.

Finding a common definition of the concept of minorities is very complex. Nevertheless, until a few years ago, a sort of "soft" consensus on the notion of the minority prevailed in Europe, whereby a minority was described as a group of citizens of a state, constituting a numerical minority and holding a non-dominant position in that state, endowed with ethnic, religious or linguistic characteristics which differ from those of the majority of the population (Plasseraud 2010). Ethnic communities sometimes develop from generations of integrated, former migrants in nation states. Since 1945, "national models" for dealing with cultural differences, emerging in Europe as a result of de-colonization, have evolved along with the arrival of migration waves which led to cultural diversity and the formation of new ethnic communities in many countries. Policies towards these ethnic minorities varied between assimilation of individuals (regardless of their cultural uniqueness) and integration of entire ethnic minorities which maintain their own cultures, languages, and religions. The construction of ethnic minorities and their integration with the majority society depend on the immigrants' characteristics as well as on the attitude of receiving states and societies. Ethnic minorities could be excluded by dominant minorities based on their racial or cultural difference. They can also have collective and communal attitudes and perceptions, based on a common culture, religion, and history. Thus, an ethnic group can be defined as a social construct built both on an assignment to an inferior social position by the dominant minorities and a self-definition centered on the minority's own culture, community, and history. Ethnic minorities vary in their inner strength and vitality, while dominant societies and states differ in exclusion policies towards them. However, ethnic minorities always suffer from some exclusion (Castles et al. 2014).

One of the concepts central to social integration of ethnic minorities within the majority is the social network. Social networks are sets of links based on kinship and ethnic origin (Rebhun and Lev Ari 2010). These networks help ethnic minorities cope with the economic, cultural, and social challenges of their integration. The size of these networks is determined by the number of people in a given group. The members can be loosely or tightly bound to one another. In tightly bound networks, the individual has frequent contacts as well as common identities and activities with the other members. In loosely bound networks, the individual is connected with other people on the basis of a single activity. If all the members of a network are connected to each other, the network is very tightly bound (Avenarius 2012). In some cases, social networks provide minority groups with financial help for housing, information, and help in finding work, social assistance, and emotional support (Avenarius 2012; Koser 2010).

There are three possible social circles of integration into the host culture that help understand the process involved in feeling "at home" in the majority society: the inner circle comprising home (family), the church (religion), and the school (education); secondly, public spaces shared by the majority and ethnic minorities, such as shops and markets; finally, cultural events and traditions that are usually reserved for the majority (Haug et al. 2007). According to the transnational theory, these social ties can be also found in diverse geographic and social spaces (Rebhun and Lev Ari 2010; Lev Ari 2008; Vertovec 2010). The media, the internet and social networks help reduce a sense of alienation and difference (Sheffer 2003).

In an era of living in the global village, cultural and social ties might be anchored in a variety of geographic spaces situated beyond national borders, namely transnational spaces (Lev Ari 2008; Rebhun and Lev Ari 2010; Vertovec 2010). Ethnic minorities might participate in transnational communities. This process has a substantial influence on the patterns of their integration in the majority society and sometimes generates multiple loyalties, split between two or even more countries (Levitt and Glick-Schiller 2004; Rebhun and Lev Ari 2010).

Moreover, these social spaces have more branches and minorities remain in contact with their national group in different places across the globe as well as with the native-born from their ethno-religious group (Levitt and Jaworsky 2007). Ethnic minorities can act simultaneously in different transnational spaces, creating a diverging set of mutual social, economic, cultural, and political ties.

Although most minority groups suffer from one form of discrimination or another, some constitute a "privileged" ethnic minority. In addition to having social and cultural rights in the country in which they live, they enjoy high socio-economic status. One prominent example of a privileged minority group is that of American Jews, who have "become white" over the generations (Brodkin 1998). Jews suffered for decades from discrimination and racism, but following their move to the suburbs – a process that began after World War II – and after improving their level of education, they experienced upward mobility from the working to the middle class, similarly to Poles, Irish, and Italians (Brodkin 1998; Horowitz 2008).

Thus, Jews generally integrate well into the society in which they live from the social, cultural, professional, and economic perspectives, even if they remain a distinct ethno-cultural group. As such, they are particularly vulnerable to attacks from the underprivileged, who direct their resentment towards mainstream society at Jews (Alidadi et al. 2012; Ben-Rafael 2017).

Antisemitism, in the most simplified caption, is a negative perception of Jews. Perceptions of antisemitism imply that some kind of phenomenology exists exterior to those who report about it. Clearly, every person or group of persons tends to report their perceptions of that phenomenology through the lens of their own characteristics, experiences, and, admittedly, biases. Jews' prevalent status as a minority in the society as a whole typically generated parallel positions of Jews versus the hegemonic others in different places (DellaPergola 2020c; Graham 2018). Classic antisemitism is defined as beliefs that Jews are bad by nature and cause disasters to their "host" societies. Furthermore, antisemitic myths accuse Jews of controlling banks and businesses, and incorporate the practice of discrimination against Jews. Recently, "new antisemitism" had been embedded in the political left, the right, and radical Islam. It denies Jews the right to belong to the family of nations (Ben-Rafael 2017).

In the next section, previous research findings regarding socio-cultural integration as well as relations between Jews and the Hungarian majority, including antisemitism, will be presented.

Patterns of Integration Among Jews in Contemporary Hungary: Previous Studies

Historically, Jews favored and were favored by multinational structures that were non-exclusive and culturally non-committal. Clearly, on this account, Jews – as any other sector of European society – shared and were bound to be affected by more general trends emerging, for better or worse. Since the dissolution of the Soviet Union, the European Union has constituted the main area of residence and, hence, an influential frame of reference for Jews in Europe. Under these circumstances, the nature and quality of interactions between Jewish minorities and national majorities within European societies becomes of paramount importance.

The crucial issue is whether or not a tolerant and pluralistic environment can be created across the European continent – within the EU and outside of it – where the various components of national and religious cultures can be recognized as equally legitimate and where minority cultures not defined by a specific territory can obtain the same recognition and legitimacy as the territorially based majorities. Jews in Europe seem to be caught between two opposing challenges: hostility and antisemitism (implicit or explicit) on the part of the majority on the one hand, and acceptance by and assimilation with the society on the other (DellaPergola and Staetsky 2020). Furthermore, each local manifestation of antisemitism should be studied separately on the merits of the particular society and culture within which it occurred (DellaPergola 2020c; see also Graham 2018).

According to a 2018 FRA (Fundamental Rights Agency of the European Union) report, 41 percent of Jews aged 16–34 have considered emigrating from Europe because of antisemitism over the last five years. Antisemitism's role as the main factor encouraging emigration might be enhanced by perceptions regarding governments' responses and efforts to eliminate it, which are considered overwhelmingly inadequate. A most recent report regarding Hungary submitted by the Kantor Center (2020) claims that although the government distances itself from antisemitism, the growing far-right discourse on public platforms includes antisemitic tropes. Antisemitic incidents also include vandalism and verbal attacks (Kantor Center 2020).

The rate of antisemitic attitudes among the adult Hungarian population remained similar between 1995 and 2006. However, after a moderate rise in the following years, a significant growth of antisemitism was observed in 2009. The results indicate that while the proportion of those latent antisemitic sentiments remained nearly constant, blunt instances of antisemitism became significantly more frequent; this increase could reflect radicalization of the previously moderately antisemitic group. A more recent study, which compared data from the 2011 and 2017 surveys, analyzed the relationship between three types of antisemitism: religious, secular, and emotional. The first two represented the cognitive component of antisemitism and were composed of variables measuring one's agreement with different stereotypical statements. In turn, emotional antisemitism refers to the affective component. The results show that only measuring the cognitive components of antisemitism is insufficient and should always be complemented by the measurement of its emotional intensity (Barna and Kovács 2019).

The hypothetical explanatory factor behind the change is the rebirth of the "Christian-national" idea which appeared as a foundational element in the new Hungarian constitution, according to which the Christian culture is the ultimate unifying force of the nation, providing the inner essence and meaning of the state. In this discourse, being Christian is equated with being Hungarian. Self-declared and self-defined Christian religiosity plays the role of a symbolic marker for accepting the national-conservative identity discourse and belonging to the "Christian-national" cultural-political camp, where antisemitic prejudice occurs more frequently than in other segments of society (Barna and Kovács 2019).

Methodology and Participants

The study is based on semi-structured interviews. This method allowed us to explore relations between Jews and non-Jews, as described by the participants themselves, as part of a more comprehensive depiction of their everyday lives (Frankfort-Nachmias and Nachmias 2008). The research tool was an interview guide which included questions regarding the micro and macro levels described in the introduction section.

The interviews were conducted primarily in English, some in Hebrew or in Hungarian, with translation to English. The language proficiency of the participants, particularly in English, varied, but the researcher tried to maintain the original wording as much as possible. The "snowball" (chain-referral) sampling procedure was utilized through contacts of colleagues and friends.

The participants included seven Jewish and four non-Jewish interviewees. In the first group, most were men (five out of seven). Their age range was between 39 and 80 (average age: 55 years). As for their occupations, there were two university professors, a teacher, a computer programmer, two business owners, and a journalist. Six out of seven are native-born – it should be noted that almost all Hungarian Jews are native-born (see also Graham 2018). In addition, four non-Jewish interviewees participated in the study. Three of them are men between the ages of 28 to 64 (average age: 45 years). The group is made up of a PhD student, a lawyer, a pastor (the head of a theological college), and a university professor. All non-Jewish interviewees are native-born. It should be noted that two out of four non-Jewish interviewees have Jewish fathers. However, one of them is a pastor and the other defined himself as "Roman-Catholic." Thus, according to Jewish *Halacha* (religious laws guiding behavior in every aspect of life) and their socialization, they are non-Jewish by definition.

Micro Perceptions

Feeling "at home": "My home is Hungary"

This section will start with an analysis of themes from the Jewish point of view represented by seven interviewees. It seems that their affiliation with Hungary or, for some, Budapest in particular, ranges from strong feelings towards Hungary, through transnational affiliation (particularly with Israel), to total alienation. Their testimonies will be presented in order, along this spectrum, and integrated into a discussion at the end of this section.

K. is the one respondent who seems to be the most attached to Hungary: "My home is Hungary,"[1] he says and elaborates on his strong cultural attachment: "I'm Hungarian, I dream in Hungarian, I count in Hungarian and so on. I know Hungarian literature [...] I know Hungarian history much better than any other history."

J. also perceives Hungary as her home: "My home is Hungary. I feel good here." However, she is ambivalent regarding Hungarians – personally, politically, and culturally: "I don't like them so much [...] because of what they think [...] the politics [...]. At the beginning, we were democrats. Now it is over [...] but I do like many people here, lots of friends, the food [...] here I know how to do business."

The other Jewish interviewees express even more ambivalence regarding their feelings of affiliation with the Hungarian society. Although for G. Budapest is "home" culturally and ideologically, Hungarian people as a whole make him feel uneasy. His words contain an implicit hint of disappointment in them: "I don't really identify with the Hungarian narrative of history and this Hungarian identity. Hungarians mostly regard themselves as victims of others and this is the main narrative [...] but I feel at home in Budapest which is the town of culture and pretty much multi-cultural. It has a strong liberal tradition."

He feels at home in Hungary but mostly refers to Israel as his "second home." He further elaborates: "My son lived there for five years. One of my grandchildren was born there, so she is 'Sabra' [a colloquial term for an Israeli-born person – L.L.]. I am very proud that I have a 'Sabra' grandchild and I love Israel and when I can, I go to Israel."

P. refers to his affiliation with a broader perspective of Hungarian history, as being part of the Austro-Hungarian Empire. He states: "I would hardly say that I'm Hungarian [...]. I'm a Hungarian Jew but it's very important to understand that – not only for me but for most of Hungarian Jews – Hungary refers to when it was

---

[1] Repeated statement expressed by several Jewish participants.

Austria-Hungary [...] My family is partly from Slovakia, partly from Romania, partly from Serbia."

He does feel "at home" in Hungary but also has a transnational connection with Ukraine: "I feel at home here. At the same time, I feel [...] at home in Russia as well as in Ukraine." It seems that P. is not as rooted in Hungarian society as he claims, and reminds of someone with multiple-transnational feelings of affiliation.

S. is even more explicit and states that she does not feel at home in any country, not even in her home town: "[I don't feel at home] anywhere, I am the 'wandering Jew.' I lived in various places, lived in England for four years. In the United States [...] I am here because my family is here and I do not feel good here [...] due to politics [...] I am divorced and cannot move the children [...] I am stuck here [...]. My parents are quite old and I am the only child. This is also part of the thing."

Z., the only immigrant among the interviewees (although from another post-communist country), does not feel at home in Budapest at all: "I do not feel at home at all. No. Because those who are my age, now everybody left. Everybody is integrated in New York, probably. In New York I would feel at home." She elaborates on her antagonism towards Hungary:

> I don't understand them. It's a minefield. It was a big culture shock [...]. I thought that because I know the language it will be very easy to melt in. But then I went to law school and I was marginalized as are immigrants [...]. They have a different temperament: We invite people home immediately, we put food on the table, even if we don't have. It's a very different culture [...]. I respect them, they're very good professionals in many ways, but to make a joke I have to think four times because it could be offensive.

The four non-Jewish interviewees also expressed different feelings with regard to being "at home" in Hungary. They seem to be less ambivalent on this issue, although they are not totally committed. Some refer to particular cities or settlements which for them constitute a "home" in Hungary. Similarly to the analysis of Jewish participants' statements, their perceptions and feelings will be presented in sequence, from the most "rooted" to the one that is most critical.

L. seems to be the most attached to her family house in a small settlement near Budapest: "Feeling home is not just about place. It's also about the people around me. That for me is really important, the location as well. I live in a house with my family now, which was built at the end of the nineteenth century and the builders were my great-grandparents."

P.S. also feels at home in a specific location (Budapest) rather than in Hungary in general: "I feel at home in Budapest, Budapest is my hometown [...] I have strong connections with Budapest, I think, stronger than with Hungary. But I like Hungarian literature and music as well." In addition to that, P.S. feels at home in various other places such as Rome and Vienna, where he used to live for several years.

H. describes several "homes" in Hungary and Israel, referring to his parents' different roots and ethnic origin:

> I feel at home in Budapest, in Hungary. But not everywhere in Hungary. For instance, there is another town in Hungary in which I feel at home – Szeged. Because this was the hometown, not only because my mother was born there, but also one of my favorite people, Emmanuelle, lives there [...] I also feel at home in Israel. Because Israel is a very important place. [...] first time I was there, I was with my father and I remember we were standing at the seashore in Tel Aviv [...] looking at the sea and he told me that this is the only place besides Hungary where he would have been able or would like to live.

I., who is a pastor, describes his relationship with his homeland, Hungary, in the most controversial way: "I don't regret that I was born here, on this soil. I like and love this place and language, although I had several problems with the authorities when I was young."

It seems that for almost all native-born Jewish interviewees, Hungary feels like "home" – emotionally and culturally, although with different intensity and a certain criticism. Political issues and the Hungarian society's transition from a post-communist, relatively liberal community to a more right-wing one constitutes the basis for criticism and even disappointment, as do some cultural norms. However, two interviewees do not feel at home in Hungary: one of them is an immigrant and the other feels "stuck" there and would prefer to emigrate. Most of them also perceive Israel as a second, or equivalent, home and a few have transnational affiliation with other countries.

All non-Jewish interviewees feel very much at home in their home towns in Hungary (for some of them it is not Budapest). The connections with their Hungarian roots are more prevalent than among the Jewish participants. This is obvious given the "majority versus minority" history in Hungary, which uprooted many Jews from the countryside. However, some of the interviewees also expressed transnational affiliation with other countries. In addition, two of them who had Jewish fathers expressed strong attachment to Israel as well. One of them even expressed critical attitudes towards Hungary, although he did not specify the reasons.

Although this study is qualitative and thus not representative of the entire Hungarian population, it seems that the two groups of interviewees, both Jews and non-Jews, feel at home in Hungary and are attached to its culture and history. In addition, non-Jews seem to be more "rooted" in the country. However, there are other countries which "feel like home"; some Jewish and non-Jewish interviewees are somewhat critical towards some of its policies, although it was not always expressed explicitly and in a detailed manner.

Social Integration

Social integration, which will be presented in this section, focuses on the structure of the participants' social networks: within their own ethnic group, with the majority society or transnational ones.

Let us start with the Jewish interviewees. G., who is a secular Jew, states that he has mostly Jewish friends: "I am obviously a child of Holocaust survivors and my friends and my acquaintances are mostly Jewish; [they] come from the same background." By "the same background," G. means that his friends share the same idealistic values and political attitudes which go against Orban's right-wing regime: "Here in Budapest, we are sharply divided with my own Jewish friends who are mostly liberal, democratic, anti Orbán regime." K.'s network is mainly Jewish as well, based on his community and work as a Chabad emissary: "Although I live in Hungary, almost all my friends are Jewish, I work with Jews, I deal with Jews. Thank God, many Jews live in Budapest, so it's easy to find Jewish friends." S. also has mainly Jewish friends who she knows from "high school, with whom [she] was brought up and later – from the university."

J. describes her social life in a positive way and claims she has plenty of friends, both Jewish and non-Jewish, adding: "even my husband is not Jewish." A. reports having many non-Jewish friends, although he is very affiliated with the Neolog community. Since his time at school and university came during the communist era, no one knew who belonged to any religion:

> When I was a student in high school or at the university, it was the communist regime and this regime was against all religions [...] So, in my class there were 30 students and we never talked about religion. [...] Ten years after graduation, we met after the regime change, and we realized there that 'you are Jewish' [...]. So that's why I have a lot of friends who are not Jews and I have some friends who are Jews.

P. describes mainly professional, transnational social networks. From his words, it seems that he does not have what he calls "private" friends in either country: "So my friends are not [...] private friends but professional friends [...]. I don't have nonprofessional friends here. I have a lot of professional friends in Russia."

When asked about her best friends, Z. says she has primarily transnational networks and seems to have no Hungarian friends at all: "All my friends are from abroad. Armenia – my best friend, she's from Armenia, from Romania, from the US. I have one girl who's converted to Judaism who's Hungarian... I have colleagues with whom I get along very well [...]. I don't have any non-Jewish Hungarian friends. [...] I live here, I speak the language but no, I can't even recall one single person."

From the non-Jewish point of view, when asked about having Jewish friends, L. answered in a sarcastic manner. She jokingly referred to Jewish friends as part of a bizarre collection. Most of her friends, however, are not Jewish: "[...] of course: Lesbian Jewish friends, the best part. (Laughing) Yes. Yes. I collect them, sometimes, as I collect stamps, I collect this kind of people (laughing). No, this is just a joke, yeah, I have Jewish friends [...] Most of my friends are non-Jewish, mainly Christian Lutheran."

P.S. describes his social network as consisting of Hungarian friends, but also as transnational, since his community is an international one: "My best friends are in Hungary and in Italy. And I have friends... because of the community, which is highly international. I have very good friends in other European countries, some of them even in Africa, but most of them are in Europe."

P. S. does not have Jewish friends, although it is important to him: "It would be important for me to have Jewish friends. Among my closest friends there are none, but it's not because I am... I'm not open to them."

I., who is a pastor, initially claimed he did not have many friends, but he did not specify whether they were Jewish or not. While describing his Jewish Israeli friends, he started to recall a few: "I don't have many friends, but I have a few very good friends. For example, one is a lady who lives in Tel Aviv, she's a journalist [...]. There is another person and she comes to Hungary every August and September, there is also another teacher, a university professor."

Later, he adds: "I have lots of good friends in the Jewish community."

H. definitely prefers Jewish friends. Although he defined himself as non-Jewish, it seems that his Jewish identity is very strong, probably due to having a Jewish father who H. mentions throughout the interview: "I feel more comfortable with Jewish people. If there are two people, one of whom is not Jewish and one that is Jewish, and they are equal in all other terms, I would choose the Jewish."

Some Jewish interviewees, both secular and religious, describe social networks which are ethnic-based in their structure and constitute a kind of community with which they work and share similar values and attitudes. Others have mixed social networks – Jewish and non-Jewish – along with transnational connections. Only one Jewish interviewee seems to have no friends in Hungary and only transnational networks. One possible explanation for that might be that she is the only immigrant in the group. As for the non-Jewish respondents, they represent a spectrum: from having no Jewish friends to preferring Jews over non-Jews.

Macro Perceptions

Relations between Jews and Non-Jews – Hungary and Antisemitism: "They Smile at You but Behind Your Back, They Hate You"

When the seven Jewish interviewees were asked to describe relations between Jews and the majority society, they seemed to have different opinions. While those who are more religious expressed a rather idealized picture, those who are relatively secular and assimilated offered undeniably critical reflections. They also pointed to recent manifestations of antisemitism.

K., a religious Chabad member, has the most positive perception regarding relations between Jews and non-Jews in contemporary Hungary. He seems to believe that being Jewish in contemporary Budapest is particularly safe: "We can live a safe religious life in Hungary, nowadays. It's easy. [...]. I believe the safest place for living a Jewish life in Europe is Hungary today, there's no safer place in Europe than Hungary." He reiterates that point throughout the interview and elaborates: "You don't need to hide anything [...], so you can eat in a Kosher restaurant, [...] you can wear outside the Tzitzit, and the Kippah, so it's easy, as it was in New York, 30 years ago."

K. perceives antisemitism in Hungary as a result of the demise of the communist regime and the emergence of liberalism that followed it: "In the 90s, when the communist era collapsed, many political ideals have come up from ground zero, even the antisemitic [...], it's just freedom of speech and freedom of basic rights in a free country, can speak [about] everything, and antisemitism appeared immediately."

G. also thinks that after the fall of the communist regime things changed for the worse for Jews in Hungary: "After the Hungarian political system converted to the democratic way [...], antisemitism started immediately. Just like in other post-communist countries; this was a shock for Hungarian Jews."

Furthermore, K. emphasizes that Hungary actually had the largest number of Jewish survivors, compared with other European countries: "So this is why it hurts, the highest proportion of survivors came back to Hungary and started a new life, more than in any other country, for example: [..] The Jewish community in Poland disappeared." As a person in charge of an organization which combats antisemitism, K. is aware of data and facts on this phenomenon: "It didn't change in the last 20 years, whatever government came and went, one third of Hungarian society believes that antisemitic stereotypes are true." However, K. describes recent legislation against antisemitism: "They just try to use this rule against people who just shout antisemitic speeches, and since community dignity has been protected by law in Hungary in the last eight years, so, if someone breaks this law, he has to pay some fine."

Regarding Holocaust denial, K. says it is also forbidden by Hungarian law: "if someone says the Holocaust was not a real thing, he is punished immediately by the jury's decision."

A. who is also a religious person, expresses similar opinions to K. when it comes to Jews in Hungary. He describes them as an integral part of the country's social fabric: "Hungarian Jews are very integrated in Hungarian society, very integrated in Hungarian culture [...]. We have been here for 200 years and we have a lot of interfaces with non-Jews." Similarly to K., he perceives governmental actions against antisemitism as very efficient and firm: "[...] Antisemitic attacks, verbal attacks, are fewer and fewer every year."

G. emphasizes that most Hungarian Jews perceive themselves as part of the majority in an extreme manner which is sometimes expressed by denying their Judaism: "The majority of Hungarian Jews regard themselves as Hungarian. Liberal Hungarians. They would even reject your suggestion that they are Jewish [...] they may say that they have Jewish ancestors [...]."

S. describes Hungarian Jews in similar terms: "The majority of Jews belong to this group; they are liberal, highly educated, multi-lingual and multi-cultural."

J., who is secular, also claims that life in Hungary is easy for Jews, but compared to K. and A., she is more aware of latent antisemitism, particularly outside of Budapest: "I think that being Jewish in Budapest is easy. It happens that I hear how they speak about Jews. I hear my employees who work in my restaurant saying that Jews are thieves, it happens. Outside of Budapest, in the villages, I think it is difficult [for Jews]. In the big cities, there is no problem."

When asked directly about recent developments, J. admits there have been some incidents involving antisemitism, racism, and homophobia and refers to Hungarians' actions during WWII:

> They [the Hungarians – L.L.] do not like Jews, gypsies, immigrants... blacks, homosexuals. This is Hungary [...]. They are not ready to take responsibility. People still say: 'Enough with the Holocaust, I did not do it, what do I care?' But Hungarians helped. The Nazis had nothing to do, just to sit like that (she demonstrates sitting on a couch). If today anything would happen, I think it would be the same situation.

P. perceives the attitudes towards the Holocaust in a different way than J. He says Hungarian and secular-assimilated Jews share the same attitudes in this regard: "So, the average Hungarian believes that they have suffered as much as Jews did, and there is a big philosophical debate whether the Holocaust is part of Hungarian history or not. The assimilated Hungarian Jews naturally say it is part of Hungarian history, it is a tragedy for Hungarians as for the Jews."

However, P. briefly summarizes the situation by claiming: "There is antisemitism, there's no question, a lot. But even the strongest antisemite knows that it's forbidden to be antisemitic."

G. elaborates on his criticism towards the Hungarian government and its attitude towards the Holocaust as well as the responsibility of Hungarians in that context. This narrative appears in several of the interviews done for the purpose of this study, but G's attitude is the bluntest: "The Hungarian nationalistic government must have a new interpretation of the Holocaust which is that the Nazis are guilty and not the Hungarians [...] Hungary was an innocent angel, a victim of the Nazis. But Jews reject this message because Hungarians were deeply involved. So, Hungarian Jews are very suspicious of this new Holocaust memorial institution, memorial museum."

Z. describes contemporary antisemitism in Hungary. Even at her university, she senses antisemitic sentiments, even though there are no manifestations of the Boycott, Divestment, Sanctions (BDS) movement ("I did not meet here BDS. No"). She contrasts it with the situation when she came to Budapest: "Ten or fifteen years ago, antisemitism was only in the margins. Now we obviously see that it's in the center, now we feel it. So, even in my university, on every single social ladder, we understand that it's not an advantage to be Jewish [...]. When I came here, it was cool to be Jewish, it was sexy to be Jewish, it was the Jewish Renaissance idea."

Z. goes on to describe the acceleration of xenophobia since the beginning of the refugee crisis in Europe, which also contributed to the rise of antisemitism in Hungary: "Diversity was cool and then suddenly, when nationalism became stronger after 2010 and, especially, after 2015, when the so-called refugee crisis started, [the situation] raised hatred and [being a Jew] became more than an offensive identity and Jews were kind of stuck together and again they turned to each other."

Jewish participants voice complex perceptions of relations between Jews and non-Jews as well as current antisemitism. On the one hand, there are those who emphasize the feeling of safety as a Jew in Hungary and claim that Jews are well integrated into Hungarian society. On the other hand, all of them acknowledge the existence of both overt and implicit antisemitism, although each of the interviewees attaches different importance to it. Some claim that contemporary antisemitism in Hungary emerged after the post-communist era, as a result of liberalism which has recently turned into xenophobia of all kinds, including antisemitism. Others said that Hungary is and has been an antisemitic society for decades, but has recently expressed it in more implicit ways due to the firm government policy designed to combat antisemitism. The issue of Hungarians' responsibility for the Holocaust divides the interviewees into two groups: one claims that it is unforgivable, while the other seems to be more tolerant and attributes this denial to the Hungarians' constant self-imaging as perennial victims.

Perceptions regarding minority-majority relations in contemporary Hungary also differ according to religious versus secular affiliation. Those who are more secular tend to observe nuances of undercurrents of hate and antisemitism – despite the overt, positive, and allegedly inclusive policy of the government. Another point of view, expressed particularly by the more religious interviewees, is to acknowledge existing antisemitism, but focus on the "bright side" of current policy towards Jews and their successful integration into Hungarian majority. In the next section, non-Jewish perceptions regarding Jews in Hungary will be discussed.

Relations and Antisemitism in Contemporary Hungary: Non-Jewish Perceptions

Non-Jewish interviewees shared their personal experience and views regarding antisemitism. L. distinguishes between several groups of Hungarian Jews according to their visibility and also tries to connect that division with antisemitism: "Because if I am a non-Jewish person [...], it's easy to realize that they [Chabad] are Jews because of the hat, because of the hairstyle, the clothes, so they are visible. Actually, it's a form of antisemitism. I can believe that I am not antisemitic [...]. But with Neolog Jews it's more complicated because they are like you or me; they are not visible and they are always complaining, always [...]."

She elaborates on the description she gave and its connection with antisemitism in terms of "them" versus "us": "Antisemitism starts with thinking that they are different [...]. Because of the appearance or religious habits, but essentially they are different from us."

P. S. describes the atmosphere in his family of origin as antisemitic: "My grandfather was probably more antisemitic than my father was. My father occasionally spoke negatively about Jews, so did my mother [...] on the personal level, she had friends and she liked them, her Jewish colleagues." Although most of his family was antisemitic, P.S. himself claims he has not been. He attributes this to his religiosity as well as two socialization agents: his grandmother, who was religious, and his priest:

> As For me, I was never antisemitic because my grandmother was very religious, [...] the most Catholic person in the family. Interestingly, or maybe not, [...] she was not antisemitic [...]. It was forbidden to organize religious classes at public schools. The old priest who was there was following the Church's teachings which meant that antisemitism is bad [...]. He spoke with respect about Islam and about Judaism as well.

Although H. perceives contemporary Hungary as generally not antisemitic, he seems to be concerned about an extreme right-wing party, which he refers to as "Nazis":

> In Hungary, I think people are generally not interested in knowing who is Jewish and who is not. People usually don't know it. [...] There is, however, a political party in Hungary which is quite strong now, [...] which is far-right. [...] Its name is 'Jobbik,' an interesting name because it means right, it also means good. They are Nazis, but their popularity is not because they are Nazis but because they say the same things the communists said a long time ago and people like to hear: Ok, we'll raise the pensions, the salaries and so on. [...] This right-wing government is very much against this far right-wing movement and they [the extremists – L.L.] are very much depressed and repressed.

Contrary to others, pastor I. perceives Hungarian society as having been antisemitic for decades and even blames it for not doing enough to protect the Jews. It should be noted that I. had a Jewish father and part of his family died in the Holocaust: "We were not brave enough to defend our Jewish fellow countrymen. In my opinion, the truth is that we exploited, robbed, and killed them [...]. In Hungarian society there is quite a strong latent antisemitism which almost all political groups applied and were involved in. Even communists."

Some non-Jewish interviewees are aware of antisemitism; one of them was exposed to it as a child but is determined to fight it as an adult. Another interviewee was sensitive to antisemitism, but while her words and description of the Jewish community in Budapest implied the presence of antisemitic attitudes, she signaled no intention to fight them. Another one argues that although, on the surface, antisemitism is not an issue, its rise comes as the impact of the far-right which, for the moment, is under the control of the government. Only one of the interviewees criticizes Hungarian people as having been antisemitic for a long time and goes as far as blaming them for not doing enough to protect the Jews. He is half-Jewish and mentioned that his father was a Holocaust survivor.

The non-Jewish interviewees perceive antisemitism in a different manner than Jewish participants. While the former group seems to notice some antisemitic sentiments, the latter is more aware of their actual manifestations. Both are concerned with the problem or try to initiate a change through Christian-Jewish religious avenues, so as to address this phenomenon.

When asked about their personal motivation to be engaged with the Jewish community, L. is particularly interested in her home town's geographical area with regard to past relations between Jews and non-Jews. This inquiry is part of her academic interest as well: "The story of my family is part of the history of Hungary [...] I try to understand the representation of Jewish and non-Jewish communities [...], the economic and social connection between these groups in small cities in the countryside." In addition to her academic interest in Jewish lives in the past, she also mentions some distant Jewish roots which affect her in this regard: "Grandfather on my father's side was born in 1941 [...]. [He] was a Jew and his father's family was Jewish, but his mother was Christian [...]. When I heard about my Jewish roots, I was 13 years old [...]. Unfortunately, this line of my family tree is dead. Nobody is religious either, nobody is interested in Jewish roots except me."

P.S.'s personal interest in Jewish issues began in his childhood. He was about ten years old when he first encountered the subject of Jewish history and the Shoah. It was uncommon in Hungary to talk about it. He describes an incident which seems to have left a great impression on him:

> I was a child when I first heard about antisemitism, when I first [heard] about the Shoah, although it was suppressed. You know [...] people would not talk about it openly because the regime was not interested in it. I first came across this when I was, I think [...], ten or eleven years old. I was in class [...] and there were two boys in the class. One of them was of gypsy origin, the other was Jewish. They were both Catholic, but the father of the Jewish boy was a Jew. The half-Jewish boy insulted the gypsy boy for being gypsy, whereas the gypsy boy insulted him for being Jewish [...] The other boys at school were not kind to them. So it's not a kind thing to say to someone 'you are Jewish' or 'you are gypsy.' That was my first experience.

It seems that P.S. not only has pluralistic attitudes, but has also confronted antisemitic sentiments in his family of origin: "I sensed that there was antisemitism present among Catholics and Christians, but I never liked it, you know. I would not combat it at the time, but I didn't like it and I even contradicted my parents when they spoke badly about the Jews."

Pastor I. describes his engagement with the Jewish community due to his Jewish roots and the Holocaust, which affected his family as well: "I'm involved personally in the matter because my father was of Jewish origin and I'm also involved personally in the Holocaust because there are victims in my family."

The non-Jewish interviewees express different motives that urged them to be involved or interested in Jewish communities. While one of them has academic interest in Jewish history in her home town and very remote Jewish roots, the pastor declared that his interest stemmed from his Jewish origins and the Holocaust tragedy. Only one person from the non-Jewish group has no Jewish roots – in fact, he heard antisemitic sentiments expressed by his family and has felt compelled to stand up to antisemitism as part of his Christian values. He is not only interested in Jews per se, but in the well-being of minorities in general.

Summary

The purpose of this chapter is to answer the question of whether Jews in Hungary, particularly in Budapest, feel "at home" and integrated into the Hungarian society, or rather as a privileged minority. This subject, analyzed from the micro perspective, was accompanied by a macro point of view on minority-majority relations as well as implicit and explicit antisemitism, as perceived by Jewish and non-Jewish leaders and community activists.

The main findings of the study indicate that for almost all Jewish interviewees who are native-born, Hungary feels like "home" – "My home is Hungary," most of them said. They feel strongly attached to its history and consider themselves integral parts of its culture and language, albeit their feelings vary in intensity. Furthermore, being socialized during the communist era, most of them were brought up as non-affiliates, or secular Hungarians, who did not have to identify as Jews. Thus, they can be characterized as an integrated or even assimilated ethnic group.

However, two interviewees do not feel at home in Hungary; whereas one of them is an immigrant, the other – although native-born – has transnational affiliations. As such, they can be defined as being more segregated from the Hungarian society. None of the interviewees, however, expressed perceptions or feelings of being a marginal ethnic group in Hungary.

In comparison, the non-Jewish interviewees are more rooted in Hungary and as members of the majority; they are of course part of Hungarian culture and history. However, two interviewees had Jewish fathers and although they define themselves and were brought up as Christians (one of them is a pastor), they express either transnational affiliations or more critical attitudes towards Hungarian people and culture.

Looking at their social networks, the Jewish interviewees have a mixture of friends: some have exclusively Jewish acquaintances, regardless of their religious affiliation, some have a mixture of Jewish and non-Jewish Hungarian friends, while others prefer transnational social networks. As for the non-Jewish interviewees, the same pattern emerges: some have no Jewish friends, either by choice or due to an absence of Jews in their lives, whereas others have a few, perhaps even preferring Jewish over non-Jewish friends (the latter respondent is specifically a half-Jew).

As for antisemitism, it seems that the Holocaust plays an important part in its contemporary perceptions. It is a shadow that lurks over and emerges in most interviews. Some interviewees, both Jewish and non-Jewish, point to hidden but also overt manifestations of antisemitism which they perceive as being almost inherent to the Hungarian majority.

However, these perceptions vary particularly depending on the interviewee's level of religiosity. The more secular Jews perceive contemporary Budapest in a more critical way, although they admit that life in that city allows Jews to integrate with the majority society, at least allegedly. They sense an acceleration of antisemitism, albeit in forms that are not always overt. A possible explanation to these findings, which originate in some interviewees' words, is that those who are more religious are less critical regarding the government since they receive its support in building their own religious institutions and services. The Neologs or secular interviewees, on the other hand, seem to be more pluralistic in their attitudes and thus might expect to feel more genuinely included than in the past. However, the more religious interviewees seem to acknowledge the existence of antisemitism in Hungary as a fact, but they prefer to regard the firm actions of the current government against it as efficient and consider the integration of Jews to be extremely successful.

Non-Jewish interviewees also refer to relations between Jews and non-Jews, seeing the Holocaust as central to these relations. They believe Christian-Jewish religious organizations are bases for what they perceive as good relationships and cooperation. Antisemitism seems to be acknowledged by all of them, but in a subtler way compared to Jewish interviewees – they deem it hardly present today and note the government's firm stance against it. With one exception, all interviewees seem to be very careful with regard to the criticism of the current cabinet and the instances of antisemitism in Hungary throughout and after WWII. However, it should be noted that the non-Jewish interviewees were selected for this study due to their involvement and interest in the topic, whether academic or moral, or due to Jewish roots. Therefore, it could be expected they might have different and more positive attitudes compared to other Hungarians.

Although both Jews and non-Jews perceive Jews as a well-integrated ethnic group, it seems that the "glorious days" of Jews' impact on daily life in Budapest belong to the past. The non-Jewish interviewees perceive the primary Jewish contribution to Hungary in the cultural component, except for one who considers Jews an essential part of the city. If, hypothetically, one day Jews leave Budapest, it will "collapse," he claims. It seems those among the participants who are half-Jews voice more concerns in this regard, although they are both Christians and one of them is a pastor.

Conclusions

This qualitative study is a case-study which is limited in its results. However, the findings presented here imply that Jews in contemporary Hungary are well integrated in various fabrics of Budapest; most of them feel "at home" there and integral parts of Hungary, at least in the micro perspectives. However, some are aware of undercurrents of old and new antisemitism at the macro level – sentiments which affect Hungarian Jews' sense of integration and affiliation. At the same time, it seems Jews have never before been protected by the government to such an extent, particularly compared to other contemporary European countries. Still, the degree of legal safeguards emphasizes their vulnerability as an ethnic group, as one of the Jewish (S.) interviewees bluntly summarizes: "We think it's not the Hungarians who have to protect the Jews because we are also Hungarians. For us, it's exclusion to give that specific statement; [it] means exclusion."

These explicit and implicit streams, acknowledged by Jewish interviewees in particular (and some non-Jewish ones as well), might redefine Hungarian Jews (especially those living in Budapest) as a privileged minority rather than equal members of the majority – a status most of them have been striving to achieve for decades.

Future studies on a larger sample and utilizing quantitative methodology will increase our understanding of relations between Jews and non-Jews in contemporary Hungary. These further efforts, combined with findings from the study presented here, can serve as examples of majority-minority dynamics and suggest possible trajectories for better integration of minorities in contemporary Central Europe.

Olaf Glöckner
New Relations in the Making? Jews and Non-Jews in Germany Reflect on Shoah Memory, Unexpected Growing Jewish Pluralism, Israel, and New Antisemitism

The Nazi dictatorship from 1933 to 1945, World War II, and the Shoah ended the possibility of a German-Jewish symbiosis. For a long period of time after the war, a continuing Jewish community in Germany was deemed either utopian or undesirable. However, with the influx of a certain number of former Soviet Jews during the 1990s, who preferred immigrating to Central Europe as opposed to Israel or the United States, the situation changed considerably.

The current number of registered Jewish community members – about 90,000[1] – still makes up only one fifth of the Jewish population in Germany prior to 1933. Nevertheless, steady growth of the Jewish population during the 1990s and in the early 2000s has made space for a new Jewish pluralism, ranging from the emergence of Chassidic centres (Chabad Lubavitch) in some larger cities, the return of the Masorti movement, and Union of progressive Jews in Germany (a new liberal umbrella organization) to Ohel ha Chidusch, the German branch of the worldwide movement, Jewish Renewal, and several centers and schools of the Ronald S. Lauder Foundation. Vibrant cultural and educational centres, museums, galleries and restaurants, especially in metropolitan cities like Berlin, Frankfurt, and Munich, also sprang up in this period (Ben-Rafael, Sternberg, and Glöckner 2011).

For the time being, the question of a Jewish future in Germany has become irrelevant: from a demographic point of view, the Jewish community in the Federal Republic of Germany (FRG) has become the third strongest, after France and the United Kingdom. The German Jewish community is considered an important factor of today's European Jewish diaspora. While Jewish emigration from the former USSR states has virtually come to an end, another surprise followed in the early 2000s with the influx of mostly young Israelis. At least 11,000 Israelis currently hold permanent residency in Berlin, the capital of Germany (Kranz 2015), while others live and work in metropolitan cities like Munich and Frankfurt.

---

[1] Member Statistics of the Jewish Communities, Centrale Welfare Board of the Jews in Germany (2021), 5, accessed May 18, 2023, https://zwst.org/sites/default/files/2022-07/ZWST-Mitgliederstatistik-2021-Langversion-RZ-web.pdf.

∂ Open Access. © 2023 the author(s), published by De Gruyter. [(cc) BY-NC-ND] This work is licensed under the Creative Commons Attribution-NonCommercial-NoDerivatives 4.0 International License.
https://doi.org/10.1515/9783110783216-008

Most German political elites, authorities, intellectuals, and civic forces (like the churches) have welcomed the influx of Russian Soviet Jews from the 1990s and the substantial growth of the Jewish community. Some media reports have even described "a new love" between Jews and non-Jews in Germany. Yet life for the current Jewish community is not entirely carefree, as troubling trends have arisen: problems in demographic structure (aging), ongoing secularization in younger age cohorts, and – as a rather new problem – uncertainties caused by several violent attacks on Jewish institutions and persons (for example in Berlin, Halle, and Hamburg).

Our narrative and expert interviews with Jewish and non-Jewish key figures in public and political life mainly focussed on the question of to what extent have Jewish-non Jewish relations changed, compared to the discord prior to 1933, and the general reservation and uncertainty after 1945? We also raised other key questions like: to what extent do Jews in Germany feel integrated into today's non-Jewish majority society? What do they consider core elements of their Jewish identities? What is the meaning of Israel in their lives as Jews? How do they cope with new trends of antisemitism in Germany? As a complementary question, we wanted to know from our non-Jewish interviewees how different they consider Jewish/non-Jewish relations today? To what extent does Shoah memory (still) affect these relations? How do Jews and non-Jews cooperate in social activities, and are there new, joint strategies to combat antisemitism?

Our interviews revealed that Jews in present-day Germany do not romanticize their lives in the country of the former Nazi regime. However, they appreciate efforts by the state to promote future Jewish life, to carry out dignified politics of commemoration, and to ensure security. Antisemitism is perceived as a societal problem but not as an existential threat. None of the Jewish interview partners considered Germany as a place that is too dangerous for Jews. Memory of the Shoah is considered important, but building a Jewish future, especially for one's own children, is the more relevant issue.

A key finding of our interviews in Germany is that a new generation of young Jews has grown up neither justifying living in the "country of the offenders" nor considering themselves representatives of the State of Israel. Young Jews in Germany run their own multifaceted networks, understanding themselves as Jews but to a similar extent also as Germans. Some of them enjoy participation in public and political life, deliberately acting in both roles.

For some Jews in Germany, Israel remains an important element of Jewish identity but not the most important one.[2] While making "Aliyah" (moving to the

---

[2] It is worth noting that there has never been a large number of Jewish emigrants from Germany

land of Israel) is not typically considered an option, developments in Israel are followed closely. Among the Jewish interviewees, there was criticism of certain German media and political forces that (seemingly) try to profit from sharply criticizing Israel and Israeli politics. Our Jewish interview partners very much enjoyed an increase in interfaith and inter-cultural activities, seen as a valuable means to erase mutual stereotypes and the fear of close contact. We had two subgroups in the sample: first, Jewish theologians and artists; second was our non-Jewish interviewees, all of whom had individual experiences and ties to Israel through partnerships, political activities (from several political spectrums) or theological (mainly Christian) interest – three of them mentioned it explicitly. One could even presume that half of the interviewees were motivated by a threefold interest: being in contact with Jews/Jewish institutions in Germany with an interest in civic cooperation; being in contact with Israel as a modern Jewish centre and close ally of Germany, in political and cultural life; and finally being interested in close exchanges between Christians and Jews as an opportunity for mutual learning.

However, in one of the interviews with non-Jews, the approach was completely different. A young, left-wing politician from the former East Germany (GDR) came into contact with Holocaust survivors and then gained interest in Israel as a place of refuge for German Jews. Our non-Jewish interview partners were also sensitized to new trends of antisemitism and the assumed vulnerability of Jewish communities and individuals in the country. All of them were either actively involved in practical initiatives to combat antisemitism or they supported educational and/ or political initiatives attempting to bring Israel closer to a wider public.

It became obvious in our case study that interrelations between Jews and non-Jews in today's Germany are much more complex than decades ago, and there are reasons for this on both sides. The "Jewish landscape" in Germany has become much more diverse, as outlined above. Non-Jewish stakeholders have become much more experienced with Jewish history and current Jewish life, and have more contact with Jews than previous generations. Younger non-Jews also tend to be open-minded enough to have dialogues where mutual, amicable critique is not only possible but desired.

There seems to be, in fact, a new quality of reciprocity, mutual exchange, and agreement as to what is possible together – and what is not.

---

to Israel (Olim Chadaschim) with the exception of the early years after the proclamation of the State of Israel. See: Anthony Kauders, *Unmögliche Heimat. Eine deutsch-jüdische Geschichte der Bundesrepublik* (München, 2007).

A Short Historical Review

The roots of Jewish life in Germany date back to the fourth century, when the first Jewish settlements and communities where formed in the Rhine Valley. As in other parts of Central Europe today, despite ongoing Christianization, the Jewish minority was permitted to openly practice its religion. Relations between Christians and Jews were relatively peaceful until the eleventh century. However, during the Reformation and on the eve of the Crusade, the Jewish population in the Rhine Valley experienced its first pogrom traumas. Crusader armies, before leaving for the Middle East and Palestine, killed hundreds of Jews and destroyed their property – acts of violence that were periodically repeated across medieval times and were called into question only at the beginning of European Enlightenment and the emergence of modernity.

Despite the fact that the legal emancipation of Jews in Germany happened almost 100 years later than in France (1791), German Jewry underwent an extremely dynamic and hopeful process of inner modernization and, allegedly, successful integration into German mainstream society. At the beginning of the twentieth century and even in the interwar period, Germany had become an important country of destination for Jews from Eastern Europe – especially Russia and Poland. At the same time, German Jews who numbered in the hundreds of thousands became very successful entrepreneurs, bankers, scientists (Nobel laureates among them), artists, publicists, intellectuals, and academic theorists. Germany Jewry was widely present in metropolitan towns, especially in Berlin, but also in rural areas, where they became established, for example, in cattle trade and winegrowing.

In general, German Jews had long been very optimistic that social acceptance and integration in daily life would improve in the long run. Affiliations to the growing Zionist movement (especially in Eastern Europe) were mere exceptions among the half million Jews living in Germany by the end of the 1920s and the beginning of the 1930s.

The Nazis' rise to power in 1933 caused a paralyzing shock for German Jews who were convinced that the process of social integration had already become irreversible. Now Hitler and his allies proved, step by step, that a turning back of Jewish emancipation was indeed possible. Around 300,000 of the approximately 500,000 Jews living in Germany before 1933 managed to flee, but around 165,000 were deported to death camps in Eastern Europe during World War II and eventually killed there. At the end of World War II, only circa 18,000 Jewish people had survived the Holocaust on Germany territory, either because of a non-Jewish spouse, which offered some protection, or having lived in hiding, with the help of non-Jewish Germans. At the end of 1945, the last German Chief rabbi, Leo

Baeck, declared from his exile in the United Kingdom that "the era of German Jewry has ended once and forever."

New Beginning(s) after the Shoah

The re-establishment of local Jewish communities in several cities, which began a few weeks after May 8, 1945 (the date of capitulation of Nazi Germany), was considered a transitional phenomenon. In 1948, the World Jewish Congress called on all remaining German Jews to leave the "blood-soaked German soil." Jewish life in Germany remained outlawed for about 20 years, and the Jewish communities in Germany remained more or less isolated from the rest of the Jewish world – not only from Israel but also from other countries in the Jewish diaspora until the middle of the 1960s.

Still, a certain number of Jews decided otherwise. Despite all predictions, some of the local Jewish communities survived and stabilized their membership numbers, though on a very small scale. Finally, in 1950, a Central Council of Jews in Germany resumed its work.

From that time, the number of registered Jewish community members in Germany remained more or less the same – around 30,000 – until the 1980s. Fatalities and loss of personal belongings could be compensated by re-entry to Germany, firstly by Jewish immigrants from Eastern European states that had fled communist dictatorships (i.e. Poland and Hungary). However, during the 1970s and early 1980s it became clear that the demographic collapse of most of the existing Jewish communities would be inescapable. Hitler, observers stated while shaking their heads, would celebrate "a late victory." Germany would become, in the long run, "judenfrei" ("free of Jews").

But history changes its path, and sometimes takes surprising turns. At the end of the 1980s, very few observers expected the quick downfalls of the Berlin Wall and the Iron Curtain and the fast collapse of all the socialist regimes in the Eastern Bloc, including the Soviet Union, which finally dissolved in December 1991.

Israel and the American Jewish communities had fought for decades for the release of Soviet Jews who were hindered in leaving their countries of origin and known as "prisoners of Zion." By the late 1980s it became clear that the overwhelming majority of Soviet Jews intended to leave the country as soon as the borders opened – and they did. From the estimated two million Soviet Jews (recorded in a census in 1988), more than one million immigrated to Israel during the 1990s;

ca. 350,000 immigrated to the United States. The big surprise was that more than 200,000 Soviet Jews decided to immigrate to Germany.[3]

Revival of Jewish Community Life Caused by Immigrants From the Former Soviet Union

For complex reasons, not all of the immigrants joined the local Jewish communities but, ultimately, the number of registered Jewish community members increased from circa 30,000 to more than 100,000. In other words, the post-Soviet Jewish influx saved the very small Jewish communities in East Germany (former GDR) and also created opportunities for new, organic community building. Since the late 1990s, a few dozen new synagogues and community centres have been built across the country. Jewish kindergartens and new Jewish schools have been opened, even in East Germany. The Jewish cultural scene experienced a renaissance. In the 1990s, a discussion started about whether the model of the "Einheitsgemeinde" ("united community") was still necessary and appropriate. This discussion continues today, but a process of differentiation had already began in the late 1990s.

Jews in Berlin: Structure and Specifics After 1945/89

Berlin had the biggest Jewish community in Germany before 1933, and it was the case again after World War II and the Shoah. However, the figures are not really comparable. Some 160,000 Jews considered Berlin their home before 1933, which made up about one third of the overall Jewish population in Germany. Only about 6,000–8,000 Berlin Jews survived the Holocaust inside the city, and about 2,000 Jewish Berliners returned home after the end of World War II and the capitulation of the Nazi regime.

The Berlin Jewish community, once a bastion of liberal/Reform Judaism, counted only small groups of liberal Jews during the post-War decades. As in other cities in post-War Germany, a considerable number of Polish Jews, most of them from

---

3 See: O. Glöckner, "Immigrated Russian Jewish Elites in Israel and Germany after 1989," accessed January 10, 2022, https://publishup.uni-potsdam.de/opus4-ubp/frontdoor/deliver/index/docId/4804/file/gloeckner_diss.pdf).

dissolved displaced person camps, became part of the synagogue congregation, and most of them were accustomed to Orthodox rites and practices.

Even during intensified periods of the Cold War, the Jewish community in Berlin had the fortune of having access to rabbis and cantors from several congregations. Contracts with the Senate of Berlin assured that the relatively poor and badly appointed Jewish communities were carefully supported in terms of infrastructure (kindergartens, schools, adult schools, and others, geriatric care and assistance for preserving and cultivating the large Jewish cemeteries in the city, including those in East Berlin).

After the downfall of the Iron Curtain and German re-unification, the Jewish community of Berlin witnessed a doubling of its membership numbers, thanks to the influx of Jews from the Former Soviet Union. As the Jewish community was struggling with the integration of a few thousand new members, new Jewish networks, cultural centres, associations, Jewish kindergartens, and schools were being established even outside of the Jewish community.

The growth of Jewish communities in Germany, as a result of the Jewish influx from Eastern Europe, caught the attention of the entire Jewish world and finally led to a rethinking of attitudes towards the German Jews. For example, in 1998, the American Jewish Committee expanded its European branch with an office in Berlin. International Jewish organizations like the American Jewish Joint Distribution Committee (Joint), United Jewish Appeal (UJA), and others began offering support for Jewish projects and initiatives, especially in the educational sector. At the same time, it became clear that German political representatives, state, regional, and local administrators were willing to accompany the trend of consolidation, or even "revival," in contemporary German-Jewish life. "Those who build a house, just want to stay" is a popular saying among Jewish representatives in present day Germany.[4] There has been a great deal of symbolic policy work to ensure that the Shoah and the trauma of the German and European Jews in World War II will never be forgotten.

When the Memorial to the Murdered Jews of Europe was inaugurated in 2005, situated centrally in the heart of Berlin and within eyeshot of the Reichstag building (the historical German parliament), it was clear even to external observers that the new Germany – the "Berlin Republic" – was treading a path of commemoration that was significantly different from the politics of memory in other countries (even in the West). For a long time, Germany would become a country where Jewish newcomers were welcome, where Holocaust remembrance was anchored in so-

---

[4] https://www.juedischesmuseum.de/besuch/detail/wereinhausbautwillbleiben/ (accessed June 1, 2023).

ciety and where Jewish cultural and religious life was not only "tolerated" but also welcomed and desired.

Visions and hope during the late 1990s and early 2000s in this atmosphere of "decampment" in Germany tempted some observers to expect "a Jewish renaissance in Germany" (Pinto), which some foreign journals described as "a new love between Jews and Germans."

Dynamic Development of Jewish Organizational Life Since the Early 1990s

However, in the period from the early 1990s (starting with fall of the Berlin Wall and the re-unification of Germany/Berlin) to 2004/2005, a considerable dynamic change took place within and also beyond the Jewish community in Berlin. The number of registered Jewish community members in Germany's capital slightly more than doubled, rising from around 5,000 to approximately 11,000. Jewish communities with nearly the same number of registered members (up to nearly 10,000) are currently found in Frankfurt, Düsseldorf, and Munich. This growth was almost exclusively the result of the Russian speaking Jewish influx across the country. The few local synagogues, administrative, medical, social and educational institutions, and existing Jewish organizations did everything they could to adopt and integrate the "newcomers."

It quickly became clear that new capacities had to be organized, and sometimes quite creative and innovative solutions had to be found. For example, in 2007, the education and family centre of Chabad Lubavitch Berlin found a home in a restored and re-constructed old electric power station. The leading rabbi there, Rabbi Yehuda Teichtal, declared: "There is a certain continuity: the power station produced light, and we do so as well." Old synagogues were restored – for example the single but very large liberal-conservative synagogue in East Berlin's Rykestraße and the traditional back-yard synagogue in East Berlin's Brunnenstraße.

The massive growth of organized Jewish life in Germany during the 1990s and at the beginning of the 2000s opened up many unexpected opportunities for creative community building, and not only at the local level.

The significant growth of the Jewish communities has given room for a serious discussion about a new Jewish pluralism and a possible end of the model of the "Einheitsgemeinde" (united Jewish community). Today, more than 100 local Jewish communities exist across Germany, many of them counting only a few dozen or a few hundred members, especially those in rural areas.

A study by Ben-Rafael, Glöckner and Sternberg (2009–2011), based on a survey of more than 1,000 Jewish respondents and 25 expert interviews, revealed that the growing number of Jews in Germany, especially in the late 1990s and early 2000s, paved the way for a new Jewish pluralism, at least in terms of religious and secular identities.

(Ultra-) Orthodox	Liberal/conservative	Traditional	Secular
13,2%	22,3%	32,2%	32,3%

Ben-Rafael, Sternberg, and Glöckner (2011)

Jewish communities established long ago, especially in larger towns, are today being met by new communities, either self-proclaimed by mainly immigrants from the Former Soviet Union, or supported by foreign/ international Jewish movements and organizations like the World Union for Progressive Judaism (WUPJ)[5] on the liberal side and Chabad Lubavitch on the traditional side. Some have been inspired by renewal or grassroots movements like Jewish Renewal,[6] stemming from contemporary American Judaism and trying to combine elements of Kabbalah, Chassidism, and meditation.

In recent years, all major denominations of contemporary Judaism have been able to open a rabbinical school for their respective followers and communities: the Rabbinical Seminar of Berlin (modern orthodoxy following in the footsteps of the famous Rabbi Esriel Hildesheimer), the liberal Abraham Geiger College in Potsdam, and the Zacharias Frankel College, established by Masorti Germany (conservative). In response, the state has supported the construction of more than 30 new synagogues and community centres since the 1990s. Some of the local Jewish communities in turn have developed a very open-minded style of communication, and synagogues as well as Jewish community centres often serve as a space for joint cultural festivals, concerts, readings, public discussions, and family events.

In recent years, however, uncertainties have grown among the Jewish population in Germany. Heightened security measures have been put into place in front of and also inside Jewish community centres, partly as a consequence of deadly terrorist attacks in France (which have increased from 2012) and in response to

---

5 The WUPJ supported Jewish liberal movement in Germany ("Union Progressiver Juden in Deutschland"), though a small number of registered members in 20 local communities, is extremely active and also seeks an intensive and frequent exchange with other religious and cultural groups (including Christians, Muslims, and others).
6 Two local communities have been found in Germany, strongly affiliated with "Jewish Renewal" in the US: "Ohel Hachidusch" in Berlin and "Beth Avraham" in Munich.

the terrorist attack on the synagogue in Halle, Central-Germany (2019). Meanwhile, an open discussion has started about whether the German State is capable of sufficiently protecting local Jewish communities, and other Jewish spaces, in the event of increasing violent, anti-Jewish or even terrorist attacks. [7]

The relatively versatile Jewish landscape in present day Germany consists of a wide range of cultural projects: initiatives at local "Kulturverein" (cultural associations) and Jewish theatres; annual "Yiddish Summer Weeks" in Weimar, with the remarkable participation of Jewish musicians from all over the world; socially and politically inspired projects like the "Jewish Disintegration Congress," initiated by the publicist Max Czollek and the dramatist Sasha Marianna Salzmann at the Maxim Gorki Theater in Berlin in 2016, which brought together alternative and contemporary Jewish attitudes.

Therefore, in general, Jewish life in contemporary Germany is considered to be thriving and diverse, at least in large metropolitan towns, and compared to Jewish post-war community life until the late 1980s. However, since the change of state regulations for Jewish emigration from the Former Soviet Union in 2005, demographic stagnation has become a serious topic again. The age distribution among the Jewish population is even more unfavourable than that of the average German population.[8]

Demographic fluctuation among Jews in Germany is rather low. The overwhelming majority of Jews in Germany has no intentions of leaving the country, and the number of former Soviet Jews who returned to their former homeland(s) is significantly low. The number of German Jews who decide to resettle in Israel ("Alijah") is also very low, and this is now in sharp contrast to a growing number of Israeli citizens who decide to live in Germany, either for a longer period or even for all of their life.[9]

The Israeli community in Germany has grown significantly within the last 15–20 years, and has not yet been adequately researched. It is still too early for any conclusions to be drawn as to whether the Israelis in Germany will have any significant impact on the existing local Jewish communities in Germany or on Jewish life in this country in a broader sense. On the other hand, the very fact that thousands of Israelis, many of them descendants of former German-Jewish Holocaust survivors, decide to "return" to "Ashkenaz" says a lot about the changed atmosphere and perceived opportunities, at least for a single individual future for

---

7 Ronen Steinke, *Terror gegen Juden* (München, 2020).
8 Nearly half of the Jewish population in Germany is older than 60 years of age. See *ZWST Annual Statistics 2015*, 3.
9 Compare: Kranz (2016).

Jews. The overwhelming majority of Israelis who resettle in Germany live in Berlin (Kranz 2015, 2016; Stauber and Fortuna 2016). The number of Israeli people permanently living in Germany is estimated to be at least 20.000.[10]

Among the young Jews who have recently entered the public stage, with the explicit aspiration of not only representing Jewish life but also helping to shape German society, is the second generation of former Soviet Jews, including Astrakhan-born Sergey Lagodinsky, who is currently a member of the European Parliament for the German Green Party, and Kiev-born Marina Weisband, the former general secretary of The Pirates political party. This young generation, active and successful in politics and also in the arts, religion, and elsewhere inside and outside the Jewish scene, might be enabled to form the nucleus for an upcoming Jewish elite actively involved in modernizing the country.

At the same time, antisemitism is again realized as a serious problem among Jews in Germany, as the Second FRA study on European Jewish experience with antisemitic incidents has shown.[11] A considerable portion of Jews in Germany avoid being visibly Jewish in public, probably more so since the armed attack on the synagogue in Halle in October 2019.[12] Many Jews also avoid contacting officials or security forces after having experienced antisemitic incidents. On the other hand, all political parties represented in the German Bundestag consequently distance and condemn any public manifestations of antisemitism among their own ranks.

However, a frequent bone of contention among German politicians, and sometimes even between Jewish networks und personalities, is the discussion of resolving the Israeli-Palestinian conflict, current Israeli policy towards the Palestinians, and the anti-Israeli BDS movement (boycott – divestment – sanctions). These heated debates are also reflected in general surveys among the German population where anti-Israeli sentiments ("Israel is running a crusade of annihilation against the Palestinians," "Israelis are treating Palestinians like former Nazis did with Jews") gain significant approval ratings. However, the share of the German majority that believes in antisemitic stereotypes has more or less remained at 15 to 20 percent for decades.

---

10 Estimations in media reports go up to ca. 30,000 Israelis permanently living in Germany.
11 FRA Report 2018.
12 On October 9, 2019, during the Yom Kippur celebrations, a heavily armed young right-wing extremist in Halle (Saxony-Anhalt, Central Germany) tried to attack the local synagogue and shoot as many Jews as possible. After unsuccessfully trying to enter the synagogue in Halle, he fatally shot two people nearby and injured two others, before being overpowered and arrested by security forces.

The majority of German society is actually undergoing its litmus test as to whether the bonds between Jews and non-Jews have significantly strengthened, or whether the Jewish community will become, as a whole, isolated once again, as a non-guarded ethno-cultural minority.

Sampling, Places of Interviews, and Priority Topics

Based on this thematic context, we recruited five interview partners each, among Jews and non-Jews living in Berlin, Potsdam or nearby. For these narrative and expert interviews we applied the same standardized questionnaire as with the other countries of focus.

In our interviews with Jewish people, special attention was given to: their individual backgrounds, Jewish identities and connections to Israel, roles and positions inside Jewish communities and networks, their views on the German majority and on Jewish-non-Jewish relations, confrontations with antisemitism, their future prospects for Jewish life in Germany, and their connections with/and views on Israel. We aimed to interview respondents from different religious denominations, Jewish functionaries as well as people active in grassroots movements.

In our interviews with non-Jewish people, it was important for us to talk about: the respondents' approaches to Jewish issues and their individual motivation for dealing with Jewish topics and connecting themselves with Jewish people and networks; their perceptions of Jewish developments in Germany in recent decades; their assessments of how Jewish-non-Jewish relations have changed in post-war/reunified Germany; their views on old-new antisemitism in Germany and how to combat it, the role/possible role and opportunities of Jews to help shape contemporary German society; and their connections with/and views on Israel.

Among non-Jewish interviewees, we aimed to interview respondents from different world views and political orientations. Important for both groups was that the respondents had frequent, previous intercultural (Jewish/non-Jewish) experiences. Most of the interviews were conducted in Berlin and Potsdam. The interviews lasted between 60 and 100 minutes. We assured our interview partners of confidentiality with the interview materials and agreements in case of official citations. They were completely transcribed (and some had to be translated into English) before qualitative analysis.

Interview Analysis

The significant demographic and structural changes in German Jewish communities in the last 25–30 years have been outlined above. But what about Jews and Jewish protagonists themselves, who grew up in a unifying Germany and a Jewish world also in transition?

Hannah Dannel, a young German Jewish woman who has worked as a cultural advisor for the Central Council of Jews in Germany for about 15 years, sees the general development optimistically:

> Jews have always lived in Germany, since the 4th century – at least. And currently, there are indications that things work better inside Jewish networks and institutions, particularly in Berlin. But this is, of course, related to the size of Jewish groups and milieus here. In other cities and regions there are dynamic developments as well.[13]

Dannel sees a new trend of self-confidence among the younger Jewish generations in Germany.

> This is something new, and even when I was a schoolgirl and teenager, I wasn't aware of a greater number of Jewish peers, friends, acquaintances, at least not in the immediate surrounding. Ok, I had the opportunity then to study at the Hochschule für Jüdischen Studien Heidelberg (College of Jewish Studies), which was a great gift, and then I got to know a lot of Jewish people and activists across the country. The Jewish Student Union (BJSD) had its headquarters in Heidelberg back then and it was very active. But what we're seeing today is an impressive turn to many more Jewish initiatives and innovative projects where young Jews take part, or even initiate them. And the new thing is, they also have fewer inhibitions to go in public and show 'We are here.' Also, the kind of togetherness of young Jews from quite different backgrounds – German-Jewish, Russian-speaking, Polish, Americans, Israelis – you name it – brings hope.[14]

Dannel has lived in different parts of Germany (Bonn, Heidelberg, Berlin) and had many intercultural experiences with non-Jewish groups and milieus. "I have learned a lot from it," she says, "also finding out commonalities and differences in culture and religion. There were a lot of positive experiences, and I had no fear of showing my Jewishness. However, in some cases, antisemitic incidents did remind me of who I am."[15] Hannah says that quite a few of her Jewish coevals

---

[13] Author's interview with Hannah Dannel in Berlin, May 15, 2019 (in her office at the Central Council of Jews in Germany).
[14] Author's interview with Hannah Dannel in Berlin, May 15, 2019 (at the Central Council Office).
[15] Author's interview with Hannah Dannel in Berlin, May 15, 2019 (at the Central Council Office).

share these experiences of sometimes subtle and sometimes open antisemitic expressions in their surroundings, and she concludes: "This makes me and others, at a certain point, more careful. There are situations where you think twice before wearing a Magen David (Star of David) openly, or placing a sticker with an Israeli flag or symbol on your car. Suddenly you notice that a previous feeling of nonchalance has gone."[16]

Dr. Christian Staffa, a well-known Protestant Berlin theologian, had felt from the very beginning of his theological studies that something substantial would have to be changed among churches redefining their relations with contemporary Judaism and its representatives. For many years, Staffa served as coordinator of the humanitarian organization Aktion Sühnezeichen/Friedensdienste (Action Reconciliation/Peace Service, ASF), which brought him to Israel many times. He often worked on social and humanitarian projects with retired and poor Holocaust survivors who received medical and moral support from young ASF volunteers. Staffa also maintains contact with local associations devoted to Christian-Jewish relations, and he is renowned for raising uncomfortable, self-critical questions, including questioning the past of his own church. Already in his time as program manager of the department of democratic culture and education at the Protestant Academy of Berlin (Evangelische Akademie) he has raised the issue of Jew-Hatred by the late Martin Luther and its fatal aftermath in German society. As a protestant theologian, well familiar with modern Jewish history and Jewish religious rites, Staffa has become one of the most favoured Christian partners for discussion inside the Christian-Jewish dialogue in Germany. For a number of years, aside from all the aforementioned obligations, Staffa has also been the Christian speaker of the "Arbeitsgemeinschaft Juden und Christen" at the biannual German protestant church congress, and is director of the board of trustees at "Amcha," a German civic organization supporting and caring for impoverished old Holocaust survivors living in Israel.

"People need to understand," says Staffa, "that the Holocaust is not just an issue of commemoration. The Holocaust is not history, it is present and perceptible. Those who care might see all those manifold consequences and aftermaths in our current society."[17]

For Protestant representatives like Christian Staffa, it is a matter of course that Christians and Jews conduct an interfaith dialogue "on eye-level" in today's Germany, and that Christian believers should show solidarity with their Jewish friends whenever they are attacked or threatened by antisemitic persons or groups. Final-

---

[16] Author's interview with Hannah Dannel in Berlin, May 15, 2019 (at the Central Council Office).
[17] Author's interview with Christian Staffa, April 28, 2019 in Berlin.

ly, in 2019, Christian Staffa became the first official commissary of the Protestant Church in Germany (EKD) for combating antisemitism.

In the meantime, vibrant connections between the Jewish communities and open-minded non-Jewish German politicians have developed across the political camps and are not necessarily bound by specific intersections of Jewish and Christian culture and religion. For example, Petra Pau, a former youth and pioneer leader in the socialist GDR and a current vice president of the German Bundestag and deputy of the left-wing party DIE LINKE (the leftist party), has become one of the closest and well-known friends of the Jewish community in Germany and Berlin in particular. Pau, a popular maverick, published a widely circulated book entitled *Godless Types* (2015),[18] a first resume of her previous political carrier.

Pau reported that she had no connection to Jewish issues or Jewish persons until the fall of the Berlin Wall in late 1989. A talented organizer who held onto left-wing ideals – despite the collapse of the GDR – Pau became the head of DIE LINKE in Berlin in 1991. "I had to represent the Berlin PDS (a party in the GDR that fused with another party to form DIE LINKE, O.G.), also in contact with the Jewish community in Berlin, and it was clear to me, that this was a very specific challenge. It was the time to start meeting the Jewish representatives face to face, and you can imagine that this was a very new experience," Pau remembers. "And the Jewish representatives started to gain trust and confidence in me as a responsible Berlin politician." Pau succeeded in coming into close contact and exchange with very different Jewish groups and fractions in the German capital, including all large religious movements and Chabad Lubavitch. Today Pau is a welcomed politician in local Jewish communities in Germany, and highly esteemed for her commitment to combating antisemitism. She launched adequate legislative initiatives and supported new concepts and ways forward in the culture of commemoration of the Shoah.

Over the course of many years she has also managed to become a respected German political figure in the initially very skeptical Israeli political and public scene. "My journey to Israel in 2008 was very special," Pau remembers:

> I went to Israel officially as the vice president of the Bundestag. But then, shortly before, I got a lot of attention in the *Jerusalem Post*, attacking me indirectly as a left-wing politician. The rhetoric attack was more directed to then Foreign Minister Zipi Livni for inviting me, as they wrote, 'a communist from Germany'. Therefore, I could not complain about getting too little attention.[19]

---

18 *Godless Types* was published in 2015 by Eulenspiegel Publishing House. By 2018 the book was already in its fourth edition.
19 Author's interview with Petra Pau, in Berlin on September 3, 2019.

When asked about a frequently suspected estrangement between Israel on the one side and Germany/Europe on the other, Pau didn't confirm this concern:

> I have met German-Jewish pupils who are now completing their schooling in Israel because they said they could no longer bear the situation in their home schools in Germany. And I know there are also some elderly (citizens) who now again emphasize that Israel is the haven for all Jews, and some start the discussion again about packing suitcases. However, I don't think that this is a trend. Instead of estrangement I see a lot of intensified exchange, especially among young Israelis and Germans.[20]

At the same time, Petra Pau shows a lot of sympathy toward young Israelis moving to Berlin, either temporarily or even longer. She explained:

> You know, we have this unique scholarship program here in the Bundestag, it's called the IPS program. And I currently have a female Israeli awardee here in my office, though she is not Jewish. However, I have also had Israeli Jews in my office, and some of them stayed. One of the most surprising cases was a young Jew from Russia, who first did Alijah and is now here, living with his partner, and working for the German-Israeli society. And as mentioned, in my office I have had Christian Arab awardees, and now also have a Druse woman... Regarding the Israelis in Berlin, it is interesting to see how a lot of creative groups are mushrooming, and I am wondering who of them will also join synagogues.[21]

With her tireless commitment to strengthening her connections to both the Jewish scene in Germany as well as in Israel, Pau is anything but mainstream, being on the political left. Pau has adopted deep insights into the experiences and feelings of Holocaust survivors while meeting them frequently since the early 1990s.

Andreas Nachama, born in Berlin in 1951, grew up in a family of Holocaust survivors who recalled their experiences of the Shoah at home. His father was the famous Cantor Estrongo Nachama, and Andreas became a distinguished historian and rabbi in Berlin. He also established the central exhibition and conference centre Topographie des Terrors (Topography of Terror) in the heart of Berlin, which he has led for decades. For a time he was the chairman of the Jewish community in Berlin, and he is still the rabbi at a small synagogue in Berlin-Charlottenburg. Despite his numerous activities, Nachama takes time for interfaith dialogue, as it was ingrained in him since childhood as being imperative. "My family has a huge network of friends, a lot of Christians among them, and this for a good reason," Nachama said. "Some Berlin Christians took great risks in hiding my mother during World War II and saved her life."[22] During his early academic studies at the

---

20 Author's interview with Petra Pau, in Berlin on September 3, 2019.
21 Author's interview with Petra Pau, in Berlin on September 3, 2019.
22 Interview of the author with Rabbi Andreas Nachama, on May 15, 2019 in Berlin.

Free University of Berlin, Nachama attended courses on Christianity and Islam, and later on, when already a rabbi and in several positions as a Jewish representative, he joined the Coordination Council for Christian-Jewish Dialogue in Germany, where he has been the Jewish Chairman since 2016. Nachama is also the Jewish representative in the ambitious – and independent – Berlin project "The House of One," a planned building and communication centre where a synagogue, a church and a mosque will be accommodated under one roof. In fact, the "House of One" is designed to motivate practising Jews, Christians, and Muslims to interact with each other, at the same time strengthening their own identities – and the centre will be open to the public. The project shall also serve as a model of peaceful coexistence, opposed to all atrocities committed in the name of religion. Although the building itself, in downtown Berlin, has not yet been built, there are already joint activities, especially in the educational sphere. In 2019, the fundraising campaign had quite successful results – three quarters of the estimated costs for construction (ca. 40 million euros) had been donated. The media echo has also been rather positive. However, there were skeptical voices doubting either the concept itself, or just questioning the practicability of fruitful cooperation in such a confined space. "In recent years we have had to overcome a lot of resistance against our project, also from our own religious groups and forces," said Andreas Nachama, who adds:

> Although I think this brought us, the protagonists, even closer together. We are breaking new ground, and of course, a lot of experiences will be unprecedented. Interestingly, in this stage of preparation, I have the feeling that the representatives from the smaller religions, that means the Imam and me, have the most in common, which comes from this constellation. We are the minorities but we go straight to the public and exchange. I am very curious. In any case, this project also has its special charm by opening up opportunities to destroy long-standing stereotypes and clichés about 'the others'.[23]

Nachama said that problems of antisemitism are present in Berlin and other German spaces, but specifies:

> It didn't appear overnight, it goes back to the 1990s. It is very deplorable, there are indeed some Jewish people who leave for Israel because they feel a certain anti-Jewish climate, and they make a decision. I have a few young people in my community who don't see their future in Berlin or Germany. However, I think the bigger problem is that this society is not yet ready for a basic tolerance of otherness, at least not the majority. And when tensions between Palestinians and Israelis in the Middle East are followed in the news, people easily believe that a new conflict is imported – and this makes them even more reserved, which is a real pity of course.[24]

---

23 Interview of the author with Rabbi Andreas Nachama, on May 15, 2019 in Berlin.
24 Author's interview with Rabbi Andreas Nachama, on May 15, 2019 in Berlin.

"In the last thirty years, only one antisemitic incident has really hit me," said Nachama. "And this was of, all places, in the expert commission that analyses antisemitism on behalf of the German Bundestag."[25] At the same time, Nachama added:

> I don't want to whitewash or relativize antisemitism or Jew hatred in this country, but a general problem is that we live in a society where people behave rather intolerantly towards all kinds of minorities. If one of them is under pressure, it will hit the others as well. That's why there is already a longer tradition in Germany leading Jews to the front lines when any other ethno-cultural minority, for example Turks, is being attacked.[26]

Nachama does not profess to forecast the future of German Jewry, but notes the evolution of Berlin's Jewish community: "In the 1960s, it was expected that Berlin's Jewish community wouldn't count more than about 800 people at the beginning of the new millennium. But thanks to the Russian-Jewish influx in the 1990s, the community counted about 11,000 people in the year 2000. You see, history goes its own way," said Nachama.[27] He is glad to see that young Israelis who have made Berlin their new home have also joined his synagogue. When asked about his own considerations for Alijah at any time in his life, he replies: "I was in Israel for a half year, in the early 1970s. Though I never thought about moving there, because my theological concept is not that strongly focused on Israel."[28]

In the German capital, Nachama has found open-minded, intellectual, and spiritual counterparts in Christians. For example, Reinhold Robbe[29] is a seasoned Social Democrat politician originally from North-Western Germany and a Synod member of the Protestant-Reformed Church. Robbe, who has also been the president of the German-Israeli Society and the head of the German-Israeli parliamentarian group in the Bundestag for a couple of years says that his early encounters with woeful Jewish history started as a child when he was "poking through the library shelves for adults, randomly getting hold of the book 'The Yellow Star' by Gerhard Schoenberner.[30] After reading it, the topic never left my mind."[31] Robbe

---

25 Author's interview with Rabbi Andreas Nachama, on May 15, 2019 in Berlin.
26 Author's interview with Rabbi Andreas Nachama, on May 15, 2019 in Berlin.
27 Author's interview with Rabbi Andreas Nachama, on May 15, 2019 in Berlin.
28 Author's interview with Rabbi Andreas Nachama, on May 15, 2019 in Berlin.
29 From 1994 to 2005, Reinhold Robbe was a Bundestag Deputy for the Social Democratic Party (SPD) in Germany, and from 2005 to 2010 he functioned as the Parliamentary Commissioner for the Armed Forces in Germany.
30 Gerhard Schoenberner, *Der gelbe Stern. Die Judenverfolgung in Europa 1933–1945* (Munich, 1960).
31 Author's interview with Reinhold Robbe in Berlin, June 17, 2019.

considers it a great stroke of luck to have been socialized in the surrounding of the Protestant-Reformed Church of Ostfriesland (North-Western Germany) and says: "Christian missions to Jews were obsolete long before the Nazi era and here the debate on Christian complicity in the times from 1933–1945 started earlier than anywhere else in Germany."[32]

Still, as a teenager and then as a young adult in the early 1970s, Robbe became very committed to both the Association for Christian-Jewish Cooperation and the German-Israel Society:

> I have been witnessing how dedicated Jews and Christians have established a vibrant and candid dialogue, and I think this has changed something on both sides. Though I am not sure whether the removal of anti-Jewish stereotypes and clichés that have existed since the medieval ages, has really succeeded at the base of Christian communities.[33]

Robbe is also concerned that in some German churches, a critical debate on Israel's current policy towards the Palestinians "quickly turns into an uncritical adaption of ideological images of an enemy." Robbe is convinced that German society and politics also have a special future responsibility for the presence and protection of Jewish life in Europe, as well as for the existential security of the State of Israel:

> I am not talking about amicable political criticism, for example, regarding Israel's current politics toward the Palestinians. But when Germany joins even a few of the flood of anti-Israel-resolutions in the UN, something is obviously going wrong. And this could, of course, damage Israeli-German relations in the long run.[34]

According to Robbe, German society has failed to convey comprehensive knowledge about Jewish religion, culture, history, and the present, beyond the Nazi persecution and the Holocaust. "There was a lot of symbolic policy in recent decades, which also has its imperative, along with responsible politics of commemoration," said Robbe. "But obviously, we have failed to make the German non-Jewish population more familiar with the Jewish world in general, and this makes things more complicated since now, the first time after 1945, a considerable number of Jews has deliberately decided to make this country its home again."[35] Robbe expresses his delight about the new dynamic of Jewish life, since tens of thousands of former Soviet Jews immigrated to the FRG, especially during the 1990s:

---

32 Author's interview with Reinhold Robbe in Berlin, June 17, 2019.
33 Author's interview with Reinhold Robbe in Berlin, June 17, 2019.
34 Author's interview with Reinhold Robbe in Berlin, June 17, 2019.
35 Author's interview with Reinhold Robbe in Berlin, June 17, 2019.

> I think the Jewish community in today's Germany can expect a hopeful future. On the other hand, I also hope and wish that the Jewish leading bodies and institutions appear in public more than previously, also with forward-looking topics. Of course, commemoration to the Holocaust will remain very important, the fight against antisemitism and the support of security of Jewish communities and individuals, too. But I wish the Jewish communities would also join more projects in society as a whole, just like some Jewish protagonists are already doing in education, politics and culture.[36]

One of the shining "Jewish cultural ambassadors" in present day Germany is Jalda Rebling, a famous expert of Jewish music from the early Middle Ages to modern times, and more recently a chazan from East Berlin.[37] She addresses her Jewish and non-Jewish audience through a joint discovering of common spiritual traces, melodies, and joint prayer as well as by finding a new approach and bond to proximate nature. Rebling and her partner Anna Adam regularly tour across the region with a "Happy hippie Jew bus" whose purpose she quickly explains:

> The idea is to impart aspects of Jewish life in an unconventional way, especially to young people, wherever they are in Germany, and of course with the support of local or regional institutions or networks. "The Happy hippie Jew bus" is also designed as a kind of peace mobile. It's a rebuilt Volkswagen bus, with "Shalom" in Hebrew and "Salam" in Arabic (painted) on the side, and it is full of didactic material, all kinds of plays and games for kids and teenagers who can learn, in a playful way, something about the Jewish world. Originally, the "Happy hippie Jew bus" was only planned for a few weeks, at a Jewish cultural festival in North-Rhine Westfalia, and then it developed and (stayed) for years. Our target groups grew very diverse, and we succeeded in starting really deep conversations and exchanges. We visited elementary and high schools, vocational school classes and even a boxing club in Frankfurt. It was fascinating to see how non-Jewish young people overcame their reservations, started to ask questions, and sometimes even wanted to hear more and more about Jewish life.[38]

Rebling had already had several encounters and experiences with non-Jews during her time as a Yiddish singer in the former GDR. She succeeded in opening "rare niches" of exchange in a socialist dominated society, where Jews had barely been present in public. After the reunification she went to the United States, completed a cantorial study, and upon her return to Europe she started leading services in prominent European synagogues. After many years, however, Rebling gave up her metropolitan lifestyle in Berlin and now lives in a rural area in Brandenburg. She continues outreach activities with a non-Jewish audience, albeit in a quite different environment from her hometown of Berlin.

---

36 Author's interview with Reinhold Robbe in Berlin, June 17, 2019.
37 Jalda Rebling is also Director of Studies at the European Academy for Jewish Liturgy in London (EAJL).
38 Author's interview with Jalda Rebling in Potsdam, May 15, 2019.

Jalda was one of the founders of *Ohel Ha Chidusch* in Berlin, the first independent Jewish Renewal community in Germany, affiliated with the American-Jewish Renewal movement ALEPH. This was a coherent step in her own development as a self-confident and open-minded Jewess in contemporary Germany. Rebling emphasizes the importance in overcoming rigid and narrow-minded structures and views inside the established Jewish bodies and communities:

> I had endless talks with rabbis explaining what we do in our projects, and how we try to reach out to Jewish people in this country, and then they tell me: 'I would also like to do such things, but I cannot.' And then I ask them, for example: 'What is the problem with having gay or lesbian couples under a Chuppe – if they want that? Or making a blessing for an interreligious couple, with both partners strongly interested in Jewish issues?' Otherwise we will lose Jewish contemporaries again and again.[39]

Rebling also regularly conducts interfaith services and offers concerts with Christian and Muslim singers and artists in Potsdam, for example, where parts of the audience might have their first experience with culture and religion "of the others." In fact, her way and means of coming closer is less discussion and more spiritual music.

Joshua Spinner, executive vice president and CEO of the Ronald S. Lauder Foundation, who came from the United States to Germany in 2000, works on very innovative Jewish projects in several German cities – mostly in Berlin, Leipzig, and Hamburg. He was co-founder of the Hildesheimer Rabbinerseminar Berlin,[40] which was re-opened thanks to support by the Central Council of Jews in Germany, but mostly by the Ronald Lauder Foundation. The seminar also cooperates with the Conference of European Rabbis and the Orthodox Rabbi Conference of Germany.

Interestingly, three distinct groups can be identified among the students of the new Hildesheimer Seminar. By far the largest is the group of immigrants or children of immigrants from the former Soviet Union to Germany, all of whom speak German fluently but also are able to use their Russian language and cultural skills effectively in the communities of Germany. The second group consists of students from outside Germany, primarily Hungary, but also the occasional western European or American. The final group consists of German speakers who were born and raised in German-speaking families in Germany. "There is no special demand

---

39 Author's interview with Jalda Rebling in Potsdam, May 15, 2019.
40 The Rabbinical School of Berlin is closely oriented with the life and works of Rabbi Esriel Hildesheimer (1820–1899), one of the most famous protagonists of European neo-orthodoxy in the last third of the nineteenth century. The Rabbinical Seminar to Berlin was closed by the Nazis in 1938.

for common dominators," says Spinner, when asked about the certain cultural overlapping amongst the groups. "The Tora is the common denominator, and this offers enough inner cohesion."[41] Spinner and his allies represent a new generation of Jews that looks more into the future than back to the past. "Thanks to the influx of former Soviet Jews there is an opportunity to build Jewish life here in Germany, in the long term," says Spinner. "But a sustainable Jewish life in any country in this world is only possible with Jews who, in fact, live as Jews. We work on the infrastructure and the frame conditions for all Jews who want to live as Jews, including kosher food, and sufficient Jewish education for all age groups – in Berlin and elsewhere."[42]

Joshua Spinner notes that contacts with the non-Jewish population around the new community center in Berlin Brunnenstraße (in Berlin's Mitte district) are "pleasant and relaxed." He adds:

> Here, in this part of the city, people are well educated, cosmopolitan and accustomed to meeting others with very different outlooks. Of course, sometimes our community members feel unsettled by the news of antisemitic incidents or activities – the concern is rather about an unconfined guarantee of religious liberty, including kosher butchering and Brit Mila. Antisemitism does not affect our daily lives, but of course, all of us are vigilant. [43]

As the executive vice president of the Ronald S. Lauder Foundation, Spinner is also responsible for many Jewish educational projects across Europe. He is engaged in joint initiatives in which Jewish schools and communities develop specifically local plans for the future like *Educating for Impact*.[44] "Of course it is more difficult for Jews to live their Jewish lives in places outside metropolitan areas. But there is hope for tomorrow, especially when strong and visionary leadership is on the spot," Spinner says.[45]

Although they work in rather distinct Jewish religious and spiritual networks, what Joshua Spinner and Jalda Rebling have in common is their outreach to rather well-meaning, non-Jewish environments via uncomplicated channels and contacts.

Martin Kloke, a non-Jewish Berlin-based publicist and political scientist, has the impression that the encounters between Jews and non-Jews in Germany have not yet had a broad effect: "There is a network of contacts and co-operations between the Jewish community and a minority of non-Jewish interested individuals – activists of a religious or secular nature, friends of Israel, and academics. Sig-

---

41 Author's interview with Joshua Spinner in Berlin, July 20, 2019.
42 Author's interview with Joshua Spinner in Berlin, July 20, 2019.
43 Author's interview with Joshua Spinner in Berlin, July 20, 2019.
44 https://educatingforimpact.com/ (accessed April 5, 2021).
45 Author's interview with Joshua Spinner in Berlin, July 20, 2019.

nificant organizations in this regard would include Deutsch-Israelische Gesellschaft (DIG), Gesellschaft für Christlich-Jüdische Zusammenarbeit (GCJZ) and other NGOs that ensure that these relations are filled with life. Though, the majority of non-Jewish society doesn't participate in these things, or does so only in a small amounts."[46]

Kloke also thinks that activities to commemorate flourishing Jewish life in Germany before 1933, the Nazi Crimes in WWII, and the Shoah are carried out by only a small share of the non-Jewish population. He states:

> At the yearly commemorative ceremonies and events, Jews and non-Jews commemorate the horrors of the past, in large part, together. The 9th of November, the 27th of January and the 8th May are examples. This also happens in-between, when new 'Stolpersteine' are laid in front of the apartments or houses in which Jews previously lived before they were deported and murdered. But also in this setting, on the non-Jewish side, it is primarily official representatives of state and society, as well very engaged activists, who partake in such events and commemorate together with the Jewish community. Most members of non-Jewish society participate in these events only on a minimal level, if at all.[47]

German media, especially public channels and broadcasts, regularly try to convey information about Jewish history, culture, religion, and also the modern State of Israel. Recently, German media has also sought to introduce various Jewish protagonists living permanently or temporarily in Germany, and the media, in fact, reaches specific target groups. This might be interpreted as a helpful balancing of the media and general public focus, formerly only focused on Jewish history starting with 1933, the rise of Adolf Hitler, and ending in 1945, with the liberation of Auschwitz and the end of World War II.

Even Yan Wissmann is a descendant of German Jews in the southwest German region of Baden Württemberg. His grandparents escaped to South America in 1939. He returned to Germany and was a student activist, and became surprised about the intensity of commemoration of the Shoah in some (non-Jewish) circles:

> I think, in post-War Germany, all generations were urged to confront themselves with the extremely inhumane politics of the Nazi Regime, and with the mass crimes (…) and sometimes it became overwhelming. I don't have words to describe what happened. I think, repeating and repeating these kinds of facts, can, at the end of the day, lead to a kind of paranoia.[48]

---

46 Author's interview with Dr. Martin Kloke in Berlin, December 7, 2019.
47 Author's interview with Dr. Martin Kloke in Berlin, December 7, 2019 (emphasis by the author).
48 Author's interview with Yan Wismann in Berlin, June 3, 2019.

At the same time, Yan Wissmann, Martin Kloke, and other interview partners are aware of trends of old and modern antisemitism, partly tarnishing the joy of a new dynamic development of Jewish life in Germany – notably the construction of new synagogues and the opening of Jewish kindergartens, schools, youth centres, Jewish galleries, restaurants, theatres, film and learning festivals.

Openly antisemitic expressions and brutal, physical or even terrorist attacks are currently rare cases in Germany, but Jews as well as non-Jews confirm experiences with anti-Jewish statements and remarks. Wissmann said ironically: *"I can't see very open antisemitism, but I have already had experiences in former places of employment and in private encounters. Comments like: 'The half of Berlin belongs to Jewish people' and 'Half of the houses are Jewish real estate'. I wish that were true, but it's sadly not,"* he said laughing.[49]

Martin Kloke considers the problem on a larger scale:

> Antisemitism is an unbearable disaster for the political culture of this country, because it's virulent in all social and political milieus. One of the numerous manifestations of antisemitism includes making "the Jews" responsible for the real or imagined mistakes of Israel. Alongside the traditional forms of antisemitism among the political right, we have seen a specific hatred of Jews become virulent on the political left and in the so-called 'middle ground', which is otherwise at home in largely Muslim migrant settings. This primarily anti-Israeli antisemitism has roots in both Europe and the Qur'an. As a result, it is often not taken seriously in mainstream society, or is simply silently "tolerated", in part because antizionist resentment is widespread in the liberal mainstream, and in part because right-wing populist tendencies abuse "Islam" as a projection screen for anti-Muslim racism. One can of course debate whether antisemitism really is increasing or not. One thing is clear: hatred of Jews is showing its face more shamelessly and brutally than ever before.[50]

Again, it is especially these groups, networks, and individual personalities of non-Jewish Germans who react intensely to the new forms of antisemitism and organize vigils, Kipa-"flashmobs" or even demonstrations against demonstrations. They may even directly call politicians for more state supported measures against antisemitism.

There have been no recent explorations of distinct non-Jewish support groups accompanying Jewish communities, expressing their specific solidarity in public events and backing the Jewish communities and individual Jewish people when confronted with antisemitic incidents. Neither the composition of the groups nor their specific motivations have been studied so far. However, many solidarity ini-

---

49 Author's interview with Yan Wismann in Berlin, June 3, 2019.
50 Author's interview with Dr. Martin Kloke in Berlin, December 7, 2019 (emphasis by the author).

tiatives with Jewish communities are currently organized by Christian groups and by young anti-fascist groups.

A third group of very active civil stakeholders consists of German citizens who have some Jewish ancestors in their family tree but are not members of Jewish communities or do not consider themselves as Jews in a halakhic or ethnic way. On the other hand, they might perfectly function as connectors between a Jewish and a non-Jewish world in German society.

Dr. Thomas Feist, for example, the official commissioner of Jewish life and combating antisemitism in the State of Saxony, recalls his great grandfather who survived Auschwitz and was one of the re-founders of the Jewish community in the city of Leipzig in 1945. Feist, who also lives and works in Leipzig, and who served for two legislative periods as a deputy in the German Bundestag, grew up in a Protestant atmosphere, due to the Christian part of his family. He is an active proponent of Christian culture and sees great potential for Christian-Jewish cooperation in present day Germany. Feist also considers the Judeo-Christian connection "not as a myth but as fundamental." Regarding Germany he concludes: "This wouldn't have become a nation with such strong and prominent science and culture, if there hadn't been so many leading Jewish protagonists in those disciplines."[51] Nowadays, and also in Saxony, Feist notes "a lot of vibrant Christian and also communal initiatives helping to overcome the huge trenches and divisions that have existed before and after the Shoah." He is not contesting that some of the participating Christian initiatives may "overshoot the mark," not clearly defining their religious views and motivations, and partly promote a transfigured and unthinkingly idealized picture of Israel. Nevertheless, he says: "These groups are ready to come into contact, communicate, exchange and share experiences with Jews, here and now and face the challenge where others stay away."[52] Feist also makes a smart distinction between fundamentalist Christians supporting the Jew Mission, i. e. enhanced Christian efforts to convert Jews to Christianity, as "unacceptable" and those Christians who want to communicate their principle faith in a redemptive history: "I see no problem if groups of Christians and Jews are meeting each other, even if having some diametrically core beliefs. Important is just to talk with mutual respect and honesty." As in most German cities after World War II and until today, the Jewish inhabitants of Leipzig only represent a very small portion of the local population. "Apart from a few religious members of the community, (they are) almost invisible. However, the Jews who are in the public, in-

---

51 Author's interview with Dr. Thomas Feist in Dresden, September 1, 2020.
52 Author's interview with Dr. Thomas Feist in Dresden, September 1, 2020.

cluding the rabbi and also some artists and intellectuals, generally meet an open-minded atmosphere in this city," notes Feist.

At the same time, Feist is very concerned about the lack of knowledge of Jewish history, traditions, and contemporary Jewry in large parts of German society, a deficit that might increase a general liability to antisemitic influences, primarily induced but not only by right-wing extremist groups and networks. "We need comprehensive educational programs for the prevention of antisemitism and Jew hatred," says Feist, "and these programs should be directed especially toward young people. It is deplorable that knowledge of the longstanding, rich and changing Jewish history in Germany in general, and in the respective regions and cities in particular, is so marginal."[53]

Feist, in his role as the official commissioner of combating antisemitism in Saxony, is trying to mobilize schools and other educational institutions, and several milieus and forces of civil society, to speed up knowledge and education of Jewish history, religion, and culture. He is also a strong proponent of deploying excursions to Israel, especially for young people, "to enable them to get a picture of historical and modern Jewry." Indeed, there are programs in progress in Germany to organize excursions to Israel, even for formerly right-wing extremists, thus trying to re-socialize them, and help them to dissolve a deep-rooted concept of "the enemy." Feist states:

> Particularly in east Germany, we have a fatal tradition of distancing and animosity toward Israel, caused by 40 years of disastrous anti-Israeli propaganda by the communist regime of the GDR. This tradition still continues to have effects.[54]

Meanwhile, two controversies have arisen in German academia and the German public, regarding modern Israel and current antisemitism. The first controversy touches upon the following question: at what point does harsh critique of Israel – and under certain circumstances also political opposition – become subtly or openly antisemitic? The second controversy circles around the thesis that animosity towards Israel has become the dominating and accepted form of present antisemitism in Germany.

"Israel-related antisemitism is the dominating type of Jew-hatred in the digital age, in all spheres and at all levels of communication," states Professor Monika Schwarz-Friesel, a professor of linguistics and research expert on antisemitism in German public statements. "Traditional anti-Jewish stereotypes are now project-

---

53 Author's interview with Dr. Thomas Feist in Dresden, September 1, 2020.
54 Author's interview with Dr. Thomas Feist in Dresden, September 1, 2020.

ed onto the State of Israel and its inhabitants, and its right to exist as a Jewish State is seriously challenged, while the Middle East conflict just plays a minor role."[55]

The first controversy, in particular, continues in an extreme way and polarizes scholars – especially social scientists and cultural scientists– but also journalists and publicists. And while scholars like Monika Schwarz-Friesel argue that many antisemites use alleged critique of Israel as a massive outlet of Jew hatred, other scholars predicate that the "accusation of antisemitism" is misused to muzzle any critique of Israel. The Jewish communities, traditionally closely related to Israel, follow the discussion with huge concern, fully aware that a large section of German people, when discussing the Middle East conflict, appear unable to differentiate between Jews, Jewish communities, Jewish diaspora, and the State of Israel. "I permanently have to explain to debaters, that I am not an Israeli citizen, that I don't have an Israeli passport, and subsequently, I cannot vote for any Israeli government, and that I do not participate in Israeli politics," says Kuef Kaufmann, the head of the Jewish community in Leipzig.[56]

The heated inner-German debates about Israel might also affect, at least in the long run, the longstanding, traditional relations between Jews and Christians, maybe even in well-established platforms like the Associations for Christian-Jewish Cooperation, most of them already established in the 1950s and 1960s. At the moment, however, it seems too early to assess to what extent ongoing polarized debates about Israel and antisemitism will affect broader circles and networks frequently working at the intersections between Jews, Christians, and other ethno-cultural/ethno-religious groups in Germany. Or, in other words: it is not yet foreseeable to what extent the sustained conflict between Jewish Israelis and Palestinians in the Middle East will also considerably affect the encounters between Jews and non-Jews in Germany in the long run.

Conclusion(s)

A new quality of cooperation and mutual learning has taken shape among Jewish and non-Jewish stakeholders in Germany. Jewish leaders, artists, intellectuals, and some theologians show appreciation for a new quality of exchange "at eye-level" – also as a means to reduce mutual stereotypes and fears of interaction. Our interviews have also revealed that Jews in Germany go about different ways to develop

---

55 Monika Schwarz-Friesel on idz: https://www.idz-jena.de/wsddet/wsd8-5/ (translation by the author).
56 Author's interview with Kuef Kaufmann, Head of the Jewish Community in Leipzig, November 11, 2022.

and strengthen their Jewish identities. Israel is an important factor for many of them, but does not appear to be the most essential one. None of the Jewish interview partners were considering Alijah (immigration to Israel).

Our non-Jewish interview partners offered a significant mix of motivations for being in close contact with Jews, Jewish communities, and Israel: sensitization to the Jewish revival in Germany, individual commitment in organizations of Christian-Jewish cooperation or German-Israeli friendship, or religious interest in Judaism and Israel. Combatting antisemitism was considered as a matter of course.

Our interviews revealed that Jewish-Christian encounters in Germany are not that broad or frequent, but the existing connections show promise of liveliness and sustainability. For Jewish stakeholders in Germany, commemoration to the Shoah remains an important element of their identities. At the same time, building a Jewish future here, in Central Europe, has become a similar priority. Israel is highly appreciated as a "safe haven" for Jews across the world and as a spiritual source – solidarity with Israel thus seems a matter of course. In a few interviews with non-Jewish interviewees, sorrow was expressed that German-Israeli relations might cool down due to different opinions and politics in Israeli-Palestinian relations. One of the interview partners principally hoped for more Jewish commitment in German politics and society.

In general, our interview partners believed that there is a Jewish future in Germany, though they abstained from any predictions. All in all, German society is considered as stable. Antisemitism appears as a problem that has to be combatted. However, plans of leaving the country, due to feelings of uncertainty, seem to be rare exceptions.

Marcela Menachem Zoufalá
Ambivalence, Dilemmas, and Aporias of Contemporary Czech Jewish *Lived Experience*

To Remember—and to Forget

To be a Jew almost always means to relate mentally to the Jewish past, whether the relation is one of pride or gloom or both together, whether it consists of shame or rebellion or pride or nostalgia (Amos Oz).[1]

As Tony Judt aptly captured, the post-WWII Eastern Europe had much more "to remember—and to forget"[2] than the West. The East was originally home to larger Jewish communities, most of the Jews were murdered on local soil, and the majority of societies were more involved in anti-Jewish violence during and after the war.[3] Respective governments have instrumentalized the crimes of WWII, including the Holocaust, for their nation-building narratives; however, Jews once again did not fit into the story.[4]

After the Holocaust, two thirds of European Jewry were decimated. In Central and Eastern Europe, the Nazi extermination was followed by persecution for more than four decades under the baton of totalitarian regimes. A "new layer of resentments and memories"[5] consisting of adversities and injustice constructed by the Communist régimes was painted over the raw unprocessed traumas of the Shoah and the WWII.[6]

Only after the end of the Cold War have Jewish communities found the strength to reclaim old or create new identities and minority cultures. At the end of the twentieth century, those who embarked on a complex journey of searching for Jewish roots were often immersed into the process of "becoming Jewish" accompanied by the so-called de-assimilation.

---

[1] Amos Oz, "Poem: To Be a Jew," Jewish Journal, January 2, 2019, https://jewishjournal.com/spiritual/poetry/291731/poem-to-be-a-jew/.
[2] Tony Judt, *Postwar: A History of Europe Since 1945* (New York: The Penguin Press, 2005), 821.
[3] Judt, *Postwar: A History of Europe Since 1945*, 821–822.
[4] See: Judt, *Postwar: A History of Europe Since 1945*, 821–822.
[5] Judt, *Postwar: A History of Europe Since 1945*, 823.
[6] For the extensive study dedicated Jews in Czechoslovakia in 1945-1989, see Blanka Soukupová, Židé v Českých zemích po šoa. Identita poraněné paměti. [Jews in the Czech Lands after the Shoah. The Identity of Wounded Memory], Bratislava, Marenčin PT, 2016.

In an attempt to find "authentic Jewishness" and one's place in it, diverse, sometimes intertwined paths were discovered and followed on a personal or communal level. Longing to belong took place through practicing passionate religiosity, dedication to the Holocaust commemoration, countering antisemitism and xenophobia, or attachment to Israel, among others.

One of the instruments to navigate Jewishness has been represented by efforts to revitalize the traditional Jewish culture and environment by breathing new life into it. "Jewish spaces" is a well-known term coined by Diana Pinto in the middle of the 1990s that has evolved over the last three decades and has been periodically revisited by researchers and intellectuals interested in European Jewish life.

"There is now a new cultural and social phenomenon: the creation of a 'Jewish space' inside each European nation with a significant history of Jewish life. The first is the gradual integration of the Holocaust into each country's understanding of its national history and into twentieth-century history in general. And the second is the revival of 'positive Judaism'" (Pinto 1996, 6).[7]

After 1989, during the first decade of post-communist transition, the so-called Jewish Renaissance occurred in Central and Eastern Europe. This phenomenon, described by Ruth Ellen Gruber[8] more than two decades ago, has involved both Jews and non-Jews and in many ways has still been evolving until today. Pinto's essay and Gruber's book heralded passionate polemics on "Jewish-less Jewish revival"[9] or how to distinguish between Jewish culture and Jewish-themed culture and whether it is still at all relevant.[10]

Prague's Jewish Community in Maiselova Street in the Old Town, once part of the Jewish Ghetto, was a prominent address for many who learned or intuited they had Jewish roots or were simply curious about quickly reborn Jewish life that suddenly emerged on the surface. In both cases, the Jewish community in the 1990s was somewhat unprepared to receive high numbers of "pilgrims." Many were sent away without even being able to enter the communal premises. Due to this selective approach, several Czech people with Jewish backgrounds were rejected

---

[7] Diana Pinto, "A New Jewish Identity for Post-1989 Europe," *JPR Policy Paper 1* (London: Institute for Jewish Policy Research, 1996), accessed April 4, 2023, https://www.bjpa.org/content/upload/bjpa/a_ne/A%20New%20Jewish%20Identity%20For%20Post-1989%20Europe.pdf.
[8] Ruth Ellen Gruber, *Virtually Jewish: Reinventing Jewish Culture in Europe* (Berkeley: University of California Press, 2002).
[9] Konstanty Gebert, "What is Jewish about Contemporary Central European Jewish Culture?" in *Being Jewish in 21st Century Central Europe*, ed. Haim Fireberg, Olaf Glöckner, and Marcela Menachem Zoufalá (De Gruyter, 2020), 283.
[10] Gebert, "What is Jewish about Contemporary Central European Jewish Culture?" 283.

and never returned, remembering their often first and only encounter with a Jewish world as puzzling.

The factors that contributed to this exclusive attitude undoubtedly partly originated in twentieth century totalitarianism. Long-term persecution resulted in suspiciousness and mistrustfulness towards its surroundings.

Several conversation partners expressed an opinion that more or less has stayed the same regarding communal openness and permeability in the last three decades. However, many Jewish groups or organizations based on religious or cultural affiliation have been meanwhile established as partly or wholly inclusive and have welcomed those with partial or no Jewish roots. There is a religious reform movement, "Ec chajim," and the recently established Jewish Community Center (JCC), to name two such organizations, with all-encompassing world views. A number of Jewish "secular" organizations is listed under the umbrella of the Federation of Jewish Communities.[11]

Methodology

The study[12] introduces anthropological research that strives to deconstruct and interpret the meaning of Jewishness as a lived experience among the members of the Jewish minority in the Czech Republic today. The research topics include the self-perception and image of the world surrounding them; how Jews position themselves in their respective ambiance; do they experience a sense of belonging (sharing common destiny) on a national, transnational, global, (trans)local, or communal level; how they perceive the majority society's perspectives; and lastly, do they feel responsible for the well-being of their own community and (or) members of other minorities or even local/global majority society?[13] The research findings pre-

---

[11] "Organization," Federation of Jewish Communities in Czech Republic, accessed May 12, 2023, https://www.fzo.cz/en/about-us/organization.

[12] The article was supported by two research projects: 1) "United in Diversity"—An Interdisciplinary Study of Contemporary European Jewry and Its Reflection, which was awarded a multiyear grant under the Erasmus+ program, Key Action 2: Strategic Partnerships, by The Czech National Agency acting under the delegation of the Education, Audiovisual and Culture Executive Agency (EACEA) of the EU. The project was carried out by Charles University as a coordinating institution, The Moses Mendelssohn Center for European Jewish Studies at the University of Potsdam, Comenius University and Tel Aviv University; 2) the program "Excellence Initiative – Research University" at the Jagiellonian University in Krakow ("Jewish and Muslim Minorities in Urban Spaces of the Central Europe," project ID WSMiP.2.3.2022).

[13] An almost identical set of research topics was employed in the following OA article: Marcela Menachem Zoufalá, Joanna Dyduch, and Olaf Glöckner, "Jews and Muslims in Dubai, Berlin, and

sented in this article resulted from long-term qualitative anthropological research on Czech Jewish identity, sense of belonging, and transnationalism carried out in 2014–2022. The study's theoretical postulates employ a hermeneutic-narrative approach involving an emic perspective by highlighting the conversation partners' perception and interpretation of the reality surrounding them. The main methodological tools used to collect data were participant observation, interview, subsequent socio-cultural analysis, review of scholarly sources, literature, and press, occupied with the Jewish community's quality of life. Over 30 interviews were recorded, scrutinized, and interpreted.[14]

Participants

The fieldwork led to 31 in-depth interviews[15] with 11 Jewish women and 20 Jewish men. All conversation partners[16] were self-identified (self-ascribed) as Jews and Czechs, some of them Halachically Jewish, some of patrilineal descent, and one convert. All interview partners were eligible under the Israeli Law of Return. All the conversation partners have embraced their Jewishness openly within their social circles. Some of them have been employed or volunteered for Jewish organizations. All of them, except one, were born in Czechia or Slovakia (until 1993 Czechoslovakia). Most conversation partners lived in Prague; some lived in other major cities such as Brno, Karlovy Vary, and others. Czech was the primary conversation language, with occasional Hebrew, German or Yiddish vocabulary. Most of the interviews were carried out face-to-face and some were also online. The age of the interview partners spans between 24 and 71 years old.[17]

Warsaw: Interactions, Peacebuilding Initiatives, and Improbable Encounters," *Religions* 13, no. 1 (2021): 13, https://doi.org/10.3390/rel13010013.

14 See Marcela Menachem Zoufalá, "Ethno-religious Othering as a reason behind the Central European Jewish distancing from Israel," in *Being Jewish in 21st Century Central Europe*, ed. Haim Fireberg, Olaf Glöckner, and Marcela Menachem Zoufalá (De Gruyter, 2020). ISBN-13: 978–3110579659.

15 Additionally, dozens of concise verbal exchanges with so-called informants occurred for over a decade.

16 In line with the approach of the reflexive methodology, for the specific interviewees, the term "interview partners" or "conversation partners" rather than "respondents" was preferred to underline their essential share on the research.

17 According to different sources the number of the Czech Jews varies between 3,900 (Della Pergola, "World Jewish Population, 2020") to 20,000 (Federation of Jewish Communities in the Czech Republic). The majority of the Czech Jews lives in Prague. There are smaller communities in Brno, Plzeň, Karlovy Vary, Olomouc, Liberec, Děčín, Ostrava, Ústí nad Labem, and Teplice (ibid.).

Antisemitism as a Constant Phenomenon

While investigating the quality of life in the European Jewish context, the question that cannot be omitted is to what extent members of Jewish communities feel safe. What is their perception of antisemitism and do they have a personal experience?

Many Jewish conversation partners repeatedly claim that levels of antisemitism in the Czech Republic are shallow. This is often confirmed by the research on manifestations of antisemitism, showing that the Czech Republic is not only in the European context[18] but also worldwide a place with a relatively small number of antisemitic incidents.[19] The Federation of Jewish Communities (FJC) has repeatedly claimed that the Czech Republic is a "safe country for the Jewish community, especially compared to other countries of central and western Europe."[20] It is indisputable that physical antisemitic attacks are primarily carried out against visibly-identifiable Jews.[21] For this reason, many European (and global) Jewish

---

[18] A recent study focused on antisemitic prejudices in Visegrad countries shown in cross-country comparisons displaying the relatively low proportion of strongly antisemitic respondents in the Czech Republic (two percent). In the three remaining Visegrád countries, the rate varied between 10 and 14 percent. This applied to so-called cognitive antisemitism (traditional religion-based anti-Judaism and Conspiratorial antisemitism). In the case of strong Secondary antisemitism that includes Holocaust denial and distortion, it was again Czechia with two percent, Poland and Slovakia with seven percent, while the highest rate, at 12 percent, was found in Hungary. On the other hand, Israel-focused antisemitism/new antisemitism in its moderate or strong extent was found among 52 percent of respondents in the Czech Republic, higher than Hungary with 49 percent but lower than Poland with 71 percent and Slovakia with 58 percent. Ildikó Barna and Tamás Kohut, rep., *Survey on Antisemitic Prejudice in the Visegrád Countries* (Budapest: Tom Lantos Institute, 2022).
[19] For example, in 2021, the Federation of Jewish Communities in the Czech Republic (FJC) recorded 1,128 antisemitic incidents. In line with trends of recent years, a constant increase can be observed; the current number of incidents is 254 higher than in 2020, when 874 incidents were recorded. Ninety-eight percent of all incidents belongs to cyberantisemitism (findings from Annual report on manifestations of antisemitism in the Czech Republic 2021, published by the Federation of Jewish Communities in the Czech Republic).

FJC findings can be compared to the Police Presidium of the Czech Republic data: "In 2022, there were 25 criminal offenses against Jews. (...) There was a single criminal case involving threats to an individual or group of people with death or bodily harm; (...) there were no incidents of disorderly conduct against Jews involving desecration or attacking another. (...) Two defamation incidents and four instigating hatred incidents were recorded in 2022." "Antisemitism Worldwide Report for 2022," Center for the Study of Contemporary European Jewry – Tel Aviv University. It is important to clarify that the data from the Police Presidium are significantly lower due to solely registering antisemitic "criminal offenses" and not "incidents."
[20] Annual Report on Manifestations of Antisemitism in the Czech Republic 2021, 8.
[21] Annual Report on Manifestations of Antisemitism in the Czech Republic 2021, 5.

leaders appeal to their local community members to be inconspicuous and not appear as easy targets with kippa or Magen David on the streets.

However, even though the Czech Republic is often considered a safe haven by the international Jewish community, most of the conversation partners of this study have encountered antisemitic prejudices, both positive and negative stereotypes, similarly as being subjected to fetishization and exoticization, while interacting with the majority of society.

When asked about the outdoor wearing of Jewish symbols, such as kippa or Magen David, most of the conversation partners generally agreed it was not a problem; however, most of them eventually preferred not to identify with their beliefs publicly. The declared reasons varied from avoiding to showing off and considering these matters of a private nature. A few mentioned safety concerns or simply feeling uncomfortable. Those wearing the symbols occasionally expressed their need to appear in good taste without being too striking.

"Do You Have a Mezuzah on Your Door? Yeah, I do. On the Outside? No…"

Having mezuzah affixed to the doorposts is a certain indicator for diaspora Jews. This is not a matter of one's personal taste or body image, as mentioned earlier, but rather something permanently posted on the entry door distinguishing the space as a Jewish household, as a traditional sign that cannot be as easily undone as removing a kippa or taking down a Magen David. Having a mezuzah on the main door was an important question for many of our conversation partners. However, only one home carried it – an apartment in the building with a constantly locked street gate. The given explanation for having a mezuzah inside but not outside of the house included theft of the mezuzah by curious passers seeking an original souvenir. The predominant motive for having it inside was often a certain discomfort:

> "Did you have a mezuzah on the door?"
> "At home? No, I didn't. I had it on the other, inside door."
> "And why on the inside door?"
> "Because I didn't want to draw attention to it. Then again, I didn't really know the neighbors."

Local Unique Entanglement: Secularization, Assimilation, and Intermarriage

One of the justifications for not exposing their ethnoreligious identity externally might be the overall features of the surrounding environment. The Czech Republic is recognized as the most atheistic country in Central and Eastern Europe[22] while other countries' comfortable majorities are religiously affiliated and believe in God.[23] Czechs also do not relate Christianity with their national identity, comparable to most Western Europeans.[24] One of the local features is that a fervent religiousness manifested outwardly is relatively uncommon. Certain inconspicuousness intrinsic to the majority society is even more intense among minorities. This might be an apparent response to the twentieth-century multiple traumas mentioned above.

Another particularity of the local environment is a high rate of Czech-Jewish intermarriages in the first third of the twentieth century. For example, in the years 1928–1933 almost one fifth of marriages of Jewish people were intermarriages. In the Bohemian part of the Czechoslovakia the number was more than twice higher (43.8 percent) and in Moravia nearly every third marriage was with someone from outside of the community.[25, 26]

---

[22] "About seven-in-ten Czechs (72%) do not identify with a religious group, including 46% who describe their religion as "nothing in particular" and an additional 25% who say "atheist" describes their religious identity. When it comes to religious belief – as opposed to religious identity – 66% of Czechs say they do not believe in God, compared with just 29% who do." Jonathan Evans, "Unlike Their Central and Eastern European Neighbors, Most Czechs Don't Believe in God," Pew Research Center, July 22, 2020, https://www.pewresearch.org/fact-tank/2017/06/19/unlike-their-central-and-eastern-european-neighbors-most-czechs-dont-believe-in-god/.
[23] "Religious Belief and National Belonging in Central and Eastern Europe," Pew Research Center's Religion & Public Life Project, May 10, 2017, https://www.pewresearch.org/religion/2017/05/10/religious-belief-and-national-belonging-in-central-and-eastern-europe/.
[24] "Eastern and Western Europeans Differ on Importance of Religion, Views of Minorities, and Key Social Issues," Pew Research Center's Religion & Public Life Project, October 29, 2018, https://www.pewresearch.org/religion/2018/10/29/eastern-and-western-europeans-differ-on-importance-of-religion-views-of-minorities-and-key-social-issues/.
[25] "In Bohemia the figure was 43.8 percent, in Moravia 30 percent, in Slovakia 9.2 percent, and in Subcarpathian Rus' 1.3 percent," Petr Brod, Kateřina Čapková, and Michal Frankl, "Czechoslovakia," YIVO Encyclopedia of Jews in Eastern Europe (2010), accessed April 11, 2023, https://yivoencyclopedia.org/article.aspx/Czechoslovakia.
[26] For the history of the Jews in the Bohemian Lands written by an international team of scholars, see Kateřina Čapková and Hillel J. Kieval, *Prague and beyond Jews in the Bohemian Lands* (Philadelphia: University of Pennsylvania Press, 2021).

These figures are globally unparalleled. According to DellaPergolla, most of the Jews worldwide in the 1930s (65 percent) lived in countries with less than five percent of intermarriages and a quarter of them did not even reach one percent. The worldwide average was 5.1 percent in 1930 and 33.5 percent in 1980. In the U.S. in 2001, every second marriage was an intermarriage (54 percent).[27]

These above-mentioned patterns were also noticed by one of the first Holocaust historians in Bohemia and Moravia, Miroslav Kárný, who testified that the local Jewish experience could be characterized by a high degree of secularization, assimilation, and intermarriage.[28]

Several generations of solid assimilation and a high intermarriage rate sometimes resulted in antisemitism within the mixed families. As one conversation partner summed up: "(…) that awkward moment when my [non-Jewish] dad says to my [Jewish] mom something like 'you're all Kohn!' But not that anyone would be mad at me." Even though the stigmatized partner is predominantly the minority, there are cases where the non-Jewish family member is silently perceived as lacking a particular understanding and is not seen as "one of the tribe."

During the communist era in Czechoslovakia and elsewhere, minorities were regularly discouraged from performing their cultures and traditional customs. The population was homogenized, and manifestations of distinction were often punished. Minorities themselves were considered a threat to the collectively imposed identities of Czechoslovak socialist citizens. This authoritarian approach naturally qualified minorities for activities in dissent, and at the same time they were perceived as more vulnerable to the investigative and recruiting practices of the secret police. In other words, being openly Jewish during the totality could be seen as a sign of resistance against the régime.

"Are you wearing a Magen David around your neck?"

"I only wore it under the communists. It was a symbol of resistance to the regime. Now I'd consider it an exhibition. I don't see any reason to list it anywhere. After all, it's listed on my Wikipedia page."

Many conversation partners referred to the persecution of minorities and state-sponsored antisemitism during the Communist era. One of its peaks was undoubtedly Operation Spider carried out during the 1970s and 1980s, the so-called Normalization that followed the 1968 Prague Spring terminated by the Soviet (Varsovian pact) Invasion. As researchers agreed, an increased persecution of Czecho-

---

27 Sergio DellaPergola, *Jewish Intermarriage around the World* (New York: Routledge, 2009), 26–27.
28 Miroslav Kárný, *"Konečné Řešení": Genocida Českých Židů v Německé Protektorátní Politice* (Praha: Academia, 1991), 18.

slovak citizens of Jewish origin by the security apparatus of the Czechoslovak Socialist Republic can be observed during this period.[29]

In 1972, the Czechoslovak Ministry of the Interior initiated a "targeted mapping and registration of persons of Jewish origin (religion),"[30] their family members, and persons who had come into contact with the Jewish culture and religion in any way. Jewish organizations were also under increased control of the security apparatus.[31]

Most of the volumes were destroyed by the State Security in December 1989; however, researchers estimate that between 1972 and 1989, approximately 20,000 people were included in the Operation Spider records.[32]

How Garlic Helps Jews to Rule the World

A few conversation partners shared their direct experiences with classical antisemitic prejudices, such as "Jews have abnormal body parts," "Jews like garlic," etc.

One conversation partner recalls how she was ordering a vegetarian dinner for a trip with the Czech Union of Jewish Youth. Once the restaurant learned the meal was for a Jewish group, in an attempt to meet all customers' desires, they asked if they wanted to add a lot of garlic. "So I agreed with a certain amount of garlic to make them happy," the partner concludes with a slightly tired smile. Furthermore, she shares her long-life feeling of responsibility that she believes might be common for other small-sized Jewish communities: "For a lot of my non-Jewish friends, I'm the only Jewish person. And if I acted like a bitch, they'd take it out on everybody. That's why even with strangers, I feel the need to be on my guard and behave myself. When I go on a trip organized by a Jewish

---

29 Martin Šmok, *Through the Labyrinth of Normalization: The Jewish Community as a Mirror for the Majority Society* (Prague: Jewish Museum, 2017).
30 Michael Nosek, "Akce PAVOUK," Policie České republiky, October 6, 2022, https://www.policie.cz/clanek/akce-pavouk.aspx.
31 The registration of the Jewish population was already carried out by State Security in the 1950s when Operation "Family" was conducted. In 1962, the operation was discontinued on the grounds of "manifestation of antisemitism in counter-intelligence work." Nosek, "Akce PAVOUK." In the 1950s, the infamous antisemitic show trial against 14 members of the Communist Party of Czechoslovakia, "Trial of the Leadership of the Anti-State Conspiracy Centre Headed by Rudolf Slánský," also took place.
32 Ondřej Koutek, "Akce 'PAVOUK': Evidování židovského obyvatelstva Státní bezpečností za normalizace [Operation "Spider": the registration of the Jewish population by the State Security during the Normalization]," *Paměť a dějiny* (2017/01): 54.

organization, we're so careful to bear; it's almost unnatural, lest they say, jeez, those Jews are assholes."

Several partners experienced even raw conspiracy theories that could be reduced to claims that "Jews are wealthy, and that's why they are ruling the world" (or the other way around). Quite a number of the partners testified that conspiracy theories were to be found at the intellectual margins of society and also among highly educated people. Karol Efraim Sidon, the Chief Rabbi of the Czech Republic and former Chief Rabbi of the city of Prague, revealed an absurd encounter where he had such an experience. In an almost humorous manner, Sidon recounted that shortly after he returned from emigration and became a rabbi, he was approached by the board of directors of the Czechoslovak Commercial Bank seeking his support against the then finance minister. "We were pretty taken aback – they really expected us to be able to help them in real terms! We didn't even pray for them. Yet it was about the only thing we could do. The idea of a Jewish conspiracy and the power that Jews have is inflated everywhere in the world," he concluded.

"They are all Anti-Israel"

One younger conversation partner shared her disenchantment and sense of exclusion from her liberal left-wing social circles shaped by inherent anti-Israeli rhetoric that she perceived as not grounded in critical thinking and sadly unfair. "They are all anti-Israel, I mean really anti-Israel. On the other hand… not anti-Jewish, but anti-Israel. It's kind of weird, you know."

She spends a lot of time in the company of young leftist activists and intellectuals, who write articles on social issues that she considers brilliant and organize demonstrations that she loves to attend.

She is convinced that one should always be critical, considering the Czech Republic, any other country, "and even Israel." Further, the conversation partner expressed her disappointment that specific Israel-related issues are undebatable with her peers. "It bothers me terribly when you can't carry on a debate with someone, and it happens to me quite often, just with activist leftists, that they use words like genocide… and it just… it's not like… it's not… So yeah, we can talk about what's wrong, absolutely, but they can't just knock any debate off the table with something like that right away; it's like not true (…), and you can't argue against it…"

Perception of Majority Views

Our conversation partners, when asked about their experiences with the majority of society's attitudes towards the Czech Jews, presented the following points: many claimed that Czech people simply don't care and they might have never met a Jew, and even if they have, they may not recognize them. "Zero opinion" or "most people don't care" were some of the typical responses. At the same time, they mention deeply-rooted positive perceptions of Jews due to famous Jewish actors, writers, and artists that are considered as "ours" by the Czech mainstream society. Furthermore, after the Velvet Revolution, many non-Jewish writers, intellectuals, diplomats, and politicians willingly helped to create an embracing milieu for Jews in the Czech Republic. This strongly inclusive attitude of the Czech elites might have sprang from a "shared sense of persecution"[33] experienced together with the Jewish minority during the totalitarian era. The elites' approach is also due the moral legacy of the first Czechoslovak president Tomáš Garrigue Masaryk whose active engagement against blood libel's accusation in an antisemitic cause called later Hilsner Affair positively influenced the status of the Jewish minority and subsequently also Czech-Israeli relations. Masaryk was followed in this respect by the first democratically elected president after 1989, Václav Havel.[34]

Another factor potentially contributing to rather favorable or at least neutral stances towards Jewish minority and Israel was bluntly framed by one interview partner in the following words: "(…) as the anti-communism is going on now, it is also connected with that; if we say we are anti-communists, we cannot do what the communists did – to be like anti-Jews and anti-Israel."

The described process could be naturally detected in many post-totalitarian political decisions and the general shaping of the political culture. The guiding principle was negative delimitation against the former regime.

One of the emerging topics of majority-minority relations was the relatively low visibility of the Czech Jews, which several partners assessed as somehow natural: "I don't think they're [Czech majority] even really addressing it. Because Jews are not particularly visible in society, they don't think about them at all."

---

[33] "Israel Studies in Poland, Czech Republic, and Germany: paths of development, dynamics, and directions of changes," Journal of Israeli History, Joanna Dyduch, Marcela Menachem Zoufalá & Olaf Glöckner (2023) https://www.tandfonline.com/doi/full/10.1080/13531042.2023.2212891
[34] Dyduch, Glöckner, and Menachem Zoufalá, "Israel Studies in Poland, the Czech Republic, and Germany: Paths of Development, Dynamics, and Directions of Changes."

"Let People Know we Live Here and are Totally Normal!"

"And I just have the feeling that they [the Czech public] don't see us at all, and this is why it's necessary to do these events to let people know that we [Jews] live here and that we're completely normal. That's the basic principle of fighting against people being afraid of you and thinking, who knows what." The partner then describes how members of the Union of Jewish Youth attend together Prague Pride or pro-refugee demonstrations with giant banners including stars of David. "I would like to see [Jewish] people more in the public space..." she suggests.

"Let the Muslim Woman be Here, But Don't Wear the Hijab, let the Jew be Here, but Let Him Eat Pork"

One conversation partner, while asked about the future of Jews in Europe, contemplated that he would like to see an inclusive future rather than "to flee to an independent state and ghettoize ourselves." He shared his concerns that Europe is heading towards "going armored," and he would like to have it more "connected and intertwined." He followed this up with a description of the situation of Jews and other minorities in the Czech Republic, where according to his observation Jews can live their Jewishness safely and comfortably but only at home. "If I'm openly expressing my origins and my beliefs, that's where things can get messy." He continued with the following comparative examples: "Let the Muslim woman be here, but don't wear the hijab, let the Jew be here, but let him eat pork. That's very Czech, I think, let the gays be gays, but don't hold hands outside." By pointing out the limited tolerance or rather acceptance he perceives among the majority of society, he repeatedly emphasized that these attitudes do not represent a problem for himself as he is not religious.. He criticized it, however, on behalf of those who may "need to visibly claim that, need to live by the rules more than, say, I do, or are religious... it's going to be hard for them."

And elsewhere:

> Get in, believe what you want at home, but don't drag it out. I won't have a problem with it, but it can be difficult for someone whose Judaism is more intense.

Another conversation partner expressed his perceptions about the majority of society's views on Jews quite bluntly: "As long as the Jews are cute to cuddle, fine, but the moment they should be above them [the majority society], they go crazy. And I think it's been here battered by communism. When you look at those kids' movies, every school is always the same, right? There's this little boy running out with his satchel; his daddy's picking him up, and his mommy's cooking at home, right, and there's no Jew."

Other Minorities

A Tiny Step Away From Being a Muslim to Being a Jew

Even though we never directly asked conversation partners about their attitudes towards other minorities, many of them simultaneously opened those topics with antisemitism. They shared concerns mainly regarding Muslims in Europe and their well-being, pointing out general unacceptance by the majority of society. According to recent polls, 65 percent of the Czech population has a favorable view of Jews, while almost the same number, 64 percent, has an unfavorable opinion of Muslims, and 66 percent for Roma.[35] Negative perspectives predictably grow with higher age and lower education. The Muslim and Roma minorities are often perceived as stigmatized, and the level of negative prejudices from the majority society is generally extreme. Jews, on the contrary, are prevalently seen as a privileged minority with an elevated social status, stereotyped as well-educated, intelligent, and wealthy, serving as a positive reference group for a large part of Czech society. More than half of Czechs (51 percent) would accept Jews into their family while only 12 percent would accept Muslims.[36]

It is crucial to remind readers here that a large part of the anthropological fieldwork was carried out during and after the so-called refugee crisis where the EU widely criticized the Czech Republic for not accepting enough people escaping from the Middle East or North Africa.

---

[35] Richard Wike et al., "European Public Opinion Three Decades after the Fall of Communism," Pew Research Center's Global Attitudes Project, October 15, 2019, https://www.pewresearch.org/global/2019/10/15/european-public-opinion-three-decades-after-the-fall-of-communism/.

[36] "Eastern and Western Europeans Differ on Importance of Religion, Views of Minorities, and Key Social Issues," Pew Research Center's Religion & Public Life Project, October 29, 2018, https://www.pewresearch.org/religion/2018/10/29/eastern-and-western-europeans-differ-on-importance-of-religion-views-of-minorities-and-key-social-issues/.

The three statements below spontaneously compared the situation of Jews with predominantly Muslim refugees, with the conversation partners noticing clearly emerging patterns of group-focused enmity:

> (...) these sort of hatreds towards some other population groups purely arise from that frustration, and that when you've got *another population group* that's being targeted, there's no need to target the Jews.

> So the antisemitism is, I think, in those people just as much as the Islamophobia, that those people are just as capable of turning against the Jews as they are now against the Muslims.

> Today, under the influence of the refugee crisis, the sleeping demon suddenly awakens, and one doesn't quite realize; one sees that it's just a tiny step away from being a Muslim to being a Jew.

Compared to Western Europe, the actual demographic figures applying to Muslim minorities of Central and Eastern Europe are relatively low[37] – similar to Jewish ones (except for Hungary, Austria, and Germany). There are ca. 20,000 Muslims[38] in the Czech Republic, with an estimated few hundred Czech Muslim converts.[39] However, the role of the Other in the imagination of the majority seems quite crucial without considering whether the minorities' presence is tangible or just imagined. Members of minorities, representing the Others, are often interchangeable[40] in the eyes of the majority, and the objective consequences of that are, on many levels, self-evident. One of the relatively recent examples par excellence from the Central European neighborhood can serve local demonstration against accepting Muslim refugees, which escalated into the burning of an effigy of an ultra-Orthodox Jew holding the flag of the EU.[41]

---

[37] Statista Research Department, "Estimated Muslim Populations in European Countries as of 2016," Statista, February 28, 2023, https://www.statista.com/statistics/868409/muslim-populations-in-european-countries/.

[38] "Europe's Growing Muslim Population," Pew Research Center's Religion & Public Life Project, November 29, 2017, https://www.pewresearch.org/religion/2017/11/29/europes-growing-muslim-population/.

[39] For a demographic overview and original findings on Muslim-Jewish relations in the Czech Republic, see Zbyněk Tarant, "Jews and Muslims in the Czech Republic – Demography, Communal Institutions, Mutual Relations."

[40] See e.g. Jiří Smlsal, "Kontinuita Stereotypů. Židé, Romové, Muslimové," Migrace Online, May 17, 2016, https://migraceonline.cz/cz/e-knihovna/kontinuita-stereotypu-zide-romove-muslimove.

[41] "Protesters Burn Effigy of Orthodox Jew at Anti-Immigration Protest in Poland," i24NEWS, November 20, 2015, https://www.i24news.tv/en/news/international/europe/93019-151120-protesters-burn-effigy-of-orthodox-jew-at-anti-immigration-protest-in-poland.

Ambiguity Towards Muslims

In some Czech Jews' testimonies, Muslims were perceived not only as another even more vulnerable European minority but also, simultaneously, as potential perpetrators of antisemitism. A few conversation partners expressed this ambivalence, showing sympathy or even responsibility for Muslims' safety and well-being on the one hand, while palpable undercurrents revealed a sense of jeopardy or even dire predictions about the European Jewish future on the other.

One of the conversation partners introduced his views, saying that since the establishment of Israel the diaspora had partly lost its justification. With a seemingly stoic attitude, he let himself be heard that "(...) with the increase in the Muslim population of Europe, antisemitism will rise in those traditional countries and end up with Jews leaving or ceasing to be Jews."

Another voice expressing duality in the perception compared the two minorities through the majority lens, attributing the role of a more suitable scapegoat to the Muslims: "(...) the hatred or the need to find an enemy leans now in a different direction, you don't recognize the Jew that easily, and there are so few of them; I'm not saying there are more Muslims, but it's easier [to delimit themselves] against the perceived or real danger." Here, the particular antagonistic perception of Muslims as potential victims and "perceived or real danger" materializes in one sentence.

Some of the younger interview partners, however, expressed unequivocal solidarity or even a sense of guilt for having another minority to "shield" them:

> (...) But now it will take some time before we become the center of attention, like the Muslims are today. That, unfortunately, or fortunately, is how it is. I'm worried about it, as part of a minority, I feel responsible for how other minorities are doing, and whose situation is not ideal.
>
> *Do you yourself wear any symbols out on the street?*
>
> I do, and I don't care. When we attend demonstrations, we have badges that say SuperJew, and so on.
>
> *So you have no problem walking through Prague wearing a SuperJew badge?*
>
> Maybe in time I will have a problem, because people say I look like an Arab (laughter), so in time I'll have a problem taking a walk with my looks. And then maybe that Jewish star will, on the contrary, save me.

The surge of the xenophobia and Islamophobia that has accompanied the so-called refugee crises allowed the Czech Jews to identify with Muslims and emphasized their minority consciousness. In some cases, it amplified the gap between them and the majority of society and strengthened their Jewish affiliation: "I have a terrible problem with how people treat issues of race and ethnicity. It's so important to me that it's how I differentiate between people I want to talk to and people I don't want to talk to. And that's the one crucial marker that I feel more people in the [Jewish] community see the same way I do."

Ingathering of the Exiles

The relationship of Czech Jews to Israel is often immersed in intense nostalgia and protectiveness blended with a certain ambivalence potentially rooted in a growing difficulty of self-identification with a distant and rapidly changing Middle Eastern country.[42] Another significant perspective common for Jews globally was the perception of Israel through safety lenses. Israel represents an ultimate refuge "if things would go wrong." This generally pragmatic aspect of the diaspora attitude transmuted in the following account into the partially unconscious search for belonging and authenticity that, surprisingly, for the author of the statement, was found in Israel:

> Many years ago, I was in Israel at a youth meeting, and a large proportion of the people did not arrive because the Iraq war had just started, so the first thing I got in Israel was a gas mask. A lot of people simply didn't arrive because their parents would not let them go there. I spent 14 days in Israel with European Jews, and it was a very happy time, which for me was very interesting because they were interesting people, we had interesting lectures, and moreover, it was in Israel, and I had room and board. But I realized that for me, absolutely the most important thing was that it was as if I somehow seemed to lose vigilance. Although I was in a country where Scuds with nerve gas could start falling at any time, I felt very safe there. I, who just walks around, and for 43 years now, have been saying that there is no antisemitism in the Czech, had to admit to myself that even though there are a lot of things to be afraid of in Israel, at the same time, there are things one doesn't need to worry about because everyone is Jewish. Some are not Jews, of course, but it is a Jewish majority society, and the people share the idea that we are all in the same boat.

It may appear seemingly paradoxical that this specific conversation partner represents a diasporic Jewish intellectual par excellence for his surroundings, even to a certain extent distancing himself from Israeli society. In parallel, he has retroactively harmonized an essential part of his life story with the biblical promise of

---

[42] See Menachem Zoufalá, "Ethno-religious Othering as a reason behind the Central European Jewish distancing from Israel."

the Ingathering of the Exiles,[43] one of the principal foundations of Zionist narratives contributing to the concept of the negation of the diaspora.

Discussion

The quality of life of the Czech Jewish diaspora can be described as one the highest in Europe, if not worldwide, after the Velvet Revolution. According to statistics, antisemitism is generally on relatively low levels in the long run, with anti-Jewish violence in particular almost nonexistent. Czech Jews are mostly rushing to confirm this; however, it is also necessary to determine their comparative framework and point of departure. The Central European distinct settings that emerged from twentieth-century disastrous ideologies may play a role in these favorable assessments that are being issued no matter how complex the real circumstances might be. Most of the interview partners, while asked specifically about their personal day-by-day experience with antisemitism, eventually provided several examples. Nevertheless, they often perceived these cases as irrelevant, worthless to mention, or even an inherent part of the Jewish experience.

Several conversation partners mentioned that the relatively flat level of antisemitism might also result from the lower visibility of Jews in the public space. This applies to previously discussed wearing of religious symbols, such as kippa or Magen David, and the Jewish voice in public debate. There might be many different factors contributing to this status quo.

Besides the aftermath of the already discussed twentieth-century traumas, and the limited size of the local Jewish community that receives naturally less attention, it can also be kept in mind that the Czech environment does not commonly create optimum conditions for strong nationalism and fervent religiosity – that applies to both majority and minority population.

Czech Jews were one of the most assimilated diaspora communities in the first half of the twentieth century. The number of intermarriages before WWII was globally unique, with more than four out of ten Jewish people married to someone outside of the community. Considering these figures, Czech society back then seems convincingly liberal and open. Nevertheless, recently extensive research revisiting the image of "Masaryk's Czechoslovakia" as the democratic island, the only

---

[43] Deuteronomy 30: 1–5.

liberal state in Central Europe equalizing minorities, has challenged this long-standing perception.[44]

One of the crucial points of this research is represented by a number of interview partners being preoccupied with other minorities' well-being, as expressed in their accounts. It can even be claimed there is a widely shared discomfort among the Czech Jews originating in concerns of growing xenophobia, Islamophobia, and Antigypsyism targeting Muslims, Roma, and recently Ukrainian refugees. Islamophobia has been rising as a repercussion of the so-called refugee crisis since 2015. Antigypsyism is a constant phenomenon in the Czech Republic, widely accepted even in educated circles and repeatedly criticized by the EU. The considerations extended to other minorities spontaneously emerged among the conversation partners, mainly while answering questions about antisemitism. This outcome reconfirmed the unchallenged position of Jews as a certain indicator, metaphorically known as a canary in the coal mine regarding the overall atmosphere in the society.

The xenophobia targeting other minorities has made Czech Jews reconsider their own status and, in some cases, feel more vulnerable and strengthen their ties to the Jewish community, where they felt more understood and that it was appropriate to share their concerns.

Perception of Muslims oscillates between identification with another minority group currently in the "center of attention" to apprehending them as potential carriers of antisemitism. In some cases, Jewish interview partners felt guilty for helplessly witnessing as other minorities, not exclusively the Muslims, were "taking a bullet" (instead of them) by channeling the majority of society's xenophobic attitudes.

Stanisław Krajewski, a Polish Jewish intellectual and one of the contributors to the earlier featured debate on Jewish revival in Central Europe, shared a provocative perspective on the de-assimilation of Jews after the collapse of the Iron Curtain, claiming it was, partially, the non-Jewish interest in the "Things Jewish" that encouraged Jews with troubled, conflicted identities to rediscover their roots and heritage.

"If there is a general interest, then the whole atmosphere becomes different, and [Jewish] people are much more ready to overcome their fear and feeling of

---

[44] Tatjana Lichtenstein, *Zionists in Interwar Czechoslovakia: Minority Nationalism and the Politics of Belonging* (Bloomington: Indiana University Press, 2016).

being inadequate (...) when they try to explore or get closer to the Jewish culture and traditions,"[45] he noted.

Analyzing this observation through the prism of post-colonial cultural studies, a certain inverse parallel with Said's renowned concepts formulated in Orientalism[46] can be drawn. "The Other," here represented by Jews, learned about themselves through the eyes of the hegemonic society, this time in an overwhelmingly positive manner clearly communicating that being Jewish was now not only appropriate but even appreciated. One can only ask to what extent this attitude is a step towards the normalization of majority-minority balanced and mutually beneficial coexistence or a phase of cultural appropriation characterized by fetishization and exoticization of the Jew.

This approach most likely enhanced Jewish self-acceptance and approving perception. For most of society, it may represent an exit strategy to mitigate failure after vainly seeking to fill the abysmal void left by the missing Jews. A certain nostalgia for Jews can be traced in many places where they once lived throughout Europe to North Africa and, recently, even the Middle East. This feature is often reflected by popular culture and its manifestation varies, assuming the nature of the local environment. Interestingly, there is a flowing tendency to portray the Jews not only as stereotyped figures in a reductive manner but increasingly as multidimensional universal characters, retroactively acknowledging their whole authentic presence.

Jews were always present in Europe in sufficient numbers to channel socioeconomic crises repercussions, as the ancestral Other being for centuries instrumentalized as a screen to project majorities' inner and outer struggles.

Compensatory mechanisms of an unofficial affirmative action spontaneously activated after the end of the Cold War in Central and Eastern Europe came too late for many Jews. After the long twentieth century, the invitation to the table providing a particular advantage compared to other minorities may look suspicious and appear as another instrument of othering. Those members of the Jewish community in Czechia who accepted the privilege given by the majority often prefer to maintain the mentioned inconspicuousness and low profile, carefully following the societal mood so as not to be too different (too Jewish) and fall out of favor.

---

[45] Stanislaw Krajewski, "The Concept of De-Assimilation as a Tool to Describe Present-Day European Jews: The Example of Poland" (2022), https://www.eurojewishstudies.org/conference-grant-programme-reports/report-a-jewish-europe-virtual-and-real-life-spaces-in-the-21st-century/.
[46] Edward W. Said, *Orientalism* (Vintage Books, 1979).

The findings of this long-term qualitative research are not entirely encouraging. Conjointly with the global decline of democracy lasting almost two decades,[47] visibly growing nationalism, nativism, and populism, European Jews once again experience the role of those who are here to be blamed (or praised) for ruling the world, having too much power or as a novelty of the twentieth and twenty-first century, for the Israeli-Palestinian conflict. In parallel, we witness an apparent surge among those who eventually embraced their Jewish roots by finding a distinct path and formulating a new story: often, however, co-creating the story with those who share identical values and motivations rather than joint ethnic backgrounds.

---

[47] "Global Freedom Declines for 17th Consecutive Year, but May Be Approaching a Turning Point," Freedom House, New Report, March 9, 2023, https://freedomhouse.org/article/new-report-global-freedom-declines-17th-consecutive-year-may-be-approaching-turning-point.

Barbora Jakobyová, Eduard Nižňanský, and Olaf Glöckner
Jewish Experiences and New Encounters in Slovakia

A visible and stable Jewish life in Slovakia was first established in the second half of the nineteenth century by Jews emigrating from Bohemia, Moravia, Austria, and Poland. Jewish pluralism developed in many European countries during that time period, and Slovakia was no exception. Apart from traditional Orthodox communities, Neolog communities were founded – a form of modernized religious Jewry in central eastern Europe – influenced by the Neolog movement in Hungary. Traditional Jewry had been flourishing decades earlier, partly due to the charismatic Rabbi Moses Schreiber (1762–1839), better known as Moshe Sofer (Chatam Sofer). Sofer created his own Orthodox school (Yeshiva) in Pressburg (after 1918 Bratislava) and became a mentor for thousands of young Talmud and Tora students. Some historians argue that Moshe Sofer's Yeshiva was the most influential Jewish space in central Europe until World War II.[1]

Following Jewish emancipation in 1896, many Jews adopted the Hungarian language and customs to advance in society. Many Jews moved to cities and learned professions; others remained in the countryside, mostly working as artisans, merchants, and shopkeepers.[2] Jews gradually created the middle class that the Slovaks did not have, while antisemitism continued to grow. Jew-hatred continued to grow, especially on the Christian side, and lined with typical stereotypes ("Jews murdered Christ"), on an economic level ("Jews exploit Slovaks"), and on the national level ("Jews are not Slovaks, they speak Yiddish, Hungarian, German"). After the First World War and unifying Czechoslovakia as an independent state, anti-Jewish riots broke out in the Slovak part of the new State. However, these riots quickly ended. The democratic and parliamentary Czechoslovak Republic gave the Jews all civil and political rights. The Jews accepted Czechoslovakia as their state. They could also apply for Jewish nationality.

---

1 https://www.aish.com/jl/h/48956361.html (accessed December 15, 2021).
2 Barbara Hutzelmann (2018), "Einführung: Slowakei" [Introduction: Slovakia], in *Slowakei, Rumänien und Bulgarien* [Slovakia, Romania, and Bulgaria]. *Die Verfolgung und Ermordung der europäischen Juden durch das nationalsozialistische Deutschland* [The persecution and murder of European Jews by National Socialist Germany], ed. Barbara Hutzelmann, Mariana Hausleitner, and Souzana Hazan (München, 2018), S. 18 f.; furthermore: Thomas Lorman, *The Making of the Slovak People's Party: Religion, Nationalism and the Culture War in Early 20th-Century Europe* (London: Bloomsbury Publishing, 2019), 47/48.

However, during the 1930s, antisemitism increased again, now fostered by economic Judeophobia during the Great Depression and steered by the politics of the Nationalist Hlinka's Slovak People's Party. During the Czechoslovak Republic, this party never won more than one third of the votes in Slovakia in democratic elections. The party then merged with several other nationalist ones in November 1938 and finally became like the Hlinka's Slovak People's Party – Party of Slovak National Unity, the dominant political body of the Slovak State. Spiritual mentors and party chairmen Andrej Hlinka (chairman from 1913–38) and later Jozef Tiso (chairman from 1939–45) became Slovak *priests*. Under Tiso,[3] Slovakia remained unoccupied in the early 1940s, while the State became a close ally of Nazi Germany,[4] a dictatorship, and collaborated with Germany until the end of the war in 1945. From then on, antisemitism became state politics, not only resulting in the exclusion of Jews from social life. Under Tiso, Slovak authorities went as far as offering "financial compensation" to Nazi Germany for the deportation of Slovak Jews.[5] These deportations continued into the fall of 1944 after German troops occupied Slovak territory to quash the Slovak National uprising. During World War II, German and Slovak authorities deported more than 70,000 Jews from Slovakia, many of them ending up in the Nazi death camps in occupied Polish territory. Precise figures are still unclear, but it is estimated that from the Jewish-Slovakian population, which counted 136,000 people before the war, between 68,000 and 100,000 were killed.[6]

After World War II, the number of Jews in Slovakia was estimated at 25,000. At that time, many of the remaining Slovak Jews decided to emigrate, even more so after the communist takeover in February 1948 and – just a few months later – the declaration of the State of Israel. Israel became the safe haven, but a considerable number of Slovak Jews also managed to emigrate to the USA. During the communist period, lasting from early 1948 until 1989, organized Jewish life steadily de-

---

[3] See: Eduard Nižňanský, "Die Vorstellungen Jozef Tisos über Religion, Volk und Staat und ihre Folgen für seine Politik während des Zweiten Weltkrieges." in *Religion und Nation: Tschechen, Deutschen und Slowaken im 20. Jahrhundert*, ed. Kristina Kaiserová, Eduard Nižňanský, Martin Schulze-Wesel (Essen: Klartext, 2015), s. 39–82; James Mace Ward, *Priest, Politician, Collaborator: Jozef Tiso and the Making of Fascist Slovakia* (Ithaca, NY: Cornell University Press, 2013).
[4] See "Treaty of Defence between Germany and Slovakia," in *Eduard Nižňanský, Slowakisch-deutsche Beziehungen 1938–1941 in Dokumenten I* (Prešov: Universum, 2009), S. 304–306.
[5] See Ivan Kamenec, *On the Trial of Tragedy. The Holocaust in Slovakia* (Bratislava: H&H, 2007); Eduard Nižňanský and Katarína Psicová, *Antisemitismus und Holocaust in der Slowakei in Dokumenten deutscher Provenienz von 1938 bis 1945* (Banská Bystrica: Múzeum SNP, 2021).
[6] David M. Crowe, *The Holocaust: Roots, History, and Aftermath* (Boulder, CO: Westview Press, 2008), 447.

clined, additionally hindered by aging, assimilation, and the hostile politics of the regime against any religious life and activities.

Only with the peaceful revolution in Czechoslovakia in 1989 (and Slovak independence in 1993) were some religious and cultural Jewish structures re-constructed and renewed, though – as we witnessed in our series of expert interviews – by protagonists with a long breath and prodigious self-confidence. In terms of identity, some Slovakian Jews today identify as religiously Jewish while others as ethnically Jewish, with the former outweighing the latter. Most recently, religious observance seems to be on the rise – children and youth of mixed marriages are also returning to the community and studying Judaism. Today, Bratislava and Košice have active, Orthodox synagogues: the Heydukova Street Synagogue in Bratislava and the Pushkinova Street Synagogue in Košice. Kosher food is available in Bratislava and Košice, but almost impossible to find elsewhere in the country.[7]

Agreeing that a Jewish future in Eastern Europe can only be built on a very solid educational foundation, starting with early age groups, the Ronald Lauder Foundation has opened a Kindergarten (Lauder Gan Menachem) in the Slovakian capital. The globally active Chassidic movement Chabad Lubavitch has also been running an enlarged educational center in the heart of Bratislava's historic Old Town since 2000, including a Hebrew school named "Tora Or" (Light of the Tora).[8] However, the rebuilt and newly established structures of Jewish life in Slovakia, formerly home of vibrant, dynamic, and self-confident Jewish communities in several cities of the country, still appear as kind of "a drop in the bucket."

Due to limited capacity, our interview sample in Slovakia exclusively concentrated on a half dozen interviewees, most of them Jewish functionaries and intellectuals, but with perceptibly varying world views and at least gradual deviations regarding their perspectives on a Jewish future in the country. The Jewish interviewees revealed a clear awareness of demographic weakness and limited future prospects for the very small Jewish communities in the country, which is not surprising when considering that today's Slovak-Jewish population is no more than 2,600 in number,[9] most of them living in Bratislava and in smaller Jewish communities in Košice, Prešov, Banská Bystrica, Zvolen, Žilina, and Nové Zámky.

To commemorate the murdered Jewish population, a number of monuments and commemorative plaques, including plaques with the names of the murdered

---

[7] World Jewish Congress, Slovakia, accessed on December 15, 2021, https://www.worldjewishcongress.org/en/about/communities/SK.
[8] https://www.chabadslovakia.com/templates/articlecco_cdo/aid/584089/jewish/Hebrew-School-Tora-Or.htm (accessed May 22, 2023).
[9] Institute for Jewish Policy Research/JPR, Slovakia, accessed December 15, 2021, www.jpr.org.uk/country?id=294.

Jews, were erected. At the Jewish cemetery in Zvolen there is a list of Holocaust victims and in front of the cemetery there is a monument to Slovaks who helped Jews during the Holocaust and were awarded the "Righteous Among the Nations" award. Every year, the names of not only the Jewish victims but also the Slovaks who saved them are read there. September 9 (the adoption of the racial so-called Jewish Code from 1941) is a memorial day of the Slovak Republic.

The Jewish interview partners were encouraged to describe how they currently experience and see organized Jewish life in the country, what makes their individual Jewish identities distinct, and how they consider Jewish/non-Jewish relations in Slovakia today. We also asked about their experiences with antisemitism, and to what extent old-new antisemitism might affect their individual lives, and the day-to-day lives of the local Jewish communities. Sharing biographical experiences was welcomed, so some interviewees gave insight into specific life experiences.

Surprisingly, almost all of the interview partners were carefully optimistic about Jewish issues. They are certainly aware of the community's tiny size (compared to before World War II), and nowadays they face problems similar to most other diaspora communities in Europe: aging, secularization in the younger generations, trends of assimilation, declining interest in Jewish issues, and a lack of sufficient infrastructure, at least in smaller cities.

On the other hand, our interview partners, especially those with special functions in the Bratislava community, expressed a resolute and active pragmatism ("to make the best of it"), proudly raised the flag, and committed to *not* departing from Jewish traditions, personhood, and community activities.

Slovak Jews feel foremost like *Slovak citizens* and secondly as ethnic or religious Jews, and they obviously feel well integrated into the non-Jewish majority society. Actual trends and incidents of antisemitism are carefully noticed, but not considered an existential threat. Critical attention is paid rather to growing nationalism and historical revisionism. Our non-Jewish interview partners shared similar concerns regarding growing nationalism, but also referred to a vibrant Jewish community, with open doors for interested non-Jews and a readiness for more dialogue. However, due to the small number and size of the Jewish communities, the frequency and scope of joint Jewish-Christian activities and projects seem to be limited, and rather concentrated on Jewish *history*. A great deal of respect is shown for Slovak Christian schools, which frequently organize site visits with their classes to Auschwitz.

Some uncertainties have emerged since right wing populist/right extremist parties and parts of the the clergy developed new forms of mutual sympathy and interest in cooperation – which inevitably raises memories of the disastrous bonds and collaborations under the Tiso-regime in World War II. However, as our interviewees told us, uncertainty is rarely caused by open antisemitism or hostile attacks but rather by far right-wing rallies and celebrations under the guise of "new patriotism." The trend obviously meets the majority society's wishes to place its own sufferings in World War II in the foreground, despite Slovakia being a long-time ally of Nazi Germany until 1944. Thus, the commemoration of the tragic fate of distinct minorities under Tiso and Nazi Germany, including the deportation and annihilation of the overwhelming majority of Slovak Jews, is not directly contested but is in danger of becoming downplayed or gradually ignored.

Our non-Jewish interviewees, however, embodied the opposite of such current trends. They have found an approach to Jewish topics, Jewish networks, and people by simply acknowledging and considering the fate of the Slovak Jewish population during World War II.

The Jewish interview partners very much appreciated contacts with interested non-Jews. Most of them also argued that Slovakia could be one of the most secure places for Jews in the world. The trust in politics and authorities seems unshaken for the time being, a position also shared with interview partners in other countries in our project's focus.

Both our Jewish as well as our non-Jewish interview partners had high professional qualifications and were of varying ages and gender. All were well-integrated in their professional fields and had optimal networks in their private networks, which may contribute to them feeling at home in their city of residence, as well as in their native country. A.A., a young successful female author (non-Jewish), who publishes books on Jewish history and present day Slovakia admits:

> So, I feel at home in my house, but in general I feel at home in Bratislava, in Slovakia. I would say that I am a local patriot and that I'm interested in exploring the whereabouts of my city and maybe country, but I can't say about myself that I would like to travel outside of the country.[10]

A Jewish scientist and pensioner, Egon Gál, made a quite optimistic remark when saying: "I feel at home here, in Bratislava. I have been living in this city for quite a long time (...) I feel normal. I have no problems. I'm happy to live here and I feel good."[11] K.S., a Jewish, middle-aged businesswoman, also situated in Bratislava, said when asked where she would feel most at home:

---

10 Interview with author and historian A.A., in Bratislava, March 29, 2020.
11 Interview with Egon Gál., in Bratislava, April 4, 2020.

> So, I feel at home, I don't know, so I'm travelling, that is where I feel at home, you know, that's when I'm with Hashem or whatever in order to be fine. But I live in Bratislava, and my main social circles, that's what I, and before that I (indiscernible) to live in Bratislava, I've lived here all my life.[12]

Jewish and non-Jewish interview partners were pleasantly surprised when asked about the *presence of Jews* in their closest circles of friends. Also, the Jewish respondents didn't consider it a meaningful criterion to choose friends primarily by cultural, ethnic, or religious belonging.

In this regard, K.S., the businesswoman from Bratislava, said: "My main social circles are businesspeople, intellectuals, mainly non-Jews because there are not too many Jews here, so it would be very difficult just to be with Jews."

Egon Gál, who was also former president of the Jewish Community in Bratislava, admitted that, due to his individual and professional biography, Jews were not the most important persons in his life:

> It's hard to tell, most of my best friends are non-Jewish because I lived most of my life outside of the Jewish Community. In my academic professional specialities, there haven't been Jews in Bratislava. Admittedly, I have also good Jewish friends, and I am a long-time member of the Jewish community here, and so my relation to Jewish people, community members, is also good. For some time I was President of Jewish community (in Bratislava, O.G.), so I had a lot of friends there as well."[13]

Professor Martin Muránsky, a non-Jewish professor of philosophy at the University of Bratislava, and very well acquainted with the Jewish scene in Slovakia's Capital, said:

> Choosing my friends because they are Jewish? This is not my case. I never choose my friends because of being Jewish or non-Jewish. I didn't. Today I do not accept this thing [sic] this differentiation of people on two sorts, you know. I didn't have that kind of socialization. I am lucky that I am not a victim of this differentiation in my life. So, but after all I was aware of who is or who is not Jewish in my circle of friends.[14]

Obviously, Jewish and non-Jewish interviewees in Bratislava did not feel any constraint or strong motive to find friends in specific ethno-cultural, religious, or political groups. Or, conversely, to join any networks or communities due to needing a sense of collective belonging. On the contrary, they saw it as a matter of course to choose friends in their professional fields or through cultural or intellectual inter-

---

12 Interview with K.S., a businesswoman, in Bratislava, March 28, 2020.
13 Interview with Egon Gál in Bratislava, April 4, 2020.
14 Interview with Professor Martin Muránsky in Bratislava, April 5, 2020.

ests. Thus, drawing from our interviews in Bratislava, the boundaries between Jewish and non-Jewish networks appeared to be quite permeable and flexible. Strategies of mutual alienation seemed – 80 years after the Shoah – irrelevant. Being aware of the disastrous fate of their ancestors nearly 80 years ago, the Jewish interview partners felt well-affiliated with their current places of residence.

Like all Jewish communities and organizations in the former Eastern Bloc, Slovakian Jews also had to fight a permanent struggle of survival against assimilation and communist repression on the one side and against fatalism and institutional regression on the other. However, it seems that the pressure by the communist system was much more problematic than the relations with non-Jewish neighbours or any occurrences of antisemitism. So, unsurprisingly, the end of the Cold War and the political and social transformation from 1989/90 was very much welcomed by the interview partners.[15] From that time onward, it was possible to develop new structures and programs, also supported by Israel and Jewish organizations in the western world. Some of the interview partners also admitted that after the end of the communist regime, it was the first time they felt free to live as Jews in public, not fearing any restrictions or negative repercussions from the state.

The entire political and societal shift created great incentives for the very few but still persistent local Jewish communities in Slovakia. Dr. Tomáš Stern, today's Head of the Jewish Community in Bratislava, tried to draw a realistic balance "30 years later":

> Admittedly, from the demographic point of view, we have a very small Jewish collective in Slovakia today. We have about 2,000 men and women who are registered as belonging to the Jewish religion, half of them live in Bratislava. Across the country, there are 12 local Jewish communities, but the JC in Bratislava is covering half of the people. Four rabbis are active in the country, among them one liberal, but in general the communities are following the orthodox rite. In Bratislava, also non-Halachic Jews can become members of the community, albeit with some constraints, for example they cannot join the Minjan. Of course, we are happy to have them with us, and the Bratislava community considers itself a 'United Community', covering people from all thinkable congregations. Though, in fact, small communities like ours need a very strong coherence, and this is rather safeguarded by keeping the Jewish tradition in its original essence. As for Bratislava, we have a Jewish kindergarten and a Sunday school, more educational structure would be desirable. But this is what we can build on, we are grateful for this.[16]

---

[15] Interestingly, this is at least partly in contrast to some statements which our colleague Lilach Lev-Ari got during her interview series among Jews in contemporary Budapest. Here, for example, unsolved problems in the post-Communist period in Hungary were blamed for an increase in antisemitic incidents. See in this volume: Lilach Lev-Ari, "Feeling 'At Home' or Just Privileged Minorities? Perceptions of Jewish and non-Jewish Respondents in Contemporary Budapest."
[16] Interview with Dr. Tomáš Stern in Bratislava, January 20, 2022.

Regarding the perspectives of the Jewish communities in Slovakia, Tomáš Stern says:

> The number of our members is not that big, but we feel – unlike 30 years ago – that we can do something, that we have opportunities to work on our future. It will remain very important to commemorate to the Holocaust. But I think we are also committed to think on our future, to the positive parts of our history and there is a lot of creative potential among our believers. There is a Jewish Museum in Bratislava, we have a very modern JC journal called 'Kehila', we have our own TV, where we produce TV-stand ups, documentaries, discussions, etc., and we have an open door for interested people who want to contact us. This is also the case in contacts with Christians.[17]

While Bratislava and Košice have active Orthodox synagogues, Jewish religious and cultural pluralism in Slovakia seems more distinct than expected at first glance. Egon Gál offered a broader insight when explaining:

> Now there are all generations in the community. We have a kindergarten, we have a Sunday school, we have various holidays which are visited by all generation, families. (…) We have two Rabbis. One is Liberal, one is Orthodox. But, the community is one, and it is structured more by generation, less by political view or religious. (…) Most of the internal offers are used by old people, because young people have their families, their employment. There are a lot of discussions and cultural programs in the community. (…) There are also various clubs in the community. But it is very similar like in other religious communities. There are clubs of seniors, club of young families, and each of these clubs has its own program, and there is B'nei Brith.[18]

While some of the interview partners viewed the certain plurality inside the Jewish community of Slovakia as a strength and an advantage, at least one JC member, considering himself to be traditionally Jewish, harshly opposed:

> We are trying to live as a unified body, but it's a fantasy. After the revival of Judaism here in Slovakia in 1990, there was a very strong trend of the survivors to open up the community, also to mixed couples and to *all* people with any Jewish grandfathers or grandmothers, which was very complicated. (…) They wanted to found, as they call it, a Reform kehilah, but the state didn't allow them because what they understand (of) reform was, it doesn't mean religious. (…) We just stopped the process, we started fighting, we came back to kehilah and that's all. So we are here and they are there and let's see what will happen in the future.[19]

---

17 Interview with Dr. Tomáš Stern in Bratislava, January 20, 2022.
18 Interview with Egon Gál in Bratislava, April 4, 2020.
19 Interview with L.A., an economist, in Bratislava, March 28, 2020.

Others appeared quite pragmatic, or even rather open-minded when asked about the opportunities of cooperation and interconnectedness with non-Jewish population groups, especially regarding culture and arts. Egon Gál said:

> We have to cooperate with them because we are such a small group. We wouldn't survive without cooperating with the non-Jews. So I don't think there is any problems you know. What is this politics on the other side, the average life needs a cooperation. We cooperate. They cooperate with us, we have friends from non-Jewish groups and they have Jewish friends. (...) Culturally, we are who we are, they are who they are. (But) the music it's an international language. So you know ...the Danube river is a very special river in Europe, longest river in Europe. And all the nations around the Danube they have very similar music, so now there are other singers from Serbia, the lady who comes to sing Yiddish because we were looking for a lady speaking Yiddish. She's not Jewish, but did speak Yiddish language, so it's a ... culturally it's a gain. Culturally, it's not any confrontation.[20]

A veteran board member in Bratislava also spoke positively about the situation between Jews and non-Jews:

> I see no problem in the relationship between Jewish society and non-Jewish society. There are some problems on the individual level. But such problems are also among Jews, among some Slovaks and some Hungarians, some Slovak and some Czech people.[21]

As in many other European countries with a remarkable Jewish population, joint initiatives between Jews and Christians in Eastern Europe mainly began in the 1990s. The aims are manifold, spanning from mutual learning of spiritual and theological views to organizing interfaith events and holding critical dialogues about the failure of Christian-Jewish relations in the past. The third aim, however, is a source of contention, stemming from the role of the Catholic church in Slovakia and the Tiso regime. Josef Tiso, who served as the President of the Slovak Republic during World War II, was not only a politician but also a Roman Catholic priest. As Eduard Nižňanský and Katarína Bohová describe in another chapter of this volume, collaboration between societal forces and the Nazis brought Slovakia – up until the national uprising in 1944 – extremely close to the National Socialists. Most Catholic priests, being in political positions during the Tiso regime, did not intervene when the Slovak Jews were deported from their homes. Slovak Jews were the first to be murdered in the Majdanek and Auschwitz-Birkenau death camps. Since a considerable number of Catholic priests had been mired in Tiso's regime, and the church still has not developed a self-critical attitude about its

---

20 Interview with Egon Gál in Bratislava, April 4, 2020.
21 Interview with a board member of the JC Bratislava, April 3, 2020.

own involvement in this dark historical chapter, leading representatives of the current Jewish population believe that interfaith dialogue is not yet fathomable. Thus, Tomáš Stern states:

> Christian and Jewish representatives share a lot of contacts in Slovakia, and there is, for example, a longstanding project between the Catholic University of *Trnava* and the Jewish community. And there is, aside [from] the theological, also a vibrant cultural exchange and finally a lot of joint commemoration ceremonies, as for example on last September 9th (2021), the day of adoption of the anti-Jewish race laws by the Tiso regime. Most members of the Slovakian government came there to the ceremony at the Holocaust memorial of Bratislava, including the prime minister and president of the parliament. I am acquainted with some of the leading politicians, deeply rooted in Christian faith, and they consider the anti-Jewish crimes during the years from 1941 to 1944 as horrific, as well. However, until today the Catholic Church of Slovakia did not succeed in doing a public condemnation of the crimes against Jews under the rule of Josef Tiso. When the Pope was visiting Slovakia last year, we had a certain hope, but he did also not mention the name of Tiso. It seems that we have to wait for such words a bit more. Though, again there are regular, helpful contacts with church dignitaries, including the archbishop, who, by the way, strongly supports memorial service on January 27th, the day of the liberation of Auschwitz.[22]

For Tomáš Stern and the other leading figures of Jewish communities in Slovakia, it is beyond question that dialogue activities with Christian institutions will maintain, and the general prospects are seen carefully optimistic. At local places, Christian-Jewish activities might be rather limited, due to the currently very small numbers of Jews in Slovakia. Frequent Jewish-Christian activities seem to be feasible only in Bratislava and Kosice. Though, as several of our interview partners confirmed, there are, in fact, interested protagonists on both sides, primarily motivated by the joint search for theological commonalities as well as the deep interest and dismay among non-Jews regarding anti-Jewish politics and criminal collaboration with Nazi-Germany during the Holocaust.

Martin Muránsky, who had many Jewish friends in the Slovak capital, formulated an inevitable, in his view, requirement for understanding the situation of Slovakia's Jews under Tiso:

> You have to have the immediacy, if you wish to further understand something. You have to educate yourself as much as possible, but you also have to have a proximate experience, you know? You have to listen to the stories from the people who really survived something that you never survived – the kinds of memories and tragedies that you haven't had in your family. So, this combination is for me very important because it can be lost in your tragedies and losing ... and being lost means that you are not able to create bridges to others. Or you can be lost in your abstract educational conventions. You know, I'm asking myself what

---

22 Interview with Dr. Tomáš Stern in Bratislava, January 20, 2022.

happened here and how could this happen here. And I try to work most with things within this important question, not to be lost and not to be ignorant.[23]

This set of problems is, at least in certain circles and milieus of Slovakian society, currently hotly debated, and contemporary writers are playing an important role in this regard. One of the most discussed books in this context is Denisa Fulmeková's novel *Lily of the Valley: Rudolf Dilong's Forbidden Love*, based on the true love story of a Catholic priest and the author's Jewish grandmother. Catholic priest Rudolf Dilong cooperated with the Tiso government in World War II, and thus – by using his individual channels and contacts – he was able to save his Jewish beloved. The story grows even more unique when the young Jewish woman becomes pregnant and gives birth to their baby.

With her acclaimed novel, Fulmeková has sparked many different reactions and resonance, as she described:

> After publishing this book, I was very curious what the public would say about this book. And this book has awakened or incited very controversial reactions and opinions. (...) I was invited to the northern part of the country, Orava, to be a judge in a literature competition. However, I was not officially introduced to competitors. I was anonymously sitting as a judge in this competition because they were afraid that the local priests would get angry if they said that I was the granddaughter of a priest.
>
> During one discussion about my book I was verbally attacked by men who said that I don't value the legacy of the Slovak State. Other reactions were quite positive because people often wrote to me about some relics and some old documents or they reminisced about that era. But I think that the most open-minded discussion that I have witnessed was at the senior club of Jewish society in Bratislava. I read them a poem by Rudolf Dilong, which was written for my grandmother on her fiftieth birthday. And the ladies that were attending the discussion told me that they forgive Rudolf Dilong because he wrote such a beautiful poem for a woman.[24]

In circles like those described by Fulmeková – and also among our non-Jewish interview partners – the tragic fate of the overwhelming majority of Slovak Jews and the close collaboration of Tiso's regime with Nazi Germany is an important topic. However, other milieus are intensively working on a white-washing of the past, supported by nationalist or even right-wing extremist organizations. Thus, the aforementioned Bratislava historian and author A.A. notes:

> I think the most important fact that influences the relations between the Jewish community in Bratislava and the rest of the society is the fact that the population of the Jewish commu-

---

23 Interview with Martin Muránsky in Bratislava, April 5, 2020.
24 Interview with Denisa Fulmeková in Bratislava, April 5, 2020.

nity compared to its pre-Holocaust state both in Slovakia and in Bratislava is tiny. So they might not be that visible in society, but I still feel that antisemitism is on the rise. It is related to the tensions in the society and to the rise of the popularity of the extreme right, especially with young people. This is one of the problems in Slovakia now. And I think it also complicates the relations with the Jewish community.[25]

As we already learned from other authors in this volume, parts of the Jewish population in central and eastern Europe are unnerved by the new trends of growing nationalism and right-wing populism, not necessarily openly antisemitic but clearly creating myths of national innocence during the occupation in World War II, praising fighters for national liberation and independence and downplaying acts of collaboration and complicity. On the other hand, Jewish community members also show their appreciation with new initiatives at schools to confront Slovakian teenagers with the crimes that were committed 80 years ago. Bratislava businesswoman and member of the Jewish community K.S. explained:

> It's a very difficult question, you know. During the last 30 years (...) the Jews were commemorating the tragedy of the Jews, but now maybe it's much better because it is in the schools. The historians are teaching the kids about the history including this topic, which means the Holocaust and so on and so on. Slowly, slowly it will come. There is a new generation and I think this new generation partially, they, you know ... because they are taking them to Auschwitz. (...) So I don't know what is at the end of the process, but the elite, they are trying to do the best, they are pushing the kids to understand what happened. To explain the history to them, and to really give them a reason for cooperation, but it's just the beginning of the process, it's very difficult for me to define.[26]

Our interview partners seemed to be aware that antisemitism in Slovakian society still exists, though seldom shown openly, but very much present in several society milieus. At the same time, the Jewish interview partners emphasized that they – personally – feel secure in their homes in Slovakia. Physical attacks on Jews currently seem to be rare in Slovakia. Antisemitic statements are being carefully monitored, especially concerning the new upward trend of right-wing populism and historical revisionism. However, the situation is not considered unbearable, as reported by the media, for example, from several places in Western Europe.

L.A., the economist from Bratislava, stated:

> Everywhere in Europe there's a problem with antisemitism. All the world is now in transformation, so the paradigm of the twentieth century ended in 2014. In my eyes, from 1914 until 2014, that was the twentieth century, beginning with the First World War and ending with the

---

[25] Interview with author and historian A.A., in Bratislava, March 29, 2020.
[26] Interview with K.S., a businesswoman, in Bratislava, March 28, 2020.

Russian-Crimean war. The Arabic, you know, they called it Spring, and so on. (...) Now all the world is going to be transformed into something, we don't know what it will be. So of course, there are also antisemites in Europe, but I don't think we are the main problem for them now.²⁷

Egon Gál considers the situation more or less similarly:

> There are some problems, but they are rather hidden. Nobody would look you in the eye and tell you: "I don't like you because you are Jewish" or something like that. My brother, who was in politics, had problems with his Jewishness. But if you are not in public life, like me, usually you don't have this problem. I never had problems with my Jewishness in my adult life. Admittedly: we have a political party that is explicitly anti-Jewish. And if you read internet discussions, anonymous discussions, so you find that there's something anti-Jewish, I don't know. But in public life, there is no problem.²⁸

Interestingly, one of the non-Jewish interview partners, an author and historian, considered the problem of antisemitism in Slovakia as being quite significant:

> Yes, there is a problem with antisemitism. It doesn't surface that much, mostly occasional violent acts or acts of vandalism, but it's very present in Slovak society in the form of hoaxes, conspiracy theories, and maybe also at the level of the church. (...) Some members of Slovak clergy, but not the church in general, but some members have a problem with antisemitism, for sure.²⁹

This view was rather contradicted by Martin Muránsky who stated:

> More or less all of this anti-Semitic agenda is digitalized. And this hate speech agenda is a very modern phenomenon and I would say that this is the first problem what we have to tackle when we are talking about the resources of anti-Semitism in Slovakia. But the security on the streets, the kind of security agenda that they are really afraid of like in the western part of Europe where 45% of Jews who are thinking about emigration, that's not the case here. I would say that now, the situation here is, compared to other EU member States, better.³⁰

Regarding the threat of historical revisionism, Tomáš Stern says:

> Indeed, the are some trends and attempts of historical misrepresentation. And we have to note that one party is inside the parliament that openly acts as fascists. However, the majority of deputies from all other parties are clearly avowing themselves to anti-Fascism. Also the

---

27 Interview with L.A., an economist, in Bratislava, March 28, 2020.
28 Interview with Egon Gál in Bratislava, April 4, 2020
29 Interview with author and historian A.A. in Bratislava, March 29, 2020.
30 Interview with Martin Muránsky in Bratislava, April 5, 2020.

acting president, Zuzana Čaputová, is making clear that fascism and anti-Semitism won't be tolerated at all. This is, of course, encouraging for our community.[31]

In summary, it appears that Jews in Slovakia witness incidents of antisemitism. When such events occur, Jews do not live with the illusion that Jew hatred has disappeared. However, they are more concerned by some current trends of right-wing populism and historical revisionism, but do not feel seriously menaced in their daily lives or for their personal safety. Those who deal with the topic simply for political interest consider the situation of the Jews in Slovakia more secure than in Western Europe, and partly also than in other countries of the former Eastern Bloc. This does not say that our respondents would be completely unworried, and of course they welcome and support, for example, special educational programs for children and teenagers for elucidation on and prevention of antisemitism, including teaching about the Holocaust and site visits to memorials and former concentration camps.

At the same time, there seems to be a certain confidence that the "modus vivendi" of living together with the non-Jewish majority in Slovakia will work quite well in the long run. Even the idea of a Christian-Jewish occident in cultural terms is not completely denied. Beyond this, the non-Jewish interviewees, like Martin Muránsky from the Comenius University, also saw significant progress in Christian-Jewish relations, though maybe more enhanced "from the top" than "from below." Our interviewee stated:

> When I see these activities of this Confederation of Slovak Bishops and the Central Union of the Jewish Religious Communities, they have really coordinated activities. They introduce even in Vatican there are many commissions, or there are not many, but there are commissions for inter-religious relationships. And there is also a commission about the relationship between Catholics and Jews. As far as I see in this field they are really aware of the importance of having good common perspectives, about living together and not denying the specific religious autonomy of Jewish people.[32]

Martin Muránsky also underlined that Jews are able to play a key role in local places and municipalities when it comes to the real challenges for the politics of commemoration but also for initiating, at the very least, the re-construction and restoration of Jewish buildings and places to their condition prior to 1941, as they have become heavily decayed during the Cold War and State Communist Regime:

---

31 Interview with Dr. Tomáš Stern in Bratislava, January 20, 2022.
32 Interview with Martin Muránsky in Bratislava, April 5, 2020.

I would say in local politics, you have this big initiated event introducing the Day of Holocaust Remembrance or this new definition of antisemitism. You have many regional initiatives. Almost not bad. But you see, in it Slovakia based policies which make it available to people, or visible for the people. Step by step you see this trust, I would say, that the future is here.[33]

In such a light, it is not surprising that, according to our interviews and talks, emigration from Slovakia is not a serious consideration, also not to Israel – the modern Jewish state, which pro-actively canvasses for "Alija," i.e., coming home to the land of the forefathers.

Our interviewees revealed that contemporary Israel is an important pillar of their Jewish identities, although the motivation to move to Israel appears to be weak or non-existent. Some of the elderly interview partners described that they had thought about Alija several times in their lives. However, they decided against it either for personal reasons (no complete consensus among their families) or for professional reasons (no comparable perspectives as experts in their professional fields, partly also due to advanced age).

K.S., the businesswoman in Bratislava, explained what Israel means to her:

Israel is what I absolutely inherently need. We need it for our kids. I'm absolutely aware that we need the State of Israel because of security, and we need something that we can fight, you know for us, for our lives. That's emotional. Economically, I led some big Israeli investments and these developed in Slovakia. Socially, I have some friends in Israel, and from Israel I also have some Jewish friends from other countries. (…) And yes, I considered Aliyah after 1989 (…) and after the split of Czechoslovakia, I thought that I would go to Israel and continue my life in Israel but (…) at the time I couldn't convince my former spouse.[34]

One of the Board members of the Jewish community in Bratislava said:

It's very important to have a strong Israel (…) They do care about what's happening to the Jewish communities all around the world. (…) In-between all these scenarios it's nice to have Israel. So it's important culturally because it helps the younger generation develop its identity, travelling, seeing the country. Economically, again, a lot of opportunities. Israel is a start-up nation, you know, making us proud and creating possibilities for some of us who have the will and the potential to further develop their economic enterprises. Israel, as a start-up place, or at least as a place of some ideas is very nice to have and to visit. For a Jew, it's very important to have this backstage.[35]

---

33 Interview with Martin Muránsky in Bratislava, April 5, 2020.
34 Interview with K.S., a businesswoman, in Bratislava, March 28, 2020.
35 Interview with a board member of the JC Bratislava, April 3, 2020.

For complex reasons, our Jewish interview partners had no intention to move to Israel and do not intend to do so in the future. Our non-Jewish interview partners had neither personal experiences with Israel nor had they temporarily visited the country. However, they expressed much understanding of the fact that Jews around the globe consider Israel as an important element of their identities.

Martin Muránsky, for example, was also quite responsive to the ongoing Israeli-Palestinian conflict and other conflicts in the region when saying:

> I'm not a member of the Jewish Community. For me the Israel question is more abstract than an existential question. I can say that for people who survived the Holocaust, the State of Israel is an existential imperative. And for 16 million Jewish people around the world it is good to know that Israel keeps statehood, and that works very well. So, this is my first sentence. If I look on the sides of the victims of the Holocaust – and the survivors –, I wish to have a sacred place for me and I wish to have a place which has justified roots. I am also aware that Israel has been, from the very beginning, in this tragic situation of the unsolved Middle East conflict. Though, what is the lesson to be learned for me? That you have to be really very careful in the human history and in present situations. As it looks now, for example, the Christian-Jewish tradition is more or less completely losing ground now in the Middle East. However, I still hope and wish that for all minority members it will remain worthy and safe enough, to keep living there.[36]

In general, the small size and the limited opportunities of Jewish communities in Slovakia today embody only a fraction of the formerly numerous and vibrant Jewish community. Nevertheless, it does not appear to be a reason "to throw in the towel" – at least not for the active protagonists. For example, Egon Gál is impressed by the various activities inside the Jewish communities – starting from religious service in two congregations – traditional-orthodox and neolog – via cultural programs to clubs and intellectual events. However, he also notes: "Most of the visitors (of the communities, O.G.) are elderly people. Furthermore many of the clubs and circles in the community are also characterized by a dominance of elderly people. But this is similar to other religious communities, as for example the churches."[37]

What our interview partners described mirrors more or less similar situations in the Jewish communities of the other countries we focused on. A certain demographic decline is to be expected during the coming years and decades, except Slovakia – and other countries in Central and Eastern Europe – might face a greater influx of Jews from other regions of the world. As we have also heard in the interviews, more young Ukrainians are expected to come to Slovakia in the long run, at least in Bratislava, and among them, for example, Jewish students. Also, in Brati-

---

36 Interview with Martin Muránsky in Bratislava, April 5, 2020.
37 Interview with Egon Gál in Bratislava, April 4, 2020.

slava, some young Israelis have already gained a foothold, not at least as IT experts working for Israeli companies in the country.

The Jewish community in Bratislava is obviously willing to keep its door open, at the same time fighting against an exotic or special image. In this sense, K.S., a businesswoman and an active member of the Jewish community in the capital, summarized the situation in simple terms:

> Some people said that we are a specialty, that Slovak Jewry is something special. Nothing's special. We are Jews living in Slovakia, that is how we see it. We are Jews living in Slovakia, so for us the brothers are in Israel, the brothers are in Canada, everywhere. So it was never just to call our community Slovak Jewry. It's a Jewry living in Slovakia, so now it's again – let's see how it will proceed.[38]

---

[38] Interview with K.S., a businesswoman, in Bratislava, March 28, 2020.

Olaf Glöckner, Marcela Menachem Zoufalá
Jews in Poland: Between Cultural/Religious Renewal and New Uncertainties

In the context of European-Jewish history of the twentieth century and the Shoah, the fate of Polish Jewry could be considered as dramatic in particular. About three million Jews had their home in Polish territory before the outbreak of World War II, but only a few hundred thousand survived the Nazi German occupation (mainly by timely evacuation into the former Soviet Union). Though, when Polish Jewish survivors in greater numbers returned to their former home places after the end of the war, many of them were received with aversion, hate or even lethal hostility.[1] The pogrom of Kielce in summer 1946 appeared as the harshest proof that hatred of Jews continued, in line with anti-Jewish discrimination during later decades in Communist Poland, now camouflaged as "anti-Zionism."[2] When a targeted state communist campaign against alleged "Zionist agents" drove tens of thousands of Jews to flee the country in 1968, organized Jewish life in Poland finally seemed to be a thing of the past.

Seen from this perspective, the re-establishment and moderate growth of some local Jewish communities since the 1990s – i.e., after the end of the Communist regime – appears in a certain way, just like the unexpected growth of local Jewish communities in Germany in the late 1990s, due to the influx of former Soviet Jews.

In all the countries of the former Communist "East Bloc," Jewish communities – if present at all – were living in the shadows, and this was the case in Poland as well. Though, after the end of the Cold War and the transition process of the East-

---

[1] As Carla Tonini writes, the book of Jan T. Gross, *Fear. Anti-Semitism in Poland after Auschwitz* (published in 2006), in particular sparked a sharp debate in Polish public and society on the widespread Polish hostility against Jewish Holocaust survivors immediately after their return from concentration/death camps or from exile. Gross writes that pogroms occurred in the eastern regions of the country and in the district of Krakow, while fifteen hundred were killed trying to get back their properties. See: Carla Tonini, "The Jews in Poland after the Second World War.

Most Recent Contributions of Polish Historiography," *Quest. Issues in Contemporary Jewish History. Journal of the Fondazione CDEC* 1 (April 2010), accessed May 31, 2023, https://www.quest-cdecjournal.it/the-jews-in-poland-after-the-second-world-war-most-recent-contributions-of-polish-historiography/.

[2] See: Jarosław Dulewicz and Joanna Tokarska-Bakir, ""An Unfinished Story": Genealogy of the Kielce Pogrom Victims (Selected Problems and New Research Possibilities)," *Scripta Judaica Cracoviensia* 18 (2020): 163–188, accessed May 31, 2023, https://www.ejournals.eu/Scripta-Judaica-Cracoviensia/2020/Volume-18/art/19397/.

ə Open Access. © 2023 the author(s), published by De Gruyter. [CC BY-NC-ND] This work is licensed under the Creative Commons Attribution-NonCommercial-NoDerivatives 4.0 International License.
https://doi.org/10.1515/9783110783216-011

ern European countries aiming to form Western style democracies, new opportunities and perspectives for organized Jewish life became reality – partially by intensifying contacts to Jewish organizations in Western Europe, to Israel, and to the American-Jewish community. However, the individual commitment of outstanding personalities with a special bond to Polish-Jewish history should not be omitted. Undoubtedly, for example, American-born Michael Joseph Schudrich has played a crucial role in re-vitalizing organized Jewish life in Poland for many decades. Schudrich, who grew up and studied in New York City, among others at Columbia University and at the Yeshiva University, settled on behalf of the Lauder Foundation to Warsaw in the early 1990s, where he has continued to work – with few hesitations – until today. His own grandparents had been Polish Jews, and they emigrated to the United States before World War II and the Shoah. Since 2005, Schudrich is holding two citizenships: American and Polish. He considers his work as the Chief Rabbi of Poland in the following way: "That is the story of Polish Jews today. When Jews around the world discuss Poland, they have an obligation not only to remember the past, but also the work being done to bring as many Jews here in Poland back to the Jewish people. This is our real challenge."[3]

Not only individual protagonists "from outside" but also experienced organizations like the Ronald S. Lauder Foundation and Chabad Lubavitch began to start activities in and with Jewish communities in Poland in order to stabilize Jewish life on-site, to provide for the needy and to work on the future of the local communities, especially by enhancing educational programs. However, Jewish life on site still depends on local stakeholders and activists – people who are ready to invest time and energy, and who are motivated to participate in committees and engage in administrative work in the longer run.

Nowadays, Jewish life in contemporary Poland is mainly based on communities in Warsaw, Kraków, Wrocław, Łódź, Katowice, Szczecin, Gdańsk and a few other cities, all together counting not more than 10,000 members.[4]

Quite similar to the interview series in Germany, a sample of Jewish and non-Jewish interview partners who are often present in public, share responsibilities, and shape public discourse on the Jewish/non-Jewish relations was approached. Twelve women and men were willing to give an in-depth interview, eight of them with a Jewish background and four non-Jews (committed to projects and activities such as research on Jewish history and contributing to the culture of remembrance, or being active in Christian-Jewish initiatives).

---

[3] *The Jewish Chronicle*, November 5, 2009, accessed April 9, 2023, https://www.thejc.com/news/israel/murdered-sisters-are-daughters-of-former-radlett-rabbi-1ypH3xahvCo91YKw3lANmV.
[4] World Jewish Congress, Jews in Poland, accessed April 9, 2023, https://www.worldjewishcongress.org/en/about/communities/PL.

We focussed on question(s) such as to what extent relations between Jews and non-Jews have changed after the end of communism and if rapprochement is possible according to their opinions. We have also asked to what extent Jews in Poland feel accepted and integrated into non-Jewish majority society; what they consider as core elements of their Jewish identity today; the meaning of Israel for their life as Jews; and also their perception of ongoing nationalistic and antisemitic trends and tendencies in Poland. The non-Jewish interview partners were primarily asked for their specific motivation(s) to familiarize themselves with Jewish topics as well as to contact and exchange with Jewish people and institutions. We were also interested to learn about their impressions and perceptions of a growth of Polish nationalism (and patriotism) and possibly also of new manifestations of antisemitism. We established initial contacts with (Jewish) intellectuals in Warsaw and with (Jewish and non-Jewish) protagonists of NGOs, with all further contacts resulting from the "snowball principle." Most of our interviewees preferred to appear anonymously in later citations, thus we decided to keep all quotes anonymous. The (first) names used here are fictional and do not indicate any connection to our interview partners.

Interestingly, the most active Jewish leaders we interviewed (mainly in Warsaw) offered a somewhat moderate perspective by being reluctant to join the "revival euphoria" supported by some media. These attitudes did not directly contradict Ruth Ellen Gruber's thesis of a rather "virtual Jewish life" currently present in Eastern Europe.[5] In parallel, these conversation partners offered astonishing inviews into local community dynamics that showed growing Jewish pluralism, despite the statistically limited size of this minority in Poland.

The Jewish interviewees spoke of an atmosphere of departure in some synagogues, projects, and Jewish interest groups, especially in Warsaw – although not typical for the general scene. They also reported on outstanding inner Jewish commitment, despite certain difficulties, to reach the younger generation. "We have to compete with lots of alternative offers aiming to our Jewish youth, especially in the cultural scene," Krzysztof, one of the leading Jewish representatives in Warsaw, told us. However, according to some of the Jewish interviewees, a certain number of young Polish Jews become very religious and observant. As in other countries under focus in this project, young people have discovered the wealth and beauty of Jewish tradition to an extent that was impossible for their parents who had grown up in a state-socialist, anti-religious vicinity. The next generation started to rebuild Jewish identities.

---

5 Ruth Ellen Gruber, *Virtually Jewish: Reinventing Jewish Culture in Europe* (University of California Press, 2002).

Currently, those young Jewish adults, who are deeply involved in new outreach projects, try to remain realistic and not succumb to euphoria. Thus, Blanka, one of the most active protagonists in the past 20 years, promoting youth initiatives but also being involved in programs to consolidate local Jewish communities, assessed soberly:

> To me, the future of Jewish life in Poland seems very difficult. And I don't see guarantees for the next 20 years. Why? Because we are too assimilated. There is no vision within the Jewish community how to build this community. It's very compulsive how the community operates in all Poland. We have eight Jewish communities. (...) All together it's maybe 2,500 Jews. People who were born, with Polish roots.[6]

The same interviewee reflected on the problem of fluctuation among young Polish Jews, such as in the metropolitan cities. For example, it would be difficult to find an appropriate Jewish partner, given the relatively small number of Jews permanently living in the country. Blanka stated:

> Many of us don't have a perspective to find a Jewish partner. And it's very difficult to live a Jewish life without [a] Jewish partner because nobody in Poland who is 'like normal thinking' wants to have [a] Jewish life or raise children in [the] Jewish tradition because it's very difficult to be Jewish here.[7]

According to some of the Jewish interview partners, there is – indeed – a certain trend among young Polish Jews to become religious and – along with that – quite active in local Jewish places. But then, due to the lack of a wider infrastructure to guarantee the possibility of an observant Jewish lifestyle and also to find a Jewish partner, at least some of them decided to head for Israel or any other flourishing Jewish places in the Western world.

We have the impression that all of the interview partners had strong ties to Israel, either by family bonds, connections with friends, or just feeling emotionally attached. In one of the Jewish cultural centres in Warsaw we met Natan, a young man who explained a more detailed way of his individual relation to Israel:

> Israel is very important to my identity, my sense of belonging, the language and the country – I translate from Hebrew to Polish, it's one of my jobs. Though, I don't want to call it a job because it doesn't bring in money, I translate for example Shmuel Agnon's stories, I already got a prize for that (laughs). So it's the language and the Israeli culture. Jerusalem is a very important thing for me, I lived there and it's very important. (...) I go there once a year I think, with friends or just to visit my family. But it's a different thing when you just go for a week to

---

6 Interview with Blanka in Warsaw, May 13, 2019.
7 Interview with Blanka in Warsaw, May 13, 2019.

hang out in Tel Aviv or just going to visit your family and spend a week there, but in a lot of sense, Israel was always important for me and my family, even in Communist times. We loved these Israeli post stamps on all these letters... It was always very exotic.[8]

As we could see, strong ties to Israel might embody an important factor for individual and collective Jewish identities in Poland, among religious as well as among secular Jews. However, immigration to Israel ("Aliyah") was only seriously considered by one of the interviewees. Hanna decided to move to Tel Aviv, while being in a partnership with an Israeli man, and wanted to create a family in the near future.

Regarding religious affiliation, some interviewees underlined that they consider themselves less religious or completely secular and their Jewishness was primarily defined by cultural heritage and Jewish intellectualism. Some even referred back to "East Bloc times," claiming that some of the then existing organizational structures and the cultural activities have been inspiring and reliable. Thus, Dawid, a middle-aged publicist, working for an arts journal for a couple of years, told us:

> There is a general claim that Jewish identities have changed with the system turn after the end of the Cold War, and especially with the new Jewish structures, offers and institutions. But there were Jewish organizations before. There was no Lauder foundation and no Jewish community like 'Kehila' but there was TSKŻ (Social and Cultural Association of Jews in Poland) and other organizations. We never hid our Jewishness and we never – I never experienced the change of the system like a change of my own identity. I know that there are people who say that that they experienced that. They hid, they concealed their Jewish identity during these times and then everything burst out, but it's not my story.[9]

Maja, considerably experienced in the leadership of the Jewish community of Warsaw, justified her Jewish public commitment and activity with neither religious nor cultural or intellectual reasons while arguing in a European-Jewish context:

> First of all, the future of the Jewish people in Europe depends on the future of Europe. If the future of Europe is going to be in the grey zone of constant conflict management and populism, security threats, physical – security instability, rising conspiracy theories etc. then I'm afraid generally most Europeans will not be happy in Europe. That's going to change the world we live in, unfortunately, and it's not about Jews, it's about us as European citizens. If it goes about Poland, I do not believe that there will ever be hundreds or thousands of Jews living in Poland, because it means they would have to come from somewhere. They would have to move from somewhere and I do not see – in this political situation – from where. However, I believe that it's extremely important to care about the safety and the

---

8 Interview with Natan in Warsaw, May 15, 2023.
9 Interview with Dawid in Warsaw, May 14, 2023.

well-being of the Jewish life in Poland because it's our historical home, for Jews around the world, no matter if you are from Poland or not, I'm talking about numerous concentration camps, death camps, cemeteries, material heritage. It's extremely important to keep the memory of the Jews here in Poland, to keep this place safe because we need to come here.[10]

In addition, professional Jewish historians feel a sense of mission when dealing with the (mostly tragic) past of Jewry in Poland. They try to convey knowledge on the centuries long Jewish history inside Polish society, as an important element of a new interrelationship primarily between Jews and Christians. They simultaneously emphasize the joint experiences from disastrous periods of time, where both groups suffered in at least partly similar ways. Six million Polish civilians have been murdered in World War II under Nazi occupation – three million Jews and three million non-Jews. Adam, currently one of the most important Jewish exhibition curators in Poland, a historian and at the same time religiously active, formulated desired aims while not avoiding a generally dire European context:

> We need to remember that Poland hasn't been a free country after 1945. Also, we need to remember strong changes at the end of the 1960s, and also John II. activities in the 1980s. And regarding current challenges, we are not in the vacuum. Similar problems are all over Europe. Fear of strangers, for example, fear of social descent, and diffuse fears stimulated also by overly problematic reports in the media. From the past, we should learn where stigma can lead to. I believe that prejudice could be defeated by education, education and again education. I remember, a few years ago, it was still very difficult for many politicians in this country to say "Jew", because it was used like a curse word.[11]

The non-Jewish interview partners usually had key emotional experiences as young adults when attending memorial places of the Shoah, meeting Holocaust survivors or doing voluntary work for civil organizations who aimed for reconciliation. Later on, they engaged in activities to promote mutual respect and challenge surfacing trends of historical revisionism and antisemitism. Thus, Milena, one of our interviewees, a young woman in her early 30s, who accompanies Polish youth groups and school classes to "lieux de memoire," sites of memory, in her leisure time and organizes meetings with eyewitnesses, said:

> I cannot say that there was any one-dimensional reason, why I have been such a long time active in educational work on Jewish history. I would say this was a kind of process, and the realization that we are facing an unusual crime – the attempted murder of a whole people

---

10 Interview with Maja in Warsaw, May 10, 2019.
11 Interview with Adam in Warsaw, May 14, 2019.

and a whole culture. Today, in our educational activities, we work closely together with Jewish individuals and organizations, and we share a lot of mutual learning.[12]

Similar to the German interviewees, we met people who had developed their specific interest in Jewish issues and Jewish contacts by exploring religious commonalities and differences (between Christians and Jews), or by attending longer stays or internships in Israel. However, the dialogue between Christians (especially Catholics) and Jews in Poland has seemingly reached its potential. Thus Szymon, a Jewish publicist, stated:

> [The dialogue] is always within the social bubble, an intellectual thing. When you gather five intellectuals and one rabbi and two priests in one room it's very important to know that you don't have enough of an impact. Of course, the church has its own agenda so they participate in various Jewish events (…) but it's like an official thing. There is a day of Judaism in the church so I think for the intellectual life it's important. The Catholic intellectual life is divided in sides, there are some liberal Catholics but it's a minority within a minority, so this official church intellectual life is almost non-existent. The clergy is definitely not an intellectual thing but within the very conservative Catholic Church you can find people who like Jews and you can find some conservative Catholic intellectuals who don't like Jews, so it's like that.[13]

Regarding social effects and possible "fruits" of an enlarged Christian-Jewish dialogue, expectations are set rather lower, compared to other countries. This might be rooted, at least partly, in some statements of Catholic representatives in public, sometimes repeating old anti-Jewish stereotypes typical for centuries. An additional, problematic factor affecting Jewish-Christian relations is the growing nationalism – an old-new nationalism that often includes the assumption that "Polish" is synonym for "catholic."

Undeniably, Catholicism has a prominent importance in Polish collective identity. And for many people, being a good Polish patriot is interchangeable with being a good Catholic. Public discourses on national identity oscillate around the quest for "fundamental values," and – unlike some other countries explored in this study – considerable parts of society and even politics strongly hark back to religious values (faith, holiness of the family, and others). This trend might not necessarily lead to the exclusion of other population groups – like non-Catholics and non-Christians – but it might impede the public interreligious and intercultural dialogue and exchange in a substantial way.

Marta, a Jewish manager in her late 30s, described what such nationalist attitudes could mean for the Jewish (and other) ethno-cultural minorities:

---

12 Interview with Milena in Warsaw, May 14, 2023.
13 Interview with Szymon in Warsaw, May 15, 2023.

> If you want to raise a child in Poland your child will have a religious Polish education. For many parents and teachers, it is a matter of fact, to raise Polish pupils as 'good Catholics'. It makes it much more complicated for the parents and the kids, if the latter shall be raised in Jewish values and tradition. I heard many times from Polish boys that I'm a nice and clever woman but they don't want to build a family with Jewish children. And it doesn't mean that they don't want to raise them to be Jewish. They just don't want to have Jewish children by blood. (...) Being Jewish by blood means that you are second category person you are not the same like the others, just like being with defects.[14]

Polish officials would probably deny that such attitudes are a widespread behavior pattern, and the most recent revival of organized Jewish life in several cities of the country is declared as a welcome enrichment for society. Antisemitic actions are sharply condemned, and governmental politics towards the Jewish communities express a receptive positive attitude, including the commitment to preserve Jewish heritage. Thus, in December 2017, the Polish Ministry of Culture and National Heritage assigned 100 Million Złoty for the endowment fund for the renovation of the Jewish Cemetery in Warsaw. The same institution, in cooperation with the Jewish community, enacted conservatory guidelines that aim to halt any works that endanger the existence of cemeteries.[15]

However, only a few weeks later, at the beginning of 2018, the Polish parliament, the Sejm, passed a new law[16] according to which it will be a punishable offense to ascribe responsibility to the Polish nation for crimes committed by National Socialist Germany. This law is extremely questionable, due to some obvious Polish cases of former collaboration with Nazi Germany under occupation. This also includes crimes of murder against the Jewish population, like in the case of Jedwabne, a small city where at least 300 Jews were killed by Polish neighbors in July 1941, when the German Wehrmacht invaded the city and ousted the former Soviet occupation troops.[17]

Thus, the Jewish communities in Poland are currently torn between public and State-supported well-meaning, but also State-sponsored trends of historical re-

---

14 Interview with Marta in Warsaw, May 13, 2019.
15 Anna Chipczyńska, "Preserving Jewish Cemeteries as an Actual Challenge in Contemporary Poland," in *Being Jewish in 21st Century Central Europe* by Haim Fireberg, Olaf Glöckner, and Marcela Menachem Zoufalá (Berlin and New York: De Gruyter, 2020), 300.
16 The bill states that "whoever accuses, publicly and against the facts, the Polish nation, or the Polish state, of being responsible or complicit in the Nazi crimes committed by the Third German Reich ... shall be subject to a fine or a penalty of imprisonment of up to three years." BBC, "Poland's Senate passes controversial Holocaust bill,"
February 1, 2018, https://www.bbc.com/news/world-europe-42898882.
17 Jan T. Gross, *Neighbors: The Destruction of the Jewish Community in Jedwabne, Poland* (Princeton University Press, 2001).

visionism (and "whitewashing" from cases of collaboration during the Holocaust) and obvious discomfort stemming from antisemitic incidents.

According to our Jewish interviewees, antisemitism in Poland is currently not perceived as an existential threat but nevertheless a problem to cope with. Gabriela, one of the Jewish community leaders, told us in the interview:

> So far yes, we hear lots of unpleasant antisemitic incidents, lots of verbal hate speech. That's what I wanted to say. Not being beaten up like in the streets of Belgium or France but definitely being threatened. Though, I would never tell the people: "Do not wear a Kippa!" or "Do not wear a Shtreimel!" I would tell them about the consequences, about what could happen.[18]

Despite the above-mentioned rather unpleasant trends, many of our interview partners stressed that they feel, especially in metropolises like Warsaw, "at home" and as part of the overall Polish society. Szymon confirmed:

> I belong to Warsaw, I definitely do, it's not the only town where I lived but it's a place where I have so many friends, so many connections, so I think I have a very strong sense of belonging. Half of my friends have Jewish ancestry, more or less. Most of my friends are liberal academics or intellectuals or journalists (...) So I live in a bubble and I think I have a strong sense of belonging to this bubble which is partly Jewish. Do I have a strong sense of belonging to the country or to the state which is represented by this government? No.[19]

Statements like this gave the impression that those who have a strong Jewish identity and are prominent in public do feel connected with Polish civil society and urban life, but are also aware of their position of (cultural) "outsiders."

The diversity of Jewish lifestyles and perspectives in contemporary Poland have an intriguing impact on the inner dynamics. Orthodox and traditional communities work away from rather liberal groups, intellectual circles, milieus, and networks understanding themselves primarily as "culturally Jewish." Among the committed religious forces providing external support, while carrying their own political agendas, is the Chassidic movement Chabad Lubavitch that gained enormous ground in many of the Eastern European countries after the end of the Cold War. In contemporary Poland, however, it didn't achieve comparable success like in other countries of Central and Eastern Europe.

Generally, the various Jewish communities and organizations do respect each other but certain religious and political disagreements cannot be overlooked. Powerful dissents appeared, during the interviews, while contemplating on how to preserve the long and rich former Jewish history in the country, on how to relate to

---

18 Interview with Gabriela in Warsaw, May 16, 2019.
19 Interview with Szymon in Warsaw, May 15, 2019.

Polish society if nationalism grows further, and on how to deal with current forms of antisemitism. There are a few Jewish men and women who decided to leave the country because of either fearing a drastic increase of antisemitism and Judeophobia in the coming years or not finding a satisfying manner to live a full-scale Jewish life anywhere in the country. On the other hand, our interviewees witnessed reverse trends. Currently, young people settle in Poland from Israel, either for professional self-fulfilment, founding start-up companies in the Polish market or just using the opportunity of getting local citizenship due to their Polish Jewish ancestry.[20] However, the number of those Israelis who come to Polish metropolitan cities for long periods has been rather small, and not comparable – for example – with the growing community of Israeli Jews in Berlin or Barcelona.

However, there are some more partly quite surprising developments that might also strengthen and stabilize the Jewish communities in Poland in the longer run, and prevent an advancing demographic decline. A rather new phenomenon is the intention of not a few Polish people to check their ancestors' descent. There is historical proof that greater numbers of Jewish children had been (secretly) adopted by Christian families in Nazi-occupied Poland which is what often saved their lives, but they then became "invisible" as Jews.[21] Many of those originally Jewish children have never been told after 1944/45 about their descent, either in order to avoid psychological breakdowns and trauma, or just to keep the (Christian) family status and atmosphere as it had been for years. Also, the prevailing antisemitic and anti-Zionist atmosphere in Communist Poland could have been a grave reason for the Christian/non-Jewish adoptive parents and grandparents to conceal their offspring's original roots. Within recent decades, especially among young Polish people – as almost everywhere in Europe and in the Western world –, there is a tendency to search for new and modern identities, also by looking back to the own family histories.[22] In case of Jewish roots discovery, some of the bearers willingly (re-)turn to Jewish identities. In some rare cases, this shift may even result into a "Chazara B'teshuva" (return to Judaism) and – if necessary – also conver-

---

[20] A similar regulation is in effect in Germany. Descendants of the former German-Jewish "Jekkes" who had settled worldwide during the 1930s, after fleeing the so called "Third Reich," can nowadays apply for German citizenship and are usually approved for that, after checking the verifying documents. It is to assume that one of the strong motivations for applying for Polish or German citizenship is the prospect of also becoming a "citizen of the European Union."

[21] See: Renee Ghert-Zand, "Polish hidden Jews embrace 'hip' ancestry," *The Times of Israel*, October 30, 2014, accessed May 31, 2023, https://www.timesofisrael.com/polish-hidden-jews-embrace-hip-ancestry/.

[22] Katka Reszke, *Return of the Jew: Identity Narratives of the Third Post-Holocaust Generation of Jews in Poland* (Academic Studies Press, 2013).

sion.²³ It might be too soon for concluding how many of these people who re-discover their Jewish lineage will in fact return to Jewish religion and culture, and – all the more crucially – how many will join local Jewish communities and play active roles there.

Some of those rediscovering their Jewish roots might become additionally encouraged when seeing the growing interest of Polish non-Jews in Jewish history, culture and tradition, not only among interested Christian circles but also among civil rights activists, artists, local historians, educationists, and others, as for example in the *White Stork Synagogue* in Wroclaw, where the Jewish community closely cooperates with the Bente Kahan Foundation and the Department of Jewish Studies of Wrocław University. The synagogue does not only offering religious service, but also exhibitions, film screenings, workshops, lectures, concerts, and theatre performances.²⁴

The Jewish Community Center (JCC) in Krakow also became a symbol of reconciliation especially given the role played by non-Jews in its revival. For example, non-Jewish volunteers are crucial for helping out on Shabbat, when Jews are not supposed to work.²⁵

As the research outcomes made apparent, Jewish life is not only understood as a domain of religious communities and synagogue activities. In parallel, a high number of cultural activities is being performed. These events enhance the Jewish cultural heritage per se and in parallel integrate Jewish culture, arts, and lifestyle into a broader society. This applies, at least partly, to Polish Jewish Intellectuals who experience the hyphenated identity, as Polish (democrats) and as part of the Jewish world that should contribute to promote civil society. As Paweł, a former political dissident and well-known Polish intellectual, declared:

> Even in times of State-Socialism, we had sensitized Jewish protagonists who tried to combine Jewish tradition, Jewish values with working for democracy and a better society. There is no reason to hide Jewish traditions of thought and the very long experiences in Jewish people's fight for freedom and justice. I think it is also important for Jews in this country to show their concern when government's policy seems to turn predominantly power politics, a trend we can also see in other European countries, and even in Israel.²⁶

---

23 Those Polish people, firstly discovering their Jewish family roots and then joining the Jewish communities in Poland, should not be intermixed with former non-Jewish, often Christian-socialized converts who also enter the local Jewish communities.
24 https://fbk.org.pl/en/synagogue/history-of-the-synagogue/ (accessed April 5, 2022).
25 Yardena Schwartz, "40 Miles From Auschwitz, Poland's Jewish Community Is Beginning to Thrive," i*TIME*, February 27, 2019, accessed April 5, 2022, https://time.com/5534494/poland-jews-rebirth-anti-semitism/.
26 Interview with Paweł in Warsaw, May 15, 2019.

Vice versa, within recent decades parts of the Polish (non-Jewish) civil society have increasingly become sensitized not only by the Jewish traumas in World War II and the Holocaust, but also by the tentative comebacks of (organized) Jewish life in some places of Poland, especially since the end of the communist period. Theologians, artists, historians, and even some politicians have developed their interest in supporting and accompanying the renewal of Jewish life in the country. As Geneviève Zubrzycki recently indicated, the pro-Jewish euphoria of Polish elites may represent attempts to erase the equal sign between Polishness and Catholicism; to redefine the national identity in a more embracing and multidimensional manner.[27]

Our interviews among non-Jewish Polish citizens who are closely connected with Jewish issues revealed that the younger generation in particular has developed a growing interest not only in the fate and history of Jewish people who became victims of the Shoah. There is also an increasing interest in exploring Jewish impacts on Polish history in general, in interactions between Jews and non-Jews before and also after World War II. However, this has also resulted in some governmental decisions for preserving Jewish history and culture, remarkably beyond the care for Jewish cemeteries, as for example with the museum of the Ghetto uprising in Warsaw, currently under construction. In the most ideal case, these general moves of approach to Jewish history and culture – as part of Polish history and culture – could be completed by painful but maybe wholesome joint attempts to undergo the years of Nazi occupation and the subsequent times of renewed antisemitism. Such a readiness among many Polish Jews and non-Jews seemed to be given, and the open discourses on Jewish/non-Jewish relations during WWII, as they firstly appeared at the beginning of the 2000s, have aimed exactly in this direction.

Nevertheless, many "disturbing factors" also belong to the current reality for Jews and non-Jews in Poland, aside from the growing nationalism and – probably intertwined with it – the so-called competitive victimhood. Decades ago, politics and civil society started with new forms of commemorative culture (dedicated to the annihilated Jewish population). Nationalist and revisionist movements have tried to counter this trend, blaming politics and society for exaggerating the crimes against the Jewish population or for efforts to neglect memory of non-Jewish victims and non-Jewish resistance. The term "double Holocaust" thus resulted. In a certain way, such trends flow into claims that national resistance against Nazi Germany was, principally, also combined with attempts to protect

---

[27] Geneviève Zubrzycki, *Resurrecting the Jew: Nationalism, Philosemitism, and Poland's Jewish Revival* (Princeton University Press, 2022).

and to solidarize with pursued Jews (we can see these trends in Poland as well as in Hungary and in Slovakia). Such tendencies might put Jewish communities and their representatives in a quite uncomfortable situation: on the one hand they know that close solidarities with Jews were very rare under Nazi German occupation. On the other hand, a number of such cases did occur, and, of course, commemoration to non-Jewish victims should not be downplayed.

Summary

Organized Jewish Life in Poland is currently only visible in a few cities and local places – first of all, but not only, in Warsaw, Krakow, and Wroclaw. Aside from local communities who witness a certain revival of Jewish religion and tradition especially among young people – a generation that already grew up in the post-communist era – Jewish intellectuals and artists are also quite active in the public scene. Like in other countries under focus, joint events and cultural weeks, co-organized by Jews and non-Jews, work quite successfully. There is also a tradition of Christian-Jewish dialogue, though, as it seems, not yet affecting broader Christian communities. Antisemitism in Poland seems to be on the rise – as almost everywhere in Europe – but is obviously not permanently worrying for the Jewish population.

In particular, left-liberal Jewish intellectuals expressed a certain discomfort when talking on nationalist trends in the country, though they did the same when talking about political trends in Israel. Religious interview partners were less critical and emphasized their appreciation in particular for the Polish governmental care for Jewish history preservation.

Strong bonds to Israel seem to be typical for both the local Jewish communities but also for Jewish intellectuals and artists. In addition, Jews in Poland feel a bit unsettled by the somewhat cooled relations between the Jewish and the Polish State since 2018/19. In a certain way, migration movements take place in both directions: Polish Jews are leaving Poland for Israel and (young) Jewish Israelis settle in Poland (mainly Warsaw). To what extent the small but vibrant local Jewish communities in contemporary Poland will stabilize in the near future is not yet recognizable. Predictably, key figures of the Jewish communities see the realization of the full potential of Jewish life in Poland intertwined with the future of Europe.

Marcela Menachem Zoufalá and Olaf Glöckner
Afterword

For many decades, Jewish life in Europe was a synonym for the Holocaust, and post-war Europe was, to a certain extent, rebuilt with the Shoa as a cornerstone of its identity and the primary purpose of existence. Scholars view this historical event in even broader contexts – as defining for all of humanity. Dan Diner introduces the concept of "the rupture of civilization"[1] (*Zivilisationsbruch*), which attributes both a universal and particular dimension to the Holocaust: "This universal crime was perpetrated against humanity in the medium of the extinction of a particular group, namely the Jews."[2] Aleida Assmann comprehends the Holocaust as a "universal symbol with a global resonance"[3] that gained its fields of action through representations such as images, films, books, events, and discourses. Despite its global impact, Assmann, however, also remarks that the historical memory of the Holocaust is close-knit with Europe and World War II. Therefore, it is not unexpected that European Jewish communities have remained suffering from the consequences of the Holocaust – in terms of demography, impacts of intergenerational traumas, and collective uncertainties between Jews and non-Jews.

In parallel to these challenging perceptions, it became apparent that the emerging culture of commemoration has gradually gained an uncontested role in public life. Simultaneously with the cultivation of remembering, a powerful societal consensus led mainly by the political elites on combating antisemitism and strengthening Jewish communities has been established. Predictably, the scale of such efforts varies from country to country.

One of the primary aims of this study was to evaluate the status quo and potential fundamental shift of once seemingly irreparably damaged relations between Jews and non-Jews. The authenticity assessment of such a significant change should involve consideration of whether most developments naturally arise or are instead compulsive demarcation or artificial dialogue scenarios. In any case, what may even start as positive advancements initiated as a top-down approach must be subsequently implemented in highly functioning grass root societies to succeed in the long run.

---

1 Dan Diner, *Gegenläufige Gedächtnisse. Über Geltung und Wirkung des Holocaust, Toldot 7* (Göttingen: Vandenhoeck & Ruprecht, 2007).
2 Ibid.
3 Aleida Assmann, "The Holocaust – a Global Memory? Extensions and Limits of a New Memory Community," in *Memory in a Global Age*, edited by A. Assmann and S. Conrad (London: Palgrave Macmillan, 2010), https://doi.org/10.1057/9780230283367_6.

At the same time, it shall not be omitted that the Jewish population also dramatically influences whether a "normalization" of mutual relations will be fulfilled. One of the noteworthy concepts in Judaism "repair of the world" (Tikkun Olam) holds Jewish people accountable not only for their own moral, spiritual, and physical prosperity and eudaemonia but for the flourishing of humanity as a whole. This significant principle has been globally materialized in the activities and efforts of numerous Jewish individuals and organizations. Veritably, this guiding idea of assuming responsibility for the benefit of the entire society strongly resonates with the "idealistic aspiration to advance a better world," which the European Union recognized and self-declared as one of its fundamentals.[4]

In this very universe of discourse, the EU strives to reconfirm its position as a worldwide "normative power" by encouraging peaceful coexistence, equality, solidarity, respect to diversity, social inclusion, and non-discrimination, to name just a few of the basic democratic principles and human rights promoted globally by the EU. The above-mentioned implies that it would be in the best interest of European Jewish communities to pursue these common goals by becoming active and well-organized proponents of European values and the integration process.

According to the latest assumptions, EU leadership openly relies on European Jews taking a "central role in improving and promoting inter-religious and inter-community relations within Europe"[5] and, besides the conventional fight against antisemitism, expanding their scope and involving "other categories of racial and religious discrimination, including, of course, Islamophobia."[6] This is seen as a particular opportunity to battle "the logic of exclusion,"[7] representing one of the principal roots of the twentieth century Jewish catastrophe.

Therefore, the crucial research question of the following study should be to determine whether European Jews identify with the expectations vocalized above and whether they are equipped to carry on the fight for human rights and democratic principles as a perennial forerunner of other minorities. Are they prepared to actively assist the European Union with promoting and implementing its fundamental yet universal values and policies? And further, are Jewish communities willing and able to mediate between the EU and other European minorities? The topics resulting from qualitative anthropological research in European Jewish communities may serve as impulses for upcoming scholarships.

---

4 Shared Vision, Common Action: A Stronger Europe, 2016, https://www.eeas.europa.eu/sites/default/files/eugs_review_web_0.pdf.
5 Sharon Pardo and Hila Zahavi (eds.), *The Jewish Contribution to European Integration* (Lanham, 2020).
6 Ibid.
7 Ibid.

Undoubtedly, Western Europe represents, partially due to its (post)colonial history, a highly diverse ethnocultural and ethnoreligious environment, including the Jewish population as the de facto oldest minority on European ground. In the former state-communist Eastern Bloc, such exchanges were not desired. Moreover, the respective regimes pursued distinct, often latent, anti-religious policies. Consequently, an impartial dialogue between Jews and non-Jews was delayed in certain parts of Central and Eastern Europe until the 1989 political turn, epitomizing even today an "uncharted territory."

However, since this dialogue has begun, an interest in the Jewish religion and tradition, local Jewish histories and culture, and contemporary Jewry has occurred on quite a massive scale for a variety of reasons. Motives may range from persistent feelings of guilt (particularly in Germany), Philo-Semitic tendencies, cultural appropriation, and exotification, to name a few that are loaded with complex emotions, to historical, sociological, anthropological, theological, in brief scientific explorations, sharing a coherent attempt to gain an understanding of "the other culture" that has been present on the continent for almost 2,000 years.

There are indeed many reasons on the side of the Jewish population to engage more intensively with their surrounding culture, that is, by a decisive part of individual members of the minority perceived as their native culture.

Jews from the liberal Jewish spectrum might develop a lively engagement with Christian (and Muslim) culture. Jewish activists and intellectuals shared accounts of joining "Societies for Christian-Jewish cooperation" to highlight the fatal connections between religious (and related) anti-Jewish prejudices, unquestioned "normal" discrimination, and periodic outbreaks of violence across many centuries. Intentional interfaith and cross-communal network building involves analytical work to find similarities and significant differences between worldviews while searching for common cultural experiences.

There are also other, problematic reasons for seeking interreligious alliances that are worth mentioning to complete the picture. Those are in a similar manner based on the mutual connection of Christians and Jews, this time affiliated with fundamentalist ideologies. Their intentions are not uncommonly tainted by inclinations to reinforce themselves at the expense of the Muslims, who are being stereotyped and reduced as a security threat.

The interreligious dialogue, or rather trialogue among Jews, Christians, and Muslims, is an inevitable part of the process of restoration and reconciliation. Along these lines, initiatives, both top-down and bottom-up, take place. An inspirational Berlin's "House of One" includes all aspects necessary for progressing this path. Interestingly, the project found its mirror image in Middle Eastern Abu Dhabi, where the Abrahamic Family House was recently inaugurated.[8]

Jewish and non-Jewish artists play music and theater in many European places and organize film festivals together. Intercultural encounters with theological and philosophical exchange are increasingly popular. The revival of Jewish art and culture, not infrequently carried out by non-Jewish artists and activists, is often and well-meaningly accompanied by the media. Unsurprisingly, many activities might go unnoticed – and there are indeed many informal contacts, cooperation, and networking occurring in semi-private settings.

The overall findings favor the assumption that the coexistence of Jews and non-Jews in many countries in Central and Eastern Europe is less problematic than in any historical period. However, the question remains whether this seemingly positive turn from former hostility or parallel realities to gradually successful shared lives is a temporary phenomenon staged by politicians, civil society activists, and artists or a stable trend that extends into the communal neighborhoods. Most results showed, however, mixed outcomes on this essential topic; therefore, follow-up research would be highly beneficial.

In Hungary, Poland, the Czech Republic, Slovakia, and Germany, where the research project "United in Diversity" focused on current Jewish life and the relations between Jews and non-Jews nearly eight decades after the Shoah took place, crucial findings about dynamic structural developments, a new Jewish self-awareness, creative social participation, evolving forms of mutual rapprochement and understanding, but also increasingly influential old demons of revisionism and antisemitism, were captured in this book. Europe may face its most significant challenges today – internally and externally. Although relatively weak in demographic terms, the Jewish communities are willing and able to contribute to the continent's future with all their experience and potential. Our study impressively demonstrated this.

---

[8] M. Menachem Zoufalá, J. Dyduch, and O. Glöckner, "Jews and Muslims in Dubai, Berlin, and Warsaw: Interactions, Peacebuilding Initiatives, and Improbable Encounters," *Religions* 13, no. 1 (2022): 13.

Bibliography

Aarons, Victoria, and Alan L. Berger. *Third-Generation Holocaust Representation: Trauma, History, and Memory.* Evanston: North Western University Press, 2017.

"Act No. 338/2020 Coll. of 4 November 2020 amending Act No. 125/1996 Coll. on the immorality and illegality of the communist system and amending and supplementing certain acts." https://www.slov-lex.sk/pravne-predpisy/SK/ZZ/2020/338/. Accessed May 31, 2022.

Actes and Documents du Saint Siège relatifs à la Second Guerre Mondial. Edited by P. Blet, R. A. Graham, A. Martini, and B. Schneider, I–XI. Cita del Vaticano 1970–1981.

Adamczyk-Garbowska, Monika, and Magdalena Ruta. "Od kultury żydowskiej do kultury o żydach." In *Następstwa zagłady Żydów. Polska 1944–2010*, edited by Feliks Tych and Monika Adamczyk-Garbowska, 715–732. Lublin: Wydawnictwo Uniwersytetu Marii Curie-Skłodowskiej, 2012.

ADAP Serie E, Tom 1, 272 (Document no. 150).

ADL surveys on antisemitic attitudes worldwide (Hungary). n.d. https://global100.adl.org/country/hungary/2019. Accessed June 20, 2023.

Ahren, Raphael. "Decrying 'betrayal,' Hungary Jews say Netanyahu ignoring them." *Times of Israel*, July 20, 2017. https://www.timesofisrael.com/decrying-netanyahu-betrayal-hungary-jews-say-pm-ignoring-them/. Accessed June 20, 2023.

AJC Survey of American Jews on Antisemitism in America. n.d. https://www.ajc.org/AntisemitismSurvey2019. Accessed June 19, 2023.

Alidadi, K., M. Foblets, and J. Vrielink, eds. *A test of faith? Religious diversity and accommodation in the European workplace.* Ashgate, 2012.

"An expert opinion of the Institute of History of the Slovak Academy of Sciences on Ferdinand Ďurčanský." Website of The Institute of History, Slovak Academic of Sciences. n.d. http://www.history.sav.sk/index.php?id=durcansky. Accessed October 31, 2021.

"An expert opinion of the Nation's Memory Institute." Website of the Nation's Memory Institute. n.d. https://www.upn.gov.sk/data/pdf/historicke-hodnotenie-FD.pdf. Accessed October 31, 2021.

Annual Report on Manifestations of Antisemitism in the Czech Republic 2021. Prague, Czech Republic: Federation of Jewish Communities in the Czech Republic, 2021. https://www.fzo.cz/en/wp-content/uploads/VZ21EN_elektronick%c3%a1-data.pdf. Accessed June 19, 2023.

Answer given by Hans van der Broek in the European Parliament. Website European Parliament. Parliamentary question – E-2343/1997(ASW). https://www.europarl.europa.eu/sides/getAllAnswers.do?reference=E-1997-2343&language=EN. Accessed October 31, 2021.

"Antisemitische Vorfälle 2018." n.d. https://report-antisemitism.de/documents/2019-04-17_rias-be_Annual_Antisemitische-Vorfaelle-2018.pdf. Accessed June 19, 2023.

"Antisemitism Worldwide Report." The Kantor Center, n.d. http://kantorcenter.tau.ac.il/general-analyses-antisemitism-worldwide. Accessed June 19, 2023.

Antisemitism Worldwide Report for 2022. Center for the Study of Contemporary European Jewry – Tel Aviv University, April 17, 2023. https://cst.tau.ac.il/antisemitism-worldwide-report-for-2022/. Accessed June 20, 2023.

"Antisemitism Worldwide 2019 and the Beginning of 2020." n.d. https://en-humanities.tau.ac.il/sites/humanities_en.tau.ac.il/files/media_server/humanities/kantor/Kantor%20Report%202020_130820.pdf. Accessed June 19, 2023.

"Antisemitism Worldwide 2018 General Analysis." n.d. https://en-humanities.tau.ac.il/sites/humanities_en.tau.ac.il/files/media_server/humanities/kantor/Antisemitism%20Worldwide%202018.pdf. Accessed June 20, 2023.

"Antisemitism Worldwide 2013 General Analysis." n.d. https://en-humanities.tau.ac.il/sites/humanities_en.tau.ac.il/files/media_server/humanities/kantor/Doch_2013.pdf. Accessed June 20, 2023.

"Antisemitism Worldwide 2011: General Analysis." n.d. https://en-humanities.tau.ac.il/sites/humanities_en.tau.ac.il/files/media_server/humanities/kantor/research/annual_reports/GA-ALL_8.pdf. Accessed June 20, 2023.

Assmann, A. "The Holocaust – a Global Memory? Extensions and Limits of a New Memory Community." In *Memory in a Global Age*, edited by A. Assmann and S. Conrad. London: Palgrave Macmillan, 2010.

Assmann, Aleida. *Der lange Schatten der Vergangenheit*. München: C. H. Beck, 2006.

Assmann, Aleida. *Erinnerungsräume*. München: C. H. Beck, 2010.

Avenarius, C. B. "Immigrant networks in new urban spaces: Gender and social integration." *International Migration* 50, no. 5 (2012): 25–55. https://doi.org/10.1111/j.1468-2435.2009.00511.x Accessed June 20, 2023

Axelrod, Toby. *Jewish life in Germany: Achievements, challenges and priorities since the collapse of communism*. JPR Report, 2013.

Baka, Igor. *Židovský tábor v Novákoch 1941–1944* [The Jewish Camp in Novák 1941–1944]. Bratislava, 2001.

Bandler, Kenneth. "On my Mind: The battle for France." *The Jerusalem Post*, September 29, 2015. http://www.jpost.com/Opinion/On-my-mind-The-battle-for-France-419428. Accessed June 20, 2023.

Barak, M. *Native-born minority/ homeland minority*. Center for Educational Technology, 2006 (Hebrew).

Baranovič, Štefan, ed. *Ferdinand Ďurčanský (1906–1974). Zborník zo seminára o Dr. Ferdinandovi Ďurčanskom, ktorý sa konal pri príležitosti jeho nedožitých deväťdesiatych narodenín v Rajci 8. 12. 1996* [The yearbook from seminar about Dr. Ferdinand Ďurčanský, which was held on the occasion of his not live ninetieth birthday in Rajec on December 8, 1996]. Martin: Matica Slovenská, 1998.

Barna, Ildikó, and Árpád Knap. "Antisemitism in Contemporary Hungary: Exploring Topics of Antisemitism in the Far-Right Media Using Natural Language Processing." n.d. https://www.theo-web.de/ausgaben/2019/18-jahrgang-2019-heft-1/news/antisemitism-in-contemporary-hungary-exploring-topics-of-antisemitism-in-the-far-right-media-using Accessed June 20, 2023.

Barna, Ildikó, Tamás Kohut, and Katalin Pallai, together with Olga Gyárfášová, Jiří Kocián, Grigorij Mesežnikov and Rafal Pankowski. "Modern Antisemitism in the Visegrád Countries – Countering Distortion." Research Gate, February 2021. https://www.researchgate.net/publication/349360020_Modern_Antisemitism_in_the_Visegrad_Countries_-Countering_Distortion/link/602c7321a6fdcc37a82fffb5/download. Accessed June 19, 2023.

Barna, Ildikó, Anikó Felix, Grigorji Mesežnikov, Rafael Pankowski, and Veronika Šternová. "Contemporary Forms of the Oldest Hatred: Modern Antisemitism in the Visegrád Countries." In *The Noble Banner of Human* Rights, 303–338 Leiden: Brill Nijhoff, 2018.

Barna, Ildikó, and András Kovács. "Religiosity, religious practice, and antisemitism in present-day Hungary." *Religions* 10, no. 9 (2019): 1–16. doi:10.3390/rel10090527. Accessed June 19, 2023.

Bibliography

Barna, Ildikó, and Tamás Kohut. *Survey on Antisemitic Prejudice in the Visegrád Countries*. Budapest, Hungary: Tom Lantos Institute, 2022. https://tomlantosinstitute.hu/files/en-205-sapvc-20220420-done-rc-online-new.pdf. Accessed June 19, 2023.

Bauer, Yehuda. "Whose Holocaust?" *Midstream* (November 1980): 42–46.

Bauer, Yehuda. *Rethinking the Holocaust*. New Haven; London: Yale University Press, 2001.

BBC. "Poland's Senate passes controversial Holocaust bill." February 1, 2018. https://www.bbc.com/news/world-europe-42898882. Accessed June 19, 2023.

Bell, David Andreas, Marko Valenta, and Zan Strabac. "A comparative analysis of changes in anti-immigrant and anti-Muslim attitudes in Europe: 1990–2017." In *Comparative Migration Studies* 9, no. 57 (2021). https://comparativemigrationstudies.springeropen.com/articles/10.1186/s40878-021-00266-w. Accessed June 19, 2023.

Ben Johanan, Karma. *A Pottage of Lentils, Mutual Perceptions of Christian and Jews in the age of Reconciliation*. Tel Aviv: Tel Aviv University Press, 2020.

Ben-Rafael, E. "Belgian Jews and neo-antisemitism." *Contemporary Jewry* 37, no. 2 (2017): 275–293.

Ben-Rafael, Eliezer, Olaf Glöckner, and Yitzhak Sternberg. *Jews and Jewish Education in Germany Today*. Leiden/Boston, 2011.

Bernstein, Julia. "Antisemitismus an Schulen in Deustchland." Beltz Juventa, 2020.

Bernstein, Julia. "Mach mal keine Judenaktion!" n.d. https://www.frankfurt-university.de/fileadmin/standard/Aktuelles/Pressemitteilungen/Mach_mal_keine_Judenaktion__Herausforderungen_und_Loesungsansaetze_in_der_professionellen_Bildungs-_und_Sozialarbeit_gegen_Anti.pdf. Accessed June 19, 2023.

Blacher Cohen, Sarah, ed. *From Hester Street to Hollywood: The Jewish-American Stage and Screen*. Bloomington: Indiana University Press, 1983.

Borschel-Dan, Amanda. "British Jews fight to regain the Labour party they once called 'family.'" *Times of Israel*, November 9, 2017. https://www.timesofisrael.com/british-jews-fight-to-regain-the-labour-party-they-once-called-family/. Accessed June 19, 2023.

Boyd, Jonathan. "Jewish life in Europe: Impending catastrophe, or imminent renaissance?" *Institute for Jewish Policy Research*, November 2013. http://www.jpr.org.uk/documents/Jewish%20life%20in%20Europe%_20-%20Impending%20catastrophe%20or%20imminent%20renaissance.pdf. Accessed June 19, 2023.

Braham, Randoph L. "Hungary: The Assault on the Historical Memory of the Holocaust." In *The Holocaust on Hungary: Seventy Years Later*, edited by Randolph L. Kovacs and Andreas Kovacs. Budapest: CEU Press, 2016.

Brandmüller, Walter. *Holocaust in der Slowakei und die katholische Kirche* [The Holocaust in Slovakia and the Catholic Church]. Ph. C. M. Schmidt, 2003.

Brod, Petr, Kateřina Čapková, and Michal Frankl. "Czechoslovakia." YIVO Encyclopedia of Jews in Eastern Europe, 2010. Accessed April 11, 2023. https://yivoencyclopedia.org/article.aspx/Czechoslovakia. Accessed June 19, 2023.

Brodkin, K. *How Jews became white folks and what that says about race in America*. Rutgers University Press, 1998.

Büchler, R.Y. "Jewish Community in Slovakia before the World War II." In *Tragedy of the Slovak Jewry*, 5–26. Banská Bystrica: Múzeum SNP, 1992.

Bucholc, Mrta, and Maciej Komornik. "The Polish 'Holocaust Law' revisited: The Devastating Effects of Prejudice-Mongering." n.d. https://fra.europa.eu/sites/default/files/fra_uploads/fra-2018-experiences-and-perceptions-of-antisemitism-survey_en.pdf. Accessed June 19, 2023.

"Budapest politicians tour new holocaust museum described as shocking." *Hungarian Free Press*, May 7, 2015. http://hungarianfreepress.com/2015/05/07/budapest-politicians-tour-new-holocaust-museum-described-as-shocking. Accessed June 19, 2023.

Buryła, Sławomir. "(Nie)banalnie o Zagładzie." In *Mody v kulturze i literaturze popularnej*, edited by Slawomir Buryła, Lidia Gąsowska, and Danuta Ossowska, 139–172. Kraków: Universitas, 2011.

Campaign Against Antisemitism. *The Antisemitism Barometer*. n.d. https://antisemitism.uk/barometer/. Accessed June 19, 2023.

Čapková, Kateřina, and Hillel J. Kieval. *Prague and Beyond: Jews in the Bohemian Lands*. Philadelphia: University of Pennsylvania Press, 2021.

Castles, S., H. De Haas, and M. J. Miller. *The age of migration: International population movements in the modern world*. The Guilford Press, 2014.

Cherry, Robert, and Annamaria Orla-Bukowska, eds. *Rethinking Poles and Jews: Troubled Past, Brighter Future*. Rowman and Littlefield, Lanham, 2007.

Chipczyńska, Anna. "Preserving Jewish Cemeteries as an Actual Challenge in Contemporary Poland." In *Being Jewish in 21st Century Central Europe*, by Haim Fireberg, Olaf Glöckner, and Marcela Menachem Zoufala, 291–298. Berlin/ New York: De Gruyter, 2020.

Cohen, Ben. "Time to cut ties with Poland's government." *Cleveland Jewish News*, n.d. https://www.clevelandjewishnews.com/columnists/ben_cohen/time-to-cut-ties-with-poland-s-government/article_a63548ae-e415-11eb-8c51-7f25126c7692.html. Accessed June 19, 2023.

Commission for Religious Relations with the Jews. Dicastery for Promoting Christian Unity. Vatican State. n.d. http://www.christianunity.va/content/unitacristiani/en/commissione-per-i-rapporti-religiosi-con-l-ebraismo/commissione-per-i-rapporti-religiosi-con-l-ebraismo-crre/en.html. Accessed June 19, 2023.

Constitution of The Slovak Republic. Website of President of Slovak Republic. n.d. https://www.prezident.sk/upload-files/46422.pdf. Accessed October 31, 2021.

Cotler, Irwin. "The Laundering of Antisemitism under Universal Public Values." In Kantor Center Report, Antisemitism Worldwide 2019 and the Beginning of 2020. n.d. https://en-humanities.tau.ac.il/sites/humanities_en.tau.ac.il/files/media_server/humanities/kantor/Kantor%20Report%202020_130820.pdf. Accessed June 19, 2023.

"COUNCIL FRAMEWORK DECISION 2008/913/JHA: of 28 November 2008, on combating certain forms and expressions of racism and xenophobia by means of criminal law." n.d. https://eur-lex.europa.eu/legal-content/EN/TXT/?uri=celex%3A32008F0913. Accesssed June 19, 2023.

Czapliński, Przemysław. "Prześladowcy, pomocnicy, świadkowie." In *Zagłada. Współczesne problemy rozumienia i przedstawiania*, edited by P. Czapliński and E. Domańska, 155–181. Poznań: Wydawnictwo Poznańskie Studia Polonistyczne, 2009.

Czapliński, Przemysław. "Zaglada jako horror: Kilka uwag o literaturze polskiej 1985–2015." *Zagłada Żydow. Studia i materialy*, no. 2 (2016): 393.

Debois M., Sergio I. Minerby, and J. Vigoder. *The Catholic Church – from Enemy to an Ally?* Jerusalem: The Hebrew University, 1993.

DellaPergola, Sergio. "Jewish Demography in the European Union – Virtuous and Vicious Paths." In *Being Jewish in 21st Century Central Europe*, edited by Haim Fireberg, Olaf Glöckner, and Marcela Menachem Zoufla, 17–56. Berlin: de Gruyter, 2020.

DellaPergola, Sergio. *Jewish Intermarriage around the World*. New York: Routledge, 2009.

DellaPergola, S. "Jewish perceptions of antisemitism in the European Union, 2018: A new structural look." *Analysis of Current Trends in Antisemitism* 40, no. 2 (2020c): 1–86.

DellaPergola, S., and D.L. Staetsky. *Jews in Europe in the turn of the millennium: Population trends and estimates.* JPR Report. Institute for Jewish Policy Research, 2020.
DellaPergola, Sergio. "World Jewish Population, 2020." In *American Jewish Year Book 2020*, edited by Arnold Dashefsky and Ira M. Sheskin, vol. 120, 273–370. Cham: Springer, 2022. https://doi.org/10.1007/978-3-030-78706-6_7. Accessed June 19, 2023.
DellaPergola, S. "World Jewish population, 2019." In *The American Jewish year book, 2019*, edited by A. Dashefsky and I. M Sheskin, vol. 119, 263–356. Berman: Jewish Databank, 2020b.
Dialogika-Resources/Documents-And-Statements/Jewish. Council on Centers of Jewish-Christian Relations. n.d. https://ccjr.us/dialogika-resources/documents-and-statements. Accessed June 19, 2023.
Diner, Dan. *Gegenläufige Gedächtnisse. Über Geltung und Wirkung des Holocaust.* Toldot 7. Göttingen: Vandenhoeck & Ruprecht, 2007.
Dreyfus, Jean-Marc, and Eduard Nižňanský. "Jews and non-Jews in the aryanization process comparison of France and the Slovak State, 1939–1945." In *Facing the catastrophe: Jews and non-Jews in Europe during World War II*, 13–39. Oxford: Berg, 2011.
Dulewicz, Jarosław, and Joanna Tokarska-Bakir. ""An Unfinished Story": Genealogy of the Kielce Pogrom Victims (Selected Problems and New Research Possibilities)." *Scripta Judaica Cracoviensia* 18 (2020): 163–188. https://www.ejournals.eu/Scripta-Judaica-Cracoviensia/2020/Volume-18/art/19397/. Accessed May 31, 2023.
„Ďurčanského sochu zatiaľ neodstránia. Mesto chce stanovisko od historikov" [The monument of Ferdinand Ďurčanský will be not removed yet. The city wants an expert opinion from historians]. *Denník Sme*, February 24, 2011. https://myzilina.sme.sk/c/5781369/durcanskeho-sochu-zatial-neodstrania-mesto-chce-stanovisko-od-historikov.html. Accessed October 31, 2021. (in Slovak)
Ďurica, Milan S. *Jozef Tiso (1887–1947), Životopisný profil* [Jozef Tiso 1887–1947, a biographical profile]. Bratislava, 2006.
Ďurica, Milan S. *Dejiny Slovenska a Slovákov* [The History of Slovakia and Slovaks]. Bratislava: Slovenské pedagogické nakladateľstvo, 1995.
Dvorník, Francis. *Byzantine Mission among the Slavs: SS. Constantine-Cyril and Methodius.* New Brunswick, New Jersey: Rutgers University Press, 1970.
Dyduch, Joanna, Olaf Glöckner, and Marcela Menachem Zoufalá. "Israel Studies in Poland, the Czech Republic, and Germany: Paths of Development, Dynamics, and Directions of Changes." In *Israel Studies as a Global Discipline, Journal of Israeli History*, edited by Derek Penslar and Johannes Becke. 2023. https://www.tandfonline.com/doi/full/10.1080/13531042.2023.2212891. Accessed June 19, 2023.
"Eastern and Western Europeans Differ on Importance of Religion, Views of Minorities, and Key Social Issues." Pew Research Center's Religion & Public Life Project, October 29, 2018. https://www.pewresearch.org/religion/2018/10/29/eastern-and-western-europeans-differ-on-importance-of-religion-views-of-minorities-and-key-social-issues/.
Engelking, Leszek. "Laleczki na sprzedaż: Zabawa w Holocaust i handel Holocaustem." In *Holokaust v české, slovenské a polské literature*, edited by Jiří Holý. Praha: Karolinum, 2007.
Engelking, Leszek. *Nowe mity: Twórczość Jáchyma Topola.* Łódź: Wydawnictwo Uniwersytetu Łódzkiego, 2016.
EU Agency for Fundamental Rights (FRA). *Discrimination and hate crime against Jews in EU Member States: experiences and perceptions of antisemitism.* November 2013. http://fra.europa.eu/en/pub

lication/2013/discrimination-and-hate-crime-against-jews-eu-member-states-experiences-and. Accessed June 19, 2023.

EU Agency for Fundamental Rights (FRA). *Major EU antisemitism survey planned for 2018*. December 13, 2017. http://fra.europa.eu/en/press-release/2017/major-eu-antisemitism-survey-planned-2018. Accessed June 19, 2023.

EU strategic plan for combating antisemitism and fostering Jewish Life (2021-2030). n.d. https://commission.europa.eu/strategy-and-policy/policies/justice-and-fundamental-rights/combatting-discrimination/racism-and-xenophobia/combating-antisemitism/eu-strategy-combating-antisemitism-and-fostering-jewish-life-2021-2030_en. Accessed June 19, 2023.

Eurobarometer survey on Antisemitism in Europe, January 22, 2019. https://ec.europa.eu/commission/presscorner/detail/en/MEMO_19_542. Accessed June 19, 2023.

"Europe's Growing Muslim Population." Pew Research Center's Religion & Public Life Project, November 29, 2017. https://www.pewresearch.org/religion/2017/11/29/europes-growing-muslim-population/. Accessed June 4, 2023.

Eurostat. Statistics Explained. Ageing Europe – statistics on population developments. n.d. https://ec.europa.eu/eurostat/statistics-explained/index.php?title=Ageing_Europe_-_statistics_on_population_developments. Accessed June 4, 2023.

Evans, Jonathan. "Unlike Their Central and Eastern European Neighbors, Most Czechs Don't Believe in God." Pew Research Center, July 22, 2020. https://www.pewresearch.org/fact-tank/2017/06/19/unlike-their-central-and-eastern-european-neighbors-most-czechs-dont-believe-in-god/. Accessed June 19, 2023.

"Experiences and perceptions of antisemitism: Second survey on discrimination and hate crime against Jews in the EU." n.d. https://fra.europa.eu/sites/default/files/fra_uploads/fra-2018-experiences-and-perceptions-of-antisemitism-survey_en.pdf. Accessed June 19, 2023.

Fabricius, Miroslav, and Ladislav Suško, eds. *Jozef Tiso: Prejavy a články 1913–1938* [Jozef Tiso: Speeches and Articles 1913–1938]. Bratislava: Historický ústav SAV, 2002.

Fabricius, Miroslav, and Hradská, Katarína, eds. *Jozef Tiso: Prejavy a články 1939–1944*. [Jozef Tiso: Speeches and Articles 1939–1944]. Bratislava: Historický ústav SAV, 2007.

Félix, Anikó. *Antisemitism Report 2019–2020*. MAZSIHISZ, n.d. https://mazsihisz.hu/files/public/filecache/ma__medialibrary_media/657/7657/antiszemita_incidensek_2019-2020_eng_FINAL.pdf. Accessed June 19, 2023.

Fireberg, Haim. "Confronting New Antisemitism: From Working Definition to Model Law and Back." n.d. https://en-humanities.tau.ac.il/sites/humanities_en.tau.ac.il/files/media_server/0001/unedited.pdf. Accessed June 19, 2023.

Frankfort-Nachmias, C., and D. Nachmias. *Research methods in the social sciences*. Worth Publishers, 2008.

"Freedom House," "Global Freedom Declines for 17th Consecutive Year, but May Be Approaching a Turning Point." *New Report*, March 9, 2023. https://freedomhouse.org/article/new-report-global-freedom-declines-17th-consecutive-year-may-be-approaching-turning-point. Accessed June 19, 2023.

Freeman, Hilary. "Why, as a British Jew, I'm terrified by the anti-Semitism suddenly sweeping my country." *The Daily Mail*, August 9, 2018. http://www.dailymail.co.uk/debate/article-2720381/Why-British-Jew-I-m-terrified-anti-Semitism-suddenly-sweeping-country.html. Accessed June 19, 2023.

Fundamental Rights Agency (FRA) Report: Experiences and perceptions of antisemitism – Second survey on discrimination and hate crime against Jews in the EU, December 2018.

Gábor, Fináli. "We have no example of being able to live as Hungarians." https://www-szombat-org.translate.goog/hagyomany-tortenelem/nincs-mintank-hogy-lehet-magyar-zsidokent-elni?_x_tr_sch=http&_x_tr_sl=hu&_x_tr_tl=en&_x_tr_hl=en. Accessed June 19, 2023.
Gardista, February 9, 1943. Joachim Gauck in Düsseldorf: „Mich erschreckt der Multikulturalismus". *Rheinische Post online*, April 20, 2018.
Gebert, Konstanty. "What is Jewish about Contemporary Central European Jewish Culture?" In *Being Jewish in 21st Century Central Europe*, edited by Haim Fireberg, Olaf Glöckner, and Marcela Menachem Zoufalá, 283–290. De Gruyter, 2020.
Głowiński, Michał. „Wielkie zderzenie". *Teksty Drugie*, no. 3 (2002): 199–211, 206. https://rcin.org.pl/Content/55867/WA248_70610_P-I-2524_glowin-wielkie.pdf. Accessed June 19, 2023.
Goldberg, Jeffrey. "French Prime Minister: If Jews flee, the Republic will be a failure." *The Atlantic*, November 10, 2015. http://www.theatlantic.com/international/archive/2015/01/french-prime-minister-warns-if-jews-flee-the-republic-will-be-judged-a-failure/384410. Accessed June 19, 2023.
Graham, D. *European Jewish identity: Mosaic or monolith? An empirical assessment of eight European countries*. JPR/Report, Institute for Jewish Policy Research, 2018. http://archive.jpr.org.uk/object-eur183. Accessed June 20, 2023.
Gross, Jan T. "Eastern Europe's Crisis of Shame." September 13, 2015. https://www.project-syndicate.org/commentary/eastern-europe-refugee-crisis-xenophobia-by-jan-gross-2015-09?barrier=accesspaylog. Accessed June 19, 2023.
Gross, Jan T. *Fear. Anti-Semitism in Poland after Auschwitz*. New York: Random House, 2007.
Gross, Jan. *Neighbors: The Destruction of the Jewish Community in Jedwabne, Poland*. Princeton University Press, 2001.
Gruber, Ruth Ellen. *Virtually Jewish: Reinventing Jewish Culture in Europe*. Berkeley: University of California Press, 2002.
Gruntová, Jitka. *Oskar Schindler. Legendy a fakta*. Praha: Naše vojsko, 2014.
Hackett, Conrad. "5 Facts about the Muslim Population in Europe." Pew Research Center, November 29, 2017. https://www.pewresearch.org/short-reads/2017/11/29/5-facts-about-the-muslim-population-in-europe/. Accessed June 19, 2023.
Haug, B., G. M. S. Dann, and M. Mehmetoglu. "Little Norway in Spain: From tourism to migration." *Annals of Tourism Research* 34, no. 1 (2007): 202–222.
Hausleitner, Mariana, Souzana Hazan, and Barbara Hutzelmann. *Die Verfolgung und Ermordung der europäischen Juden durch das nationalsozialistische Deutschland 1933–1945*. Band 13 Slowakei, Rumänien und Bulgarien. Berlin/Boston: Walter de Gruyter GmbH, 2018.
"Here's the Joint Declaration of the Prime Minister of Poland and the Prime Minister of Hungary." November 26, 2020. https://abouthungary.hu/news-in-brief/heres-the-joint-declaration-of-the-prime-minister-of-poland-and-the-prime-minister-of-hungary.
Hiemer, Elisa-Maria, Holý, Jiří, Firlej, Agata, and Nichtburgerová, Hana. *Handbook of Polish, Czech, and Slovak Holocaust Fiction: Works and Contexts*. Berlin: Walter de Gruyter, 2021.
Hilberg, Raul. *Perpetrators, Victims, Bystanders: The Jewish Catastrophe, 1933–1945*. New York: HarperCollins, 1992.
Hilberg, Raul. *The Destruction of the European Jewry*. Third Edition. New Haven: Yale University Press, 2003.
Hlavinka, Ján, Ivan Kamenec, and Martin Clifford. *The Burden of the Past Catholic Bishop Ján Vojtaššák and the Regime in Slovakia (1918–1945)*. Bratislava: Dokumentačné stredisko holokaustu, 2014.
Hlavinka, Ján, and Eduard Nižňanský. *Pracovný a koncentračný tábor v Seredi 1941–1945* [The Labor and Concentration camp in Sereď 1941–1945]. Bratislava, 2009.

Hoffman Yitzik, "Christianity as told to our Children – the Description of Christianity." In History Textbooks in Israel, 1948–2005, M.A. Thesis by Dina Porat, Tel Aviv University, 100. July 2006, Hebrew.

Holý, Jiří. "Arnošt Lustig's Colette, dívka z Antverp – Between Historical Facts and Fiction." In *The Holocaust in the Central European Literatures and Cultures: Problems of Poetization and Aestheticization / Der Holocaust in den mitteleuropäischen Literaturen und Kulturen: Probleme der Poetisierung und Ästhetisierung*, edited by Reinhard Ibler, S. 142–231. Stuttgart: bidem-Verlag, 2016.

Horowitz, B. "New frontiers: 'Milieu' and the sociology of American Jewish education." *Journal of Jewish Education* 74, no. 1 (2008): 68–81.

Hrabovecká, Hilda. *Ruka s vytetovaným číslom* [Hand with a Tatooed Number]. Bratislava, 1998.

Hradská, Katarína. "The Status of Jews in Slovakia under the 1st Czechoslovak Republic." In *Emancipation of Jews – Anti-Semitism – Persecution in Germany, Austria-Hungary, in Czech Countries and in Slovakia*, 131–138. Bratislava, 1999.

Ibler, Reinhard. "Introduction." In *The Holocaust in the Central European Literatures and Cultures: Problems of Poetization and Aestheticization / Der Holocaust in den mitteleuropäischen Literaturen und Kulturen: Probleme der Poetisierung und Ästhetisierung*, edited by Reinhard Ibler, S. 7–10. Stuttgart: ibidem-Verlag, 2016.

IHRA. "What Is Antisemitism?" International Holocaust Remembrance Alliance. n.d. Accessed June 4, 2023. https://www.holocaustremembrance.com/resources/working-definitions-charters/working-definition-antisemitism. Accessed June 4, 2023.

Inotai, Edit. "Sense of Impunity Lies behind Hungary Official's Antisemitic Attack on Soros." *Balkan Insight*, November 30, 2020. https://balkaninsight.com/2020/11/30/sense-of-impunity-lies-behind-hungary-officials-antisemitic-attack-on-soros/. Accessed June 19, 2023.

Janssen, Madeleine. „So soll es Polen und Ungarn an den Kragen gehen." An interview by Madeleine Janssen with Michael Roth, the German Minister of European Affairs. *t-online. Nachrichten für Deutschland*, August 21, 2020. https://www.t-online.de/nachrichten/ausland/eu/id_88431006/eu-europastaatsminister-michael-roth-will-polen-und-ungarn-sanktionieren.html. Accessed June 19, 2023.

Jewish Leadership Council. *Jewish Community Leaders Meet with Prime Minister David Cameron*. January 10, 2013. http://www.thejlc.org/2015/01/jewish-community-leaders-meet-with-prime-minister-david-cameron-3.

Judt, Tony. *Postwar: A History of Europe Since 1945*. New York: The Penguin Press, 2005.

Kamenec, Ivan. *Po stopách tragédie* [On the trial of tragedy]. Bratislava: Archa, 1991.

Kamenec, Ivan. "Štátna rada v politickom systéme Slovenského štátu v rokoch 1939–1945" [The State Council in political system of the Slovak state in 1939 to 1945]. *Historický časopis* 44 (1996): 221–242.

Kamenec, Ivan. "The Escape of Rudolf Vrba and Alfréd Wetzler from Auschwitz and the Fate of Their Report." In *Uncovering the shoah: resistance of Jews and their efforts to inform the world on genocide – Odhaľovanie Šoa: odpor a úsilie Židov informovať svet o genocide*, edited by Ján Hlavinka and Hana Kubátová, 101–112. Bratislava: HÚ SAV, 2016.

Kamenec, Ivan. *Jozef Tiso: Tragédia politika, kňaza a človeka* [Jozef Tiso: The Tragedy of a Politician, Priest and Man]. Bratislava: Premedia, 2013.

Kamenec, Ivan, Vilém Prečan, and Stanislav Škorvánek. *Vatikán a Slovenská republika (1939–1945) Dokumenty* [Vatican and Slovak Republic 1939–1945]. Bratislava: SAP, 1992.

Kantor Center. *Antisemitism worldwide 2019 and the beginning of 2020*. 2020. humanities.tau.ac.il/sites/humanities_en.tau.ac.il/files/media_server/humanities/kantor/Kantor%20Center%20Worldwide%20Antisemitism%20in%202019%20-%20Main%20findings.pdf. Accessed June 19, 2023.

Kárný, Miroslav. *"Konečné řešení": Genocida českých židů v Německé protektorátní politice*. Praha: Academia, 1991.

Kern, Miroslav. „Sociológ Vašečka o 70 rokoch od nástupu komunizmu: Chýba nám tu múzeum totality" [The sociologist Vašečka about 70 years since onset of Communism: We lack the museum of totalitarianism]. *Denník N*. February 23, 2018. https://dennikn.sk/1034803/sociolog-vasecka-o-70-rokoch-od-nastupu-komunizmu-chyba-nam-tu-muzeum-totality/. Accessed October 31, 2021.

Kertész, Imre „Wem gehört Auschwitz?" *Die Zeit*, no. 48 (1998).

Khader, Bichara, "Muslims in Europe: The Construction of a 'Problem'". *OpenMind*. n.d. https://www.bbvaopenmind.com/en/articles/muslims-in-europe-the-construction-of-a-problem/. Accessed June 19, 2023.

Kirchick, James: Is Germany capable of protecting its Jews?, in: *The Atlantic*, April 29, 2018 https://www.theatlantic.com/international/archive/2018/04/germany-jews-muslim-migrants/558677/. Accessed June 19, 2023.

"Kolektív Historického ústavu SAV, Stanovisko ku knihe M. S. Ďuricu: Dejiny Slovenska a Slovákov" [Expert opinion on the book by M. S. Ďurica: History of Slovakia and Slovaks]. *Studia historica Nitriensia* 5 (1996): 285–291.

"Kompetenzzentrum Für Prävention und Empowerment." n.d. Accessed June 4, 2023. https://zwst-kompetenzzentrum.de/?lang=en.

Koser, K. "Introduction: International migration and global governance." *Global Governance* 16 (2010): 301–315.

Koutek, Ondřej. "Akce 'PAVOUK': Evidování židovského obyvatelstva Státní bezpečností za normalizace" [Operation "Spider": the registration of the Jewish population by the State Security during the Normalization]. *Paměť a dějiny* (2017).

Kovács, András. "Antisemitic Prejudices and Dynamics of Antisemitism in Post-Communist Hungary." In Proceedings / International conference "Antisemitism in Europe Today: The Phenomena, the Conflicts," November 8–9, 2013. https://www.jmberlin.de/sites/default/files/antisemitism-in-europe-today_4-kovacs.pdf. Accessed June 19, 2023.

Kovács, András. Hungary: Hungary since 1945. YIVO Encyclopedia of Jews in Eastern Europe. 2010. https://yivoencyclopedia.org/article.aspx/Hungary/Hungary_since_1945.

Kovács, András, and A. Aletta Forrás-Biró. *Jewish life in Hungary: Achievements, challenges and priorities since the collapse of communism*. The Institute for Jewish Policy Research (JPR), 2011. Aaccessed June 19, 2023.

Kovács, András. "Hungarian Intentionalism: New Directions to the Historiography of the Hungarian Holocaust." In *The Holocaust in Hungary: Seventy Years Later* by Randolph Braham and Andras Kovacs, 443–459. Central European University Press, n.d. Kindle Edition.

Krajewski, Stanislaw. "The Concept of De-Assimilation as a Tool to Describe Present-Day European Jews: The Example of Poland". Conference Paper at the International Conference "A Jewish Europe? Virtual and Real-Life Spaces in the 21st Century, May 3–5, 2022; Co-organized by University of Gothenburg and University of Southampton in Sweden.

Kranz, Dani. "Forget Israel—The Future is in Berlin! Local Jews, Russian Immigrants, and Israeli Jews in Berlin and across Germany." *Shofar* (2016). https://archive.jpr.org.uk/object-ger220. Accessed June 19, 2023.

Krištúfek, Peter. *Ema a Smrtihlav*. Bratislava: Artforum, 2014.

Kubovi Aryeh, Leon. "The Silence of Pius XII and the Origins of the 'Jewish Document'". In *Yad Vashem Studies* VI, 7–22. Jerusalem, 1967.

Lartey, Jamiles. "Jewish Community Centers in US Receive Nearly 50 Bomb Threats in 2017 so Far." *The Guardian*, February 4, 2017. https://www.theguardian.com/world/2017/feb/04/us-jewish-community-centers-bomb-threats. Accessed June 19, 2023.

Lefkovits, Etgar. "Berlin official: German kids tired of Holocaust." *The Jerusalem Post*, March 10, 2008. https://www.jpost.com/international/berlin-official-german-kids-tired-of-holocaust. Accessed June 19, 2023.

Lev Ari, L. *The American dream: For men only? Gender, immigration and the assimilation of Israelis in the United States*. LFB Scholarly, 2008.

Lev Ari, L. *Contemporary Jewish communities in three European cities: Challenges of integration, acculturation and ethnic identity*. De Gruyter, 2022.

Levitt, P., and N. Glick-Schiller. "Conceptualizing simultaneity: A transnational social field perspective on society." *International Migration Review* 38, no. 3 (2004): 1002–1039. DOI: 10.1111/j.1747-7379.2004.tb00227.x. Accessed June 19, 2023.

Levitt, P., and B.N. Jaworsky. "Transnational migration studies: Past developments and future trends." *The Annual Review of Sociology* 33 (2007): 129–156.

Lewis, Jerry. "Nearly half of British Jews say they have no future in Europe, study finds." *The Jerusalem Post*, January 14, 2015. http://www.jpost.com/Diaspora/Nearly-half-of-British-Jews-says-they-have-no-future-in-Europe-study-finds-387693. Accessed June 19, 2023.

Lichtenstein, Tatjana. *Zionists in Interwar Czechoslovakia: Minority Nationalism and the Politics of Belonging*. Bloomington: Indiana University Press, 2016.

Linde, Steve. "New UK Jewish leader: I want to meet Muslims." *The Jerusalem Post*, June 25, 2015. http://www.jpost.com/Diaspora/New-UK-Jewish-leader-I-want-to-meet-Muslims-407127. Accessed June 19, 2023.

Lustig, Arnošt. *Nemilovaná (Z deníku sedmnáctileté Perly Sch.)*. Praha: Odeon, 1991.

Lustig, Arnošt. *Lovely Green Eyes*. Translated by Ewald Osers. New York: Arcade Publishing, 2002.

Lustig, Arnošt. *Colette. Dívka z Antverp*. Praha: Mladá fronta, 2013.

Macionis, J.J. *Sociology*. Pearson, 2017.

Marshman, Sophia. "From the Margins to the Mainstream? Representations of the Holocaust in Popular Culture." *eSharp* 6, no. 1 (2005): 1–20. https://www.gla.ac.uk/media/media_41177_en.pdf. Accessed June 19, 2023.

Menachem Zoufalá, Marcela. "Ethno-religious Othering as a reason behind the Central European Jewish distancing from Israel." In *Being Jewish in 21st Century Central Europe*, edited by Haim Fireberg, Olaf Glöckner, and Marcela Menachem Zoufalá, 185–206. De Gruyter, 2020. https://www.degruyter.com/document/doi/10.1515/9783110582369/html. Accessed June 19, 2023.

Menachem Zoufalá, Marcela, Joanna Dyduch, and Olaf Glöckner. "Jews and Muslims in Dubai, Berlin, and Warsaw: Interactions, Peacebuilding Initiatives, and Improbable Encounters." *Religions* 13 (2021): 13. https://doi.org/10.3390/rel13010013. Accessed June 19, 2023.

Mendes, Meir. *The Vatican and Israel*. Jerusalem: The Hebrew University, 1983 (Hebrew).

Mesežnikov, Grigorij. „Prezentácia vzťahu Európska únia – Slovensko hlavnými politickými aktérmi" [Presentation of the European Union – Slovakia relations by the main political actors]. *Medzinárodné otázky* 8 (1999): 17–51.

Minerbi Sergio I. (2006), Pope John Paul II and the Jews; An Evaluation, Jerusalem Center for Public Affairs – JCPA), *Jewish Political Studies Review* 18:1-2

Moravcsik, Gyula. Constantine Porphyrogenitus: De Administrando Imperio (Second revised ed.) Washington D.C.: Center for Byzantine Studies, 1967.

Naamat, Talia. *The Legal Significance of the Working Definition: Recent Trends and Case Law*, 27–31. Justice, Spring 2020. https://www.ijl.org/justicem/no64/#27/z. Accessed June 19, 2023.

Nešťáková, Denisa, and Eduard Nižňanský. "Swedish interventions in the tragedy of the Jews of Slovakia." *Nordisk judaistik* 27, no. 2 (2016): 22–39.

Nešťáková, Denisa, and Eduard Nižňanský. "Regulating of sexual relations between Jews and non-Jews by ordinance Number 198/1941 Coll. of Slovak laws in times of the Slovak State." In *Women and World War II. Judaica et Holocaustica 7*, 89–118. Bratislava: Stimul, 2016

Neusner, Jacob. *A Rabbi Talks with Jesus*. Revised edition. Montreal and Kingston: McGill-Queen's UP, 2000.

"NEVER AGAIN" Association. n.d. https://www.nigdywiecej.org/en/. Accessed June 19, 2023.

Nižňanský, Eduard. „Der Holocaust in der Slowakei in der slowakischen Historiography der neunziger Jahre." *Bohemia* 44 (2003): 370–388.

Nižňanský, Eduard, and Barbora Jakobyová. „Lokální aktéri počas holokaustu. Prípad dvoch katolíckych kňazov z Dolného Kubína: Ignác Grebáč-Orlov a Viktor Trstenský" [The local actors during the holocaust. The case of two Catholics priests from Dolný Kubín: Ignác Grebač-Orlov and Viktor Trstenský]. In *Historik a dejiny: v československom storočí osudových dátumov*, 59–86. Bratislava: Veda, 2018.

Nižňanský, Eduard. *Politika antisemitizmu a holokaust na Slovensku 1938–1945* [Slovak Politics of anti-Semitism and the Holocaust in Slovakia 1938–1945]. Banská Bystrica: Múzeum SNP, 2016.

Nižňanský, Eduard. „Die Vorstellungen Jozef Tisos über Religion, Volk und Staat und ihre Folgen für seine Politik während des Zweiten Weltkriegs." In *Religion und Nation: Tschechen, Deutsche und Slowaken im 20. Jahrhundert*, edited by Kristina Kaiserová et al., 39–83. Essen: Klartext, 2015.

Nižňanský, Eduard. "Anti-Semitic Policies of Jozef Tisos during the War and before the National Court." In *Policy of Anti-Semitism and Holocaust in Post – War Retribution Trials in European States*, edited by Mičev, Stanislav et al., 113–148. Banská Bystrica: Múzeum SNP, 2019.

Nižňanský, Eduard. „Die Machtübernahme von Hlinkas Slowakischer Volkspartei in der Slowakei im Jahre 1938/39 mit einem Vergleich zur nationalsozialistischen Machtergreifung 1933/34 in Deutschland." In *Geteilt, besetzt, beherrscht*, edited by Monika Glettler et al., 249–287. Essen: Klartext Verl, 2004.

Nižňanský, Eduard. "Expropriation and deportation of Jews in Slovakia." In *Facing the Nazi genocide: non-Jews and Jews in Europe*, 205–230. Berlin: Metropol, 2004.

Nižňanský, Eduard. "On relation between the Slovak majority and Jewish minority during the World War II." *Yad Vashem studies* 42, no. 2 (2014): 47–89.

Nižňanský, Eduard. Die "Arisierung" jüdischen Vermögens in der Slowakischen Republik. In *Eigentumsregime und Eigentumskonflikte im 20. Jahrhundert: Deutschland und die Tschechoslowakei im internationalen Kontext*, 373–412. Essen: Klartext Verlag, 2018.

Nižňanský, Eduard. "Die jüdische Gemeinde in der Slowakei 1938/39." In *Jahrbuch 2000*, 116–133. Wien: DÖW, 2000.

Nižňanský, Eduard. "Die Deportation der Juden in der Zeit der autonomen Slowakei im November 1938." In *Jahrbuch für Antisemitismusforschung 7*, 20–45. Frankfurt/Main: Campus, 1998.

Nižňanský, Eduard. „Die Aktion Nisko, das Lager Sosnowiec (Oberschlesien) und die Anfänge des "Judenlagers"." In *Jahrbuch für Antisemitismusforschung 11*, 325–335. Berlin: Metropol, 2002.

Nižňanský, Eduard. "Payment for the deportations of Jews from Slovakia in 1942." In *Discourses – diskurse*, 317–331. Praha, 2008.

Nižňanský, Eduard. "The discussions of Nazi Germany on the deportation of Jews in 1942 – the examples of Slovakia, Rumania and Hungary." *Historický časopis*, no. 59 (2011): 111–136.

Nižňanský, Eduard et al., eds. *Slowakisch-deutsche Beziehungen 1938–1941 in Dokumenten I. Von München bis zum Krieg gegen die UdSSR*. Prešov: Universum, 2009.

Nižňanský, Eduard. „Der Holocaust und die Slowakei." In *Meine zwei Leben* by Lotte Weiss, 173–194. Berlin: LIT, 2010.

Nižňanský, Eduard. "The history of the escape of Arnošt Rosin and Czeslaw Mordowicz from the Auschwitz-Birkenau concentration camp to Slovakia in 1944." In *Uncovering the shoah: resistance of Jews and their efforts to inform the world on genocide – Odhaľovanie Šoa: odpor a úsilie Židov informovať svet o genocide*, edited by Ján Hlavinka and Hana Kubátová, 113–134. Bratislava: HÚ SAV, 2016.

Nižňanský, Eduard, and Ivan Kamenec, eds. *Holokaust na Slovensku 2. Prezident, vláda, Snem SR a Štátna rada o židovskej otázke (1939–1945). Dokumenty* [Holocaust in Slovakia 2. President, governement, parliament SR and State Council about Jewish question (1939–1945). Documents]. Bratislava: NMŠ, 2003.

Nižňanský, Eduard, ed. *Holokaust na Slovensku 4, Dokumenty nemeckej proveniencie. 1939–1945* [Holocaust in Slovakia 4. The documents of German origins. (1939–1945)]. Bratislava: NMŠ, 2005.

Nosek, Michael. "Akce PAVOUK." Policie České republiky, October 6, 2022. Accessed May 13, 2023. https://www.policie.cz/clanek/akce-pavouk.aspx. Accessed June 19, 2023.

"Nyilatkozatháború Után Visszavonta Gázkamrázós Írását Demeter Szilárd." Szabad Európa, November 29, 2020. https://www.szabadeuropa.hu/a/nyilatkozathaboru-utan-visszavonta-gaz kamrazos-irasat-demeter-szilard/30974746.html. Accessed June 19, 2023.

„Odhalenie busty Ďurčanského spustilo policajné vyšetrovanie" [The unveilling of a bust of Ferdinand Ďurčanský started a police investigation]. *Denník Pravda*, June 14, 2011. https://spravy.pravda.sk/regiony/clanok/210914-odhalenie-busty-durcanskeho-spustilo-policajne-vysetrovanie/. Accessed October 31, 2021.

Official text of the Joint Declaration of the prime minister of Poland and the prime minister of Hungary, November 26, 2020. https://abouthungary.hu/news-in-brief/heres-the-joint-declaration-of-the-prime-minister-of-poland-and-the-prime-minister-of-hungary. Accessed June 19, 2023.

"Organization." Federation of Jewish Communities in Czech Republic. n.d. Accessed May 12, 2023. https://www.fzo.cz/en/about-us/organization. Accessed May 12, 2023.

Ostachowicz, Igor. *Noc żywych żydów*. Warszawa: Wydawnictwo W.A.B., 2012.

Oz, Amos. "Poem: To Be a Jew." *Jewish Journal*, January 2, 2019. https://jewishjournal.com/spiritual/poetry/291731/poem-to-be-a-jew/. Accessed June 19, 2023.

Pardo, Sharon, and Hilda Zahavi, eds. *The Jewish Contribution to European Integration*. Lanham, 2020.

Paulovicova, Nina. "The Unmasterable Past? Slovaks und the Holocaust: The Reception of the Holcoaust in Post-communist Slovakia." In *Bringing the Dark Past to Light. The Reception of the Holocaust in Post-Communist Europa*, edited by John-Paul Himka and Joanna Michlic, 549–590. Lincoln/London: Univerzity of Nebraska Press, 2013.

Paulovicova, Nina. "Mapping the Historiography of the Holocaust in Slovakia in the Past Decade (2008–2018). Focus on the Analytical Category of Victims." *Judaica et Holocaustica* 10, no. 1 (2019): 46–71.

Pinto, Diana. "A New Jewish Identity for Post-1989 Europe." *JPR Policy Paper.* London: Institute for Jewish Policy Research, 1996. Accessed April 4, 2023. https://www.bjpa.org/content/upload/bjpa/a_ne/A%20New%20Jewish%20Identity%20For%20Post-1989%20Europe.pdf. Accessed April 4, 2023.

Plasseraud, Yves. National minorities/ new minorities: What similarities and differences in contemporary Europe? *Erudite,* September 12, 2019. https://doi.org/10.7202/1064037ar. Accessed June 20, 2023.

"Pope Francis's statement." Website of the Conference of Bishop of Slovakia. n.d. https://www.kbs.sk/obsah/sekcia/h/dokumenty-a-vyhlasenia/p/dokumenty-papezov/c/sk2021-prihovor-papeza-frantiska-pri-stretnuti-so-zidovskou-komunitou. Accessed October 31, 2021.

Pope Francis and Rabbi Abraham Skorka. *On Rome and Jerusalem, Conversations between A Pope and a Rabbi.* Jerusalem: Tobypress, 2014. Originally published in Spanish as *Sobre el cielo y la tierra.* Beunos Aires: Editorial Sudamericana, 2010.

Porat, Dina. "Five Popes, Four Visits, Two Declarations: Relations between the Catholic Church and the Jewish People and state following the Holocaust from a Israeli Perspective." *Kivunim Hadashim* (new directions) 34 (May 2016, Hebrew): 33–40.

Porat Dina. "Recent Efforts by the Catholic Church to Abate Antisemitism in the Wake of the Holocaust." *Justice* 58 (2016): 7–11.

Porat Dina. ""Tears, Protocols and Action in a Wartime Triangle": Pius XII, Roncalli and Barlas." In *Christianesimo nelle storia* 27, 599–632. Bologna University Press, 2006.

Porat, Dina. "The International Working Definition of Antisemitism and Its Detractors." *Israel Journal of Foreign Affairs* 3 (2011). https://www.osservatorioantisemitismo.it/wp-content/uploads/2013/03/kantorcenter_dporat_definition_of_antisemitism.pdf. Accessed June 19, 2023.

Porat, Dina, and David Bankier. *Roncalli and the Jews During the Holocaust, Concerns and Efforts to help.* Jerusalem: Yad Vashem, 2014.

Porat, Dina, Ben-Johanan Karma, and R. Braude. *In Our Time: Documents and Articles on the Catholic Church and the Jewish People in the Wake of the Holocaust.* Tel Aviv University Press, 2015.

Protesters Burn Effigy of Orthodox Jew at Anti-Immigration Protest in Poland. i24NEWS. November 20, 2015. https://www.i24news.tv/en/news/international/europe/93019-151120-protesters-burn-effigy-of-orthodox-jew-at-anti-immigration-protest-in-poland. Accessed June 19, 2023)

Rebhun U., and L. Lev Ari. *American Israelis: Migration, transnationalism, and diasporic Identity.* Brill, 2010.

"Religious Belief and National Belonging in Central and Eastern Europe." Pew Research Center's Religion & Public Life Project. May 10, 2017. https://www.pewresearch.org/religion/2017/05/10/religious-belief-and-national-belonging-in-central-and-eastern-europe/. Accessed June 19, 2023.

Reszke, Katka. *Return of the Jew: Identity Narratives of the Third Post-Holocaust Generation of Jews in Poland.* Academic Studies Press, 2013. https://www.jstor.org/stable/j.ctv2175r5n. Accessed May 31, 2023.

Rich, Dave. "Antisemitism in the radical left and the British Labour Party." *The Kantor Center.* January 2018. http://kantorcenter.tau.ac.il/sites/default/files/Dave%20Rich%20180128.pdf.

Rosen, David. "Reflections on the Recent Orthodox Jewish Statement on Jewish – Catholic Relations." In *Bulletin of the Association of the Friends and Sponsors of the Martin Buber House,* 7. 2019.

Rosenfeld, Alvin H. *A Double Dying: Reflections on Holocaust Literature*. London: Indiana University Press, 1980.

Rosenfeld, Alvin H. *The End of the Holocaust*. Bloomington: Indiana University Press, 2011.

Rothberg, Michael. *Traumatic Realism: The Demands of Holocaust Representation*. Minneapolis: University of Minnesota Press, 2000.

Rothkirchen, Livia. "The Situation of Jews in Slovakia between 1939 and 1945." *Jahrbuch für Antisemitismusforschung* 7 (1998): 46–71.

Rudee, Eliana. "'Cholent Festival' Brings Jewish Culture to Hungary via Food, Music, Traditions." Jewish News Syndicate, January 31, 2022. https://www.jns.org/cholent-festival-brings-jewish-culture-to-hungary-via-food-music-traditions/. Accessed June 19, 2023.

Said, Edward W. *Orientalism*. Vintage Books, 1979.

Sanchez, Raf. "Theresa May says there can be 'no excuse' for anti-Semitism as she marks Balfour centenary with Netanyahu." *The Telegraph*, November 2, 2017. http://www.telegraph.co.uk/news/2017/11/02/theresa-may-says-can-no-excuse-anti-semitism-marks-balfour-centenary/. Accessed June 19, 2023.

Schlagwein, Felix. Rising anti-Semitism in Hungary worries Jewish groups. Deutsche Welle. December 17, 2020. https://www.dw.com/en/rising-anti-semitism-in-hungary-worries-jewish-groups/a-55978374. Accessed June 19, 2023.

Schwaez-Friesel, Monika, and Jehuda Reinharz. *Inside the Antisemitic Mind; The language of Jew-hatred in contemporary Germany*. Brandeis University Press, 2017 (Kindle edition).

Schwalbová, Manca. *Vyhasnuté oči*. [Quiescent Eyes]. Bratislava, 1964.

Shared Vision, Common Action: A Stronger Europe. A Global Strategy for the European Union's Foreign And Security Policy. June 2016. https://www.eeas.europa.eu/sites/default/files/eugs_review_web_0.pdf. Accessed June 19, 2023.

Sheffer, Gabi. *Diaspora politics: At home abroad*. Cambridge University Press, 2003.

Shimoni Stoil, Rebecca. "American Jews voted 70%-25% in favor of Clinton over Trump, poll shows." *Times of Israel*, November 10, 2016. https://www.timesofisrael.com/american-jews-voted-70-25-in-favor-of-clinton-over-trump-poll-shows/. Accessed June 20, 2023.

Sirotnikova, Miroslava German, Edit Inotai, Tim Gosling, and Claudia Ciobanu. "Democracy Digest: Poland and Hungary Refuse to Back down over EU Veto." Balkan Insight, November 27, 2020. https://balkaninsight.com/2020/11/27/democracy-digest-poland-and-hungary-refuse-to-back-down-over-eu-veto/. Accessed June 19, 2023.

Sister Rose's Passion. Director Oren Jacoby. Storyville Production, 2004.

Sladovníková, Šárka. "The Film Colette – Risk of a 'Modern' Approach to the Depiction of the Holocaust." In *Der Holocaust in den mitteleuropäischen Literaturen und Kulturen: Probleme der Poetisierung und Ästhetisierung*, edited by Reinhard Ibler, 243–254. Stuttgart: ibidem-Verlag, 2016.

Slovak Law Code 1940, Constitutional Act No. 210/1940 Coll.

Slovak Law Code 1941, Govt. Reg. 198/1941 Coll.

"Slovakia. Population: Demographic Situation, Languages and Religions." Website of the European Education and Culture Executive Agency. n.d. https://eacea.ec.europa.eu/national-policies/eurydice/content/population-demographic-situation-languages-and-religions-72_en Accessed October 31, 2021.

Smith, Mitch. "Anonymous Bomb Threats Rattle Jewish Centers Across Eastern U.S." *The New York Times*, January 9, 2017. https://www.nytimes.com/2017/01/09/us/bomb-threats-jewish-centers.html. Accessed June 19, 2023.

Smlsal, Jiří. "Kontinuita Stereotypů. Židé, Romové, Muslimové." Migrace Online, May 17, 2016. https://migraceonline.cz/cz/e-knihovna/kontinuita-stereotypu-zide-romove-muslimove. Accessed June 19, 2023.

Šmok, Martin. *Through the Labyrinth of Normalization: The Jewish Community as a Mirror for the Majority Society.* Prague: Jewish Museum, 2017.

Sniegon, Tomas. *Vanished History. The Holocaust in Czech and Slovak Historical Culture.* Berghahn Books, 2017.

Soukupová, Blanka. *Židé v Českých zemích po šoa. Identita poraněné paměti.* [Jews in the Czech Lands after the Shoah. The Identity of Wounded Memory], Bratislava, Marenčin PT, 2016.

Štefánek, Anton. *Základy sociografie Slovenska* [Foundations of the Sociography of Slovakia]. Bratislava, 1944.

Strauss, Elissa. "The JCC Bomb Threats Confirm That Jewish Parents Are Right to Be Afraid." *Slate Magazine*, January 19, 2017. https://slate.com/human-interest/2017/01/the-jcc-bomb-threats-confirm-that-jewish-parents-are-right-to-be-afraid.html. Accessed June 19, 2023.

Šústová Drelová, Agáta. "Čo znamená národ pre katolíkov na Slovensku?" [What does the "nation" mean to Catholics in Slovakia?] *Historický časopis* 67 (2019): 385–412.

Szabó, Miloslav. ""Clerical Fascism"? Catholicism and the Far-Right in the Central European Context (1918–1945)." *Historický časopis* 66 (2018): 885–900.

Szabó, Miloslav. *Klérofašisti. Slovenskí kňazi a pokušenie radikálnej politiky (1935–1945)* [Clerofascists. Slovak priests and the temptation of radical politics]. Bratislava: Slovart, 2019.

Szabó, Miloslav. "Zwischen Geschichtswissenschaft und Wissenschaft. Der Holocaust in der slowakischen Historiographie nach 1999." *Einsicht* 11 (2014): 16–23.

Tablet. An eight paper series, October–December 2002, by researchers of Heythrop College, Faculty of Theology, Philosophy, Christian Spirituality, Divinity.

Tarant, Zbyněk. "Jews and Muslims in the Czech Republic – Demography, Communal Institutions, Mutual Relations." In *Being Jewish in 21st Century Central Europe*, edited by Haim Fireberg, Olaf Glöckner, and Marcela Menachem Zoufalá, 185–206. De Gruyter, 2020. https://www.degruyter.com/document/doi/10.1515/9783110582369/html. Acccessed June 19, 2023.

Thalassinos, Eleftherios I., Mirela Cristea, and Graţiela Georgiana Noja. "Measuring active ageing within the European Union: implications on economic development. Equilibrium." *Quarterly Journal of Economics and Economic Policy* 4 (2019): 591–609. https://www.ceeol.com/search/viewpdf?id=925494. Accessed June 20, 2023.

"The conclusions of Casablanca Conference." Encyclopedia Brittanica, n.d. https://www.britannica.com/event/Casablanca-Conference. Accessed October 31, 2021.

"The speech of the Pope John Paul II. in Slovakia." Website of The Conference of Bishops of Slovakia. https://www.kbs.sk/obsah/sekcia/h/dokumenty-a-vyhlasenia/p/dokumenty-papezov/c/navsteva-svateho-otca-v-sr-1995. Accessed October 31, 2021.

"The statements by the Conference of Bishop of Slovakia." Website of Conference of Bishop of Slovakia. https://www.tkkbs.sk/view.php?cisloclanku=20210913093. Accessed October 31, 2021.

"The statement by the Slovak government." Website of Slovak government. https://www.vlada.gov.sk/vyhlasenie-vlady-sr-k-umiestneniu-busty-f-durcanskeho-v-rajci/ Accessed October 31, 2021.

"The summary from the meeting of the Municipial Council in Rajec, held on 19 May 2011." Website of slovak municipial Rajec. http://www.rajec.info/files/16995-ZAPIS20110609.pdf. Accessed October 31, 2021.

"The Treaty between the Slovak Republic and the Holy See." http://spcp.prf.cuni.cz/dokument/kon-sr.htm. Accessed October 31, 2021.

"The written questions by Hedy d'Ancona in the European Parliament." Website of the Members of the European Parliament. https://www.europarl.europa.eu/sides/getDoc.do?pubRef=-//EP//TEXT+WQ+E-1997-2343+0+DOC+XML+V0//EN. Accessed October 31, 2021.

"The written questions by Leonie van Bladel in the European Parliament." Website of the Members of the European Parliament. https://www.europarl.europa.eu/sides/getDoc.do?type=WQ&reference=E-1997-2469&language=EN. Accessed October 31, 2021.

"The written questions by Otto Bardong in the European Parliament." Website of the Members of the European Parliament. n.d. https://www.europarl.europa.eu/sides/getDoc.do?pubRef=-//EP//TEXT+WQ+E-1997-2644+0+DOC+XML+V0//EN. Accessed October 31, 2021.

Tomczok, Marta. *Czyja dzisiaj jest Zaglada? Retoryka – ideologie – popkultura*. Warszawa: IBL, 2017.

Tonini, Carla. "The Jews in Poland after the Second World War. Most Recent Contributions of Polish Historiography." In *Quest. Issues in Contemporary Jewish History. Journal of the Fondazione CDEC*. April 2010. https://www.quest-cdecjournal.it/the-jews-in-poland-after-the-second-world-war-most-recent-contributions-of-polish-historiography/. Accessed May 31, 2023.

Trepte, Christian. "Between documentary and provocation – New tendencies (not only) in contemporary Polish Holocaust literature." *Slovo a smysl*, no. 29 (2018): 171–184.

Trepte, Christian. "Kinder und Enkel des Holocaust erzählen. Neue Perspektiven in der polnischen Holocaustliteratur." In *The Holocaust in the Central European Literatures and Cultures: Problems of Poetization and Aestheticization / Der Holocaust in den mitteleuropäischen Literaturen und Kulturen: Problem der Poetisierung und Ästhetisierung*, edited by Reinhard Ibler, 39–57. Stuttgart: ibidem Verlag, 2016.

Trigano, Shmuel. "A Journey Through French Anti-Semitism." In *Jewish Review of Books*. Spring 2015. https://jewishreviewofbooks.com/articles/1534/a-journey-through-french-anti-semitism/. Accessed June 19, 2023.

Vago, R. "The quest for the 'authentic' Central Europe." In *Being Jewish in 21st Century Central Europe*, edited by H. Fireberg, O. Glöckner, and M. Menachem Zoufalá, 3–16. De Gruyter, 2020.

van Alphen, Ernst. "Playing the Holocaust." In *Mirroring Evil: Nazi Imagery/Recent Art*, edited by Norman L. Kleeblatt, 65–83. New York: Jewish Museum, 2002.

van Alphen, Ernst. "Playing the Holocaust and Playing with the Holocaust." In *Holocaust Fiktion: Kunst jenseits der Authentizität*. Edited by Dirk Rupnow and Iris Roebling-Grau, 151–162. Paderborn: Wilhelm Fink, 2015.

Vertovec, S. "Conceiving transnationalism." In *The Creolization reader-studies in mixed identities and cultures*, edited by R. Cohen and P. Toninato, 266–277. Routledge, n.d.

Vincze, Zsófia Kata. "The 'Missing' and 'Missed' Jews in Hungary." In *Being Jewish in 21st Century Central Europe*, edited by Haim Fireberg, Olaf Glöckner and Marcela Menachem Zoufalá (eds.), 115–143. Berlin: de Gruyter, 2020.

Vitale, Monica, and Rebecca Clothey. "Holocaust Education in Germany: Ensuring Relevance and Meaning in an Increasingly Diverse Community." *FIRE: Forum for International Research in Education* 5, no. 1 (2019): 44–62. https://files.eric.ed.gov/fulltext/EJ1207646.pdf.

Vnuk, František. *Mať svoj štát znamená život* [Having own state means life]. Bratislava, 1991.

von Schnurbein, Katharina. "European Union Activities in Combating Antisemitism in 2019." In Kantor Center Report Antisemitism Worldwide 2019 and the Beginning of 2020. n.d. https://en-humanities.tau.ac.il/sites/humanities_en.tau.ac.il/files/media_server/humanities/kantor/Kantor%20Report%202020_130820.pdf. Accessed June 19, 2023.

Vrba, Rudolf. *I Cannot Forgive*. Vancouver, 1997.
Ward, James Mace. *Priest, Politician, Collaborator: Jozef Tiso and the Making of Fascist Slovakia*. Ithaca and London: Cornell University Press, 2013.
Weinthal, Benjamin. "German Intel: Migrants Will Bring Anti-Semitism." *The Jerusalem Post | JPost.com*, October 26, 2015. https://www.jpost.com/Diaspora/German-intel-Migrants-will-bring-anti-Semitism-430058. Accessed June 19, 2023.
Wetzler, Alfréd. [as Lánik, J.]. *Čo Dante nevidel* [What Dante Did not See]. Bratislava, 1964.
Wike, Richard, et al. "European Public Opinion Three Decades after the Fall of Communism." Pew Research Center's Global Attitudes Project. October 15, 2019. https://www.pewresearch.org/global/2019/10/15/european-public-opinion-three-decades-after-the-fall-of-communism/. Accessed June 19, 2023.
Yiftachel, O. "The homeland and nationalism." In *Encyclopedia of nationalism*, 359–383.
Academic Press, 2001.
Zubrzycki, Genevieve. "Nationalism, 'Philosemitism' and Symbolic Boundary-Making in Contemporary Poland." Comparative Studies in Society and History 58, no. 1 (2016). https://www.cambridge.org/core/journals/comparative-studies-in-society-and-history/article/nationalism-philosemitism-and-symbolic-boundarymaking-in-contemporary-poland/3BEF2AB1798A5399D1F686C7F45DE439. Accessed June 19, 2023.
Zubrzycki, Geneviève. *Resurrecting the Jew: Nationalism, Philosemitism, and Poland's Jewish Revival*. Princeton University Press, 2022.

About the Authors

Katarína Bohová holds a double degree in History and Slovak Language and Literature from the Faculty of Arts at Comenius University in Bratislava (2013–2019). In 2021 she started working on her Ph.D. in the General History Department at the same faculty. In her dissertation she analyzes the Image of Enemy in European history in the twentieth century. She also focuses on antisemitism and the Holocaust in Slovakia in 1939–1945.

Haim Fireberg was (until he recently retired) a Research Associate at the Kantor Center for the Study of Contemporary European Jewry, Tel Aviv University, and head of research programs at the Center. His main foci of research are the social and demographic situation of Jewish communities in Europe, urban history of the Jewish community (H'Yishuv) in Palestine in the twentieth century and during the first decade of the State of Israel, and the study of virtual Jewish communities (maintaining Jewish and Israeli life in cyberspace). Fireberg is also active in monitoring and researching contemporary antisemitism, concentrating on Europe, and was in charge of analyzing violent incidents worldwide. His most recent publications include: *Being Jewish in 21st Century Germany*, edited together with Olaf Glöckner (Berlin/Boston: De Gruyter, 2015); and *Being Jewish in 21st Century Central Europe*, edited together with Olaf Glöckner, and Marcela Menachem Zoufalá (Berlin/ Boston: De Gruyter, 2020). Currently, Fireberg (with partners) conducts vast social and cultural research in five main Jewish communities in Europe.

Olaf Glöckner, PhD, is a Senior Researcher at the Moses Mendelssohn Centre for European-Jewish Studies in Potsdam (MMZ). He is also Lecturer at the Historical Institute and at the Department of Jewish Studies at the University of Potsdam. Glöckner's main foci of research are Jewish Migration, European Jewry after 1989/90, German-Israeli relations, and modern antisemitism.
Glöckner has worked and participated in several empirical studies on Jewish migration, Jewish education, and Jewish experiences with modern antisemitism (including Studies on Antisemitism for the Fundamental Rights Agency 2012/13 and 2017/18). Currently he is involved in the EU-funded projects "'United in Diversity' – An Interdisciplinary Study of Contemporary European Jewry and its Reflection" and "EUphony – Jews, Muslims and Roma in the 21st Century Metropolises" as well as in the joint research project "ASJust – Struggling of the Judiciary in Germany with Anti-Semitism."
Among Glöckner's recent publications are: *Being Jewish in 21st Century Central Europe*, edited with Haim Fireberg and Marcela Menachem Zoufalá (Berlin/ Boston: De Gruyter, 2020); *Das neue Unbehagen. Antisemitismus in Deutschland heute*, edited together with Günther Jikeli (Hildesheim: Olms, 2019).

Jiří Holý is a Professor at the Department of Czech Literature and Comparative Literature and Head of the Centre for the Holocaust and Jewish Literature at the Faculty of Arts, Charles University in Prague. In 1994/1995, he served as Assistant Professor at the University of Regensburg. He was also a Visiting Professor at Humboldt Universität (1999/2000), at Universität Wien (2004/2005, 2008/2009), and at Universität Leipzig (2014/2015). Together with Dr. Marcela Menachem Zoufalá, he coordinated the multiannual EU project *"United in Diversity." An Interdisciplinary Study of Contemporary European Jewry and Its Reflection*.
Prof. Holý specializes in literary science and research, mainly within the area of Czech Literature and Jewish Topics in Literature and Culture. His main publications in recent years include *Handbook of*

Polish, Czech, and Slovak Holocaust Fiction: Texts and Contexts (editors E.-M. Hiemer, J. Holý, A. Firlej, and H. Nichtburgerová) (Berlin: De Gruyter, 2021); "Jews and Jewishness in Cinema and Literature: The Case of the Czech Republic," in *Being Jewish in 21st Century Central Europe*, edited by H. Fireberg, O. Glöckner, and M. Menachem Zoufalá (Oldenbourg: De Gruyter, 2020), 165–184; "Jurek Becker: Jakob der Lügner (with H. Nichtburgerová)," in *Holocaust. Zeugnis. Literatur. 20 Werke wieder gelesen*, edited by M. Roth and S. Feuchert (Göttingen: Wallstein Verlag 2018), 152–168; "Die Namen auf den Mauern der Pinkas-Synagoge in Prag," in *Texte prägen*, edited by H. Kenneth et al. (Wiesbaden: Harrassowitz, 2017, 415–432; and "Nontraditional Images of the Shoah in Literature and Film: Comedy and Laughter," *Holocaust Studies* 23, no. 1–2 (2017): 208–221.

Barbora Jakobyová is a Ph.D. student at the Interwar and WWII History Department at the Institute of History of the Slovak Academy of Sciences in Bratislava. She received her Master's degree in History at the Faculty of Arts, Comenius University in Bratislava, where she completed her university studies with the defense of a Master's thesis on World War II as the object of propaganda in the press. Her subsequent research was devoted to the history of a Jewish community in the city of Dolný Kubín, in which Jakobyová, together with Professor Eduard Nižňanský, explored in the local context the larger topic of the Holocaust in Slovakia. Her current doctoral research under the title "Medico-social care for children in Slovakia in the interwar period" on the example of the functioning of relief administration and counseling bureaux for mothers and children concerns history of childhood, poverty, hunger, and humanitarianism after the WWI as well as (de)population discourse in interwar Czechoslovakia. Her most recent article "Population Crisis in Interwar Czechoslovakia: Building up a Healthy Family" was published in the *Journal of Family History* 48, no. 3 (2023): 293–308. https://doi.org/10.1177/03631990231161505.

Lilach Lev Ari is an Associate Professor at Oranim, College. She is the dean of the Faculty of Graduate Studies and a lecturer. Her research interests include human migration, gender and migration, contemporary Jewry, ethnic identity and identification, ethnic minorities and integration, stratification, intercultural encounters, acculturation and multiculturalism.
Lev Ari has published the following books: *The American Dream –For Men Only? Gender, Immigration and the Assimilation of Israelis in the United States* (2008); *American Israelis, Migration, Transnationalism, and Diasporic Identity* (2010 with Uzi Rebhun); *Contemporary Jewish Communities in Three European Cities: Challenges of Integration, Acculturation and Ethnic identity* (2022); as well as various publications in scientific journals such as: *Contemporary Jewry, The Journal of Heritage Tourism, Higher Education, Tourism Recreation Research*, and *Journal of Multilingual and Multicultural Development and Religions*.

Marcela Menachem Zoufalá, PhD. is a cultural anthropologist, lecturer, and researcher at the Centre for the Study of the Holocaust and Jewish Literature, Faculty of Arts, Charles University. Her research interests include Jewish and Israel Studies, specifically the quality of life of contemporary European Jewish communities in the context of a sense of belonging, transnationalism, and antisemitism. In the field of Israel Studies, her research interests combine Mizrahi Studies, ethnicity, and gender. Recently, she has focused on Jewish-Muslim relations from a transurban comparative perspective. Marcela has (co-)authored and (co-)edited several monographs and articles, including: "Israel Studies in Poland, Czech Republic, and Germany: paths of development, dynamics, and directions of changes," in *Journal of Israeli History*, with Joanna Dyduch and Olaf Glöckner (2023); and "Ethno-religious Othering as a reason behind the Central European Jewish distancing from Israel," in *Being Jewish in 21st Century Central Europe*, edited by Haim Fireberg, Olaf Glöckner, and Marcela Menachem Zoufalá (Berlin/ Boston: De Gruyter, 2020). She is a principal investigator of the international project "Jews, Muslims, and Roma in the 21st Century Metropolises." She is also a member of the Jewish and Muslim Minorities in Urban Spaces of Central Europe research team. Marcela Menachem Zoufalá is the European Association of Israel Studies' vice-president.

Eduard Nižňanský is a member of the Department of General History at the Faculty of Arts of the Comenius University, Bratislava. In his research, Prof. Nižňanský focuses on the Holocaust, National socialism, and international relations in 1933–1945. He has published 20 monographs and 100 scientific studies (published in Slovakia, Czech Republic, Poland, Romania, Austria, Germany, Great Britain, Israel, and USA). He has lectured in Olomouc (Czech Republic), Krakow (Poland), Vienna (Austria), Karlsruhe, Freiburg, Saarbrücken (Germany), Jerusalem, and Beer Sheva (Israel).
Among his publications are "The Holocaust in Slovakia" (six volumes); "Slovak-German relationship 1938–1945 in Documents" (two volumes – Slovak-German); "The Jewish Community in Slovakia between the Czechoslovak Parliamentary Republic and the Slovak State in the Central European Context" (Prešov: Universum 1999, Slovak); "Nazism, The Holocaust, The Slovak State" (Kalligram 2010, Slovak); "The Policy of anti-Semitism and the Holocaust in Slovakia 1938–1945" (Banská Bystrica: Múzeum SNP, 2016, Slovak); "Antisemitism und Holocaust in der Slowakei in Dokumenten deutscher Provenienz 1938–1945" (Banská Bystrica: Múzeum SNP, 2021, Slovak – German). Nižňanský also served as the editor of *Judaica et Holocaustica* (12 annual volumes).

Dina Porat is the former head of the Kantor Center for the Study of Contemporary European Jewry. She also served as head of the Department of Jewish History of the Rosenberg School for Jewish Studies, and as incumbent of the Alfred P. Slaner Chair in Antisemitism and Racism, all at Tel Aviv University. She served as the Yad Vashem chief historian until 2021, and is currently its academic advisor.
Prof. Porat has been awarded prizes for some of her many publications (including the National Jewish Book Award for her biography of Abba Kovner, published by Stanford University Press) and the Bahat Prize for her new book on Jewish revenge after World War II; she was TAU's Faculty of Humanities' best teacher for 2004, got the Raoul Wallenberg Medal for 2012, appeared on the 50 leading Israeli scholars list of the Marker Magazine in 2013 and Forbes' list of the 50 leading women in Israel in 2018, and was a visiting professor at Harvard, Columbia, New York, Venice, and Hebrew universities. Her main research interests include contemporary and classic antisemitism, history of the Holocaust, Zionism and the Jews of Europe, the "Final Solution" in Lithuania, and Jewish-Catholic relations since World War II. She served as an expert for Israeli Foreign Ministry delegations to the UN world conferences and as the academic advisor for the International Task Force on Holocaust Education, Remembrance, and Research (now IHRA).

Index of Persons

Adam, Anna   152
Adamczyk-Garbowska, Monika   53
Agnon, Shmuel   202
Alphen, Ernst van   54, 68
Alter, Daniel   101
Ancona, Hedwig "Hedy" de   34
Ansky, S.   57
Aristotle   68
Assmann, Aleida   51, 53, 56, 63, 68, 213

Baeck, Leo   137
Baka, Igor   25
Bardong, Otto   34
Bauer, Yehuda   51, 53, 68
Becker, Jurek   64
Ben-Rafael, Eliezer   141
Benedict XVI   76
Berger, Gottlob Christian   19
Bernstein, Julia   106
Bezalel, Judah Loew ben   57
Bieńczyk, Marek   67
Biľak, Vasil   40
Bladel, Leonie van   34
Borowski, Marek   90
Brandmüller, Walter   29-31
Broek, Hans van der   35
Brons, Aart   83
Brunner, Alois   19
Buryła, Slawomir   56, 68
Burzio, Giuseppe   20, 30, 44
Buzalka, Michal   45

Čaputová, Zuzana   42, 194
Chabon, Michael   56, 57
Chalupecký, Ivan   46
Chernivsky, Marina   105
Chicago, Judy   53, 68
Cieslar, Milan   61
Churchill, Winston   47
Constantin, Saint *see* Cyril, Saint
Cotler, Irwin   107
Cunningham, Philip   84
Cyril, Saint   41

Czapliński, Przemysław   62
Czollek, Max   142

D'Amato, Joe   51
Dannel, Hannah   145
Demeter, Szilárd   98
Deodato, Ruggero   51
Dilong, Rudolf   191
Diner, Dan   213
Dlugoš, František   46
Dostoevsky, Fyodor   58, 60
Duda, Ján   46
Dumas, Alexandre *fils*   58
Ďurčanský, Ferdinand   7, 36-40, 49
Ďurica, Milan Stanislav   28-33, 35, 36, 46, 49

Eichmann, Adolf   19
Eisik, Dan   83
Elizabeth II   84
Engelking, Leszek   54, 65, 68

Feist, Thomas   157, 158
Fináli, Gábor   99
Fisher, Eugene   84
Francis I   42, 48, 72, 77, 79, 80, 85, 86, 97, 190
Frank, Anne   52, 55, 60
Fulmeková, Denisa   191

Gál, Egon   185, 186, 188, 189, 193, 196
Gary, Romain   57
Gauck, Joachim   103
Girelli, Leopoldo   83
Głowiński, Michał   67, 68
Gojdič, Pavel   45
Göth, Amon   55
Gross, Jan Tomasz   61, 69, 199
Gruber, Ruth Ellen   162, 201
Grysa, Tomasz   71, 80-82

Havel, Václav   171
Heisler, András   94
Herzl, Theodor   76
Hildesheimer, Esriel   141, 153

Index of Persons

Hitler, Adolf 14, 18, 98, 136, 137, 155
Hlavinka, Ján 25, 44, 46
Hlinka, Andrej 8, 182
Hlinka, Anton 14
Horthy, Miklós 97
Hrabovec, Emília 29, 46
Hrabovecká, Hilda 23
Hradská, Katarína 25, 29
Hilberg, Raul 24, 26
Hubenák, Ladislav 26

Ildikó, Barna 96, 112
Ickx, Johan 47

Jakobyová, Barbora 25
John XXIII 73, 75
John Paul II 45, 75, 76, 79, 81, 86, 204
Judák, Viliam 46, 47
Judt, Tony 161
Jurčaga, Peter 46, 47

Kalita, Marek 63
Kamenec, Ivan 11, 21, 27, 29, 44, 46
Kamiński, Mariusz 92
Kárný, Miroslav 168
Karvaš, Imrich 24
Kasper, Walter 85
Katzir, Ram 54
Kaufmann, Kuef 159
Kawalerowicz, Jerzy 64
Keneally, Thomas 55
Kertész, Imre 53-55
Klein, Felix 104
Klínovský, Karol 46
Kloke, Martin 154-156
Knap, Árpád 96
Koch, Kurt 71, 72, 77, 80-82
Koffman, Joshua 85
Korec, Ján Chryzostom 46
Kovács, András 95, 112
Krajewski, Stanisław 178
Krall, Hanna 57
Krištúfek, Peter 56, 65-70
Kuboš, Ján 46, 47

Lacko, Martin 38
Lagodinsky, Sergey 143

Langer, Lawrence 52, 53, 55, 68
Lanzmann, Claude 55
Lapid, Yair 89
Lárišová, Petra 25
Lehrer, Abraham 105
Levi, Primo 54
Levinthal, David 54
Leyen, Ursula von der 109
Libera, Zbigniew 54
Lipscher, Ladislav 27
Livni, Zipi 147
Lônčíková, Michaela 25
Lörinc, Alexander 44, 46, 47
Ludin, Hanns Elard 18, 19, 30
Lustig, Arnošt 56-61, 64, 69

MacDougal, Russell 83
Mach, Alexander 10, 11, 17, 18, 25, 27, 28, 33, 46, 47
Májek, Stanislav 46
Marshman, Sophia Francesca 53, 54, 56, 68
Masaryk, Tomáš Garrigue 171, 177
Mečiar, Vladimír 7, 21, 31, 32, 35, 36
Medrický, Gejza 24
Merkel, Angela 102
Methodius, Saint 41, 42
Mičev, Stanislav 19
Michalkiewicz, Stanisław 90
Michela, Miroslav 25
Mikuš, Jozef 30
Mňačko, Ladislav 58
Morávek, Augustín 13
Mosiński, Jan 90
Morawiecki, Mateusz 97
Mulík, Peter 38, 46
Muránsky, Martin 186, 190, 193, 194, 196
Mussolini, Benito 47

Nachama, Andreas 148-150
Nachama, Estrongo 148
Nižňanský, Eduard 25, 29
Nurowska, Maria 58

Obama, Barack 89
Ogórek, Magdalena 90
Orbán, Viktor 79, 97, 121
Ostachowicz, Igor 56, 62-65, 68-70

Index of Persons

Pakula, Alan Jay   54
Pankowski, Rafał   90
Pasinowski, Władysław   62
Pau, Petra   100, 101, 147, 148
Paul VI   75, 81
Pavel, Ota   67
Pels, Peter van   52
Petranský, Ivan   46
Pinto, Diana   1, 162
Pius X   76
Pius XII   31, 47, 73
Piwowarski, Krystian   62
Pizzaballa, Pierbattista   81-83
Prečan, Viliam   29
Putin, Vladimir   79

Radičová, Iveta   39
Rebes, Julian   see Ostachowicz, Igor
Rebling, Jalda   152-154
Reinharz, Jehuda   106
Robbe, Reinhold   150-152
Romero, George A.   63
Roncalli, Angelo Giuseppe   see John XXIII
Roosevelt, Franklin Delano   47
Rosen, David   81, 82, 84-86
Rosenfeld, Alvin Hirsch   53, 54, 56, 60, 68
Rothberg, Michael   52, 68
Ruta, Magdalena   53
Rutha, Bogdan   56
Rybárik, Ján   37, 38
Rzońca, Bogdan   90

Sabach, Michelle   83
Said, Edward   179
Salner, Peter   26, 29
Salzmann, Sasha Marianna   142
Scheiber, Sándor   112
Schick, Ludwig   101
Schnurbein, Katharina von   107
Schoenberner, Gerhard   150
Schreiber, Moses   see Sofer, Moshe
Schudrich, Michael Joseph   200
Schuster, Josef   102
Schwalbová, Manca   24
Schwarz-Friesel, Monika   101, 106, 158, 159
Ševčíková, Zuzana   25
Sidon, Karol Efraim   170

Simon, Attila   25
Skorka, Avraham   79, 81, 85, 86
Škorvánek, Stanislav   29
Škvorecký, Josef   67
Slavkovská, Eva   32
Słobodzianek, Tadeusz   62
Slota, Ján   36
Sofer, Moshe   181
Soros, George   98
Spiegelman, Art   55, 64, 69
Spielberg, Steven   53, 55
Spinner, Joshua   153, 154
Staffa, Christian   146, 147
Stav, David   83
Stegner, Jerzy   56
Stern, Tomáš   187, 188, 190, 193
Sternberg, Yitzhak   141
Stolov, David   81, 83
Styron, William   54
Sush, Darren   68
Szewc, Piotr   67

Tarantino, Quentin   55, 64
Teichtal, Yehuda   140
Thering, Rose   84
Tiso, Jozef   9-12, 14, 15, 17, 19, 20, 25, 27-33, 35, 38, 42, 43, 46, 48, 49, 62, 182, 184, 185, 189-191
Tomczok, Marta   62, 64
Tondra, František   45
Tonini, Carla   199
Topol, Jáchym   56, 65
Trstenský, Viktor   45
Tuka, Vojtech   9, 10, 17, 25, 27, 28, 33
Tusk, Donald   62

Vašečka, Michal   40
Vašek, Anton   44
Vasiľ, Cyril   46, 47
Vicze, Kata   99
Vnuk, František   28, 46, 49
Vojtaššák, Ján   4, 7, 30, 41, 43-49
Vrba, Rudolf   23
Vrzgulová, Monika   25

Weisband, Marina   143
Wetzler, Alfred   23

Wiesel, Elie 54
Wisliceny, Dieter 13, 16, 25
Wissmann, Yan 155, 156
Witiska, Jozef 19
Woodman, Donald 53

Zavacká, Katarína 26
Zemecki, Robert 60, 61
Zlatoš, Štefan 30
Zubrzycki, Geneviève 92, 93, 210

www.ingramcontent.com/pod-product-compliance
Lightning Source LLC
Chambersburg PA
CBHW020228170426
43201CB00007B/351